T·H·E
JEWISH
MESSIAHS

T·H·E JEWISH MESSIAHS

From the Galilee to Crown Heights

HARRIS LENOWITZ

New York   Oxford

OXFORD UNIVERSITY PRESS

1998

Oxford University Press

Oxford   New York
Athens   Auckland   Bangkok   Bogotá   Buenos Aires   Calcutta
Cape Town   Chennai   Dar es Salaam   Delhi   Florence   Hong Kong   Istanbul
Karachi   Kuala Lumpur   Madrid   Melbourne   Mexico City   Mumbai
Nairobi   Paris   São Paulo   Singapore   Taipei   Tokyo   Toronto   Warsaw

and associated companies in
Berlin   Ibadan

Copyright © 1998 by Harris Lenowitz

Published by Oxford University Press, Inc.
198 Madison Avenue, New York, New York 10016

Oxford is a registered trademark of Oxford University Press

Library of Congress Cataloging-in-Publication Data
Lenowitz, Harris.
The Jewish messiahs : from the Galilee to Crown Heights
/ Harris Lenowitz.
p.   cm.
Includes bibliographical references and index.
ISBN 0-19-511492-2
1. Jewish messianic movements—History.
2. Messiah—Judaism.   I. Title.
BM615.L39   1998
296.3'36—dc21   97-29980

1 3 5 7 9 8 6 4 2
Printed in the United States of America
on acid-free paper

PREFACE

I began this work after I had received invitations to speak to the Society of Independent Scholars in San Diego and to the department of religious studies at the University of California, San Diego, in the spring of 1993. In my lecture to the department of religious studies I wanted to talk about Yakov Frank's peculiar use of metaphor. I decided to put that talk in perspective for the Society of Independent Scholars by providing the members with a general introduction to the topic of Jewish messiahs. When I had finished the lectures, I felt that I could now write an accessible account of all the Jewish messiahs, rather than postponing it, as I had originally intended, until I had finished my work on Frank. I would like to thank Seymour Cain, of the society, and David Noel Freedman and William Propp, of the department of religious studies, for offering me these opportunities to develop my thinking on the topic.

My study of Jewish messiahs had begun with Frank in 1976. While preparing materials for *A Big Jewish Book* (1978) with Jerome Rothenberg, I came upon the Hebrew translation of a Polish work on Frank and have spent the years since then studying Jewish messiahs and Jewish messianism, along with messianism in general. Two matters that had been thrust aside in the study of the topic, particularly since the nineteenth century, began to occupy my attention. In the scholarly literature, the Jewish messiahs themselves have not received as much attention as has the theological and national concept of messianism, and the texts that present all the messiahs in their own words, or in the words of their contemporaries, have never been presented or studied as a group. I determined to approach the topic in a way that would refocus attention on the messiahs in their stories—how they were alike and how different, and what themes they might all have in common.

I have been forced to sketch out a long and complicated history in this work and so to resist detailed inquiries into many events, personalities, and social backgrounds. The work of great scholars on these topics over many years has enabled me to do this, since I can rely on what they have done and on the continuing exploration of others. Even so, no work such as this could have been done by a single individual without the support and attention of others, among them my university and college and the department of language and literature and the Middle East Center. I would like to thank a few others here and relieve them of responsibility for what I have done with their advice and suggestions.

Professor John J. Collins of the University of Chicago was of great help to me, providing direction in assembling the first and second chapters, particularly that part which treats of Jesus. Professor Martin Jaffee of the University of Washington guided me in clarifying other parts of the first chapter, especially that part of the second chapter dealing with Bar Kosiba. A meeting with Professor David Gitlitz of the University of Rhode Island in 1995 opened my way into the exploration of crypto-Jewish culture, particularly that of the New World. Professors Abraham Duker and Chone Shmeruk were invaluable to me as my work on Yakov Frank began and progressed. My friends Drs. Phyllis and Michael Walton provided me with important insights and direction into the world of the sixteenth century, into magic and its child, science. Professor Joseph Dan, the Scholem Chair in Jewish Mysticism at the Hebrew University, has been a good friend for many years, and his good, clear work has helped me formulate much of my thinking here, particularly in achieving balance among competing messiahs. Many readers for several presses, whose names I do not know, made comments on parts of the work as it was growing that were important urgings. Of those who read the whole manuscript carefully I must mention first my mother, Itta Freed Lenowitz, and Professor Raphael Patai for the kind attention they brought to the task. Toward the end of the writing I made the acquaintance of Professor Matt Goldish of the University of Arizona. I am grateful to him for his friendship and for the carefulness and the sympathy he has shown for a project which, in its drive to simplify so much, has had to leave so much obscure. As for Kathryn Wyer: she has helped me in reading texts in languages in which I am not expert, guided me through anthropological materials, and provided important insights to me. But I am indebted beyond telling, as are all who read and enjoy the book, to my dear Kathy, for her impelling me to see things clearly and write them understandably.

Translations of the works are mine unless otherwise noted. I have chosen to retain the peculiarities of the various accounts rather than make them consistent; this should help retain the flavor of the originals.

San Diego, New York, Ramat David   H. L.
1993–1998

CONTENTS

T·H·E
JEWISH
MESSIAHS

1

INTRODUCTION
The Ritual and the Accounts

Wherever Judaism has been, its messiahs have arisen. From the first century BCE to the present, they have stepped forth to rescue, as it were, the religious polities of the Jews. They have contended against Rome in Israel. Exiled, they have risen in arms to ride across the plains and mountains of Islamic Persia, wandered the shores of the Mediterranean all but alone, and yet frightened the pope to death; tailored and cobbled in Inquisition Spain and Portugal; called upon the Jews of Italy to repent; strided through the halls of the Vatican and the courts of the Holy Roman Empire; returned to the land of Israel to walk the hills of Safed for a time; had visions and spread their teachings along the Rhine; made the first group voyages to resettle the land of Israel in early modern times; conducted orgies in the role of virtual divinities in Turkey; roamed at the head of caravans across the Carpathians, traversing the rivers of Walachia and Podolia; languished in noble prisons in Turkey and Poland; cured ailments; quickened the wombs of barren women; eaten, drunk, sung, and prayed the world into its repair through the pale of settlement, and into the heartlands of Russia and Brooklyn; hiked the deserts and clambered up the mountains of Yemen to conquer satyrs. They have walked through the walls in which they have been imprisoned. They have flown through the air, and they have walked across the water and through the water and have sailed over the water on their scarves to reach freedom. They have died in ignominy and returned from the grave in glory. They have always sought to rescue their people from oppression. But they have always failed to overcome the oppressors. Their own people have feared them and reviled them and rejected their offer of redemption.

The title they have chosen, or let others apply to them, connects them to messianism, a doctrine that combines religion and politics in its promise of salva-

3

tion. Since salvation for the Jews has never been achieved, Jewish messiahs have continued to appear at the darkest moments, as well as at those hours when promise briefly glimmers. When they feel the time is right, when a segment of Jewish society feels a rising existential threat, messiahs take upon themselves their ancient occupation and emerge to lead those who can see only an unacceptable present and an impossible future. The messiah cannot save himself or his following or the larger society to which they belong, and as he and his movement flicker out, their dying light illuminates that society, setting despair and hope into balance again and bringing back meaning to daily life.

The Romans crucified Jesus and killed Bar Kosiba in battle. At least two Persian messiahs also died in battle, and David Alroy was either executed by the Persian government or beheaded by fellow Jews at the government's order. The Holy Roman emperor sent Shlomo Molkho to be burned to death, and David Reubeni to die a victim of the Inquisition. Isaac Luria died young; Hayim Vital lived to old age; both died in a state of disappointment but of natural causes. Shabtai Zvi died on the estate to which he'd been sent by the Ottoman sultan after he had saved himself from execution by converting to Islam. Yakov Frank died in his own noble court in Offenbach after converting to Christianity and receiving the title of baron. At this point, we can say without equivocation that all Jewish messiahs are dead. The fact of their deaths is the proof of their failure. The Jewish messiahs have failed to achieve cosmic redemption; they have failed to guide their followers through the apocalypse to youth, wealth, and eternal life. Nevertheless, the fact that they continue to arise—and we can predict that a Jewish messiah will arise again—suggests that they do achieve what they mean to achieve; they do not fail to be messiahs.

THE CONTROVERSY OVER JEWISH MESSIAHS: DELIVERERS OR CHARLATANS?

What is that achievement? The irrationality and violence of the Jewish messiah cults have caused many Jewish scholars to shy away from the topic altogether. The modern Jewish scholars who have dealt specifically with actual Jewish messiahs tend to get caught up in the issue of whether these figures are dangerous or beneficial to Judaism and Jews. They, like others, are intent on defending their judgments of these messiahs, which have been passed in accord with their feelings, as Jews, about Judaism.

The strong emotions aroused by the subject are apparent in the controversy between two important modern Jewish scholars, Aaron Z. Aeshcoly and Gershom Scholem. Aeshcoly's feeling toward messiahs was clearly sympathetic. His argument was in the tradition of the activist messianic theory, which holds that humans can redeem the world, either bring on the messiah through their deeds or hold his arrival at bay. Aeshcoly emphasized the treason of the generation of the messiah, contrasting its failure with the messiahs themselves, who did their best to show their people the way but were unable to overcome the weakness of their communities and, for that reason alone, failed to achieve salvation.[1]

By contrast, Scholem's distrust of messiah figures led him to highlight in his work any immoral or violent incidents, even if only rumored, in their careers; he never explicitly called a messiah a charlatan, but his treatment of them showed no sympathy. Of them all, Scholem thought the most of Shabtai Zvi, a crucial figure in Scholem's re-visioning of Jewish history. It must be said though that Scholem felt that Zvi was a creature of Nathan of Gaza, his prophet, on the one hand; and described Zvi as a psychotic, on the other. Scholem's position rejected actual Jewish messiahs, in the tradition of those rabbinic authorities who have habitually opposed messianic candidates as they arose. In fact, Scholem maintained that Jewish messianism, stripped of its messiah and resupplied with a conservative public and private ethics, has made a great contribution to the endurance of the Jewish people, even to its preservation and perhaps its deliverance, including the building of the state of Israel. It is of some interest to note that for a moment, while young, Scholem thought he was the messiah. (See M. Brenner, "From Self-declared Messiah to Scholar of Messianism," *Jewish Social Studies* 3,1 [Fall, 1996]).

Rather than defending the Jewish messiahs as deliverers whose societies failed them, or condemning them as charlatans or madmen who deceived their societies for their own ends, I will explore here the figure of the messiah himself and the relationship between him and his followers and the outside world, as expressed through the primary and secondary accounts of these episodes. To my way of thinking, Jewish messiahs are central figures in rituals that are performed by Jewish societies in disarray; the rituals include their own sad endings, which are both inevitable and necessary. The accounts of the rituals participate, then go on to program later performances of the ritual.

THE MESSIANIC RITUAL

Why have Jewish messiahs arisen time and time again, only to be rejected by everyone but a small group of followers, and perhaps even to be killed by those forces in the larger society that consider the messiah a threat to stability and their domination of the Jewish population? Is it because the latest Jewish messiah has no knowledge of the existence of previous messiahs, or of their fates? On the contrary, there is ample evidence that later Jewish messiahs know a great deal about the failures of their predecessors. Messiahs are aware of their own roles and the history of the ritual. The followers as well as the opponents of the messiah must share his awareness to varying degrees. Yet they all act out their parts to the end, as if they were players in a dramatic performance. This performance is the ritual of the messiah and is occasionally reenacted when some members of the society perceive the community as being under intolerable stress. The Jewish community and the larger society are partners in the ritual dance of destruction; they come together to destroy the messiah, then move apart to resume their old positions in the status quo. In the context of the ritual, the messiah does not actually ignite the flames of the apocalypse; rather, his immolation sheds light on what a society must do in order to go on.

I understand rituals to be practices carried out by members of a traditional society whereby the identities of the individuals within the society are achieved and their relations with each other are determined. Familiar acts having known outcomes, rituals reassure their participants of their place in the world. Far from motivating change, the performance of the messiah ritual confronts society with a counterpart that it can only reject, allowing it, in fact, to endure chaos.

From the time of the Romans' conquest of the land of Israel in 66 BCE until the modern state of Israel was formed in 1948, Jews have lived, whether in the land of Israel or in other lands, as subordinate minority communities within stronger and dominant majority cultures and polities. The degree of oppression exercised on Jewish communities by the dominant group has varied, but the fundamental power relationship has not. This situation has created the awareness among Jewish societies and individuals that the continuation of their self-constructs as Jews and members of Jewish communities may be threatened at any time. The threat need not be in the form of a renewed severity that may lead to extinction by cruel force; it may come in the form of a new liberty that proffers the benign dissolution of social strictures, or both at once. In a messianic performance, some members of the society who perceive an existential threat respond by seeking to change themselves and their situation completely, while the institutions of the community—highly traditional, concerned with self-preservation, and fearful of the messiah's radical agenda—resist and, at last, reject that change. The messianic movement and its surrounding society cooperate in a ritual that generates the cult and then destroys it.

In the end, with the destruction of the messiah and his movement, there is no change in the status quo. The immediate conflict—between the messianic movement and the Jewish community and the external society—has been resolved, but the resolution is only temporary; the fundamental conflict, between Jews and the external society, remains. It seems that the purpose of the messianic movement is to allow the Jewish community to continue functioning as a Jewish minority, while the continued existence of the Jews in this situation makes it likely that future messianic events will occur.[2]

It is not surprising that, within Jewish society, messianism has been able to attract followers in its quest to overcome threats to its existence and to gain liberation and redemption—salvation—for the Jewish people. The appropriate symbols and idea of messianism have been an intrinsic part of Jewish society since biblical times; the term "messiah" first appears in the Hebrew Bible. A messianic movement can manipulate these symbols to mobilize a following. The symbols have the power to draw the following because they are familiar but they do not have to remain static and irrelevant to the current situation. Each messianic movement distinguishes itself from its predecessors by reconstituting traditional symbols so that they correspond with the movement's own circumstances and with the peculiar stresses under which the followers, the leader, and the larger society operate.

The most powerful symbol in Jewish messianism is the messiah himself, who will lead the Jewish people to salvation. A messianic movement thus requires a central living figure, who, on the strength of his own will and that of his following, inhabits the symbolic role of messiah and provides the center around which the cult develops. Many messiahs, as I shall note, have shown themselves to be unique, even bizarre characters; yet the role does have a certain requirement: The personality of the messiah, along with his ability to wield the symbols of the divine and carry out symbolic acts that engage divinity in a close personal relationship, must attract a following whose perceptions of reality have already been unsettled by outside stresses.[3] Although realistically the ultimate goals of messianism are unattainable, the messiah and the followers create together an alternative reality; the charismatic relationship between the messiah and the followers is necessary for both of them and allows each to define their common activity as nonpsychotic, however unsympathetic the larger society around them may be to their view.[4] In order to maintain the relationship, the central figure must be acutely sensitive to the needs of the following—which may alternate between permissiveness and absolute authority. Even the most authoritarian figure may occasionally be seen appealing to the following as his companion. Together they seek to reappropriate an image of themselves as whole functional beings through means that are, unfortunately, predisposed by the role they play in the cult. The group is conservative in its perceptions of itself and will not acknowledge that any adjustment, in the messiah-follower relationship or in the methods it employs to achieve its goal, has taken place even when such changes have in fact occurred. The movement's interests are immediate; its demands are absolute and cannot be adapted to the reality of the world outside the cult. It is unstable and unable to maintain itself; it is never able to resolve its status as a marginal group or to integrate its ideology with that of the larger society. Since the success of a messiah cult depends, ultimately, on the victory of the messiah, and since the messiah must eventually die, the cult must fail, either upon the messiah's death or whenever it can no longer maintain its hope in his triumphant reappearance. Once the performance ends, its symbols are put away. While some of the effects may modify social routines, the messianic movement itself dissolves, awaiting a new circumstance and new personae to reenact the order of things.

Often thought the most successful messianic movement in Judaism, Christianity achieved its power and endurance largely by abandoning the goals and society of Jesus and his disciples following his death. Within Judaism, Jesus is not regarded as a fulfilled messiah, and the Jesus Christ of Christianity is generally thought of as the retrospective application of a name to a host of sociohistorical events and identities that neither he nor his immediate following had much to do with. Christianity in fact ceased to be a messianic movement and became instead a revitalization movement. Unlike the messianic ritual, revitalization movements do result in widespread societal change. Following Jesus' performances of the messianic ritual, the Jewish community remained a minority, oppressed by Roman rule; meanwhile, Christianity extended and transformed Jesus' movement into a force which took over and revitalized the Roman empire, guaranteeing its continuation, arguably until the Islamic conquest of Constantinople.[5] Jewish messianic movements keep the pattern of the ritual alive so that a new messiah might arise to step beyond the boundaries of acceptable change, thereby reminding society where the boundaries are and permitting it to exist within these boundaries. The ritual performance falls outside the conventional space of the society; it must end so that society can go on.[6] The society has taken from the performance what it needed, and the performance comes to an end, often along with the performers.

Most of the periods and places of Jewish history never produced any messianic ferment. In fact, despite what I have said about the messianic ritual being performed as a means to relieve stress within the Jewish community, no Jewish messianic movements are recorded during the period of the Crusades, when Christian armies, passing through Europe on their way to Jerusalem, massacred thousands of Jews; nor did a Jewish messiah arise in the period before or during the Holocaust. Why should this be the case? Were these events simply too abrupt, too traumatic, too comprehensively disastrous for the entire Jewish population to allow a messianic movement the chance to rise and fall? Or was it just a coincidence that an appropriate messiah figure did not appear to lead such a movement in those times and places? It does seem that the messianic ritual requires instability of a particular degree, neither too great nor too little, but it needs just enough despair or just enough hope to tip the balance. When the environment either enforces massive and detailed control or provides complete liberty, these movements do not commonly arise; when the situation is one in which neither the individual nor the group can find its place, they do.[7] I would like to go beyond this and predict the moments when more performances will occur or even to look back and say, "This situation, or this, brought about the last movement." But I find that this is not possible, any more than predicting an earthquake or explaining one that has happened.

It is understood that, in general, earthquakes tend to happen where earthquakes have happened before. Earthquake experts can't predict why an earthquake will occur at a certain place or intensity, or explain why one earthquake did occur but another didn't, because, they say, "We don't have enough data. We don't have all the history of all the earthquakes even in one area; we don't know exactly what pressures are applied to a given area, and from what quarter, with what force; we don't know the exact composition of the earth at all points where pressure bears." And so it is, too, with messianic movements: However common the pattern of cause and result may be to the events, each—as much as the individuals performing in the ritual—expresses the pattern differently.

Messianic events take place at points of pressurized confusion. They tend to run into each other—chronologically or geographically; religion does not cause them but only provides them with an expressive mode. But how much confusion is necessary for a messiah's appearance to develop into a movement of any size? How much pressure is necessary on how many? How much pressure on any single individual? Economic, political, social pressure? How can one draw up an equation that will take all these variables, as they act on each other, into account? And where can such data be found, and by what methods? How can one look back and say, "This condition guaranteed a messianic outburst that did (or did not) happen?" The Jewish case alone shows that preconditions are not apparent: Ease or poverty, or perceptions of either, for example, do not determine either the occurrence of an event or the participation of any individual in it; events of a distant past may play as important a part as present circumstances.

Although this work, then, will attempt to give a picture of the social, economic, political, and religious conditions at the time of each of the Jewish messianic movements it considers, it will not specify the precise causes for these movements, for I believe this to be impossible. What this work will equip, is the investigation of the succession of Jewish messiahs it describes within the context of a ritual performance that is repeated over and over in Jewish history.

As I stated earlier, the Jewish messianic ritual employs symbols and images that come out of Jewish society and tradition, including the accounts written by and about earlier messiahs. The very first "messiahs" are those mentioned in the Hebrew Bible.[8] The accounts of the biblical messiahs show them to be qualitatively different from the postexilic ones. The biblical accounts nevertheless supply many of the symbolic features that later accounts employ. It is worthwhile now, therefore, to consider exactly what "messiah," literally the "anointed one," signifies in these primary accounts.[9]

KING, PROPHET, PRIEST — THE BIBLICAL MESSIAH

Three figures are anointed in the Bible—the king, the prophet, and the priest. Each of these is anointed with oil as he assumes his role. Gradually, these three different roles are transformed and at last combined in a single figure by the postexilic period who would be capable of performing all three functions. He would be the victorious king of a unified nation; he would critique social conduct and prophesy a specific date for the reign of the nation's God over the whole earth; he would exemplify the pure, holy attributes that are required of an officiating priest. As the combination is melded and transformed, the lines that differentiate the functions are erased. The act of anointing itself disappears altogether by the time of the destruction of the Second Temple in the first century CE.

At the beginning of the history of kingship in the Bible, Hannah prays at a shrine, and her prayer is answered: She has a son, Samuel; he becomes a prophet; he anoints the first king. The last lines of her prayer are: "Yahweh [God] will judge the compass of the earth. He will enable his king. He will exalt the fame of his anointed one" (1 Sam. 2:10). In criticizing the regnant priestly clan of Eli, Yahweh promises that the time will come when they will be replaced by other priests who will "serve my anointed one [the king] for all time" (1 Sam. 2:35). This verse distinguishes between the priest and the king in both their hierarchic relationship and in the matter of anointment: The king is indeed the anointed one. It soon becomes clear that the prophet is to carry out the anointing and confirm the relationship: Yahweh tells Samuel, "Tomorrow at this time I will send you a man from the lands of Benjamin and you shall anoint him as the leader of the forces of Israel and deliver them from Philistine power" (1 Sam. 9:16). The military role of the anointed one receives emphasis here: He is to command the army and to deliver it from an enemy that has the upper hand, not to lead an army in an invasion. As the anointed one, his person is inviolable. David, who will replace Saul as the anointed one, swears by Yahweh that he will take no action against Saul because "[Saul] is Yahweh's anointed one" (1 Sam. 24:7). David's words intimate Saul's replacement, but only if Yahweh determines to bring it about. Already at this point, there is some role confusion regarding anointment and office. Samuel, a prophet, does not really want to anoint Saul king; in hard language, he warns the Israelites against kings. However much the precise language may derive from a later period, after Israel had gotten a good taste of monarchy, Samuel's unhappiness is heightened in the narrative when Saul assumes some of Samuel's duties, neglecting those assigned to himself. Samuel had understood that Saul's duties were to be strictly limited to military leadership against the Philistines, and he is enraged when Saul ordains sacrifices after Gibeah (1 Sam. 14) and again at Gilgal (1 Sam. 15), acting in Samuel's role and against his specific order. The conflict between a nonmilitary figure—yet one who is a leader in his own right in religious and advisory spheres—and the king-messiah recurs, as shall be seen with other messiahs.

Moses, a prophet, sees to the anointment of Aaron and his heir, Eleazar. The Aaronide priesthood, actually established later than the time of the events described here, holds the tradition that a prophet took them as priests from a special subgroup, the Aaronides, itself drawn from a tribe, the Levites, distinguished from all other tribes in terms of landholding, residence, income, and status. Verses 3, 5, and 16 of the fourth chapter of Leviticus bring out the nature of the relationship between the priest and the congregation of Israelites, depicting acts that have resulted in discord between humans and Yahweh and the atonement for them. In the first of these passages, the "anointed priest" (never referred to as the "anointed of Yahweh") has made an error that has affected all the people. The terms of the sacrifice then required of him are the same as those required of an anointed priest who acts on behalf of the congregation whenever it errs and discovers its mistake (Lev. 4:13–21). In this legal codification, the priest is treated as if he were the entire congregation, as an abstract entity rather than as an individual human being.

The instructions for the ceremony whereby the high priest is anointed are given in Exod. 29 and 40, and in Lev. 6–9 and 21. The priest is anointed along with other items of the sacred service—in particular, the Tabernacle and the altar. In effect, he is made an item of holy service, like the altar and its utensils. Like them, he must not come in contact with various impurities (Lev. 21); also like them, he serves as an instrument for fulfilling God's purpose, while maintaining communication between the people and God. The priest's duties and consecration thus make him a holy implement rather than an Israelite or even a human being. His consecration strips him of personal power as he becomes the conduit for the All-Powerful.

If it is the prophet who carries out the unction that creates the king and the first priest, it is important to look at how the nature of the prophet who performs the unction is formulated. Of the three, he must be the original anointed one since the other two base the legitimacy of their claims on his unction. But is the prophet anointed into his task? When Isaiah says that he has come to comfort the anguished people of Israel (Isa. 61:1), he maintains that "Yahweh has anointed me." Most references to the anointment of a prophet are postexilic. Isaiah's metaphor—that God has anointed him—indicates at least that no king or priest has done so or does so generally; rather, it appears that prophets, acting as agents of the divine, anoint other prophets. This tradition may be associated with the much earlier episode in which Elijah is instructed to "anoint Hazael to be king of Aram; Jehu, son of Nimshi, to be king of Israel; and Elisha, son of Shaphat of Abel-meholah, to be prophet in your place" (1 Kings 19:15–16). The actual ceremony of anointing never appears in descriptions of the commissioning of the prophets. When Yahweh himself appoints a prophet, he does something other than anoint him. It may be, then, that Isaiah's claim includes more than one metaphor. As is necessary, the origins of the rite of anointment, like the rite itself, disappear. The prophet, like the priest and the king, is more than a simple individual; he is in some way the representative of his people and becomes a target for anyone seeking to dominate the people. In order to protect him from such threats, he is designated as messiah—though, as noted previously, he might never have undergone anointment—and given divine protection from (foreign) kings, as when kings are instructed not to harm "my anointed ones, my prophets" (Ps. 105:15). This verse, not to mention the history of Amos and his antagonists, the high priest Amaziah and King Jeroboam, shows the continuing difficulty the messiahs—king, prophet, or priest—have in making room for each other. The prophet, together with the priest and king, fills a representational role for the divine and stands at a certain distance from the rest of the community and humanity. All three claim to be carrying out orders; they are all playing roles assigned, in detail, by a superior. This emptying out of human characteristics and the replacement of free choice by divine mandate are two constant and important conditions of all subsequent messiahs and their followers alike.

The biblical accounts of anointment make it clear that messiahs have a peculiar relationship with the divine.[10] They are God's anointed, just as they are the anointed ones of the people. God ordains their entry into an intermediary, nonhuman existence; the oil of unction transmits divinity, through the persona of the anointing one, to the one anointed. The prophets do not die, or more specifically, do not die human deaths—in particular, Moses doesn't; nor does Elijah. The anointed one is taken as a partner by God, with all the benefits and liabilities that that entails. Ps. 20:7 makes it clear that the king is to be recognized as a protégé of God: "I know that Yahweh delivers his anointed one, responds to him with his mighty, delivering right arm from his holy place in the sky." David expresses the same notion in the narrative of 1 Sam. 24:7 (cited preciously). God and the king are associates. Anyone who attacks the king attacks Yahweh (or Elohim); foreign kings attack both at once, inseparably, in Ps. 2. God stakes his claim of authority over Israel on his assertion that he has never let harm befall a (righteous) king (Ps. 105:15, cited above). When Samuel calls for witnesses to his innocence, he calls equally on Yahweh and on his anointed one, King Saul (1 Sam. 12). As an associate of Yahweh's, the anointed one may even be taken as a relative. The king is adopted, if not actually sired, by God in Ps. 2:7 (compare it with 2 Sam. 7:14; Ps. 89:26–27), in a formulaic recognition: "You are my son; I have sired you today." A quasi-divine nature is established, in the preexilic period, for the messiah to possess forever or for as long as those biblical texts remain potent.

Supernaturalism comes to enrich the portrait of the king-messiah, as the political necessities of the Davidic dynasty demand theological validation. Poems sung by the cult promise the dynasty of David eternal rule: "To the one of the great saving victories of his king I will sing, to the one who loves his anointed, David and his line, forever" (2 Sam. 22:50–51). Long after Jereboam's rebellion, when the Davidic family lost its unity and half its lands, and close to the period following its complete dispossession in the defeat of the southern kingdom (586 BCE), the first hues of a far-distant and divinely executed fulfillment of this promise begin to appear. The sun has set on this time and this land, and a new sun will rise over a new land, in a new sky. The king became an idealized figure in the new history of the books of Chronicles, magnificent and worshipful. Zechariah discarded everything personal about David and substituted Solomon, the king of peace, as a model.[11] The prophet saw his contemporary, Zerubbabel, the scion of the Davidic line, as the one who met the criteria; he would return the people from captivity and rebuild the temple. The promise made to a broken and scattered people in Isa. 11, describing the nature of the future king and the future world, contains most of the rudiments on which the postbiblical expectations would come to rely for their image of the messiah-king. The new Davidic king would administer an era of absolute world peace, of universal Yahwism, of the return of the exiled people of Israel, through mighty waters, to its land. This prophet determined that his prophecy, in its fulfillment, would face up to the disastrous presence of war, death, defeat, and exile and the defeat of the king; justify this history; and compensate its agony with blessedness. In chapter 26, the Book of Isaiah describes its own times as Israel's "birth pangs" and compares the struggle to the travails of a pregnant woman who bears nothing (see the discussion in chapter 2 and the applications of this concept in chapters 6 and 7). In its formulation, it promised the rewards of resurrection as a subsequent stage. The dead of the wars and the generations preceding them would be resurrected to live under the king's righteous rule in the new world. The substitution of future deeds for present ones, of distant fulfillment for proximate promises, and the tinting of the present moment in supernatural colors, characterize these texts. They characterize Jewish messianic movements from then on.

The idea of a messiah who might fail as a national leader in the face of enemies and even fall in the struggle became tenable, gradually, some time after these developments. The idea nourishes the struggles of each messiah who comes to reinvest his predecessor with his own person rather than discrediting him (and so casting doubt on his own claim). The amalgamation of the three roles—prophet, priest and king—permitted the followers of later messiahs to choose interpretations that would allow them to maintain loyalty in spite of any disaster. A potential messiah might fail to achieve redemption on a predicted date and thus fail as a prophet. Yet he could continue to offer a determined following the hope of success as their king and national leader. He could in fact die or disappear, as did Zerubbabel, and still not be considered a failure.[12] Given the king's role as a dynast, a following could see the death of its messiah as an opening for his successor, the one who would complete the task. By referring to the history of David, a follower could easily discard the priestly and prophetic ideals of holiness and see a successful hero-king as the messiah even if he were unholy, immoral, impure. The prophecies that required a Davidic messiah disqualified the priestly lineage, the Levites. A holy priest, representing God, shouldn't make the compromises that a national leader needs to make, and yet, based on the history of a conjoint national and cultic leadership, a follower might demand that a priestly figure play an important role in a messianic movement. If greatly disappointed over the conduct of the king, a messianist might even replace the king and the prophet with a priest-king, an Aaron. Under the impact of what actually happened to kings, prophets, and priests in the face of crises, these multiple ways of understanding or explaining the role of the messiah established a broad range of expectations, almost any of which, met in some way or another, might satisfy a following.

By the time of the Second Temple, the Davidic lineage was lost. Yet the popular longing for a victorious king persisted, along with the image, the rough lineaments of his figure and deeds. The Davidic lineage of the messiah who appeared became a matter that could be determined in retrospect. The successful messiah would be taken as a scion of David if his achievements—unification and victory—established his bona fides. No messiahs, in the sense that the term "messiah" means a restorative figure who engages an actual and dominant enemy, actually appeared from 538 BCE (the end of the Babylonian exile) until the first century CE, when a flurry of them suddenly came forward. None had appeared since the beginning of the expanded application of the term in the biblical texts. In fact, the symbolic act—anointing—that initially defines the messiahs has itself either disappeared completely from royal office by the time of the return from the Babylonian exile, *though not necessarily from the designation of the central figure* (including preeminently the priest),13 or has been limited to Isaiah's metaphor of anointment in the spirit (Isa. 61:1).

Having begun this brief survey of the biblical literature on messiahs and messianism with the assertion that the term was applied to three sorts of human social functions and that the term had to do with anointing those who performed them in their positions, I find that the symbol of the anointed king and priest has been deprived of anointment in fact as a result of historical changes in the society. The oil itself has been lost, stored away for the end of time, reflecting the culture's awareness of its losses and the improbability of their being resupplied. The groundwork for change and variation in the transformation of these important symbol systems had been laid during the exile, but it remained largely unemployed for various reasons. The most significant of these was that the gap between what the Jews actually had and the ideal they hoped to attain had remained relatively narrow.

The term "messiah" as it is applied after the exile and the return to Israel thus lacks two elements present before that time: the anointing oil and a king of the Davidic lineage. The postexilic figure designated as messiah is so called in order to assert a continuing association with holy and royal anointment in spite of the disappearance of the two most important elements of the term's definition. The supernatural attribute of eternal life and the shape-changing capacity of the messiah figure as prophet-*cum*-king-*cum*-priest are trans-human qualities that are possessed by the messiah as sociopolitical emblems. In taking the appelation "messiah" and assuming the central role in the ritual an individual allows himself to be emptied out, discarding his former self in order to become an object of holy ritual service. In the act of his self-destruction—or self-sacrifice—he is reborn as the messiah, in the ritual, and in the accounts of the ritual.

This discussion will be taken up again in chapter 2, where I will note that the early Jewish rebellions following the exile establish the model of messianic movements for Judaism, and that the special cultic ritual in which a central figure acts as a "messiah" develops alongside the progression of the biblical term from a direct application to a symbolic usage. The concept of a Jewish messiah, and the term's application to the figures presented in this book, thus join the biblical definition together with the functional definition in a uniquely fitting way.

THE ACCOUNTS OF THE JEWISH MESSIAHS

This book focuses on the accounts of actual Jewish messiahs. By "accounts" I mean all fundamental texts, written and spoken, by messiahs and about messiahs by their adherents, proponents, and antagonists. Documents that contain such accounts include letters written by or about messiahs, biographies or autobiographies, histories, dream accounts, tales told by messiahs, miracle tales told about messiahs, and satires. When something new is added to an account that, otherwise, is not original, I take the addition, and perhaps the whole account in which it has been placed, as fundamental; likewise, fundamental accounts may also give other, older materials—such as biblical prose, poetry, or prophecies, and other traditional genres a new spin. Histories that lack the element of charged, personal involvement are not included, unless they are all that remain, since they are not fundamental constituents of the messiah event.

I was first drawn to these accounts because I wanted to know how messiahs felt about themselves, particularly about their being superhuman, either in their nature or in their destiny or both. I wanted to examine their own words wherever possible; otherwise, the words of followers or antagonists who had had immediate contact with them. These accounts do reveal a lot about the characters of the Jewish messiahs, and my main purpose in presenting them in this book is to allow readers the chance to see these often very peculiar figures through primary narratives. As literary works, the accounts are often of great value in themselves. When we examine them as a collection, they offer insight into Jewish messiahs and the messianic ritual. It is clear that these narratives cannot be taken as factual reports of the messiahs and their deeds; whatever "facts" might have been available are marshaled in them to guide the messiah and his followers in what they are doing and are then used again, after the event has occurred, to show how it was successful, how that messiah was and is real, or how it failed and that messiah was not in fact the messiah.

I believe that these accounts are best understood not as individual narratives, isolated from each other, but as a series of texts that move forward in time and appear in endless variations, with each new narrative displaying the influence of its predecessors. Some narratives are the instruments of the messianic events themselves, created by them in order to spread their message. I will use the term "hagiography" for such narratives rather than coining a new one. Other accounts are antimessianic, anti-hagiography; they seek to tell the same tale but with a different intention. In the same way that hagiography is the literary act of pro-claiming a messiah, anti-hagiography dis-claims him. Anti-hagiography is directed against hagiography and, as time goes on, neither literary form has any need of a present messiah in order to reproduce itself. Anti-hagiographies—the shortest is the slam, "false christ"—have been written by Jews against Jewish messiahs (the *toldot yeshu*; see, among others, the "Counter-history of Jesus," p. 48; the Karaite anti-hagiographies against the Persian messiahs, pp. 71–78; and the poems of the Frances brothers against Shabtai Zvi, pp. 162–165); by Christian authors against Jewish messiahs (Pfefferkorn's account of Asher Lemlein, pp. 100–101) (and against Mohammed in the medieval Spanish satires on his domestic life); and by Moslem authors—along with Jewish authors—against the Jewish messiahs of Yemen (see chapter 10).

Hardly a single messiah event fails to include an active public-relations effort supporting or opposing the messiah, with accounts that witness for others what they say occurred for some. Both kinds of accounts serve as guides for the messiahs and their followers, carrying the seeds of the messianic ritual from one circumstance to another. The previous accounts portray figures who were once recognized as the messiah; even though these figures turned out to be unsuccessful, they still provide models of what the real messiah should be like; they delineate the expected messiah for a new candidate as well as for his potential followers and opponents. When we consider any particular account, then, we can find characterizations that suggest the realization, improvement, or disintegration of this model in the person of the current messiah contender.

An account is influenced not only by previous accounts in its attempt to defend (or attack) a candidate as the true messiah, for portraits of the expected messiah are similarly found in biblical literature, as I have noted, and in rabbinic theology, as I will explain in individual chapters. The account is one of the components of a messianic event, just as the participants are and just as the social, political, and economic contexts are, but it acts to collect the others and give them point. The accounts of a messiah of a given time and place will use the language of the tradition to show him saving the group from disintegrating under stress or failing to do so. A portrait of the messiah and his deeds as either "credible" or "false" must be drawn—and the more expectations a messianic candidate is made to meet, the more credible he will appear. Historical texts establish present accounts and provide reference points for future accounts. It is a commonplace of rabbinic interaction with the Bible, for example, that there is no temporal sequence within the Bible when one looks back to it from a postbiblical perspective.[14] Everything happens at one time; chronological order means nothing. This holds true with the addition of every successive layer of literature and produces a sort of readable palimpsest, a text of texts. A relationship clearly exists between the deeds of a messiah and the texts that pass them along, and between these texts and the deeds of the next messiah and the texts that transmit those deeds. In a way, the deeds themselves are only tributaries, providing a new supply of raw materials to the dynastic lineage of the texts.

Not every account will display each of the three textual threads—biblical literature, rabbinic theology, and previous accounts of messiahs—in equal measure, or even be influenced in the same way by any particular category. Nor should it be assumed that the heavy influence of preexisting ideas of the messiah precludes innovations in the way a new candidate will appear. Despite the Bible's importance in establishing the "messiah" as a traditional role in Jewish thought, and the impact of subsequent rabbinic literature and accounts of messianic contenders in maintaining this role, it is necessary to understand that the supporter or opponent of a current

Jewish messiah draws upon the authorities of the past not only to address past expectations, but also to oppose the current expectations and hopes of the other side. The ritual, while reenacting the past, must also confront the present.

As the Jewish messiah cult begins to form, separating from and seeking to replace the society, the religion in place will necessarily be impacted, along with other structures such as those of the economy and the polity (to the degree that these can be separated from religion in Jewish cultures that are often only dependencies in the societies within which they exist). The religious leaders, who want to maintain their authority and power, become attentive to the literature of messianism, and so does the messiah who appears. The rabbis find grounds in this literature for rejecting the messiah. The messiah, drawing on the same textual sources, finds grounds for substituting his authority for that of the rabbis. We often find that messiahs come in clusters, several in succession or several in one region. This phenomenon demonstrates that messiahs may be most influenced by other messiahs close by, and that the accounts of these messiahs guide and stimulate their actions. The importance of the accounts increases spectacularly after Jesus' death, and they contain all we can know of the representation of the leader of the cult. The leader is the focus of attention here; though he is but one part of each event, he is an everpresent one, and we have never had all of the leaders of the important Jewish cults presented together in a single study.[15]

The textual substructure, the repository of messianic symbols, imposes no limits on the discourse. The liberality of Jewish interpretation of the Bible sustains minority opinions, discarded arguments, fantastic tales and intertextual and antitextual readings, while interpretations of other interpretations and the histories of preceding messiahs (including the Jesus of Christianity and Mohammed, the prophet of Islam) participate in shaping new interpretations and histories. The lack of agreement between biblical definitions of the messiah and his concerns—or definitions that are elaborations of biblical definitions—and messiahs incarnate is striking. The theories and the human being are engaged in a bloody war in which the rabbinic leadership after 135 CE discourages and combats any form of messianic activism.[16] The Jewish theologian and philosopher Franz Rosenzweig wrote that the followers of the false messiahs "bleed as sacrifices on the altar of the people's eternity; [the stronger ones, whose strength of hope does not allow them to be deceived], serve as priests before the altar."[17]

Clearly, the formation of any particular account involves a complex process of influence and innovation. At the beginning of each chapter of this book, and in my commentary on specific texts, I will elucidate what influences are discernible and what innovations have been made in each case. This work will show that, in spite of my observations about variety in Judaism, the messiahs choose from a limited array of futures, although these have some common determinative features that are a bit surprising.

I hope that this will provide some guidance for the reader's appreciation of the texts as a central feature in the continuum of Jewish messianic events. Each chapter will distinguish the Jewish messiah under discussion by describing briefly what is known about the social, political, economic, and religious context for each messianic movement. This will include the mention of other messiahs who appeared in the same period or location, who were perhaps of less significance or simply are not found in texts that survive, as well as any innovations in rabbinic messianic theology of the period. A brief life history of the messiah under discussion will also be given.

My analysis of the cultural imagery that appears in the accounts, together with the explanation of the overall context in which messianic events occur, should provide the reader with some understanding of the phenomenon of the Jewish messianic ritual. In the conclusion, I will discuss one group of symbols and symbolic acts—acts of separation and abandonment—because this category seems to me to organize most of the common features and themes of the texts within the structure of the messiah events. Some of these common features relate the messiah to his following and include the physical lineaments of the messiah, his immortality and the immortality of his soul, his old and new names, the part his family plays in his tale, and his attachment to his home and its cultural patterns. Other features relate both the messiah and his following to their time, which is seen as leading up to the end of the world or as the apocalypse itself: the occurrence of magic, miracles, and true prophecy; the reappearance of the Lost Tribes; the introduction of new practices and a new law. The feature that stands out most in these events is that the followers seek their own destruction, modeling themselves on their leader, a charismatic, wounded individual fatally determined to present his case dramatically before the world that has robbed him of his meaning.

Of all the accounts, the most revealing are those the messiah gives of himself; of all these self-accountings, the richest resource we have is the account Yakov Frank (the subject of chapter 8) gives of himself; his dicta go far beyond all other accounts in terms of quantity, period of time covered, engagement with the messianic tradition, and variety of rhetoric (persuasive, pensive, revelatory, concealing, satirizing). Due to the multiplicity of these functions, the dicta invariably expose one thing while hiding another. They bring us into direct contact with what Isidore Ducasse, in speaking of Shakespeare, called "the brain of the jaguar."

AN EXAMPLE

There is one passage, in one account in particular, that I believe vividly illustrates my idea of the nature of these texts. When the messiahs tell their own stories to their followings, they manipulate the theological fantasies and the accounts of their predecessors to establish themselves and their doings as both traditional and revolutionary, derived from tradition and succeeding where others have failed. They manipulate their listeners, too; and themselves? What do they think of themselves?

408. You have heard about a certain man who was called David Bar-David, who became a messiah and very many followed him. He, seeing finally that it was not finished, was led to the sultan, and the sultan said to him: Show me some miracle from those which you can do. He answered him: I will throw myself into the sea before your eyes and will return alive. He drowned in the sea and very many people who followed him threw themselves into that sea and all drowned. But now I don't

want anybody to die, as it clearly stands: *Ki loy echpauc bemaus haroscho;* I don't desire the death of an evildoer. My will is to make sure that you will be able to come to eternal life. (*The Words of the Lord* [*Yakov Frank*])

In this homily, Yakov Frank, an eighteenth-century Jewish messiah from south Poland, is speaking to his inner circle of followers. On the surface, the homily makes the simple statement that even though one sins, one may escape mortal punishment (the punishment of mortality itself) and be led onto the right way by the speaker. What Frank really seeks in the speech is his listeners' adherence. We must understand that the summons "you have heard" implies that their adherence is in doubt. Most interestingly, we can see the speaker build his argument, and we can consider, given the artful construction of the preachment, what Frank thinks of his audience; what he might have thought of himself lies just beneath that.

His chief persuasive device is to gain his audience's sympathy by recalling for them knowledge he and they share. He says, "You have heard . . ." In his historical prologue, he talks about another messiah, in details that surely are not known to them, but are similar to some they might know. In using this technique, Frank advances his position among his audience; he is one of them, one who knows what they know, and more. In fact they cannot know these details.

The historical messiah Frank first tells them about is David Alroy (see chapter 4). He employs a name for him that resembles that in one account of Alroy— David Al-David (used in Ibn Verga's *shevet yehuda;* see chapter 4)—but reformulates it to evoke the most prestigious claim of the king-messiah, to be from the lineage of King David. Considering the connotations of his own chosen family name, Frank, it is clear that he is counterposing himself to David, the son of David, and not to Bar-David's credit. The motif of the king who calls upon the messiah for miraculous proof comes from Ibn Verga's account as well, but the deaths of the messiah's following are drawn from the account of another messiah, Moses of Crete. Around 450 CE (see the full account in chapter 2) this Moses led his followers to the sea, promising them that they would cross dry-shod over to the land of Israel. Many of them jumped into the sea and drowned; Moses himself fled. Even though there are points where this account resembles the accounts of Alroy, it is not exactly like this; Frank bridges the two. Alroy never jumped into the sea, promising to return alive, and consequently he did not drown. Nobody followed him into the sea and drowned. None of this happens in any account of Alroy. But similar things, close enough to it to hold the audience together, may be remembered from the accounts of Alroy and/or from accounts of other messiahs, including that of Moses of Crete. Alroy did work wonders, including one in which he floated across a river on his scarf. The king's men could not follow him, nor could they catch him later when they crossed the river in boats. In combining the two accounts, Frank leaves out a significant point from the tale of Moses of Crete, the fact that he fled, and inserts another, invented point to replace it: Alroy drowned. Alroy, too, makes a successful escape in the river-crossing incident. Frank suppresses the messiah's flight, which had been an important element in both the Alroy account and that of Moses of Crete, preferring not to put the idea of abandonment by their leader into the heads of his listeners. Instead, Frank drowns his messiah, leaving him the errant messiah of a mistaken following but not a betrayer. In one account, a satire of anti-hagiographic treatment, many followers were swindled into believing that they would be lifted from their rooftops in Baghdad and would fly to Israel. Frank prefers to keep the idea of fraud out of his listeners' minds entirely and does not say that Alroy consciously tricked his following; instead, he dies with them in the sea. Frank's messiah is willing to risk his life to prove his faith. Other famous messiahs were required to prove themselves by returning from death: One of them, a Yemenite cited in Maimonides' letter (see chapter 10), loses his head; another, Shabtai Zvi (see chapter 7), changes his faith instead. In addition to all these vaguely recalled details woven into the story of the bad messiah, motifs from the accounts of Jesus may be present as well: He was of Davidic lineage, as it were; he said he would return from a bloody death; at one point he does walk on water; and many of his followers did die hard deaths themselves. There was even a beheading—that of John the Baptist—that might, again vaguely, stir the audience to recall that both the Yemenite messiah mentioned above and David Alroy were said to have been beheaded (again, in Ibn Verga's account).

Having gained his audience's support by presenting himself as one of them, as one who knows more than they do, Frank concludes that their messiah (he) is a much better messiah than the one he tells them about: He won't trick them; he won't die; if they follow him, they won't die; and even if they should sin (betray him), they can be forgiven and will, in either case, live forever.

An essential, traditional part of this restatement and lesson is Frank's provision of an appropriate scriptural support. Like Frank's history of David Bar-David, the verse is in fact new and improved, and, like that narrative, it seems familiar. The citation resembles three verses from Ezekiel; but it is an essence of them shaped to Frank's needs. Each verse (Ezek. 18:23, 18:32, and 33:11) sounds very much like the one Frank recites. (I will use the same system to transliterate the Hebrew that Frank's transcribers used.) In the first, *hechopauc echpauc maus roscho* ("Do I indeed desire the death of the evildoer?"), the verse continues, "No, rather that he repent and live"; in the second, *ki loy echpauc bemaus hames* ("For I do not desire even the death of the dead"), the verse continues, "but they must return/ repent and live"; in the third, *im echpauc bemaus horoscho* ("Not the death of the evildoer do I desire"), the verse continues, "let the evildoer turn back from his way and he will live." The amalgamation Frank constructs from these three verses promises his grace and extends eternal life to all. While the proof is from something every listener will hear as the Bible itself, the proposal itself is a new one, lacking the requirement of repentance—the threat—implying that Frank will see everyone through safely.

When I think of a man saying that he is more than a man, that he is divine, or that he has a divine destiny, proving it in various ways and thereby assuming power over other people's fortunes and their very lives, I want to know, "Does he believe it? How does he feel about that, really?" In looking closely at Frank's homily, I detect artifice: He desires the absolute commitment of his audience; he convinces them that he should have it by using skillful rhetoric. To say either that "he does that naturally, unself-consciously," or that "he is aware of his trickery, he is sincere, he is false, he is insane," we will need to know much more about him and his followers, and about the others like him and their followers. The most important resource we have is the accounts, like this homily, that the leaders and followers tell themselves as they try to carry out their visions, and the accounts they and others tell about them later.

THE TERM "JEWISH MESSIAH"

The origin and initial applications of the term messiah have been discussed, as has the ritual nature of the messianic event. The subject of this work—Jewish messiahs through their texts—has been defined. It remains only to specify precisely my own usage of the term "Jewish messiah" in this work. I use the term "Jewish messiah" in a broad functional sense, including all manner of central figures who act as leaders of Jewish messianic movements. These figures may call themselves messiahs, though generally they prefer to have others call them that. They may call themselves prophets or kings or priests, or take or receive other titles, such as leader or prince (nasi').[18] Since some of these terms may be used for other individuals without imputing messianic status—and since other terms, such as mother of the messiah (see chapter 5), may be used for those who function as leaders of messianic movements—the nomenclature must be taken into account, but what the individuals do must determine what the label means. It is often the case, for example, that those who prophesy the coming of messiahs turn out to be the messiahs they have prophesied. The term "messiah" thus presents itself as the most inclusive one. As will be seen, my broad application of the term permits the largest number of figures to be presented and studied together. If the term were restricted only to those who are anointed (as the literal meaning implies), no one could qualify from the period of the Second Temple until the present. Any further limitations on the application of the term—to king, say, as opposed to prophet—would clearly impose severe constraints on the field of study. Taking into account the polemics underlying the application of these terms in the early accounts[19]—written chiefly by opponents of the leaders and their followers, and often of Jews and Judaism in general—and attending to the activities of the leaders and their groups, their social function, and their common endings, one concludes that at least those authorities set against the messiahs did not clearly and consistently distinguish among their varieties. The Jewish messiahs have continued to be lumped together, most commonly and simply as "false messiahs." My conviction that each Jewish messiah is unique and deserving of individual attention is actually what brought about this book. The fact that a book like this has not been written before arises, I presume, from the confusion that stems from one's desire to expose or to deny, even to conceal, phenomena that might be thought scandalous or shameful or unworthy, phenomena that might interfere with one's own self-esteem as a Jew. In the image of the mirror that breaks as the messiah looks into it, I find the messiah's doubt and fear. In the image of the brightness that is a common feature of the physiognomy of the messiah, so blinding that one cannot peer into it, I find the desire not to look at what is there.

BIBLIOGRAPHIC NOTE   The important literature is cited here in the notes. In addition to the literature mentioned, there are several recent collections of messianic studies in English that testify to the continuing, if not increasing, interest in the topic. Three are particularly useful: J. H. Charlesworth, ed., *The Messiah* (Princeton, 1987); J. Neusner, W. Green, and E. Frerichs, eds., *Judaisms and Their Messiahs* (Cambridge, 1987); and M. Saperstein, *Essential Papers on Messianic Movements and Personalities in Jewish History* (New York, 1992). My approach to anointment and the messiahs in the discussion of the biblical messiah is new, I believe, only in associating some of the acts of anointment (those that involve inanimate holy objects) with others (those of the prophets, kings, and priests). The key points of the discussion in regard to human anointment have often been explored, most recently in John J. Collins, *The Scepter and The Star* (New York, 1995), pp. 20–48; and earlier, at greater length, in Joseph Klausner, *The Messianic Idea in Israel* (New York, 1955), pp. 13–243.

2

THE ISRAELITE MESSIAHS

Jesus of Nazareth and Shim'on bar Kosiba and Their Forerunners

The postbiblical usage of the word "messiah" connects the messiah with the end of time and its mysteries. It is associated with reinterpretations of biblical verses and certain literary works, such as the Apocrypha and Pseudepigrapha, the Qumran material, and rabbinic doctrines as they appear in the early literature or in the canon of the New Testament.[1] Sacrificing a present throne, the messiah now gains a distant one instead, ultimately (by the middle of the second century BCE) one in Heaven at the end of this era. The messiah of the apocalypse is essentially a fantasy, never to come true in this world or in this time except through God's will and effort. Yet the lineaments of this fantasy figure and the apocalyptic drama shape the expectations of the real followings of real messiahs and thus control what they attempt to do, or what they are said to have done.

The incarnate messiahs after the exile combine this-worldliness and apocalypticism in different proportions. The accounts of the first messiahs that responded to the aggressions of foreign rulers on the soil of the land of Israel—from the Maccabees through Shim'on bar Kosiba (this traditional English transliteration of *kosiva* and *kokhva* will be used throughout)—have no apocalyptic agenda at all. The primary goal of these messiahs was to rid society of alien impositions, mostly by military means. While Bar Kosiba became the epitome of the militant messiah, Jesus—who actually appeared more than a century before Bar Kosiba, although their accounts develop alongside one another—is the first to incorporate apocalyptic themes. The accounts of Jewish messianic events after Bar Kosiba generally enhance the apocalyptic, fantastic elements. The biblical prophet, with his intimate connections to the divine court and world, reenters here as the cosmic voyager, returning with cargoes of new imagery and theology and tales of the messiah who is waiting to be called. While the messiahs of these events may act as political, religious, and military leaders (this-worldly messiahs), their stories inevitably elevate their deeds to miracles and themselves to divine heights. Their character mixes together reality and surreality. As this-worldly messiahs, they seek to enable their community to overcome oppression and continue into the immediate local future. As apocalyptic messiahs, they strive to achieve fantastic objectives: eternal life, mastery over the physical world, utter contentment. These apocalyptic features, which come to predominate in our own modern understanding of what a messiah is, originally develop as peculiarly Jewish characteristics, extrapolated from Jewish tradition, applied in a new way by Jewish rabbinic scholars and mystics and then by messiahs themselves and their adherents.

This chapter will trace the history of the first militant Jewish movements that opposed foreign rule, from the Maccabbees to Bar Kosiba. It will then cover the development of apocalyptic themes within rabbinic theory as a means of rejecting militant this-worldly messiahs, and the subsequent adoption of apocalyptic themes in the accounts of one of these messiahs, Jesus. The focus on the accounts of Jesus and Bar Kosiba will illustrate the contrast between the two as messianic figures as well as the process through which both are rejected by contemporary rabbinic opinion.

THE MACCABEAN REVOLT AND THE RULE
OF THE HASMONEANS

According to the texts, the Maccabean-led rebellion against the Hellenistic Syrian rule of the Seleucids was sparked in 168 or 167 BCE by the disdainful and provocative way in which the rulers treated the popular religion. The Hasmoneans—Jews who ascended to power in 143 BCE, following the successful revolt—lacked Davidic lineage. None of the Hasmonean princes claimed to be from that house, or to be divine (which they might easily have done, following the model of other foreign leaders), or to have been divinely sent. The dynasty cooperated in the disintegration of a peculiarly Jewish culture, took possession of the priesthood, and opened the way, toward the end of its rule, for foreign powers again to set upon what they would better have left alone—the religion of the Jews. But the Maccabean legend itself confirmed and glorified the principle of armed revolt against a superior force as an act of national redemption. With but a single exception, armed resistance came to be the most important constituent of the messiah's activity in the land of Israel until the fall of Bar Kosiba at Betar in 135 CE, and the expectation of victory would be active in subsequent messianic events until the expulsion from Spain, over sixteen centuries later. Fearless courage and physical strength remained the most important qualities of the messiah for a long while. None of the Hasmoneans themselves could be the messiah, though, since they ultimately failed to bring about the complete restoration of a divine state. And since the situation worsened for Jews after Pompey settled a Hasmonean quarrel and Rome gained control of the territory, subsequent messiahs who followed the example of Yehuda ben Mattityahu (called Maccabee, "the Hammer") were found to lack a quality necessary to accomplish the

Redemption. This quality was identified as holiness. The rabbinic attack upon the legend of the Maccabees as national saviors entirely removes the Maccabees from the reconsecration of the temple and is used to support the rabbis' claim to sole authority in determining the nature of the messiah and authenticating messianic claimants.[2] Shaye Cohen differentiates the two accounts:

> In the [account in 1 Macc. 4:36–59] the Maccabees purify the temple precincts, make new utensils, reinstitute the sacrificial cult, and establish the new holiday. [In Babylonian Talmud—hereafter, TB—Shabbat 21b], instead of emphasizing the Maccabean victory and purification of the Temple, the rabbis ascribe the origins of Hanukkah to a miraculous event: A cruse of oil that should have been exhausted after only one day provided oil for eight days until a new supply could be readied. This story is not mentioned in the First Book of Maccabees, which states simply that "the Jews lit the lamps," and gives no reason for the eight-day duration of the festival. The rabbinic story thus "demilitarizes" Hanukkah, commemorating a deed of God, not a deed of man. The rabbis followed a quietist political policy and did not admire revolutionaries who fought against the state.[3]

JEWISH REBELLIONS AGAINST ROME, THROUGH THE BAR KOSIBA REVOLT

The Roman general Pompey conquered the Maccabean kingdom of Judah in 63 BCE, thus initiating centuries of Roman rule over the land of Israel. Rome's policies of taxation and military occupation, capped by its disregard for the religion of the populace, provided fertile ground, washed with blood, for one messianic candidate after another. It is true that several of the names mentioned in Josephus during this period might refer to some of the same people, but his descriptions give more of an impression of a quasi-dynastic line of rebels. Some rebels were in fact related, some might have been, and some might just have chosen names that appeared alike. From the period after "order" was reinstituted, under Archelaus in 6 CE, until the war that culminated in the destruction of the temple in 70 CE, we encounter (in Josephus and in the New Testament) one, two, or three messianic contenders known as Yehuda or Theudas; Jesus of Nazareth; Menahem, the son of the Yehuda known as "the Galilean"; and Simon (Shim'on), the son of Giora. The last to appear in the land of Israel[4] (one or two others appeared, meanwhile, in the Diaspora) was Shim'on bar Kosiba, who operated in the south rather than in the Galilee, where the others had arisen. The texts speak of these figures as leader or king, and as messiah only in that meaning.

Josephus, while willing enough to describe the Maccabean revolt as righteous (since it wasn't against Rome), refers to three of the Galilean messiahs as brigands (armed opponents of Roman rule).[5] They appeared shortly after Herod died, when Roman armed force was weakened and confusion reigned. As Josephus noted, "There were ten thousand other disorders in Judea; . . . a great number put themselves into a warlike posture. . . . There was Judas, the son of that Ezekias who had been head of the robbers; which Ezekias was a very strong man, and had with great difficulty been caught by Herod." This Judas gathered a number of men "of profligate character" from Sepphoris and attacked the palace in the Galilee, plundering the armory and the treasury and arming his men. Then, Josephus said, he "became terrible to all men, tearing and rending those that came near him, . . . in order to raise himself to royal dignity." Appearing in 6 CE, Judas is the best documented of the rebels.[6] Josephus even identifies him as the initiator of the fourth philosophy among the Jews, that of the Zealots.[7] This is the most violent philosophy of the four and so may be identified with the activities of the preceding Galilean messiahs. This is perhaps why Josephus associates Judas here with the Galilee rather than with the east side of the Jordan, as he does elsewhere. Josephus holds the Zealots responsible for all the violence against Rome that led to the destruction of the temple. According to Josephus, the cause of Judas' revolt was a census ordered by a Roman senator and consul, Cyrenius; Judas considered the Roman census a violation of Jewish liberty and the kingship of God, and called for its violent rejection. Both Judas and his men are said to have been obdurate and courageous, insistent on the loyalty of the populace, and religious in the sense that Judas assumes the assistance of God in his victories and brings a priest, Zadok, in with him. Josephus mentions the disdain Judas' party showed for torture and death. Josephus does not make Judas' fate explicit, but there is a reference to his rebellion and death in Acts 5:37; he is said to have died, having rebelled against Roman taxation, and to have had many followers, who later were scattered.

The next figure Josephus mentions is Simon, a son of Judas, tall, robust, and handsome, who crowned himself king, excited at the opportunity disorder presented. When his forces met the Romans, they "fought rather in a bold than a skillful manner" and were defeated. Simon and his brother James were crucified on the orders of Alexander, the procurator.

The third of Josephus' rebels, Athronges (in Hebrew, *etrog;* "citron," the fruit associated with the holiday of Sukkot), was also tall, with strong hands, and had been a shepherd, with no claim to the throne through wealth or family: "This man thought it so sweet a thing to do more than ordinary injuries to others, that although he should be killed, he did not so much care, if he lost his life in so great a design." He took the crown; ruled for some time with the advice of an appointed council; and killed many, both Romans and the king's forces, eventually leading his men in a senseless campaign of cruelty against Jews and Romans, soldiers and civilians alike, before he was finally subdued. These three figures had in common, daring, passion, physical stature, and a hatred for foreign domination. All demanded loyalty from the populace. In this regard, the kingly figure of Saul comes to mind; and in his pastoral simplicity, the figure of David arises from the description of Athronges.

During the rebellion of Judas the Galilean, another sort of messiah, a prophet-magician, made his first appearance: Theudas is mentioned in Acts, immediately preceding the verse on Judas' revolt and death, and by Josephus in *Antiquities of the Jews* (bk. 20, chap. 5). The author of Acts sees Theudas and Judas as similar in their presumption, their failure, and the disaster that came upon those who believed in them or obeyed them. In this account, both Theudas and Judas represent the wrong way to go about bringing the kingdom of God to power; they are mere men. Their failures are contrasted with the victory and exaltation of the slain

Jesus. Josephus' description directs our attention to the characteristic that distinguishes Theudas from Judas.[8] He writes that "a certain magician named Theudas persuaded a great part of the people to take their effects with them and follow him to the river Jordan; for he told them he was a prophet, and that he would, by his own command, divide the river, and afford them an easy passage over it; and many were deluded by his words." The Romans slew many of his followers. Theudas himself was taken alive and beheaded, and his head was brought to Jerusalem. Unlike Judas, Theudas was a magician who set out to work a miracle, like that of Moses. In doing so, he was the first to model himself on Moses; much later, some rabbinic arguments and many messiahs would take Moses, rather than David, as the messianic ideal.

In the New Testament we hear of other messiahs, apart from Jesus. In Acts 21:38, Paul is taken for one while on his way into Jerusalem, where he expects to meet death. The chief captain of the soldiers asks Paul if he can speak Greek and then accuses him of being "that Egyptian, who made such an uproar a short while before and led four thousand murderous men out into the wilderness." Paul denies this and is given permission to address the people nearby, in Hebrew. Josephus gives us additional information about the Egyptian (see *Antiquities*, bk. 20, chap. 8, par. 6; and *Wars*, bk. 2, chap. 13, par. 5): A prophet who summoned his following to the Mount of Olives, the Egyptian promised that the walls of Jerusalem would fall so that they might enter the city. Four hundred were slain, but the Egyptian escaped, never to be heard from again. Josephus says that he had thirty thousand followers and describes him as a "false prophet."

The last messiahs to have as their unique goal the immediate political emancipation of the Jews in the land of Israel appeared between Jesus' death and the end of Bar Kosiba's revolt. These were Menahem, the son or perhaps grandson of Judas the Galilean; Shim'on bar Giora; and the first to wage his war outside the land of Israel, a man named either Lukuas or Andreas.

In 66 CE, Menahem captured the Roman arms at Masada (Herod's palace), came "in state" to Jerusalem and put the Roman garrison there under siege. His attempts to break into the chief fortress, the Antonia, were not successful, but the king's men surrendered in fear, and many Romans were caught and slain. The following day, two priests who had been helping the Romans were killed. Eleazar, the priest who had started the war by refusing Roman offerings in the temple, gained control of the Antonia fortress, remaining a barrier to Menahem's rule. It was at this time that Josephus himself arrived in Jerusalem. He was at first afraid to go out of the temple's inner court and he emerged only in disguise as a member of the rebels' party (*The Life of Flavius Josephus*, par. 5). He would probably have remained in disguise had the rebels been more successful, but from this point on, the Romans had the upper hand, and Menahem and his men were eventually killed—either slain on the spot or captured, tortured, and slain in the ensuing internecine struggle.

Several groups of resisters continued to struggle against Rome even after the destruction of the temple in 70 CE. They included the *sicarii* (dagger-men), the Idumeans, and others less well known. Two such groups had leaders whom Josephus mentions by name—John of Gischala and Shim'on bar Giora. The first of these, from a wealthy family, was a political and religious moderate who sought power without going to war. No claims to kingship can be associated with him. Ultimately, his forces were absorbed into those of Bar Giora, whom Josephus describes as strong and courageous. After failing to gather much support among other rebel groups, Josephus notes, Bar Giora left Masada for the mountains: "There he proclaimed liberty to those in slavery, and a reward to those already free, and got together a set of wicked men from all quarters." His band carried out attacks, wounding and robbing the Roman forces and the rich, pro-Roman Jews. Due to the appeal of his program, which supported the poor against the rich, freed the slaves, and promised vengeance, "his army grew . . . and a great many of the populace were obedient to him as to their king" (*Wars*, bk. 4, chap. 9, par. 3). Shim'on united and led the remaining forces that struggled within Jerusalem in the last days of the rebellion. His final ignominy calls for attention since some of his deeds can also be found in other messianic careers. Taking some close followers with him, along with some miners, to show them the way, he attempted to escape from the Romans into caverns beneath the city. When he failed to make good his escape, he donned the purple-bordered, white robes of a Roman aristocrat and, rising up out of the cave, he revealed himself to the Romans and surrendered. In their triumphal celebration, the Romans led him into the forum with a rope around his head, tormenting him along the way, and slew him there (*Wars*, bk. 7, chap. 6, par. 1). Rome closed Jerusalem to Jews, and the parties of the enduring resistance returned to the Galilee and the Judaean wilderness.

The first rebel figure who appeared outside the defeated homeland sought to foment revolution against Rome throughout the lands of the eastern and southern Mediterranean, about 40 years after the destruction of the temple and the capitulation of the populace of the land of Israel. Dio Cassius calls this rebel Andreas (*Roman History*); Eusebius calls him Lukuas (*Ecclesiastical History*, bk. 4, chap. 2). He led a Jewish revolt against Rome and its local representatives in the years 115–117 CE; he began the revolt in Libya (in the city or region of Cyrene) and, after its success there, it spread across north Africa to Egypt and Cyprus and threatened the stability of the government in Mesopotamia. Eusebius dates the start of the uprising before the appearance of Lukuas, who continued it and gave it new life. Both Dio and Eusebius assert that the number of people killed by the rebels was very high, and that the number of Jews slain by the Roman forces and their allies (particularly the Greeks of Alexandria) was likewise enormous. Dio writes in fact that 220,000 Romans and Greeks perished in Cyrene and Egypt and that a similar number was killed on Cyprus. He also writes that thereafter, Jews were not allowed to set foot on the island, so perhaps all the Jews of Cyprus were killed at that time. The west-to-east movement of the revolt might indicate that it was headed for the land of Israel; the ferocity that Dio says the rebels displayed toward their enemies is more typical of a religio-political war (as are the numbers of the dead in the accounts) than of a mere political struggle. The complete extermination of opponents and the lack of any continuation of the conflict indicate a messianic outburst, but neither Dio nor Eusebius speaks of the leader as a messiah or king. The movement may not have been a messianic one at all. Furthermore, its interests might not have lain in a return to power in the land of Israel. The leader might not have had any messianic pretensions, although the texts make it seem that he did. He might only have been seeking to establish self-rule for Jewish communities outside Israel; or he might have been setting out, step by step, to recapture the land of Israel itself.

RABBINIC DOCTRINE IN THE PERIOD OF ROMAN RULE:
THE APOCALYPTIC MESSIAH

Given the failure of all these attempts, Rome came to represent evil itself, an opponent transformed into a principle of opposition to the divine, or at least to the Jews, who perceived themselves and their possession of the land of Israel as divinely ordained, all the more so as possession became untenable. This transference of political reality into the realms of fantasy finds its place in another sort of writing about the messiah—the classical rabbinic texts. Certain matters are common to the two types of accounts—those which are theoretical and those which claim to record events—but the rabbinic interpreters set themselves up as arbiters, first, of acts being recalled, and thereafter, of contemporary society. Phenomena associated with particular messianic events, earlier or contemporary, appear within rabbinic theory largely in order to show how the rabbis denied these phenomena and were right to do so. In spite of the power of rabbinic interpretation and rabbis themselves in Jewish society, their ideas about the messiah determine neither what a following expects nor what a messiah does; the ideas are variables and the messiahs and followers choose their way among them as they see fit. As each movement falters, rabbinic theory does play a part in its collapse, lowering hopes and discouraging potential adherents. Rabbinic theory also influences public perception of the outcome of each event, emphasizing its uniformly unhappy result. A theology that rejects actual messiahs burgeons as the details of each failure vary. The accounts of continuing believers, on the other hand, do not exactly regard the attempts as failures. Instead, they take refuge in a (relatively limited) number of fantasies.

What we have of rabbinic doctrine concerning the messiah largely postdates the destruction of the Second Temple in 70 CE. The germane discourses from before this date, as they are recorded in later, classical sources, speak simply of the character and appearance of the messiah: He relieves Israel of the oppression of foreign domination; he is pious; he is Davidic. They do not associate him with eschatological elements or miracles. Although the Davidic line had disappeared by the time of the Hasmoneans, there was no rush to find prophetically recognized claimants. After the destruction of the First Temple, none of the priests or messiahs laid claim to his position on the basis of lineal descent from David, until the claim was made on behalf of Jesus. Redemption was possible and depended on a united effort by the people, perhaps entailing strict adherence to time-honored religious conduct. After the fall of the Second Temple, all this changes. Redemption must counter evil, a metaphysical phenomenon given flesh in the presence of Rome on holy soil. The doctrines of redemption had first begun to change when Pompey took the reins for Rome in 63 BCE, and with the fall of the temple, redemption became something that would occur beyond the time of the individual or even the world, and that would be achieved by options that were metaphysical and a subject of debate. The Pharisees determined the outcome of the debate as it touched on the execution of policy. These sages were dismayed in the face of the defeat by Rome and resolved to follow their own course of national salvation, one that would debar a physical struggle against such odds.

If no messiah-militant could unite the populace before the destruction, then, lacking the support of the dominant party, the Pharisees, afterward, he certainly could not overcome the armed force of Rome. No messiah thereafter could succeed by proclaiming himself; only the sages could certify his candidacy, and they would not support a candidate whose platform conflicted with theirs. The fact that the messiah of Christian beliefs had a name intruded on the dominant group's desire to retain the privilege of approval and drove the debates, mentioned in rabbinic literature, over the supernatural or multiple names of the messiah.[9] The time of the appearance of the messiah became an eschatological one; imaginative discourse elaborated the general notion that the time before the messiah came would be full of horror. The dominant image of this period was drawn from the Isaiah text (26:17), which mentions the "birth pangs" of the time of the messiah. The text was originally one of despair: the travails do not produce a viable birth. Now a redemption was set in place to follow the birth pangs. So much was added to the suffering, including a turn to heresy, the forgetting of the law, and the degradation of parents and scholars (TB Sanh. 97a), that more than one authority prayed to be spared the coming of the messiah altogether. These images were little more than descriptions of the world the scholars feared, one close to the reality of their time, threatening them and their hold on a bookish, male, oligarchic rule by seniors. Descriptions of the final stage of redemption that followed the travails were likewise exaggerated. Agricultural images, among others, further removed the good time from the realm of possibility, even plausibility; the land having been irretrievably lost, the fruits of a fantasy land swelled to enormous proportions. In the same way, despite the impossibility of verifying any claim to Davidic descent, scholarly theory held firm on the prerequisite of such descent in the messiah (and it seems that the Romans deemed anyone making such a claim a rebel; cf. the lineage of Jesus in Luke). With its insistence on miracles, its antagonism toward the idea that humans can bring on the redemption under the leadership of a messiah, its unnatural, miraculous conditions, and its determination to deny paradise to those who figure on the redemption and calculate its time, together with an ethics that promotes the concepts of restraint and patience and the rewards of suffering, rabbinic doctrine moves sharply to usurp the program of national redemption.[10] The sages decide to leave such matters outside human determination.[11]

However reasonable and well-advised the rabbinic teaching was, there is in it not a little of the stoic's fear of unshackled appetite. Following messianic figures is tempting, offering an immediate and all-encompassing resolution to multiple and interwoven stresses. It possesses a seduction of its own, even, it seems, drawing the individual and the society into self-annihilation. The continued appearance of messianic candidates, then, despite rabbinic opposition, is hardly surprising. A concept with enduring power, one that could bridge the gap between rabbinic rejection and popular cravings, entered the inventory of messianic expectations at this time. This concept would prove indispensable to revolutionary movements in overcoming the disaster of apparent defeat.

THE TWO MESSIAHS

There had already existed a two-messiah doctrine—involving a holy priest and a holy king, a pairing that had actually functioned in a couple of cases.[12] Antagonism toward the Hasmonean priesthood had impelled the earlier two-messiah doctrine, decreasing the independent authority of the priest, appointed for political and economic reasons and given to Hellenizing the religion. The failed "Galilean" military campaigns in Judaea led to a new way of doubling the messiah.[13] This later doctrine, in which a messiah of the lineage of Joseph (or Ephraim) preceded a second messiah, of the house of David, preserved messianic belief in the face of repeated disasters, and retained the loyalty of those who adhered to any and all previous messiahs.[14] Through this doctrine, the Pharisees could keep their own messiah figure— now in the form of the messiah of the lineage of David—out of reach and free from contamination by natural and political inevitabilities. The doctrine became more prestigious in Judaism, facing Christian rivalry, as a parallel to the doctrine of the second coming. The idea was, in effect, a new insurance policy against ultimate failure, and strenuous efforts were made to prove its validity by referring to biblical texts. This hedge treats both the current contender and his movement as having a less than certain chance of success, and weakens total commitment to an effort in the present, thus rewarding and effectively guaranteeing the failure of any such movement. The events of the Bar Kosiba uprising displayed the new doctrine of the two messiahs—if they did not actually create the doctrine—in its most pernicious form. One authority goes so far as to say, "The issue of the Messiah and the meaning of Israel's history formed through the Messiah myth convey in their terms precisely the same position we find elsewhere in all other symbolic components of the rabbinic system and canon. . . . Israel acts to redeem itself . . . by giving up all pretense at deciding its own destiny. So weakness is the ultimate strength, forbearance the final act of self-assertion, passive resignation the sure step toward liberation. (The parallel is the crucified Christ.)"[15] Christian influence on (Jewish) messiah doctrine can also be detected in the loving attention paid, measure for measure, to the sufferings of this doomed messiah and his citizenry.

In a peculiar countermeasure to the two-messiah doctrine, the idea of the false messiah was soon developed as well; it also arose in close interaction with Christian views. During the Galilean rebellions, the term "false" was first applied to a prophet in a messianic context, paving the way for the explicit application of the term to messiahs.[16] But it was the Christian texts that coined the term *pseudochristoi* (Greek for "false messiahs"); Matthew 24:4, 6, 24; Mark 13:5, 21–22; and Luke 21:3 all use the term *pseudochristos* to refer to messianic pretenders. The Jewish tradition follows the Christian; the Greek term is borrowed and translated in the much later Hebrew term *mashiah sheker*, which reshapes and alters the previous Hebrew usage of the term "lying" (*sheker*), in connection with the witness and prophet, so that it means "false witness, false prophecy."[17] The Christian texts describe how a false messiah may be recognized, and they assert the nature of the time of his appearance, which is the equivalent of the rabbinic "birth pangs of the messiah." Having developed the doctrine of a second coming of one messiah, these basic texts have no need for two authentic messiahs, the first of them doomed to die. Instead, the false messiah causes the world to suffer, and the suffering precedes, and is essential to, the true coming of a kingdom of God—at least insofar as the identification of the false messiah identifies the true one by contrast—which will overwhelm Roman rule and replace it without war. Perhaps the doctrine of the messiah of the lineage of Joseph provokes the idea of the false messiah in the Gospels; the signs of the false messiah described in Matt. 24:26 intend to discredit Essenic figures from the city as well as the desert. The Gospels develop the theme of falseness because they have to falsify messianic contenders other than Jesus. (Acts 8:9–24 qualifies Simon Magus as the first Christian messiah.) Jewish texts don't need to develop strategies to put down competition against what is largely a chimera. Their need is to retain the adherence of the followers of all the failed messiahs from King Saul through Bar Kosiba and to direct them toward an ever-distant, inspiring illusion. After Bar Kosiba, no messianic contender arises for nearly three centuries. The term "false messiah" first finds general employment in Judaism against the Persian messiahs of the eighth century (see chapter 3), again by Jewish authors who will not allow them even the aura of holiness attached to the messiah of the lineage of Joseph. The desire of these authors is to falsify the claims of the messiahs, perhaps in order to defend their faith against Moslem accusations of gullibility, and to reject their adherents in the same way the Gospels reject Jesus' competitors. Thereafter, Jews continue to use the term against others elsewhere, as well as in retrospect, including, preeminently, Jesus.[18]

THE SIGNIFICANCE OF JESUS AND BAR KOSIBA
AS MESSIANIC FIGURES

Jesus' activity preceded the destruction of the Second Temple by some 40 years. Another 60 years separated the destruction from the rebellion led by Shim'on bar Kosiba. From the time of the Maccabean uprising in 163 BCE to the fall of Betar and the death of Bar Kosiba in 135 CE, strife and rebellion were rampant from the Galilee through the southernmost part of Judaea. Several of these rebel movements have been described above. We can assume that the Roman sources, including Josephus, exaggerate the cruelty and ambition of such movements while downplaying, even libeling, their religious motivations. The few, and partisan, sources on which we must depend do not sufficiently describe these men. We can, however, gain a sense of the range of activities of the prophets, bandits, and messiahs of this long period through an examination of two leaders—Jesus and Bar Kosiba—about whom we do have some detailed information.

The accounts we have of Jesus and Bar Kosiba developed together, responding to each other, though the men were not contemporaries. The Gospels were completed around the time of Bar Kosiba's revolt, and they are, for all practical purposes and for centuries, the true story of Jesus. The few references to Jesus in the

Talmud argue against the Christian movement and the claims the Gospels come to make on Jesus' behalf.[19] The Talmud is also antagonistic toward Bar Kosiba and thus even-handed in its opposition to flesh-and-blood messiahs. The Gospels and early Christian writings promote the idea of an atoning death and a second coming, the parousia, as properly representing Jesus' history. On the other hand, the rabbis promote the role of the *mashiah ben yosef* (the messiah of the lineage of Joseph) in order to reject the parousia and its implications of divinity (and, therefore, Jesus as he is represented in the Gospels), as well as to diminish Bar Kosiba's effort and limit the damage to national spirit following his rebellion.[20]

By the end of the second century CE, Jesus of Nazareth, to whom the term "king" is inappropriately applied since his messianic role is more like Samuel's, that of a prophet and a political leader, has ascended to victory in the minds of many, although he is still opposed by Pharisaic rabbinic views. For some Jews, he has become the true messiah precisely because he does not lead a military force against Rome in his attempt to establish the kingdom of God. After his death at the hands of the Romans, he continues to perform acts—miracles, particularly miraculous cures—that were the central element of his life as messiah. These acts occur before the second coming, giving testimony that Jesus is not really dead at all. Surviving death became a common feature in later messiah histories, as a result of the irresistible might of the governing power, which guaranteed death to messianic rebels, forcing their followers to deny that they had in fact died in order to vindicate their own continued existence. However much the early background of this element can be associated with figures such as Moses, Elijah, and Zerubbabel, it is the history of Jesus of Nazareth that concentrates the theology of physical resurrection into a requisite feature of the messiah's career.

Soon after Jesus died, as the process of his transfiguration got under way, the figure of the messiah became inextricably bound up with apocalyptic themes. The messiah became one of the characters in the fantasy of cosmic warfare, and messianic wars against real political and military forces took on some of the trappings of this fantasy. Jesus' "kingdom of Heaven" stands in opposition to the evil kingdom, that of Rome.

The accounts of Shim'on bar Kosiba, the king-messiah, enact the conflict between a continuing pressure to achieve political self-determination and a desire to resort to fantasy in order to avoid real failure. Though the texts record that an important elderly rabbinical authority, R. Akiba, recognized Bar Kosiba as the king-messiah, they also show that Akiba's opinion was derisively rejected, and that the sad outcome of Bar Kosiba's endeavor was due to his own lack of spiritual qualifications. He was considered incapable of "smelling the truth" and so was not a fit judge according to the fantastic standards of the rabbinic code, and he was found to lack sufficient piety. Bar Kosiba's reign lasted for two and a half years, from 133 CE to 135 CE, and he was the last messiah to appear in the land of Israel until the sixteenth century.

Their texts place the two messiahs in opposition to each other in several important ways. (Indeed, the two messiahs are juxtaposed by Justin, as quoted by Eusebius, cited below.) Shim'on bar Kosiba appears as a southerner and a this-worldly messiah, conservative in his religion and militant in his conduct; Jesus, a Galilean, is a messiah speaking for another world, not for the kingdom of humans. His use of the term "kingdom of God" to refer to a reign that God will soon bring about differs essentially from that of every other rebel of the period. Similar terms when used by Jesus' contemporaries and fellow messiahs, such as the kingship of God set forth in the militant program of Judas in 6 CE (cited above), denote the Jewish rejection of Roman institutions (the kingship of Rome), taxation in particular—a tradition that peaks at the time of Bar Kosiba's revolt. The stories of Bar Kosiba and Jesus, epitomizing one sort of messianism (that of Bar Kosiba) and initiating another (that of Jesus), make the texts of their lives a foundation for the realities and texts of all later Jewish messiahs.

JESUS OF NAZARETH

More has been written about Jesus than about any other Jewish messiah, yet it is quite common to find his Jewishness ignored, particularly by the traditional historians of Christianity, and even recently by Jewish writers (Sharot, for example) concerned with Jewish messiahs. None of the best modern scholars disagree on his community or context or role. He was a Galilean Jew, of the first century CE, who acted as a messiah and was taken for one. His messiahship drew on traditions that lay within the sphere of Israelite Judaism, whether rabbinic or popular. These included adherence to the common ritual practices and the laws of his community, a system that did not distinguish between religious and civil conduct. When Jesus asserts that the foundation of his faith lies in the confession known as the Shema ("Hear, O Israel, the Lord our God is one"), he may be suggesting that Judaism is reducible to this, but if so, this is surely not far from the faith of other Jews able to proclaim only this single phrase, or from that of Jews with a richer tradition, who accepted this as their confession at morning and at night, as their first and their last words. Jesus' involvement in practices like magic and in ideals like social egalitarianism was not particularly distinctive in his time. He was an apocalypticist and a prophet who proclaimed the imminence of the kingdom of God. This was not unusual either, though it did stimulate his party to bring as many people into his following as soon as possible. His social and personal program reached those who were unsatisfied with their own circumstances in the Jewish society of the time. In turn, his followers, who tended to come from the fringes of society, affected his teaching. The pattern of popular recognition and anointing of the claimant to leadership (see the Introduction) was well understood, though as objectionable to those in power in Jesus' time as it was in Absalom's. Jesus' disagreements with the civil and religious authorities fell well, if uncomfortably, within the mosaic of developing beliefs and conducts of his community.

The novelty of Jesus' program lay in its stress on a single condition for gaining contentment. The coming kingdom of God would invert the social order and bring happiness to those who were marginalized, and less happiness to those who were content at present, if the former would affect an adherence to Jesus' leadership and teaching. Rabbinic and popular tradition required adherents who sought better lives to behave according to a particular ethical or political code and, by implication, to give fealty to the rabbis as its interpreters. Jesus reordered this, though he never dispensed with adherence to the religio-civil code, or at least tacit recognition of its authority. His arguments and amendments remained within the tradition of the development of that authority. The social programs of the northern prophets from the eighth century BCE on had held that the conduct of the wealthy and the powerful brought disaster upon them and that the conduct of the poor and powerless assured their righteousness. Jesus went farther than this. He insisted that one could not be powerful or rich and be righteous, nor could one be powerless and poor and be unrighteous. A person found guilty of a crime by a court that was itself a criminal body was innocent; the poor were impoverished by a social structure that dispossessed them. Jesus was also unlike other messiahs in his apparent disinterest in developing a program for gaining power against malign political authorities (those in Rome) or for governing his kingdom when it came. In fact, his desire to be put to death in Jerusalem, in itself unique among Jewish messiahs, brings together precisely these two peculiarities of his. It would seem that he expected betrayal and disaster and sought to make use of the expectation, if not to bring it about.

His working of miracles illuminates our understanding of the messiah as a prophet. When he raises the dead, he emulates the only anointed prophet-messiahs, Elijah and Elisha. The impulse toward messianic rule and that toward messianic prophecy had never been combined in a single messiah figure prior to Jesus, nor were they combined in his nemesis, Bar Kosiba, although Jewish messiahs after the defeat of 135 CE followed Jesus in working miracles and seeking power with divine or magic support. Moses' career serves as a reference and allows even this conception of Jesus within conventional bounds. The tale of Jesus' miraculous birth to a virgin (as opposed to Isaac's birth to an elderly couple, or Samuel's to a barren woman) sets him apart, again, from common traditions as the text counterposes him and his mother, Mary, to John the Baptist and his mother, Elizabeth. Like the tale of his return from death, this innovation has to be chalked up to later influences from outside Jewish circles.

The Gospel Accounts

The source we must draw upon for an account of Jesus' life is a synopsis of three Gospels of the New Testament—Matthew, Mark, and Luke. Through these are not contemporary accounts, they are derived from some that are. They depend heavily on interpolations; furthermore, they are probably translations themselves, and it is even more likely that the accounts on which they were based were not written Greek texts, but oral Aramaic stories. The Gospels all look back on Jesus' life from the vantage point of the Crucifixion and the Resurrection, which belong to later Christian theology. The Gospels have a purpose: to proclaim truths and to exclude irrelevant or conflicting material, just as the canon of the New Testament as a whole excludes other early writings centered on Jesus.

Paul is more nearly contemporary with Jesus, but he has a particular view of Jesus that serves his own teaching and his prospectus for a particular sort of organized mission and church. The Gospel according to John is similar to Paul's letters in its expression of a theology that does not correspond to the bare-bones account of the other three Gospels, taken together or separately. It reflects a much later theology that does not make sense when examined beside the versions of Matthew, Mark, and Luke. Yet even these earlier accounts reflect the conditions and needs of an established church, one that finds itself in different circumstances and with different concerns than those of Jesus and his following in his lifetime. Their accounts have been rewritten to include later ideas, such as the virgin birth; later politics, such as the displacement of John the Baptist through a recounting of his recognition of Jesus' greater power, in speaking about him and baptizing him, and through the adding of the tale of John's nonmiraculous birth; and later traditions, such as the use of biblical material as proof texts in renderings of Jesus' nature, mission, and biography. Matthew's text alone connects the motif of the one more fit to baptize (which John mentions to Jesus) to the kingdom of Heaven, combining the messianic roles of king, prophet, and—through the motif of purification in the presence of the divine—priest.

In my effort to reconstruct the original story of Jesus, I have followed E. P. Sanders's "framework" as he has developed it in his major works and in his essay "The Life of Jesus."[21] In an attempt to portray an untrammeled Jesus, Sanders's biography reduces the accounts to a bare framework by stripping them of material that can be shown to support motives of the later Christian church, and of some material that can be shown to come from earlier or common Jewish tenets and traditions. Sanders retains material that hangs together logically. The "A" accounts, as I call this bare framework, are the simplest accounts. They are logically essential to the addition of later material of many different kinds, which is itself not essential to the A accounts. I make no judgment that the simple account is more factual, more historical, or necessarily an earlier account, but just that it is a primary account in a logical way, something that everything else is somehow connected to. Here, I have also included material from the Gospels that I refer to as the "B" accounts; these are unlikely to be original accounts in the form of separate texts or subtexts. Yet since it is part of the whole text, this material, too, has had a great influence on the development of the Jewish messianic ritual and on the accounts and conduct of later Jewish messiahs. I've only set it apart as a sort of crude example of how a text might be built up. I have thus chosen B accounts that are attached to A accounts and that display some of the richness of the many different schools of Jewish messianic speculation of their times. Regarding the tradition on which later messianic accounts depend, these accounts in the Gospels, and not the schools and documents in which the speculations may have originated, are the effective sources. My translations are based mostly on those of the New English Bible (NEB); a plus sign after the source indicates that I have taken other translations and scholarship into account in revising them.

He was born

(A) Jesus was born [in the Galilee] during the [end of the] reign of Herod. (Matt. 2:1 NEB +)

The two B accounts that follow are connected to this A account. They distinguish Jesus in several ways from contemporary pretenders who assume the garb of common Jewish traditions and differ from each other in how they do that. Whereas the other messiahs are Galileans, Jesus' own Galilean birthplace is shifted away from there to begin telling how he is not like them. It is moved to Bethlehem in the well-known text from Matt. 1 in accordance with the biblical traditions concerning the birthplace of the messiah-king (see Isa. 16:1; Micah 5:2). In the first B account of his naming, we find a name story quite like those in the Hebrew Bible, in which a hero's destiny is established. Jesus is destined to "save his people," but the account adds a new layer of theology in its explanation—he is to save them from sin, rather than from the Romans. Both B accounts include the motif of the virgin birth, unparalleled in the Hebrew Bible or the common theology of the times. The association of sexual abstinence with an encounter with the divine is similar to what happens in the theophany at Sinai, where sexual abstinence was required as a measure of purification before the giving of the law, but no births followed that encounter. Mary's kinswoman, Elizabeth, like Sarah and Rachel and Hannah, is barren for some time before conceiving, but there is no suggestion of virginity in any of these cases. In the second B account, this motif is reinforced and another name story is attached, bringing us back to the biblical motif of the king-messiah who is the "Son of God." Both B accounts below maintain that Jesus was not sired by Joseph. Joseph's role, that of a sort of gentle, feckless fool, is exalted in his abasement and virtual disappearance from the tale. The absent-father motif is not uncommon in the Hebrew Bible or later, but here it has advanced far beyond Abraham's late siring of Isaac with an elderly woman through the agency of God and has altogether replaced the human father with a divine one. Joseph the Davidide accepts his role, offering his bloodline, a model of humility and self-effacement, in the following B account:

(B) This is the story of the birth of the Messiah. Mary, his mother, was betrothed to Joseph; before their marriage she found that she was with child by the Holy Spirit. Being a man of principle, and at the same time wanting to save her from exposure, Joseph desired to have the marriage contract set aside quietly. He had resolved on this, when an angel of the Lord appeared to him in a dream. "Joseph son of David," said the angel, "do not be afraid to take Mary home with you as your wife. It is by the Holy Spirit that she has conceived this child. She will bear a son; and you shall give him the name Jesus (he will save), for he will save his people from their sins." . . . Rising from sleep Joseph did as the angel had directed him; he took Mary home to be his wife, but had no intercourse with her until her son was born. And he named the child Jesus. (Matt. 1:18–25 NEB)

(B) "You shall conceive and bear a son and you shall give him the name Jesus . . ."
"How can this be," said Mary, "when my marriage has not been consummated?"
The angel answered, "The Holy Spirit will come upon you, and the power of the Most High will overshadow you; and for that reason the holy child to be born will be called 'Son of God.' Moreover, your kinswoman Elizabeth has herself conceived a son in her old age; and she who is reputed barren is now in her sixth month, for God's promises can never fail." (Luke 1:31–36 NEB)

He grew into manhood

(A) [Joseph] withdrew to the region of Galilee; there he settled in a town called Nazareth. (Matt. 2:23 NEB +). The child grew big and strong and full of wisdom. (Luke 2:40 NEB +)

Many of the elements in the following B accounts are familiar, similar to motifs in the Bible or in Near Eastern literature in common lore. The other Galilean pretenders were noted for their hardy physiques; Moses, too, escaped murder as an infant and came to Israel from Egypt. The motif of the prodigiously intelligent child, and its implication of a divine nature and destiny, is not simply an association with the schools of wisdom, so well known from the Egyptian milieu and enshrined biblically and rabbinically in some psalms, in the tales of Solomon, and in the Book of Proverbs. Like the tales of the magi who come to the birth and the astrologers who know and tell of it, Jesus' accession of brilliance, and its display in a contest with elders at a holy site, carry an air of magic. The tale in which the motif appears builds on others as it sets Jesus above established rabbinic figures, while at the same time endorsing him as one competent in their traditions. The exaggeration of the challenge Jesus presents them comes perhaps later than the event, while the prodigious knowledge is common to the biographies of many rabbinic figures, though not to any other messiahs of the period.

(B) After [Jesus'] birth [Herod sent the astrologers who'd seen the omens of the birth of the king of the Jews] to Bethlehem [to bring back a report]. After they had gone, an angel of the Lord appeared to Joseph in a dream and said to him, "Rise up, take the child and his mother and escape with them to Egypt, and stay there until I tell you; for Herod is going to search for the child to do away with him." So Joseph rose from sleep, and taking mother and child by night he went away with them to Egypt, and there he stayed till Herod's death. . . . When Herod saw that the astrologers [had not brought back a report] he fell into a passion, and gave orders for the massacre of all children in Bethlehem and its neighborhood, of the age of two years or less. (Matt. 2:2–16)

(B) When he was twelve [his parents made the Passover pilgrimage to Jerusalem]. When the festival was over and they left for home, the boy Jesus stayed behind in Jerusalem. . . . When they couldn't find him, they returned to Jerusalem to look for him; and after three days they found him sitting in the Temple surrounded by the teachers, listening to them and putting questions; and all who heard him were amazed at his intelligence and the answers he gave. (Luke 2:41–47)

He was baptized by John the Baptist

(A) About that time John the Baptist appeared as a preacher in the Judaean wilderness; his theme was: "Repent, for the kingdom of Heaven is upon you!" (Matt. 3:1 NEB). Then Jesus came from Nazareth in Galilee and was baptized in the Jordan by John (Mark 1:9 +).

John's baptism of Jesus lies within the tradition of prophets anointing prophets. The association of the baptism scene in Matthew with monarchic power (the "kingdom of Heaven") situates the baptism within the tradition of the anointment of kings by prophets while combining these roles, through the motif of purification as a condition of being close to God, with that of the sacrificing priest. The full accounts in Mark and Luke both contain John's prophecy that a better baptizer will come—a B element; Matthew's account alone contains John's demurrer: that it is more appropriate for Jesus to baptize him, to be the Elijah to his Elisha. The immersion returns Jesus to the purity of his birth. Recognition by others reinforces this theme. Like the baptizing sectarians of the time, the account in Matthew here sees bathing not simply as a way of preparing properly for an encounter with the divine, but as a public act of penitence that gives one entry into a particular community.

He called and trained an inner group of
adherents as proponents

Messiahs seek to engage proponents as well as followers. The proponents must have persuasive techniques as well as programmatic aims and receive some training in the techniques as well as the teachings. In the A account, then, we hear of the techniques: where to find the properly disposed audience, what to say, and how to hold the audience and demonstrate the validity of the message. Among an enthusiastic crowd, very little more than a kind word and a gentle hand is needed to make an unhappy person feel better—perhaps some simple medicines, cleansing, and bandaging. The A account contains some B elements, like raising the dead, but the rhetorical imperative and the promise in Jesus' words are more like an example he uses to train his proponents. Even if these accounts have been shaped to instruct later proponents, something like them must logically have taken place.

> (A) He then went up into the hill country and called the men he wanted, and they went and joined him. He appointed twelve as his companions and gave them the power to cast out unclean spirits and to cure every kind of ailment and disease: Simon, also called Peter [the Rock]; then came the sons of Zebedee, James and his brother John, to whom he gave the name Boanerges, "Sons of Thunder"; then Andrew and Philip and Bartholomew and Matthew the tax-gatherer and Thomas and James the son of Alphaeus and Thaddeus and Simon, a member of the Zealot party, and Judas Iscariot. . . . These twelve Jesus sent out with the following instructions: "Do not take the road to non-Jewish lands, and do not enter any Samaritan town; but go rather to the lost sheep of the house of Israel. And as you go proclaim the message: 'The kingdom of Heaven is upon you.' Heal the sick, raise the dead, cleanse lepers, cast out devils." (Mark 3:13–19 + ; Matt. 10:1–7 NEB +)

> (B) (and Judas Iscariot), the man who betrayed him. (Mark 3:19)

The addition of the description of Judas as "the man who betrayed him" to the account in Mark surrenders the narrative technique of suspense and formalizes the tale, creating from it a ritual recitation that transcends the sequence of events, privileging the narrative. It sets betrayal as a formal element in the matrix of the messiah text. Even though other preceding messiah texts have the messiah involved with his chief betrayer—from Saul to Bar Kosiba—none have the messiah choose his Judas and none have the doctrine that the betrayal leads to disaster, death, and then to the throne. No full-featured betrayal like this one occurs again, but this one informs all later texts in which only some aspect of betrayal appears. Even though early rabbinic speculations include the idea that the coming of the messiah may be hastened by appropriate conduct (repentance, as noted in the baptism narrative; unity; etc.), and though some even include the suggestion that his coming may be delayed by inappropriate conduct, only the Lurianic Kabbalah, Shabbateanism, and Frankism and, to some degree, the Hasidism of R. Nahman approach the daring of the divinely commissioned betrayal as it appears in Mark.

He taught about the kingdom of God, outside the cities of the Galilee

(A) He went round the whole of the Galilee, teaching in the synagogues, preaching the gospel of the Kingdom, and curing whatever illness or infirmity there was among the people. (Matt. 4:23)

(B) His fame reached the whole of Syria. . . . Great crowds also followed him. (Matt. 4:24 NEB +)

In the A account that follows, one should note some characteristics of rhetoric that seem to have been popular at the time. In particular, the message that Jesus preaches is fitted to the group he addresses. Since he is addressing a group without much power to determine their lives—Jews, and poor Jews at that—his arguments are put forward in an unexpected way. The surprise turn, with which he begins and ends each of the discourses, engages his listeners' minds while encouraging their hopes. It is a standard feature of rabbinic argumentation and of the sermon, particularly of the form known as the *petiḥta*, which opens a longer discourse and leads the listener in to it by challenging his expectations and proposing something that seems a non sequitur. The style is entertaining, engaging the listeners in a riddle; it is, moreover, one perfectly designed to reach a group that has lost the logic of its own life and any secure expectations.

(A) When he saw the crowds he went up the hill. He sat down. When his disciples gathered around him, he began to address them: . . . "Do not suppose that I have come to abolish the Law and the prophets; I did not come to abolish, but to complete. . . . I tell you this, unless you show yourselves far better men than the Pharisees and the doctors of the law, you can never enter the kingdom of Heaven. . . . You have learned that they were told, 'Love your neighbor, hate your enemy.' But what I tell you is this: 'Love your enemies and pray for your persecutors.'" (Matt. 5:1–45 NEB +)

They arrived at Bethsaida. There the people brought a blind man to Jesus and begged him to touch him. He took the blind man by the hand and led him away out of the village. Then he spat on his eyes, laid his hands upon him, and asked whether he could see anything. The man's sight began to come back, and he said, "I see men; they look like trees, but they are walking about." Jesus laid his hands on his eyes again; he looked hard and now he was cured so that he saw everything clearly. Then Jesus sent him home and said, "Do not tell anyone in the village."

Then he called the people to him, as well as his disciples, and said to them, "Anyone who wishes to be a follower of mine must leave self behind. . . . Whoever cares for his own safety is lost; but if a man will let himself be lost for my sake and for the gospel, that man is safe. . . . If anyone is ashamed of me and my words in this wicked and godless age, the Son of Man will be ashamed of him when he comes in the glory of his Father and of the holy angels. . . . I tell you this: there are some of those standing here who will not taste death before they have seen the kingdom of God already come to power." (Mark 8:22–26, 9:1 NEB +)

John, who was in prison, heard what the messiah was doing and sent his own disciples to him with this message: "Are you the one who is to come, or are we to expect some other?" Jesus answered, "Go and tell John what you hear and see: the blind recover their sight, the lame walk, the lepers are clean, the deaf hear, the dead are raised to life, the poor are hearing the good news—and happy is the man who does not find me a stumbling block."

When the messengers were on their way back, Jesus spoke to the people about John. . . . "I tell you this: there has never appeared on earth a mother's son greater than John the Baptist, and yet the least in the kingdom of Heaven is greater than he." (Matt. 11:2–11)

Three themes are intertwined in the accounts here: Jesus as a messiah of the anointed-prophet type ("some say [you are] John the Baptist, Elijah or another prophet" Mark 8:28); Jesus as the last of that type ("I have come not to abolish prophecy but to complete it" Matt. 5:17); and the imminence of Jesus' transmutation through death into the regnant-messiah type (see Mark 9:1, which notes that the kingdom is imminent and that he is to rule it). In contrast to all prevailing doctrines, his followers are told that his death is necessary for his transfiguration and that this will happen soon, in their own time; therefore, the order of things will be upset, and is in fact in the process of being upset at this very moment. The B text having this history before it, adds details. Jesus is quite restrained and ambiguous as he replies to John through John's disciples. The restraint Jesus requires of the blind man and of his followers ("don't tell it in the village" Mark 8:26; "I give you strict orders not to tell anyone about me" Mark 8:30) keeps Jesus in compliance with his own doctrine. The blind man cannot be expected not to relate the miracle done for him by Jesus but can be enjoined to add that Jesus told him not to tell anyone. The disciples are instructed to keep the secret of his belonging among the prophets (in keeping with the tradition of Moses' instructions, in Deut. 18:9–15, to disdain magicians and those who boast of their powers), and likewise, to keep secret his expectations and predictions. But, like the secret the blind man is in fact told to tell, these secrets too are told to the disciples in order for them to be told and to have it added in the retelling that Jesus wanted them kept secret.

(B) Jesus and his disciples set out for the villages of Caesarea Phillipi. On the way he asked them, "Who do men say I am?" They answered, "Some say John the Baptist, others Elijah, others one of the prophets." "And you," he asked, "who do you say I am?" Peter replied, "You are the Messiah." Then he gave them strict orders not to tell anyone about him. (Mark 8:27–30 NEB)

He made a Passover pilgrimage to
Jerusalem in about 30 CE

The A text that follows doesn't make much—a way of actually making quite a fuss—of Jesus' knowing that there was a colt waiting for him. It does seem likely that one might be found. The way the disciples explain, as they have been instructed, what they are doing leads the village people into a state of fervor: again, Jesus promises a better future, beginning with a worse present, symbolized in the act of stealing the colt and assuring its immediate return. They elevate his seat, provide him with comfort, and construct for him a royal procession, with criers for attracting others.

> (A) They were approaching Jerusalem and when they reached Bethpage and Bethany, at the Mount of Olives, he sent two of his disciples with these instructions: "Go to the village opposite, and just as you enter, you will find there a tethered colt that no one has yet ridden. Untie it and bring it here. If anyone asks, 'Why are you doing that?' say, 'Our master needs it and will send it back here without delay.'" So they went off and found the colt tethered to a door outside in the street. They were untying it when some of the bystanders asked, "What are you doing, untying that colt?" They answered as Jesus had told them and were then allowed to take it. So they brought the colt to Jesus and spread their cloaks on it, and he mounted. And people carpeted the road with their cloaks, while others spread brushwood that they had cut in the fields, and those who went ahead and the others who came behind shouted, "Hosanna! Blessings on him who comes in the name of the Lord! Blessings on the coming kingdom of our father David! Hosanna in the heavens!" (Mark 11:1–10 NEB +)

Note that this A text from Mark has only a single animal for Jesus to ride; the B text below has two animals on which he rides simultaneously as well as a proof text. The two animals have actually been lifted from the proof text, in which the use of the Hebrew poetic device called parallelism has been misunderstood and taken as literal rather than symbolic (the "and" used in Mathew 21:2 is misleading; the juncture is more like a comma). Reliance on proof texts actually leads to such misreadings: The event itself is substantiated by the biblical verse; if the biblical verse is not literal, it is of no use in the effort; if the occurrence does not match the biblical verse as taken literally, then the event is neither factual nor, in fact, the event spoken of in the verse. The process of using proof texts itself accompanies the transition from the account of the occurrence to the account of the previous account and shows how accounts dominate the events they describe. Oddly, the association of the verse from Zechariah 9:9 with the figure of David as messiah is itself dubious. The redeemer referred to seems closer to a king of the Solomonic type—peaceful and subservient to God—than to the belligerent David.

(B) They were now nearing Jerusalem; and when they reached Bethpage at the Mount of Olives, Jesus sent two disciples with these instructions: "Go to the village opposite, where you will at once find a tethered donkey and a colt with her; untie them and bring them to me." . . . This was in fulfillment of the prophecy that says:

Tell the daughter of Zion:

"Look, your king comes to you;

humble, riding on a donkey

and on a colt, the foal of a beast of burden." [Zech. 9:9]

They brought the donkey and the colt; then they laid their cloaks on their backs and he sat on them. (Matt 21:1–7 NEB; Jerusalem Bible +)

He enacted the symbolic destruction of the temple

In the first passage of this account, Jesus destroys the temple—another will replace it—by attacking its margins, its supports. In the second passage, the suggestion is that God will throw down the temple. The prophetic demonstration, by which the prophet gives visual, vocal form to what he says, is characteristic of the prophets in the Hebrew Bible. The performance is, simultaneously, the chief feature of miraculous deeds and the stimulus to their recounting.

That God will rebuild the temple is a natural conclusion to what Jesus says, similar to that of many rabbinic positions, substantiated by prophecies that join threat and promise; but in a later passage in Mark, it is reported against Jesus that he said no human agent but *he* alone would rebuild the temple in three days.

(A) He entered Jerusalem and went into the Temple, where he looked at the whole scene; but as it was now late, he went out to Bethany with the twelve. . . . [The next day] they came back to Jerusalem, and he went into the temple and began driving out those who bought and sold in the Temple. He upset the tables of the money-changers and the seats of the pigeon-dealers; and he would not allow anyone to use the Temple court as a thoroughfare for carrying goods. . . . (Mark 11:11–18 NEB +)

As he was leaving the Temple, one of his disciples exclaimed, "Look, Master, what huge stones! What fine buildings!" Jesus said to him, "You see these great buildings? Not one stone will be left on another; all will be thrown down." (Mark 13:1–2)

He ate a final meal with his inner circle

Jesus sanctions his betrayal in the passage below. The account tells of his refusal to halt the process of his capture, imprisonment, trial and, execution. The account has a connection to the Bacchic ceremonies of the rending and consumption of the god, the *sparagamos*. Jesus adds the proffer of his own body to the blessings on the bread and wine and incorporates the Eucharist, the love feast—that is, the agape. This frees the faithful-to-the-text communicant from responsibility for his collusion in the murder of the victim, while it keeps alive the pathos. Jesus assures his companions that he will gain Heaven through their weakness and treachery. They ingest the awareness of their complicity and the knowledge that he, the greater, has taken their ignobility into account. He affirms their infirmity and substantiates their subjection to his rule for all eternity, releasing them from responsibility for their deed. Judas, left alone, punishes Judas.

(A) Now on the first day of Unleavened Bread, when the Passover lambs were being slaughtered, his disciples said to him, "Where would you like us to go and prepare for your Passover meal?" "[A man] will show you a large room upstairs, set out in readiness." . . . They found everything just as he had told them, and they prepared for Passover.

In the evening he came to the house with the twelve. As they sat at supper, Jesus said, "I tell you this: one of you will betray me; one who is eating with me." At this they were dismayed; and one by one they said to him, "Not I, surely?" "It is one of the twelve," he said, "who is dipping into the same bowl with me. The Son of Man is going the way appointed for him in the scriptures; but alas for that man by whom the Son of Man is betrayed! It would be better for that man if he had never been born."

During supper, he took bread, and having said the blessing, he broke it and gave it to them, with the words: "Take this; this is my body." Then he took a cup, and having offered thanks to God, he gave it to them; and they all drank from it. And he said, "This is my blood of the covenant, shed for many. I tell you this: never again shall I drink from the fruit of the vine until that day when I drink it new in the kingdom of God." (Mark 14:12–25 NEB +)

He was arrested and interrogated by
the high priest

In this account, an intermediary body, the Council, is imposed in the confrontation with the ruling authority (Rome) (just as the account imposes itself between the event or experience cited and the reader). The normal conduct of the court, which involves investigation and determination, has been reversed as it performs its assigned task. The conflict that is expressed in the confusion of the chief priests and the Council affects the high priest, who must force a verdict and does so in despair, demonstrating his rage and power and threatening the others with what he does to the accused.

The element of time is of singular importance in this long and detailed account. As the day begins, Jesus immediately takes control of the time of his followers. Jesus then tells his enemies that time has made them helpless against his plan. Had they wished, they could easily have taken him upon his arrival in Jerusalem and prevented his creating any disturbance at all; now, however, they have no options left, and their servants, blinded with fury at having been disarmed by Jesus' strategy, insist that he is a militant rebel and seek to deal with him as such. The account tells of other responses. For example, Judas, also incapacitated, does what Jesus has said he would do and seeks his embrace; the attendants give Peter room among them at the fire; the high priest begs Jesus to contest the conflicting and wanting accusations. Jesus refuses to take any responsibility for their decisions, frustrating them to the point of fury. They blindfold him and again identify him with the prophet-messiah. All those who spit on him, blindfold him, and taunt him seek to deny him the power to control their actions, to foresee them, and force them to fulfill his prophecy. They cover his eyes so that he may not see them, and so that they may not see themselves reflected in his gaze.

(A) He came and said to them, "Still sleeping? Still taking your ease? Enough! The hour has come. The Son of Man is betrayed to sinful men. Up, let us go forward! My betrayer is upon us."

Suddenly, while he was still speaking, Judas, one of the twelve, appeared, and with him was a crowd armed with swords and cudgels, sent by the chief priests. . . . Now the traitor had agreed with them on a signal: "The one I kiss is your man; seize him and get him safely away." When he reached the spot, he stepped forward at once and said to Jesus, "My master," and kissed him. Then they seized him and held him fast.

One of the bystanders drew his sword and struck at the High Priest's servant, cutting off his ear. Then Jesus spoke: "Do you take me for a bandit, that you have come out with swords and cudgels to arrest me? Day after day I was within your reach as I taught in the Temple, and you did not lay hands on me. But let the scriptures be fulfilled." Then the disciples all deserted him and ran away. . . .

Then they led Jesus away to the High Priest's house, where the chief priests, elders, and doctors of the law were all assembling. Peter followed him at a distance right into the High Priest's courtyard; and there he remained, sitting among the attendants, warming himself at the fire.

The chief priests and the whole Council tried to find some evidence against Jesus to warrant a death-sentence, but failed to find any. Many gave false evidence against him, but their statements did not tally. Some stood up and gave this false evidence against him: "We heard him say, 'I will throw down this Temple, made with human hands, and in three days I will build another, not made with hands.'" But even on this point their evidence did not agree.

Then the High Priest stood up in his place and questioned Jesus: "Have you no answer to the charges that these witnesses bring against you?" But he kept silence; he made no reply.

Again the High Priest questioned him: "Are you the Messiah, the Son of the Blessed One?" Jesus said, "Whatever you say." . . . Then the High Priest tore his robes and said, "We need call no further witnesses. You have heard the blasphemy. What is your opinion?" Their judgment was unanimous: that he was guilty and should be put to death. Some began to spit on him. They blindfolded him, and struck him with their fists and called out, "Prophesy! Tell us who hit you!" (Mark 14:43–65 NEB +)

He was executed on orders from the Roman
procurator, Pontius Pilate

Pilate takes up with Jesus the question of whether or not he is a revolutionary of the familiar sort, an insurgent who claims the throne as the rightful Jewish king. He expects Jesus to deny that he has claimed the kingship against the vested authority, and he is taken by surprise when Jesus is unwilling to do so. Taking Jesus' silence for acquiescence in his own condemnation, Pilate releases a real rebel, Barabbas, one who has very likely denied his participation in an uprising. Pilate too has been forced to comply with Jesus' plan. In the morning, the crowd that has been pro-revolutionary, pro-Barabbas, mocks Jesus, infuriated by their own confusion: The Romans are killing him as a rebel, but he will not act, and his inaction has compelled them to assist the Romans. They identify him as a prophet, a madman (the text below recalls Hos. 9:7: "The prophet has been driven mad by your deeds"), for declaring himself a king-messiah and prophesying a miracle that will save him, crowning his inaction with victory. Note in the account the demand the crowd, not the procurator, makes for the demonstration of a miracle as proof of his messiahship. Such a bitter cry engages rabbinic eschatological messianism rather than activist politics, as the people seek a resolution for their hopelessness.

(A) When morning came, the chief priests, having made their plan with the elders and the lawyers and all the Council, put Jesus in chains; then they led him away and handed him over to Pilate. Pilate asked him, "Are you the King of the Jews?" He replied, "Whatever you say." And the chief priests brought many charges against him. Pilate questioned him again: "Have you nothing to say in your defense? You see how many charges they are bringing against you." But to Pilate's astonishment, Jesus made no further reply.

At the festival season the Governor used to release one prisoner at the people's request. As it happened, the man known as Barabbas was then in custody with the rebels who had committed murder in the rising. . . . The chief priests incited the crowd to ask him to release Barabbas rather than Jesus. . . . So Pilate, in his desire to satisfy the mob, released Barabbas to them; and he had Jesus flogged and handed him over to be crucified.

The hour of the crucifixion was nine in the morning, and the inscription giving the charge against him read, "The king of the Jews." . . . The passers-by hurled abuse at him: "Aha!" they cried, wagging their heads, "you would pull the Temple down, would you, and build it in three days? Come down from the cross and save yourself!" So, too, the chief priests and doctors of the law jested with one another: "He saved others," they said, "but he cannot save himself. Let the Messiah, the king of Israel, come down now from the cross. If we see that, we shall believe." (Mark 15:1–32 NEB +)

Even the following B text, in which the world itself, not mortals, exhibits "signs and wonders," sees Jesus as a messiah in the sense of an anointed prophet. It connects him with his Elijah-nature, as miraculous healer and resuscitator, and suggests that he is therefore calling Elijah to save him. This is not Elijah in his role as harbinger of the king-messiah, but Elijah as prototype of the miracle-working, healing prophet.

(B) Darkness fell over the whole land from midday until three in the afternoon; and about three, Jesus cried aloud, "*Eli, Eli, lema sabachthani?,*" which means, "My God, my God, why have you forsaken me?" Some of the bystanders, hearing this, said, "He is calling Elijah." One of them ran at once and fetched a sponge, which he soaked in sour wine, and held it to his lips on the end of a cane. But the others said, "Let us see if Elijah will come to save him."

Jesus again gave a loud cry and breathed his last. At that moment the curtain of the Temple was torn in two from top to bottom. There was an earthquake, the rocks split and the graves opened, and many of God's people arose from sleep; and coming out of their graves after his resurrection they entered the Holy City, where many saw them. And when the centurion and his men who were keeping watch over Jesus saw the earthquake and all that was happening, they were filled with awe, and they said, "Truly, this man was a son of God." (Matt 27:45–54 NEB)

His disciples saw him after his death

The text below establishes Jesus as the first Jewish messiah to overcome his death in this way and is both an A- and a B-type account. The later "messiah of the lineage of Joseph" actually dies. Some messiahs who precede (and follow) Jesus do disappear in their texts: Zerubbabel, for one; another, Elijah, Jesus' model in these texts, is carried up into Heaven, but does not return, although he is expected to. The account here certifies Jesus' death, testifies to his return in a nonsymbolic, real, verifiable, and corporeal fashion, and then describes his assumption and the continuation of his power to enable his followers to perform miracles, particularly those involving a disease of some kind, including psychogenic disorders (like demon-infestation). The image of "armed words" derives from the conversion that has occurred here, from armed rebellion (the king-messiah) to ideological and unarmed rebellion (the prophet-messiah); the certain victory of the text, together with its distribution, replaces the doubtful outcome of an uprising.

(B) When he had risen from the dead early on Sunday morning, he appeared first to Mary of Magdala, from whom he had formerly cast out seven devils. She went and carried the news to his mourning and sorrowful followers, but when they were told that he was alive and that she had seen him, they did not believe it.

Later, he appeared in a different guise to two of them as they were walking, on their way into the country. These also went and took the news to the others, but again no one believed them.

Afterwards, while the eleven were at table he appeared to them and reproached them for their incredulity and dullness, because they had not believed those who had seen him risen from the dead. Then he said to them: "Go forth to every part of the world, and proclaim the gospel [news] to the whole creation. Those who believe it and receive baptism will find salvation; those who do not believe will be condemned. Faith will bring with it these miracles: believers will cast out devils in my name and speak in strange tongues; if they handle snakes or drink any deadly poison, they will come to no harm; and the sick on whom they lay their hands will recover."

So after talking with them, the Lord Jesus was taken up into Heaven, and he took his seat at the right hand of God; but the disciples went out to make their proclamation everywhere, and the Lord worked with them and armed their words with the miracles that followed. (Mark 16:9–20 NEB)

The Counter-History of Jesus (6th–7th Century CE)

The following account in an anti-hagiography. Its aim is to disgrace Jesus, and it achieves this by having Judas shame him and conquer him. Other Jewish anti-hagiographies of Jesus from the *toldot yeshu* (in Hebrew, "history of Jesus") tradition seek to do the same thing by writing that his real father was a Roman soldier named Pandar, who had intercourse with Mary during her period of ritual impurity. (The first record of this tale appears in Origen's diatribe "Against Celsus.") Many of the same elements that are found in the hagiographies of Jesus are found in the text that follows, but they have been recast in service of the defamation.

At that time the government of Israel was in the hands of a woman named Helen. In the temple stood the stone called The Stone That Yah Set Up, engraved with the letters of the Holy Name. The sages held that any who learned [the secret of] the letters could do anything he wanted by their power. The sages were afraid that if young men learned them they might destroy the world, so they tied two brass dogs to the two pillars of iron that stood at the Gate of the Burnt Offering, saying, "Whoever comes in here and learns the letters, let the dogs howl at him and the letters will leave his mind." Jesus came in, learned the letters, wrote them on a slip of parchment, slit his thigh, and laid the parchment in the wound. It caused him no pain, and the flesh closed up around the parchment. As he went out the dogs howled and the letters left his mind. When he returned home, he took a knife, cut open his flesh, and lifted out the writing. Thus he learned the Explicit Name.

Jesus returned to the Galilee as the rebellion grew and all Israel had become divided against itself. The sages came before the queen to say, "This one, our lady, is a sorcerer and will lead the world into ruin." She sent her horsemen after him, and they found him inciting the men of the Galilee by saying, "I am the son of God; it says this in your Torah." As the horsemen tried to capture him, the men of the Galilee resisted. War broke out. Jesus told them, "You have no need to fight. Trust the power of my father in Heaven." There were some birds the Galileeans had made of clay nearby. Jesus spoke the letters of the Name and they began to flap their wings. At that, the men of the Galilee prostrated themselves before him. He told them, "Bring me a millstone." They rolled it down to the seashore. He spoke the letters, set the stone upon the sea, and floated across the water in it, just as if he were sitting in a boat. The horsemen were astonished. Jesus said to them, "You tell your lady what you saw here." Then he made the spirit lift him from the water and set him on dry land. When the horsemen returned to the queen and reported what they had seen, she was amazed and trembled in fear.

Then the Elders of Israel found a certain man whose name was Judas Iscariot and brought him into the temple, before the Holy of Holies. He learned the letters of the Explicit Name engraved there on the foundation stone. He wrote them on a small parchment, slit his thigh, and laid the parchment inside. He, too, felt no pain. When Jesus and his men came into the presence of the queen and the sages she had summoned, he said, "Of me was the prophecy made: 'dogs encompassed me about; I did not fear them.'" [Ps. 22:17]. The sages entered along with Judas and began making accusations against Jesus. He responded with accusations against them and said to the queen, "It was of me that King David said, 'I will ascend to heaven, He shall receive me.'" He raised up his hands like eagles' wings and rose. Everyone was astonished. They said, "How can he fly there, between the sky and the earth?" The elders said to Judas, "Sound the letters out and rise up after him." Judas did that and rose into the sky. Everyone was astonished and said, "Oh how both of them fly like eagles." Iscariot caught hold of Jesus and flew higher, but could not force him down to earth. With the Name shared equally between them, neither could vanquish the other. When Judas saw this he played a trick: urinated on Jesus [sodomized Jesus] and made him unclean. He fell to earth and Judas along with him. (The Christians still weep for this on that night [i.e., Passover, the night of the Last Supper] and wail for what he did to him.) They seized Jesus immediately and said to Helen, "Let him be destroyed." "Or," they said, "let him say who beat him." And they put a coat over his head and banged on him with pomegranate branches, He did not know the word to use against them and they knew the power of the Name had left him. (From the Strasbourg manuscript, *ma'ase yeshu ha-notsri* [in Hebrew, "The Tale of Jesus the Christian"], as quoted in S. Krauss, *Das Leben Jesu nach jüdischen Quellen* [Berlin, 1902]).

SHIM'ON BAR KOSIBA

The accounts of Bar Kosiba testify to the stress on the Jewish population. Living in a harsh reality, Jews were torn apart by the forces that denied their own experience its meaning. From one side, rabbinic theology blamed the Jews' disaster on their own conduct, not Roman rule; from the other, their experience was annulled by being resituated in the imaginary heavens and hells and cosmic schemes of time, over which all-knowing, frightful, angelic rulers held sway. Against this, the movement led by Bar Kosiba sought to reestablish Judaean Jews in a predictable reality, lived on holy soil in accordance with traditional and dependable religious virtues. Such a life was not really possible; an accommodation with Rome did have to be reached, and the rabbinic authorities were proven right about survival as a people, if not as a nation. Bar Kosiba's rebellion, his messiahship, marked the boundaries of what was possible with blood and flames.

Shim'on bar Kosiba remained, for almost 1,800 years, a literary figure, scarcely real. That he was at all remembered as having lived, held the Romans at bay, and died testifies to the human passion to control, if not events themselves, at least the way they are recalled through narrative. His period was one known above any other for fanciful literature: Reams of Gnostic and other visions filled the entire universe of the time, so that nothing was left unknown. The Apocrypha and the Pseudepigrapha became all but canonic. Various hands did attempt to magnify Bar Kosiba's image, as will be noted, but the facts of his unredeemed death and the catastrophic end of his free Israel, rather than forcing the whole affair into obscurity, instead seem to have held his tale in place. The composers of the Mishna, the Talmuds, and the early midrashim were surely not pleased that the affair ended the way it did, but the morose tones of the history they knew resounded in a familiar way in the tale of Bar Kosiba. The final and total loss of the Jewish capital strengthened that branch of Jewish political power that had moved to the north of the land of Israel, along with its quietist philosophy. Akiba, who was tortured and slain by the

Romans in Caesarea, c. 135 CE for teaching the Torah, was now laid to rest and safely recalled in martyrology, particularly in the "Ten Killed by the [Roman] Regime," a part of the High Holidays liturgy recited until today.

The utter end of the struggle against Rome left only abstract legal discussions and disconnected memories of an extinct and therefore golden past. In their work, teachers could speak of the present and its problems with no threat of a sudden recurrence of statehood. They were free to speculate on religion and the meaning of existence outside a historical context. The rabbis dispensed with divine interference in resolving disputes just as, according to their own account, Bar Kosiba dispensed with God's help in battle. The rabbis who wrote the tales of Bar Kosiba's rebellion never mention his adherence to the law in the heat of battle. With nothing to say, no law to teach and no time for happy memories to develop, this most unpacific of Jewish leaders barely managed to hold on to a place as a morose, moral lesson in the literature of the rabbis. He reemerged as a hero and a model for Jewish behavior, particularly at the inauguration of the program of muscular (as oppsed to mental) Judaism, and pioneering Zionism toward the end of the nineteenth century. He became for young Jews a figurehead for the opposition to traditional Jewish life and its powerlessness. But no one really expected him to come forth again as he did, first from Wadi Murabba'at in 1952–1953 and then from the Cave of Letters in Nahal Hever in 1960.

Yigael Yadin was the leader of the explorations near the Dead Sea, south of Qumran, that uncovered letters from Bar Kosiba, articles of the daily life of the rebels, records of commercial transactions—in short, what remained of the real life of real free Israelites—and thus secured their freehold in Jewish reality. The devotion of the leader and his troops and their families to religious law was apparent immediately. The searchers found wool dyed purple, for making prayer shawls, the remnants of phylacteries and biblical texts. Letters dictated by Bar Kosiba himself were found, painstakingly laid out, and deciphered so that the call that came from the Judaean wilderness, in 133 CE, for ritual objects such as the lulav and the etrog, to celebrate Sukkot in the state-at-war, could be heard again. The rabbinic texts had failed to mention the devotion to the religious-and-civil law of Judaism that characterized the rebel community of the south; this finally emerged with these uncovered texts. A factual retracing of the life and deeds of Bar Kosiba requires the reinterpretation of much that was written in traditional literature and under its influence, which was generally deprecatory. The rabbis are forced to modify their antagonism toward Bar Kosiba, only because in the total disaster, many of their party fell; the Christian historians are under no such compulsion. They portray him as an ideal enemy, one who demonstrates the inefficacy of militant anti-Romanism and the doom of anti-Christianism. Bar Kosiba is best understood from the Roman texts and from the rabbinic and Christian texts when the motives of these texts are taken into account and clarified by references to the discovered documents and realia of the Dead Sea.

Bar Kosiba was born in Judaea, some 20 to 40 years before the war of 132–135 CE. The place of his birth went unrecorded, and there are no miraculous-birth tales or wondrous-youth tales about him. Nowhere is he said to be of the house of David; he might even have been from a priestly family and thus outside royal messianic lineage altogether. Though we cannot be certain of the time of its composition, the tale of R. Akiba's recognition of Bar Kosiba as the king-messiah provides some information about his age. Akiba sees Bar Kosiba as a wondrously strong man in his prime, not as an old man performing miracles; he must therefore have been under 40 years of age at the time of the rebellion. Ben Torta's retort mentions age and the grave in reference to Akiba but not to Bar Kosiba, whom he would surely have included had he been old as well, or, for that matter, very young. That he was a southerner and not a Jerusalemite—though perhaps he resided there—can be deduced from his real name and from his intimate knowledge of the wadis of the Dead Sea area and of the Judaean wilderness in general, including the population. This was where he campaigned, rather than in the city. He managed desert settlements and communications there capably, a difficult task even for someone well acquainted with sources of water and caves for storage and hideouts. He was aware of the value of each parcel of land, as we can see from the rents he levied for payment to his government. He knew the characters of the people among whom he lived and knew the means by which he could call upon their loyalties, as we can infer from his orders. Nothing connects him to Jerusalem. His real family name, Kosiba or Koziva, is the name of a location in Judaea. (The matter of his name, after the discovery of letters that bear official signatures, has largely been resolved. For some time, it was thought that his name was really Bar Kokhba, a messianic name [which means "the one of the star"] and that he was called Bar or Ben Koziba ["the fraud"], in an ironic pun—but Akiba made the pun on his real name to associate him with the text in Num. 24:17 [a star shall step forth from Jacob]; and the efforts to define Bar Kosiba by naming him continued as later sources referred to him as Akiba did in the story of his recognition, or else in opposition to the name by which Akiba called him.)[22]

Bar Kosiba is described in the secondary sources as physically strong and courageous, but not as having been wealthy or connected to any particular circle. He is not reported to have worked any miracles or cures. His letters and some secondary sources depict him as rather harsh in his recruitment tactics and in his handling of local populaces, and as particularly demanding in his direction of his officers. He is not presented as having acted graciously or kindly or as having directed others to do so. He did not refer to himself as messiah. Preferring to associate himself with the simple earthly kingship, rather than with the other-worldly divinity found in the accounts of Jesus that were contemporary with him, he called himself *nasi'* ("prince, presiding official"), the proper messiah. Since he regarded his rebellion as a restoration of the monarchy, he assumed ownership of lands, then leased them out in conformance with the latest codes, including those of the Roman governorship. He enforced Jewish agricultural laws such as tithing and the prohibition of mixtures (including seeds, and linen and wool clothing, under the same principle). Tithing became a kind of taxation, supporting his own political and military structure rather than the priesthood.

Again, we find Bar Kosiba to have been a man of rural, not urban, interests: His designs, stamped over those of the Roman coins that served as blanks, show palm trees, vines, the "four species." (In using the technique of over-stamping, the Bar Kosiba coins differ from the coins produced during the first Jewish revolt (Figure 2.1). The Bar Kosiba coins speak eloquently of rebellion; they are all over-

Figure 2.1: A Roman coin that originally showed the face of the Roman Emperor God, Nero—three letters of his name are still visible. Establishing a foundry to cast new coins from the old metal was not a priority of Bar Kosiba's. Beyond that, the defacement of the coins, like the defacement of other Roman images on vessels, and the replacement of their symbols with those of free Israel, served as standards by which the new present could be identified against the evil past from which it arose, and which it destroyed. The coins of Bar Kosiba's free Israel often include his name, Shim'on, or that of his priest, Eleazar, and the date of the year after the beginning of the war against Rome. This one, too early in the revolt for that date to be inscribed, says, rather, that it is a coin "of/for the freedom of Jerusalem." The front of the coin shows the Temple facade with the Ark visible within; the back shows a lulav and an etrog. The inscriptions are in paleo-Hebrew rather than in the Aramaic or square script and, like the use of this script in certain Dead Sea documents, display the revolutionary messianism as oriented toward a golden age, rather than a utopian era, identifying the movement with a glorious past in which its independence was innocent of any taint of foreign authority and proclaiming the renewal of that era.

stamped on Roman coins, the only such set known.) When his coins do portray the temple facade or the instruments used in temple music, the purpose is to reinforce the idea of the "holy land," by joining those images with the emblems of the biblical promise of the land. His people also over-stamped the images of gods, and other symbols of the enemy, on their Roman vessels with images of Israel. The dating of the coins, "Year one/two of the freedom of Jerusalem/Israel," affirms that the new era had already begun. Bar Kosiba was concerned about his troops' loyalty to him and demanded proof that it was strong. He seems to have been joined by a priestly coprincipal, perhaps in accordance with tradition, but, in any case, thereby ensuring the loyalty of the religious wing of his following. The head of a man called

"Eleazar the priest" appears on coins. But perhaps this is the same Eleazar, of Modi'in, who was dispatched as a traitor in the story of Bar Kosiba's death. Bar Kosiba was not an apocalypticist; he was breeding the next generation; his strong interest in their development is clear from tales of children, their studies, and their religiosity. Rabbinic sources for their own purposes show the children to have been devoted, religious students but don't credit Bar Kosiba for this. In rabbinic accounts of the brutal Roman suppression and extirpation of the population, Romans are shown concentrating their furor on the innocent young scholars.

According to all accounts, Bar Kosiba died on the battlefield. He didn't disappear; no second coming was mentioned; he wasn't viewed as the predecessor of the messiah of the days of peace. Even the story of how he died directs attention to Bar Kosiba as a physical being, betrayed by one of the traditional kin-enemies of the Jews, a Samaritan named Eleazar. After his death, his own moral weakness, overzealous haste, was held responsible, for the failure of his attempt. Everybody gained more from the stories of Bar Kosiba's death than from his death itself: The Romans explained their difficulties in putting down a rebellion in a minor province; the rabbis reestablished the displacement of the physical world by the world of the imagination; and the early church nodded its head, in agreement with God's decision to side with Rome. Bar Kosiba received a literary tribute to his dedication and his virtue, in an image used to portray his death: a snake entwined around his powerful legs, his loins, and his heart. The image, in an apocryphal tale, provides a commentary on the propaganda against him: The emblematic elements—the physical strength of a man in his prime, his progenerative capacity, and his will—are throttled by evil.

Roman Texts about Bar Kosiba and the Rebellion, by Dio Cassius and Eusebius

Dio Cassius (ca. 163–after 229) was an experienced Roman soldier and statesman. His *Roman History* deals largely with military history and is disinterested when it comes to other matters. He gives the facts of the revolt as he understands them in order to make judgments on the conduct of military rule and does not even mention Bar Kosiba.

At Jerusalem [Hadrian] founded a city in place of the one that had been razed to the ground, naming it Aelia Capitolina, and on the site of the [Jewish Temple], he raised a new Temple to Jupiter. This brought on a war of no slight importance nor of brief duration, for the Jews deemed it intolerable that foreign races should be settled in their city and foreign religious rites planted there. So long, indeed, as Hadrian was close by in Egypt and again in Syria, they remained quiet, save insofar as they purposely made of poor quality such weapons as they were called upon to furnish, in order that the Romans might reject them and they themselves might thus have the use of them; but when he went farther away, they openly revolted. To be sure, they did not dare try conclusions with the Romans in the open field, but they occupied the advantageous positions in the country and strengthened them with mines and walls, in order that they might have places of refuge whenever they should be hard-pressed and might meet together unobserved underground; and they pierced these subterranean passages from above at intervals to let in air and light.

At first the Romans took no account of them. Soon, however, all Judaea had been stirred up, and the Jews everywhere were showing great signs of disturbance, gathering together and giving evidence of great hostility to the Romans, partly by secret and partly by overt acts; many outside nations, too, were joining them out of eagerness for gain, and the whole earth, one might almost say, was being stirred up over the matter. Then indeed, Hadrian sent against them his best generals. First of these was Julius Severus, who was dispatched from Britain, where he was governor, against the Jews. Severus did not venture to attack his opponents in the open at any one point, in view of their numbers and their desperation; but by intercepting small groups, thanks to the number of his soldiers and his under-officers, and by de-priving them of food and shutting them up, he was able, rather slowly, to be sure, but with comparatively little danger, to crush, exhaust and exterminate them. Very few of them in fact survived. Fifty of their most important outposts and nine hun-dred and eighty-five of their most famous villages were razed to the ground. Five hundred and eighty thousand men were slain in the various battles and raids, and the number of those that perished by famine, disease, and fire was past finding out. Thus nearly the whole of Judaea was made desolate, a result of which the people had had forewarning before the war. For the tomb of Solomon, which the Jews re-gard as an object of veneration, fell to pieces of itself and collapsed, and many wolves and hyenas rushed howling into their cities. Many Romans, moreover, per-ished in this war. Therefore, Hadrian in writing to the senate, did not employ the opening phrase commonly affected by the emperors, "If you and your children are in health it is well; I and the legions are in health." (*Roman History*, vol. 49, pp. 12–14 [Loeb Classical Library])

Eusebius (ca. 260–ca. 339) was the bishop of the see of Caesarea and the author of the first history of the church. This history is limited to the eastern church and deals only with heresies in order to show how they were suppressed. Statements about the Jews and their war have to be read within several embedded contexts. First, Diocletian persecuted the church, particularly in the provinces. Many of its leaders were killed during Eusebius' lifetime (including his teacher). Second, Eusebius viewed the history of the world as the history of the church. Third, he saw the church as inheriting the Jewish scriptures and world and tri-umphing over the Jewish people themselves through Providence, as the church re-ceived a share in the empire of Constantine, his contemporary. Fourth, the triumph of the church over heresy, the Jews and Rome was for him the meaning of all his-tory. He thus saw Bar Kosiba in the same role as Diocletian and the biblical texts as denying the Jews their land, capital, and liberty. He propounded this view because it was "useful" for Christian posterity, not because it corrected distortion. His ac-counts of the war exerted a much greater influence on Western accounts of Jews and their leaders in rebellions than did the account of Dio Cassius.

In the following passages from the *Ecclesiastical History* and the *Chronicle*, Eusebius manipulates Bar Kosiba's unyielding expectations of his citizens in order to strike another blow against the possibility of a this-worldly, political redemption of the Jews. He ascribes control over their destiny to supernatural forces. He only reveals the endurance of the popular rebellion when he writes that it "once more progressed," and "at that time" the Jews were led by Bar Kosiba.

> The rebellion of the Jews once more progressed in character and extent, and Rufus, the governor of Judaea, when military aid had been sent him by the emperor, moved out against them, treating their madness without mercy. He destroyed in heaps thousands of men, women, and children, and, under the law of war, enslaved their land. The Jews were at that time led by a certain Bar Chochebas—which means "star"—a man who was murderous and a bandit, but who relied on his name, as if dealing with slaves, and claimed to be a luminary who had come down to them from Heaven and was magically enlightening those who were in misery. The war reached its height in the eighteenth year of the reign of Hadrian in Bethtera, which was a strong citadel not very far from Jerusalem; the siege lasted a long time before the rebels were driven to final destruction by famine and thirst, and the instigator of their madness paid the penalty he deserved. Hadrian then commanded that by a legal decree and by ordinances, the whole nation should be absolutely prevented from entering thenceforth even the district round Jerusalem, so that not even from a distance could it see its ancestral home. Ariston of Pella tells the story: "Thus when the city came to be bereft of the nation of the Jews, and its ancient inhabitants had completely perished, it was colonized by foreigners, and the Roman city that afterward arose changed its name, and, in honor of the reigning emperor Aelius Hadrian, was called Aelia. The church, too, in it was composed of Gentiles, and after the Jewish bishops, the first who was appointed to minister to those there was Marcus." (*Ecclesiastical History*, vol. 4, p. 6 [Loeb Classical Library])

> [Justin] mentions the war of that time against the Jews and makes this observation, "For in the present Jewish war it was only Christians whom Bar Chocheba, the leader of the rebellion of the Jews, commanded to be punished severely if they did not deny Jesus as the Messiah and blaspheme him." (*Ecclesiastical History*, vol. 4, p. 8)

> Hadrian's Year 16 (132 CE)   The Jews, who took up arms, devastated Palestine during the period in which the governor of the province was Tineus Rufus, to whom Hadrian sent an army in order to crush the rebels.

> Hadrian's Year 17   Cochebas, duke of the Jewish sect, killed the Christians with all kinds of persecutions, (when) they refused to help him against the Roman troops.

> Hadrian's Year 18/19   The Jewish War that was conducted in Palestine reached its conclusion, all Jewish problems having been completely suppressed. From that time (on), the permission was denied them even to enter Jerusalem; first and foremost because of the commandment of God, as the prophets had prophesied; and secondly by authority of the interdictions of the Romans. (*Chronicle*, [from Y. Yadin, *Bar-Kokhba* [New York, 1971, p. 258]])

The Letters of Bar Kosiba

Yigael Yadin, in *Bar-Kokhba*, supplies translations of the Bar Kosiba letters.[23] He provides the comparative material from Roman, Christian and Jewish sources in an appendix to his work. I have added material to his selections.

These letters demonstrate how much attention Bar Kosiba paid to religious matters. In the last letter quoted here, he provides for the supply of the "four species" for his entire army: The citron and the palm fronds, myrtles, and willows are an essential part of the holiday of Sukkot. Bar Kosiba also demands that the citrons be from crops that have been properly tithed. No mention of other holidays occurs in any of the letters; even though that may be an accident of fate, it would not be out of place to consider what this reference might imply. Bar Kosiba demands that the citrons, even though they lie at an inconvenient distance, be provided by other activists in the rebellion, "brothers," as part of the celebration of a religiously ordained agricultural holiday that summarizes his goal—the return to a life on the land, one lived according to an irrevocable covenant. He sends two men and two donkeys for their collection—a substantial commitment—recalling Moses' sending of the spies into the land at the beginning of the conquest of, or return to, Israel.

Bar Kosiba confirms the accusations of harshness leveled against him when he absolutely insists ("or else, a severe punishment") on propriety in affairs of real estate and in the conduct of his government; the delinquent Eleazar bar Hitta is to be handed over before the onset of the Sabbath so that his capture and transportation should not conflict with holy time. He does not tolerate any disloyalty, from an individual or, particularly, when groups are involved. He demands instant obedience to his orders and makes all aware of the interdependence of loyalty and rewards and penalties. A ceaseless and untiring contribution to his administration of the civil and religious law constitutes the only convincing evidence of loyalty to the cause. The order to control the herds and prevent them from harming the trees of Eleazar bar Hitta, whose fruit is to be confiscated, includes scrupulous attention to the exaction of penalties, along with a husbandman's concern for the continued productivity of the land. The penalty he imposes for harming the trees goes beyond the requirements of the Mishna.

On the twenty-eighth of Marheshvan, the third year of Shim'on bar Kosiba, President of Israel; at En-Gedi. Of their own free will, on this day, do Eleazar bar Eleazar of Hitta and Eliezer bar Shmuel, both of En-Gedi, and Tehina bar Shim'on and Alma bar Yehuda, both of Luhit in the coastal district of Agaltain, now residents of En-Gedi, wish to divide up amongst themselves the places that they have leased from Yehonatan bar Mahanayim, the administrator of Shim'on ben Kosiba, President of Israel, at En-Gedi. [A description of the land and the division follows]. . . . All is done and agreed on condition that the above four people will pay the dues of the lease of these places which they leased from Yehonatan bar Mahanayim as follows [specifications of the payments.] (Yadin, p. 176)

Shim'on bar Kosiba to Yehonatan and to Masbala. . . . "Let all men from Teko'a and other places who are with you be sent to me without delay. And if you shall not send them, let it be known to you that you will be punished." (Yadin, p. 126)

Letter of Shim'on bar Kosiba, peace! To Yehonatan son of Be'aya [my order is] that whatever Elisha tells you, do for him and help him and those with him in every action. Be well. (Yadin, p. 126)

From Shim'on bar Kosiba to the men of En-Gedi, to Masbala and to Yehonatan bar Be'ayan, peace. You sit in comfort, eating and drinking from the property of the House of Israel, and care nothing for your brothers. (Yadin, p. 133)

Shim'on bar Kosiba to Yehonatan bar Be'ayan and to Masbala bar Shim'on: "[My order is] that you will send me Eleazar bar Hitta immediately, before the Sabbath. . . . [His wheat and fruit should be confiscated] and if anyone oppose you, send him to me and I shall punish him. . . . See that the herds do not trample and destroy the trees or else—a severe punishment . . . and as for the spice orchard, let no one get anywhere near it." (Yadin, p. 128)

Shim'on to Yehuda bar Menashe at Kiryat Aravaya: "I have sent you two donkeys that you shall send with them two men to Yehonatan bar Be'ayan and to Masbala in order that they shall pack and send to the camp, toward you, palm branches and citrons. And you, from your place, send others who will bring you myrtles and willows. See that they are properly tithed and send them to the camp. [The request is made] since the army is large. Be well." (Yadin, p. 129)

Rabbinic Texts

"Esau," in the first passage below, is understood to be Rome.[24] Rabbinic authors saw the universal meaning of history in a different way than did Christian writers. The rabbis attributed the failure of the rebellion and the murder of the innocents to presumptuous conduct by Akiba and Bar Kosiba, not to the persecution of Christians by Jews. Not only does this passage say that Bar Kosiba failed to call properly on the name of God for aid in battle, but also that he even failed to observe mourning practices for the destruction of the temple, brazenly assuming the role of its restorer and counterposing human will to the will of the divine. But the rabbis and bishops join hands in justifying the role of Providence in the outcome: God ordained that Bar Kosiba should fail for his sins. A good deal—in particular, a change in national aspirations and in the policy for attaining them—had happened in order to produce this change in attitude among the Jewish leadership since the time of the Davidic court, when Joab had proclaimed, "Let us fight like men for our people and the ark of our God and let Yahweh do what he wants" (2 Sam. 10:12).

Rabbi (Yehuda Ha-Nasi') used to expound upon the verse, "The voice is the voice of Jacob but the hands are the hands of Esau" (Gen. 27:22): "The voice of Jacob screaming on account of what the hands of Esau did at Betar," and R. Yohanan used to expound, "The voice is of the Emperor Hadrian who slew eighty thousand myriad people at Betar."

And R. Yohanan said, "Eighty thousand pairs of trumpeters besieged Betar and each of them was appointed over several forces, and Ben Koziba was there with two hundred thousand men who had fingers cut off. The sages asked him in a dispatch, 'How much longer are you going to create cripples among the Jews [by making them show their bravery thus]?' He responded, 'How shall I judge them fit otherwise?' They sent in return, 'Enlist no one who cannot pull up a cedar of Lebanon.' So straightaway he had two hundred thousand of the one sort and two hundred thousand of the other sort. And when he went forth to battle he would [only] say, 'Master of the world, neither help us nor embarrass us.' That is what is meant by what is written: 'God has spurned us. Oh, you have not come forth among our troops.'" (Ps. 60:12)

What was Ben Koziba's strength like? It is said that when he went out to battle he would catch a stone from the enemy's catapults on his knee and then hurl it back and it would go on and kill several men. R. Yohanan said, "When R. Akiba saw Ben Koziba, he would say, 'A star has stepped forth from Jacob [Num. 24:17]; Kokhba has stepped forth from Jacob. This is the anointed king.'" R. Yohanan ben Torta said, "Akiba, grass will grow between your jaws and the messiah will not yet have come."

For three and a half years Hadrian surrounded Betar, and R. Eleazar of Modi'in would sit in the marketplace in the dirt and pray, "Master of the world, do not judge us this day. Do not judge us this day." Since [Hadrian] was not able to conquer [Betar], he considered retreating. A Samaritan was with him and said, "Be patient today and I will bring you to conquer it. But every day that hen sits in sackcloth and ashes brooding on her chicks you will not be able to conquer it." The Samaritan did what he said he would. He went to the city where he saw R. Eleazar standing and praying. He made out that he whispered in his ear and R. Eleazar didn't notice him. People came and told Bar Koziba, "Your companion wants to hand the city over." He sent for the Samaritan and asked him, "What did you say to him?" "If I tell you I will be telling the king's secrets [and he will have me killed], and if I don't tell you, you will kill me. It is better that you, and not the king, kill me and the king's secrets remain secret." Nevertheless, Bar Koziba was sure that it was a matter of surrendering the city. When R. Eleazar was through praying he had him brought before him. He asked him, "What did he say to you?" He replied, "I've never seen this man." [Bar Koziba] kicked him to death. At that a heavenly voice decreed, "Woe to the shepherd of idols, who leaves his flock. The sword shall strike his arm and his eye, and his arm will all wither and his eye grow all dim." (Zech. 11:17) The Holy One blessed is he said, "You who have shattered the arm of Israel and blinded his eye, that man's arm will all wither and his eye grow all dim." In an instant Betar was taken and Ben Koziba was killed. They came carrying his head to Hadrian. He asked, "Who killed this one?" A Samaritan said, "I killed him." He didn't believe him. He said to them, "Go bring me his body." They went and brought back his body and he saw a snake twined around his knee. He said, "If God had not killed this one who could have done it?" This proved that which is said: ". . . if it were not that their Rock had sold them, [that] the Lord handed them over." (Deut. 32:30)

[Thus, Bar Koziba was killed for his sin.] Betar stood for fifty-two years after the Temple was destroyed. Why was it finally destroyed? Because they lit lights on the day of the destruction of the Temple.

They killed those who lived there until horses waded in blood up to their nostrils. The blood tumbled huge boulders and flowed on into the sea, coloring it red four miles out. And Betar itself was four miles from the sea. Hadrian owned a vineyard eighteen miles square and he had a circumvallation built out of the bodies of those killed at Betar. . . .

R. Yohanan said, "The brains of three hundred children upon a single rock and three hundred baskets of phylacteries were found there . . . nine hundred bushels altogether." R. Kamaliel said, "There were five hundred schools in Betar, and the smallest had three hundred pupils. The pupils said, 'If the enemy comes after us, we will come out and kill them with our pens!' But when the people's sins brought the enemy in, they wrapped each student in his parchment and burnt him and I was the only one left." (*Lamentations Rabbah*, ed. Sh. Buber [Vilna, 1899] pp. 100–104)

It is taught that R. Eleazar the Great said, "There are two rivers in the valley of Yadayim flowing in different directions, and the Sages reckoned that [when Betar fell] they ran with two parts water to one part blood. It is taught . . . : For seven years the Gentiles fertilized their vineyards with the blood of Jews and never used manure. . . . (TB, Gittin 57–58)

BIBLIOGRAPHIC NOTE   I have found J. Klausner, *Jesus of Nazareth* (New York, 1925); M. Smith, *Jesus the Magician* (London, 1978); E. P. Sanders, *Jesus and Judaism* (Philadelphia, 1985) and *The Historical Figure of Jesus* (London, 1993); and J. Meier, *A Marginal Jew* (New York, 1991–1995) most helpful for an understanding of Jesus and the accounts of him. All these works contain lengthy bibliographies. M. Avi-Yonah, *The Jews of Palestine* (New York, 1976) provides an introduction to the historical context as well as to the revolt. A. Oppenheimer, and U. Rapoport, *The Bar Kokhba Revolt* (in Hebrew; Jerusalem, 1984); and M. Mor, *The Bar Kokhba Revolt: Its Extent and Effect* (in Hebrew; Jerusalem, 1991) have updated material, perspectives, and a bibliography.

3

THE PERSIAN MESSIAHS
Abu Isa, Yudghan, Mushka, and Serenus of Syria

From the beginning of the fifth century until the present, almost all Jewish messiahs have appeared outside the land of Israel. This has resulted in new motifs in the accounts of them, including miracles that look toward a return to Israel (the rebuilding of the temple, miraculous transportation back to Israel), alongside firm localist tendencies. The focus of this chapter is on the Jewish messiahs of Persia in the eighth century. (It includes the Syrian messiah Serenus because of his clear similarity to the Persians.) The careers of these messiahs bring together rural militant localism with the legend of the Ten Tribes and the asceticism that characterized the Mourners of Zion before them and Karaism after them. These messiahs are the direct forerunners of David Alroy, also from Persia, who is the subject of chapter 4. The first section of this chapter examines brief accounts of other Jewish messiahs from the fifth through the twelfth century, pointing out new motifs and innovations in messianic theology, with a special emphasis on the responses of Maimonides.

THE DIASPORA, EAST AND WEST, THROUGH THE TWELFTH CENTURY

After Christianity became a tolerated religion in the Roman empire (in 311 CE), only the apostate emperor Julian, who reigned from 361 to 363, turned against it. Julian's apostasy was due in part to his broad education, and in part to the distaste he developed for a Christian court in which the way to the throne lay over the murdered bodies of brothers, uncles, and cousins. He sought the renewal of Hellenistic

61

paganism and the rule of philosophy and was a constant enemy to Christianity. While his edict of 361 declared freedom of religion throughout the empire, it also ensured that contentiousness would flourish within the organized church by allowing exiled bishops to return to their sees. Certainly, a desire to denigrate Christianity motivated his support for the idea of relieving Jews of special taxes and his project to rebuild Jerusalem and the temple. Nevertheless, for a brief moment, Jews everywhere dreamed again of a renewal of power in their own land. Miraculous signs—an explosion on the building site and crosses in the sky—were imputed by Christians as the cause of the project's cessation and as testimony to its iniquity. The rebuilding of the temple—an eschatological motif, often the aim of a messiah's career—appears, from this historical moment on, as an anti-Christian design and as an anti-rabbinic one since both rabbis and Christians believed humans had no business working on the temple construction site themselves: According to rabbinic doctrine, the temple would be built in Heaven and then descend to earth; according to Christian tenets, the temple would be rebuilt by Jesus, upon his return, in a miraculous three days.

As Jews felt farther and farther away from achieving Jewish self-rule in the land of Israel, Jewish messianic movements postponed a confrontation with reality by interpreting events in the light of cosmic contexts. Since the time of the miracle-working, apocalyptically-oriented Jesus developed in the Gospels, Jewish messiahs have presented the end of their missions as the end of the world as we know it. Yet, all of them, including Jesus (if not the dominant *figuration* of him established in the late first century) have been, like the early Jewish rebels in the land of Israel, overwhelmingly concerned with local needs. The locality is no longer the land of Israel but the local people of Israel. The messiahs' distant goals, presented in their propaganda, may have been the sanctification and redemption of the people, resettled in their land, but their immediate target was freedom and self-determination for their followers.

These messiahs actually attempt to establish the conceptual land of Israel in their own locales, even as they promise a return to the land of Israel as pictured in traditional imaginative accounts. They seek to establish their own communities and govern their own lives. As they threaten to replace state authority, the state confronts them and suppresses their localized revolutionary movement by force. Disaster ensues. The state-within-the-state is internally unstable and too weak to take on a national, militarily-powerful government in a lengthy confrontation; and that is not its program. The nativist, antigovernmental, xenophobic, and violence-oriented character of such events remains an essential part of the Jewish home ritual at Passover, as the intentional community has shrunk to the area of the home. This ritual recollects Egypt, where in the spring, on the eve of redemption, the Jewish homes alone, a domestic Israel, were safe from plagues and death. Just as it incorporates so many messianic themes, including the return to Jerusalem, the common meal (seder) summons its partakers to look out of the home and read from the Haggada the appeal to God, to "spill out your wrath on the nations who have not recognized you [and have ruined us in our habitations]." This is understood to be a necessary preliminary—the execration itself is the ritual equivalent of its execution—for the arrival of the messiah's harbinger, Elijah, at every seder. He summons the Jews to freedom wherever they are and announces the onset of world peace.

A Jewish messiah next appeared in 415, amid the large Jewish population of Crete. An account of his deeds is found in the *Ecclesiastical History* of Socrates Scholasticus, a contemporary of the event from nearby.

> In the days of the emperor Theodosius the younger, who reigned from 412 to 454, a Jewish scoundrel appeared in Candia and asserted that he was Moses. He promised the Jews, of whom there were many on the island, that he would transport them without ships across the sea and bring them to the land of Judea, just as [Moses] had done for their forefathers in the time of Pharaoh, the king of Egypt, when he had led them out from slavery to redemption in the year 2154, 2,054 years before, for the incident being related occurred in 4208 approximately, in the Christian year 448. He went about saying that he was Moses and that God had sent him from Heaven to be their leader. For a year he toured the island repeating this, and he fixed a day for the exodus from there. He preached and prophesied and collected money on every side. On the appointed day, he assembled a multitude, and, coming down upon the rocks to the sea, he ordered those in front to jump into the sea. Their madness and blindness were such that they obeyed him, and so, many sank into the waves. Some fishermen who happened to be nearby charitably saved a few people, pulled them up into their boats and called out to those who remained not to jump. Because of them many of these miserable people were saved. The scoundrel fled, and I do not know what his end was; but his fraud had a good result, for many of the wretched had their eyes opened and converted to Christianity. (*Ecclesiastical History*, vol. 7, p. 33)

The messiahs after Bar Kosiba have had to promise transportation since the majority of the Jewish population after 135 CE has lived outside the land of Israel. The appearance of the messiah cited above, in the guise of Moses, arises from this simple fact and from the tradition that says that the new redemption would happen at the same time, in the same way, and under the same leadership as had the first, the one from Egypt.[1] Going across the water—any body of water now seen as the Jordan or the Red Sea—is not the only way to the land of Israel, but the natural associations of distance and borders with water create the crossing through the waves as the preferred method of passage. The same fluid that prevents migration and ensures separation from the land of Israel when converted facilitates migration. While it is easy to see the connection between this theme and such mystery waters as the Sambation River, behind which lies the land of the Lost Tribes of Israel, it is likely too that the tale of Jesus' walk *on* (over, not through) the Kineret has had some influence on this account. (Flight, too, is promised later, in Baghdad and Spain, and more recently played a part in the promotional literature of the Zionist project known as On Eagles' Wings (Ex. 19:4), which transported the Jews of Yemen to Israel in 1954.)

The act of collecting money that appears in the Socrates text remains a feature of later messianic events. Several accounts of later messiahs accuse them of swindling the gullible out of their money. In such polemics, greed is the ascribed motive for collecting money, which is thus taken as evidence of charlatanry. This argument is simplistic where it concerns the messiah. The accumulation of wealth per se is rarely the aim of the messiah; yet it may serve to symbolize that which *is* the aim—the transmutation of power. The aims of the people who donate funds are varied and more important. They include participation in the economy of salvation, in which the loss—that is, the rejection—of money and property in this world is palpable treasure laid up in the world to come. As a first step, the funds of followers are often collectivized and deposited with the messiah, who pays them out as needed. The collection of money also links the Diaspora messiahs to the Israeli messiahs, like Bar Kosiba, who collected taxes to support their military campaigns.

The scene now shifts to Syria in the period immediately following the Arab conquest of that territory from the Sassanians (ca. 645 CE), where, according to an anonymous Nestorian chronicler,

> some Jew, native of Bet Aramaye, got up in a town named Pallughta [Pumbedita?] at the point where the waters of the Euphrates separate for the irrigation of the soil, and asserted that the Messiah had come. He gathered around him weavers, [carpetmakers?], and launderers—some four hundred men. They burned down three [Christian] sanctuaries and killed the chief of that locality. A military force, however, sent from the city of Aqula, intervened, slew them with their wives and children, and crucified their leader in his own village.[2]

This passage focuses on the anti-Christian aspect of the uprising. Jewish life had continued in the eastern lands of Mesopotamia and Persia for centuries, ever since the first Diaspora in the eighth century BCE. As the Islamic empire began to expand, new political and economic opportunities became available to Jews. Note that the followers mentioned here are decidedly not the poor and ignorant. They represent a particular element of society—the artisans; the motif of the craftsman recurs for the first time since Jesus, the woodworker, one who was neither a peasant nor a member of one of the capital-endowed families of the Galilee, gained the support of a number of people who made their living in a variety of occupations other than agricultural ones. The artisan was in an ideal position as the shift toward a mixed economy became firmly established and as political changes led to new possibilities—new allies and newly weakened old oppressors—for the Jewish social economy.

These new freedoms stimulated a new, locally oriented messianism that sought autonomy not only from its Christian or Moslem rulers but also from the dominance of nonlocal Jewish communities. Two external factors contributed to the drastic messianic struggle for such changes: the battles between Byzantine and Persian forces; and the Islamic conquest of the Christian kingdoms of the Holy Land—which many Jews saw as the apocalyptic war of Gog-Màgog particularized as the war against Armilus (the name is a play on Romulus) that was portrayed in the late apocalypse known as the *Book of Zerubbabel*. This work served as a restatement of apocalypse and as a sort of latter-day Book of Daniel, with its figures and events to be interpreted and applied to current situations by its wide readership.

As mentioned in the introduction, few messiahs appeared in Europe during the period of the Crusaders, who passed through and pillaged the lands of Ashkenazic Jewry. A single Jewish messiah appears outside Islamic territory before Asher Laemlin in 1500. The episode, which occurred in Lyons, is reported in Maimonides' *Letter to Yemen*. In this letter of 1172, Maimonides, responding to a question concerning a particular messianic episode in Yemen, draws upon his limited knowledge of similar occurrences.

[In 1060] there appeared a man in [Lyons], a large center in the heart of France, which numbered more than ten thousand Jewish families. He pretended that he was the messiah. He was supposed to have performed the following miracle: on moonlit nights he would go out and climb to the tops of high trees in the field and glide from tree to tree like a bird. He cited a verse from Daniel to prove that such a miracle was within the power of the messiah: "And behold, there came with the clouds of Heaven one like a son of a man . . . and there was given to him dominion" (Dan. 7:13–14) Many who witnessed the miracle became his votaries. The French discovered this, pillaged the Jewish quarter, and put the pretender to death, together with many of his followers. Some of them maintain, however, that he is still in hiding until this very day.[3]

Flying through the air is an establishing miracle, one that proves the legitimacy of the messiah figure. In this letter, as in the Hebrew *History of Jesus (toldot yeshu)*, where Judas and Jesus are engaged in aerial combat, it does not correspond to Jewish desires to escape from disaster; it is not even associated with a distant destination.

Maimonides mentions five other messiahs in the letter—among them, Abu Isa (discussed below), David Alroy (see chapter 4), and the Yemenite claimant, about whom R. Yakov ben Netan'el, of Yemen, had written to Maimonides[4] (see chapter 10). The first of them, the first messiah to appear after the messiah of Lyons, was known as Ibn Arye ("son of the lion," a good messianic name, with its connotations of Judah, fierceness and divinely guided victory). He emerged at the time of the first Crusade (1096), but far away, in Islamic Cordoba:

My father, of blessed memory, told me that . . . there lived respectable folk in Cordova, the center of Andalusia, some of whom were given to the cult of astrology. They were all of one mind that the messiah would appear that year. They sought a revelation in a dream night after night and ascertained that the messiah was a man of that city. They picked a pious and virtuous person by the name of Ibn Arye, one who had been instructing the people. They wrought miracles and made predictions just as al-Dar'i did until they won over the hearts of all the people. When the learned and influential men of our community heard this, they assembled in the synagogue and had Ibn Arye brought there and had him flogged in public. Furthermore, they imposed a fine on him and put him under ban, because he gave assent to the professions of his adherents by his silence instead of restraining them and pointing out to them that they contradict our religion. They did the same thing to the persons who assembled about him. The Jews escaped the wrath of the Gentiles only with the greatest difficulty.[5]

In chronological order of appearance, the third messiah in Maimonides' letter was Moshe al-Dar'i:

A pious and virtuous man and scholar came from Dar'a to the province of Andalusia to study. . . . Later he left for Fez, the center of the Maghreb. People flocked to him because of his piety, virtue, and learning. He informed them that the messiah had come, as had been divinely revealed to him in a dream. Yet he did not pretend, on the basis of a divine communication, . . . that he was the messiah. He merely affirmed that the messiah had appeared. Many people became his adherents and reposed faith in him. My father and master, of blessed memory, endeavored to dissuade and discourage people from following him. However, only a few were influenced by my father, while most, nay, nearly all, clung to R. Moshe, of blessed memory. Finally, he predicted events that came true no matter what was going to occur. He would say, "I was informed yesterday—this and this would happen," and it did happen exactly as he foretold. Once he forecast a vehement rain for the coming Friday and that the falling drops would be blood. This was considered a sign of the approaching advent of the messiah, as was inferred from the verse, "And I will show wonders in the heavens and in the earth, blood and fire, and pillars of smoke" (Joel 3:3). This episode took place in the month of Marheshvan. A very heavy rain fell that Friday and the fluid that descended was red and viscous, as if it were mixed with clay. This miracle convinced all the people that he was undoubtedly a prophet. In itself this occurrence is not inconsistent with the tenets of the Torah, for prophecy will return to [the Jews] before the messianic advent. . . . When the majority of the people put their trust in him, he predicted that the messiah would come that very year on Passover eve. He advised the people to sell their property and contract debts to the Muslims with the promise to pay back ten dinars for one, in order to observe the precepts of the Torah in connection with the Passover festival, for they would never see them again; and so they did. When Passover came and nothing transpired, the people were ruined as most of them had disposed of their property for a trifling sum, and were overwhelmed with debt. When the Gentiles in the vicinity and their serfs learned of this hoax, they were minded to do away with him, had they located him. As this Muslim country no longer offered him protection, he left for the Land of Israel, where he died, may his memory be blessed. When he left he made predictions, as I was informed by those who saw him, concerning events both great and little in the Maghreb that were later fulfilled.[6]

From Maimonides' accounts, which he assembled from the reports of others, some common features emerge: The messiahs appear in urban centers; they work miracles; their movements inspire the anger of the non-Jewish population. This picture reflects Maimonides' rationalist, pacific position: that miracles are not part of the messianic specifications (they can be rationally explained and are not proof of a pretender's claim, anyway), and that the damage such pretenders inflict upon the faith of the Jews, and upon their precarious existence under Gentile domination, is not worth the risk of heeding their calls.

Maimonides develops his position on the issue of the messiah in his legal compendium, the *Mishne Torah*, condensing and summarizing rabbinic considerations of the matter, then selecting positions that meet his approval. Maimonides' conclusions have no legal bearing and do not influence messiahs or those who seek them. He quotes a rabbinic dictum (TB Sanh. 97b), "[May] the spirit of those who calculate the 'ends' expire," to support his antipathy toward the practice. Yet calculating the date of the coming of the messiah becomes a more popular activity soon after Maimonides' opinion becomes known, and he himself takes part. In spite of his assertion that the messiah need not perform miracles, miracles continue. He rejects the popular apocalyptic idea of a new order in a new era and, instead, describes the messianic age as one of plenty, with political freedom and expanded knowledge of God for Israel. A rationalist, he requires a candidate to prove himself by succeeding and denies the possibility of an unsuccessful messiah. On the other hand, he does insist that the messiah should be of the lineage of David, without explaining how this might be ascertained, and that the messiah bring all humanity together under Judaism.

Maimonides introduces a different theory on the doubling of the messiah, according to which one person passes through two stages, changing along with the changing world. Prior to Maimonides, three theories existed that might explain the deaths and defeats of messiahs. One idea proposed two messiahs, the first from the lineage of Joseph, followed by another, from the lineage of David. Another doctrine proposed the second coming of the messiah after his death and resurrection. In addition to these theoretical positions, followers frequently held that their defeated messiahs had never died but had escaped, disappearing into caves and other hiding places, and would return at any moment. Maimonides avoids the problem of how to explain a failed messiah by instituting a two-stage recognition process. A candidate, he says, may be considered the messiah "if he is a king who arises from the house of David, meditates on the Torah, occupies himself with the commandments in accordance with the oral and written Torah, and prevails on all Jews to do so and fights the battles of God." If he succeeds at all this, and if he is seen to be prepared to rebuild the temple on its site and to regather the dispersed Jews, then he is assuredly the messiah. For some time, Maimonides was the only one to find this verification procedure useful. Recently, though, it has provided the theoretical base for the aspirations of Lubavitcher Hasidim on behalf of their late rebbe, R. Menachem Mendel Schneerson (see chapter 9). Maimonides' two-messiah program rejects not only the Gospels' views but also the rabbis' idea of the messiah of the lineage of Joseph. But the mystery of proven Davidic lineage, rather than the empirical requirement of success, is the element of Maimonides' model that has had the greatest impact on future messianic events. Certain messiahs after Maimonides assert that their souls have descended, if not necessarily from David, from various rabbinic personae (by way of metempsychosis or soul wandering or progressive reincarnation). They prove able, moreover, as Maimonides says they will be, to determine the pedigrees of all Israel, aided by the holy spirit. Maimonides' doctrine of mysterious lineage underpins the claims of Isaac Luria (see chapter 6) and successive messiahs that they can identify souls and soul-parts in those around them; the possession of such an ability testifies to the fact that they are messiahs, while allowing them to refrain from explicitly identifying themselves.

One other messianic appearance occurs during the period Maimonides covers. It is not mentioned by him, but it is known through the report of an encounter in the land of Israel. The event might not have been known to Maimonides, or, having no outcome and threatening no urban Jewish population, it might not have been worth his consideration. In any case, in 1121, a Damascene convert to Judaism who is named Ovadya (after the biblical prophet, protector of converts in Jewish legend), while traveling down to Egypt, meets a certain Shlomo, a Karaite and a priest, near the settlement of Dan in Israel. Shlomo tells Ovadya that the messiah will soon come and that he himself is the one expected. Ovadya argues that the pretender (Shlomo) is not Davidic but Levitic. Shlomo's reply to this is lost. But he does say he subsists only on the fruits of Israel and milk, and he is delighted with Ovadya as a proselyte; he seeks unsuccessfully to dissuade him from leaving Israel. His affiliation with the tribe of Levi and the priests may suggest the continuation of the priestly messiah tradition.

LOCALISM, MILITARISM, AND ASCETICISM IN PERSIA

By the beginning of the fifth century, Jewish political power in the Land of Israel had all but disappeared. The goal of recovering the Jewish land remained constant, but achieving it while living and working in exile under anti-Jewish regimes nourished a conflict in Jewish values. After Baghdad became the capital of the whole Islamic world, its position as the seat of Jewish authority was refurbished. According to the rabbinic authorities in Baghdad, the value of a life lived in exile was measured by what it contributed to the redemption. Daily life was devalued in favor of a future life that would be achieved through prayers and adherence to the law, relying ultimately on supernatural intervention. Elsewhere, Jewish communities reasonably questioned this thinking. Was the only value of life in seventh-century Persia, say, to be found in its potential contribution to the restoration of the land of Israel, or didn't Jewish life, wherever lived, have some intrinsic worth? Was all Jewish life always and everywhere to be subservient to a foreign code of conduct—rabbinic tradition, the Babylonian Talmud or the Talmud of the land of Israel?

Some Jews sought to build up political-power bases in the areas where they lived in exile, with the ultimate aim of returning to a land of their own. Messianic movements of a militant character sprang up when opportunities to gain that end seemed to present themselves. The requirement that a true prophet live in the land of Israel fell away, and local figures asserted the right to determine by themselves how they would carry out their mission. They normally chose the role of the conquering messiah; local independence became a goal that was to be achieved through military action whenever possible. An awareness that there was little chance of military success—realistically, the Jewish forces were simply too weak for the task—did hamper plans for such activity, but the realization that life away from the Land had its own meaning, and could have an actual part to play in the redemption, engendered a countervailing enthusiasm.

As the Persian movements of Abu Isa, Yudghan, and Mushka, and the Syrian movement of Serenus, began in the eighth century, social upheaval provided them the opportunity and stimulus to act: The forces of Islam were on their way to defeating Christian rule but had not yet consolidated their own victory. Furthermore, a struggle for power was raging within the Islamic fold, between followers of Mohammed's family—Shiites—and the dominant Sunni imperialists. To wage a limited war against this riven but well-armed majority, the movements had to carefully assess their opportunities and methods. A shortage of resources could be overcome through cunning stratagems, such as the manipulation of local authorities, that would not require the expenditure of the few lives and weapons at hand. Programs that offered homage to the distant aim of the redemption of Israel, while promoting the independence of local action in the attainment of it, unified the supporters of three successive messiahs.

The texts that follow show that each of the three Persian messiahs incorporated elements of Islamic theology in his movement. They all supported the idea (a Moslem one) of a continuing lineage of prophets and claimed the authority to reform religious practices. Most of the new practices they required were more severe than those of rabbinic Judaism and were developed in accordance with local expectations—in particular, the emphasis on asceticism, which was associated with the discipline of the Mourners of Zion. This group, whose name comes from Isa. 63:3, is mentioned in the Roman period (the second century; see TB Baba Bathra 60b) as mourning the destruction of the temple in elegies and praying for its rebuilding and the ingathering of the scattered Jews. It is next heard of just after the Moslem conquest (in the Umayyad period). Its practices were ascetic and penitential and included regular, constant fasting and abstinence from meat and wine. A dualistic doctrine that distinguished evil and carnal inclinations from the spiritual ideals could only have reinforced the harsh and gloomy intensity of the Mourners' tradition, which gained great influence among Jews in Moslem lands, particularly Persia, where dualism was a long-standing tradition. Local Mourners' practices reinforced the local community's own authority and the authority of its leader to act independently of the Jewish power center in Baghdad. Thus the Mourners, like the messiahs, were involved with local needs, despite their preoccupation with the destruction of the temple in distant Jerusalem; mourning itself, after all, was an activity that could be conducted only outside the land of Israel, following the temple's destruction. The asceticism of the Mourners would have an important influence on the Jewish messiahs of Persia and Yemen (see chapter 9) and would be carried, through the Persian messiahs, to Karaism, an antirabbinic ideology that claimed greater loyalty to biblical law. A twelfth-century account describes the Mourners still active in Yemen.

From [Hillah] by way of the wilderness of the Land of Saba, called the land of El-Yemen, alongside the land of Shinar to the north is a journey of twenty-one days. In the wilderness there camp the Jews called Khaibar, the men of Tema. And in Tema the head of their government [dwells] and there R. Hanan the Nasi rules over them. It is a great city and their land is a journey of sixteen days among the mountains of the north. And they have great and fortified cities and the yoke of the Gentiles is not upon them, and they journey to distant lands with the tribes of Arabs, their neighbors and covenanters, to take booty and pillage. . . . And all the neighbors of the Jews fear them, and [the Jews] have among them those who work the land and own cattle. And their land is broad and among them are learned scholars, and they give them a tenth of all they have to those learned scholars who dwell in the schools and to the poor of Israel and to those who keep themselves apart in their generation, they are the Mourners of Zion and the Mourners of Jerusalem. And they do not eat flesh and do not drink wine and they wear black clothes and dwell in caves or in houses hidden away and they fast all their days except the Sabbaths and holidays. And they seek for mercy before the Holy One blessed is he upon the Exile of Israel that he be merciful upon them for the sake of his great name, and upon all the Jews, the men of Tema and Tilmas, that great city in which are about 100,000 Jews. And there is Salmon the Nasi, the brother of Hanan the Nasi, and the land is between the two brothers. And they are of the line of David for they have a document of kinship. And they dispatch many questions to the exilarch nearby in Baghdad and they fast forty days a year for the Jews who live in Exile.[7]

In this account we find a group of independent, pillaging Jews who provide financial support for the ascetic Mourners. The Persian messiahs combine asceticism with local militarism; they themselves are fierce individualists. All three Persian messiahs associate themselves with Moses, the Faithful Shepherd, as he is commonly known in midrashic literature. They, like he, have a local goal—liberation—and local rather than Israelite birth. There is much traditional literature that connects the messiah experience to the Exodus, as has been noted. Moses has an independent background as God's warrior and is arguably the Jewish equivalent to Jesus (in Christianity) and Mohammed (in Islam). As a lonely shepherd and an intimate of God, Moses typifies independence and the values of rural rather than urban life. The thread of asceticism, together with a common focus on local communities, connects Abu Isa, and the leaders who come after him, with the founder of Karaism, Anan ben David, and succeeding Karaite authorities. The Karaites, however, an urban movement rather than a rural one, as the Persian messiahs had been, relinquished military tactics. As the rule of Islam consolidated, military action became less feasible and, as had happened in Roman-dominated Palestine, the desire for a more global freedom was modulated into the quest for freedom from the authority of a particular sphere of Jewish society—in this case, the rabbinic tradition, its power base in Baghdad, and its supporters in Persia. Karaism is a missionary movement but not a militant one and is most similar to the programs of the Persian messiahs in displaying a decided diffidence toward the promotion of a return of Jews to the land of Israel. (Only one of the texts quoted below describes the intended program of the pioneer Abu Isa's revolt as an effort to go overland to Israel and seize control there rather than in Persia.) In the few karaistic homilies preached on the need for Jews to move to the land of Israel, such an act is not deemed significant as a stimulus or an immediate forerunner of the messianic age. The residue of the local autonomy encouraged by the messiahs became the mothering yeast in which Karaism grew.

Anan ben David claimed the leadership of Babylonian Jewry and was rejected at the seat of power in Baghdad. In return, Karaism, the movement he founded, rejected the continuous tradition (Rabbanism) of Judaism because it had failed to serve the needs of the society of Babylonian and Persian Jews during the early rise of Islam. The Karaites accused the rabbanite courts, in particular, of abusing the poor and of lacking concern for public health and welfare. The call of Karaism—"Search and search the Torah and judge for yourself"—went out to those seeking independence from the self-interested rabbinic authorities. Prior to the Karaites, it had been the Persian messiahs who had sought to provide exactly that localism, tailoring the practices of outside authority, as that was represented to them by Baghdad, to popular needs or rejecting them entirely. The single legal emendation we find Abu Isa ordaining removes the power of the courts to deal in divorce cases. His solution to the injustices and expenses that were likely to arise in the adjudication of such claims appears to have been typically puritanical: He outlawed divorce altogether. The process that began with the Persian messiahs—Abu Isa, Yudghan, and Mushka—and their struggles for Persian Jewish autonomy, ended in a schism between the Rabbanites and the many schools of the Karaites. Serenus' conduct and his amendments to Jewish law display another side of the struggle for local power.

ABU ISA

Yitzhak ben Yakov was active as a prophet-messiah in the first part of the eighth century near Isfahan (and so was known as al-Isfahini). He was also known as Ovadya, it seems, because he was the "servant (*oved*) of God (*Yah*)." Yet another of his names, Abu Isa, contains the Arabic form of the name "Jesus." He apparently supported the idea that both Jesus and Mohammed were prophets, at least as concerned their own peoples. He might have done so for tactical reasons and only in the presence of Moslem authorities, but there is not enough information from disinterested sources for us to be sure. If he genuinely supported the claims of these prophets, this marked the radical extent of his innovative localism. Although he did introduce new practices of prayer and daily life, these were not antagonistic toward the established strictures of the oral law. Rather, he intensified the latter in expressions of mournful longing, urging the redemption, the reclamation of the land, and the rebuilding of Zion. In following this course, he attracted a supportive local following.

The accounts that follow point out Abu Isa's artisan origins and his claim to simplicity, even illiteracy. This image of him in the accounts goes beyond the repetition of traditional themes; it rings a peculiarly pro-diasporan note in the context of this movement. The assertion of his immortality, on the other hand, is a typical feature of the messiah account.

Account by al-Qirqisani

Abu Yusuf Yaqub al-Qirqisani (from Persia) reviewed the history of Jewish sects in order to show how his own movement, Karaism, developed from, then superseded, its predecessors. He wrote his essay in the tenth century, after having traveled and read a great deal. His purpose was to show how his own views were superior to those of all the other Karaite philosopher/theologians. This work, written in 937, was called *The Book of Lights and Watchtowers* [*kitab al-anwar wal-maraqib*]. The following exerpt, and the one after it, are from Leon Nemoy, "al-Qirqisani's account of the Jewish sects and Christianity," *Hebrew Union College Annual*, 7 (1930).

Ovadia appeared after the other [Jewish] sects that have been mentioned. He was known as Abu Isa of Isfahan. He proclaimed himself a prophet. This happened

during the rule of [the caliph] Abd al-Malik ibn Marwan. It is said that he led a revolt against the [Moslem] government. Many people followed him until he had an
armed force. But he was conquered in a battle and killed. Some of his admirers say
that he was not killed but escaped to a cave in the mountains and that nothing has
been heard of him since. The most wondrous thing about him, according to his admirers, is that even though he was, in their words, an uneducated tailor and did not
know how to write or read, he composed books and shorter works, without anyone's
having taught him. In Damascus there is a group of his admirers known as Issuniyim.

The biblical prophet Amos is the first prophet to set himself at a distance
from the traditions associated with the prophetic calling. He says he is not a
prophet by lineage or occupation but a farmhand (Amos 1:1). The image of the
prophet or messiah as a common laborer attracts a disenfranchised, relatively impoverished, uneducated following. The illiterate messiah lacks adherence to the old
text and so is uniquely prepared to become literate in the newly promulgated text.
He receives the gift of literacy, and even the ability to create striking works of literature, in his encounter with the divine. The Moslem legend about the illiteracy of
Mohammed reinforces the tendency for the Jewish prophet to associate himself
with this model, especially when his community is in a Moslem society, itself an inheritor of biblical and Christian traditions.

The excerpt here comes from the first Jewish account that maintains the idea
of the nondeath of the messiah in the way that it does. It provides a simpler, though
more fantastic, explanation than the others, sacrificing universality in favor of that
which is local, familiar, and possible—a secret, hidden cave. It surrenders the flexi-
bility of a more complex explanation, preferring the blunt, if more fragile, denial of
the evidence of death itself. The cave does very well as a site for incubation and for
the passage into the underworld, remaining a plausible place to hide in a landscape
known for many caves with secret openings.

We said above that Abu Isa proclaimed himself a prophet; [he composed works
even though he was illiterate] and this could only have been by prophecy. As far as
his teachings and ideas go: he prohibited divorce, as did the Sadducees and the
Christians; he instituted seven prayer services a day, drawing upon the words of
David: "I praise you seven times a day" [Ps. 120:164]; he prohibited the eating of
flesh and the drinking of distilled liquors, not on the basis of scripture but because
God ordered him to do so, through prophecy. . . . He said that God told him to
pray the Eighteen Benedictions and the passages of the Shema', according to Rabbanite practice. But he did this only to attract the masses of the people and the
leadership to him. The Rabbanites and the public leaders reject the Issuniyim but
do not identify them with the followers of Anan [ben David] and the Karaites.

I asked Yakov ben Efraim of Egypt, "Why do you have relations with the followers of [Abu] Isa and intermarry with them when you know that they attribute
prophecy to those who are not of the faith?" He replied, "Because they do not differ
from us in the observance of holidays." This answer of his indicates that, according to
them [i.e., the Rabbanites], acting as a complete unbeliever is more excusable than

observing the holidays that they themselves made up in any way different from [the way the rabbanites do it].

Abu Isa confessed the prophetic nature of Yeshu ben Miriam and that of the Instructor of the Moslems [Mohammed] and said that each of them was sent [by God] to his people. He ordered [his own disciples] to read the Gospels and the Koran and to gain an understanding of their meanings. He said that the Christians and Moslems are required to observe their faiths just as the Jews are required to observe the one they claim. He did so for the good of his own ideas and teachings and to protect his own claim to be a prophet. If he had disavowed these two men, the people would have disavowed him, too. Thus, by recognizing these two, he hoped to bring his plans to a successful conclusion. But he was disappointed in his expectations and his hope remained a fraud.

In their legal considerations, the Rabbanites did not excommunicate the Issuniyim and did not identify them with the (later) Karaites, so the Issuniyim must have resembled the latter in important ways but not enough for the two to be considered identical. This verdict must have arisen from the fact that the Issuniyim no longer posed a powerful threat, as the Karaites did at the time this account was written.

Abu Isa's teaching concerning Jesus and Mohammed as prophets alleges that prophecy is limited neither to a particular place (the land of Israel), nor to a particular time (the period of the Bible), nor, for that matter, to a particular religion and its tradition (though only Jewish prophets bring messages of universal relevance). This assertion legitimates Abu Isa's own claim. It also provides an explanation or justification for Abu Isa's appearance and mission in Persia rather than in the land of Israel; it supports the notion of a local messiah for a local following and an independent movement, which resembles Mohammed's own political philosophy. When the text avers that Abu Isa prohibited meat-eating and the drinking of alcohol on the basis of something other than the Scriptures, one can be certain that the appeal is not only to the Mourners of Zion but to followers of Islam as well, since each of these groups followed similar traditions in this respect.

Account by Hadassi

Eshkol ha-kofer (the "cluster of camphire," which refers to Song of Songs 1:14) is by Yehuda ben Eliyahu Hadassi. Hadassi's nickname was Ha-Evel, the mourner, probably because he was a member of the Mourners of Zion group within the Karaites. In rhymes and alphabetic acrostics, he, too, is writing a sort of encyclopedia of Jewish belief as Karaites see it. Ascetic themes common to all these movements are found in his appraisals, but he asserts different motives and emphases for them. In Hadassi's account, Abu Isa forbids wine, in imitation of the Rechabites, whom Jeremiah praised not solely for their abstinence but also, more important, for their loyalty to an ancestral oath (cf. Jer. 35).

Keepers of the faith of Abu Isi, who is Ovadia of Isfahan. He said that what the prophets claimed on behalf of the messiah, "I fulfill, and God established me." He made up and established practices on his own, without the spirit of prophecy of your God.

Lazy and ignorant of the knowledge of God, he forbade man to divorce his wife, even if he find her errant, just as said the Sadducees, but not as God spake. And even obliged seven prayers before God on each and every day, in accord with the verse, "Seven times a day I praise You."

Meat he forbade and wine too, in accord with what is said of Yonadav and the Rechabites, but obliged the Issuniyim the Eighteen Blessings and the service of the shema' in its three parts, and a little more in accord with the Rabbanites who keep your flock. (eshkol ha-kofer, letters kaf–lamed–mem, from Aaron Z. Aeshcoly, Movements, pp. 141–143)

Account by al-Shahrastani

The next account is by the Moslem writter Abulfatah Muhammad al-Shahrastani, from his Book of Beliefs and Sects of Opinions [kitab al-milal wal-nahal] written in 1127. He intends to show the errors of various sectarian opinions in respect to the truth of orthodox Islam.

The Issiyim are so called after Abu Isa Ishaq ben Ya'aqov of Isfahan who was also known as Oved Elohim: that is, "one who worships God." He lived during the time of al-Mansur and his revelation began during the time of the last Umayyad king, Marwan ibn Mahmad al-Himar. Many Jews followed him. They say that he displayed signs and wonders. They believe that he marked a line around his men with a branch of myrtle when they were embattled and said to them, "Stay within this circle and the enemy's sword cannot touch you." And when his enemies approached the circle they retreated because they were afraid of the amulet or of the charm he used.

Then Abu Isa alone crossed over the line on his horse and fought the Moslems and killed many. Then he went to the tribes of Moses the son of Amram who lived beyond the wastelands in order to preach the word of God to them. They say that after he attacked the forces of al-Mansur at Ragaes, he was killed together with his men.

Abu Isa claimed that he was the emissary and prophet of the expected messiah, and he believed that the messiah had five emissaries who preceded him one after another. He believed, moreover, that God spoke to him and ordered him to redeem the Jews from the evil nations and their villainous kings. He also believed that the messiah is the most select of humans and that he himself was superior to the prophets who preceded him. He elevated the status of the Shepherd [Moses] and was of the opinion that the Shepherd was also the messiah.

In his writing he annulled the sacrifices and forbade the eating of any animal, bird or beast. He ordered ten prayers a day and decreed their times. He departed from many of the important commandments of the written Torah. (Book of

Beliefs and Sects of Opinions, from the Hebrew translation in Aeshcoly, *Movements,* p. 145f)

Letter from Maimonides

The last account of Abu Isa appears in Maimonides' famous *Letter to Yemen* (mentioned previously). In Maimonides' account, there is no mention of those peculiarities that the other historians comment on (new religious practices, asceticism, the recognition of non-Jewish prophets).

I shall now narrate to you succinctly several episodes subsequent to the rise of the Arabic kingdom from which you will derive some benefit. One of these refers to the exodus of a multitude of Jews, numbering hundreds of thousands, from the East beyond Isfahan, led by an individual [Abu Isa] who pretended to be the messiah. They were accoutered with military equipment and drawn swords and slew all those that encountered them. They reached, according to the information I received, the vicinity of Baghdad. This happened in the beginning of the reign of the Umayyads.

The king then said to all the Jews of his kingdom: "Let your scholars go out to meet this multitude and ascertain whether their pretension is true and he is unmistakably your Expected One. If so, we shall conclude peace with you under any conditions you may prefer. But if it is dissimulation, then I shall wage war against them." When the sages met these Jews, the latter declared, "We belong to the children of the district beyond the river." Then they asked them, "Who instigated you to make this uprising?" Whereupon they replied, "This man here, one of the descendants of David, whom we know to be pious and virtuous. This man, whom we knew to be a leper at night, arose the following morning healthy and sound." They believed that leprosy was one of the characteristics of the Messiah, for they found an allusion to it in the verse, "[we reckoned him] stricken, smitten of God, and afflicted" (Isa. 53:4), that is by leprosy. Whereupon the sages explained to them that this interpretation was incorrect, and that he lacked even one of the characteristics of the Messiah, let alone all of them. Furthermore, they advised them as follows, "O brethren, you are still near your native country and have the possibility of returning there. If you remain in this land you will not only perish, but also undermine the teachings of Moses, by misleading people to believe that the Messiah has appeared and has been vanquished, whereas you have neither a prophet in your midst, nor an omen betokening his coming." Thereupon they were persuaded by these arguments. The Sultan turned over to them so and so many thousands of dinars by way of hospitality in order that they should leave his country. But after they had returned home, he had a change of heart with respect to the Jews, upon whom he imposed a fine for his expenditures. He ordered them to make a special mark on their garments, the writing of the word "cursed," and to attach one iron bar in the back and one in the front. Ever since then, the communities of Khorasan and Isfahan experienced the tribulations of the Diaspora. This episode we have learned from an oral report. (*Letter to Yemen,* excerpted in I. Twersky, *Maimonides Reader* [New York, 1972], p. 459)

Maimonides' account mentions matters not found in the others and emphasizes the role of rabbinic texts in establishing the bona fides of a messiah, the role of the sages in applying the tests, and the acceptance of the texts and their interpretation by Abu Isa's following. Maimonides' sages reject Abu Isa because he is no prophet, not being from Israel, and because no sign supports his claim. This reasoning occupies Maimonides less than their rejection of the (Christian) claim that the messiah suffers. But the followers may be contending that Abu Isa, like Moses, was stricken with leprosy and cured of it as God's sign to him, which he must show to dubious Israelites as evidence of his election (cf. Ex. 4, 6–8).

YUDGHAN AND MUSHKA

Abu Isa's follower and successor, Yehuda, is also commonly known by his Persian name, Yudghan. He carried on with the teachings of his master, and some later students attached his name to teachings that explained the "inner" and "outer" meanings of the Torah, an idea that resembled beliefs about the Koran held by the Islamic sect of the Mu'tazilites. Whatever the truth of this, his assertion that some writings tell truths and make requirements that can only be grasped intuitively is useful in supporting legal and religious innovations that reject traditional authorities and hermeneutics, yet claim to be traditional. He does follow one traditional argument, which holds that reward and punishment depend on free agency.

About Mushka, who also had a Persian name, very little is known. Passionate devotion to his cause drives his suicidal determination to make war against what were by then the well-prepared forces of a stable government. He is the last of the three messianic forerunners of Anan ben David's revolution, Karaism. Interestingly, there is no claim that he survived his last battle or will return.

Account by al-Qirqisani

Yudghan [called by his followers "the Shepherd," meaning that he was the shepherd of the people of Israel] also proclaimed himself a prophet, and his disciples say that he is the messiah and lives yet, and they look forward to his return. The people of Yudghan forbid the eating of meat and the drinking of distilled liquors and engage in much prayer and fasting. And they say that the Sabbaths and holy days have been annulled in this era and are only remembrances. Some of the Karaites join them in this opinion. (*Book of Lights and Watchtowers*, quoted in Nemoy, p. 383)

Account by al-Shahrastani

[The name of this sect] comes from Yudghan of Hamadan, also known as Yehuda. He preached asceticism and earnest prayer, forbade the eating of meat and the drinking of liquor. Among those things that are passed on in his name is also his esteem for the degree of the Shepherd. . . . And he thought that the Torah has an inner and outer meaning . . . as opposed to the explanations of other Jews. He differed from them as well in his opposition to the use of logical analogy [for interpreting Scripture] and in his belief in free will, and was of the opinion that humans act as they wish. He was one of those who found reward and punishment a [theological] necessity. . . .

The followers of Mushka are to be accounted with them [the followers of Yudeghan]. [Mushka] followed the teaching of Yudghan, except that he supported opposition to those whose opinions differed from his and was in favor of warring against them. He rode at the head of nineteen men and was slain near Qum. About one of the sects of the Mushkanites it is said that they recognized the prophecy of the Elect One [Mohammed] as valid for the Arabs and other peoples, other than the Jews, since they already had a religion and a book that had come to them revealed by God. (*Book of Beliefs and Sects of Opinions*, translated into Hebrew by Aeshcoly in *Movements*, pp. 150–151)

This account is all we know of Mushka. Immediately following it, al-Shahrastani outlines a version of Arianism as followed by a Persian sect. Among its distinctions, he notes, are its traditions of asceticism and modesty.

SERENUS

This Syrian messiah of the second decade of the eighth century is reported under various names: Sari'a/Zonoria/Saur/Serenus. The period when he lived, his claim to be the messiah, and his new code of law are common to all extant texts that relate to him, however. His law code differs from that of Abu Isa, Yudghan, and Mushka in its particulars. For example, whereas Abu Isa increases the number of prayers, Serenus does not even meet minimal rabbinic standards. Such details are less important than this messiah's assertion of the right to make a new law for a new world and a new people that will stand out against the old world, the old patterns, and their failure to bring freedom and redemption. An awareness of new times and new needs is also revealed in the leniency of the responsum of the patriarch, Natronai Gaon I.

Account by Natronai Gaon

The following is from a responsum written by Natronai ben Nehemiah, religious and judicial authority and head (Gaon) of the academy at Pumbedita in Babylonia from 719 to 730.

As to your inquiry concerning a deceiver who stayed in the land of our Exile and whose name was Sari'a, who said, "I am the messiah," and people strayed after him and practiced heresy: ceased praying, [ceased] observing the laws concerning ritual slaughter, ceased keeping their wine distinct from the 'wine of [others'] oblation,' worked on the second day of festivals, failed to follow the ordinances of the sages as concerns the form of the marriage contract, like others who are major heretics, when they return [to the fold], do they require immersion or not? and what is to be their resolution? We determine: that these sinners, although they have become involved in non-Jewish acts and have denied the decisions of the sages and disdained the holidays and their commandments and made themselves unclean with corpses and carcasses, even so it is better to bring them near than to push them away. . . .Take them in and do not reject them. (*sha'arei tzedek*, in Aeshcoly, *Movements*, p. 152)

Anonymous Account

The following is from an account of somewhat dubious origin and worth.

In those days the Jews living in Spain rebelled, for there came to them a report that one named Zonoria had appeared in Syria, a swindler, who said of himself that he was the promised messiah whom they had been expecting. And all the Jews in Spain and Gallia [France] went to Syria and left their possessions behind. The emir, Ambiza, seized all their wealth, homes, and land, on behalf of the state. (J. A. Conde, *Historia de la dominacion de los arabes en España* (Madrid, 1874), p. 79, from the Hebrew translation by Aeshcoly, in *Movements*, p. 153)

Account by Bar Hebraeus

The following is from the history of the world that was written in Syriac by the Jacobite convert and bishop, Gregorius bar Hebraeus, in the thirteenth century.

At that time a Syrian man whose name was Saur said of himself that he was the messiah, and when he was captured by the governor, he said, "I was making fun of the Jews." (*Chronicon Syriacum*, from the Hebrew translation by Aeshcoly, in *Movements*, p. 153)

Account by Isidore of Badajoz

The following is from a chronicle written by Isidore of Badajoz, in the middle of the eighth century.

In those days [723 CE] the Jews were tempted away, stirred up by a Jew who called himself Serenus and announced himself the messiah and promised them the Chosen Land, and so they left behind everything they had and followed him . . . and Ambiza seized it all for the state treasury. He summoned the man Serenus to see whether he was the messiah and to let God settle the matter. (*Chronicle*, in E. Florez, *España Sagrada* [1769], vol. 8, p. 298, from the Hebrew translation in Aeshcoly, *Movements*, p. 154)

BIBLIOGRAPHIC NOTE   In addition to Aeshcoly, see J. Mann, in "Messianic Movements during the First Crusades," *ha-tekufa* 23/24 (1924–1925); I. Friedlaender, "Jewish Arabic Studies," *Jewish Quarterly Review*, III (1912–1913); R. Mahler, *Karaites* (Merhavia, 1949); Z. Ankori, *Karaites in Byzantium* (New York, 1959);

D. Lasker, "Rabbinism and Karaism: the Contest for Supremacy," in R. Jospe and S. Wagner, eds., *Great Schisms in Jewish History* (Denver and New York, 1981); L. Nemoy, *Karaite Anthology* (New Haven, 1952), "Karaites," in *Encyclopaedia Judaica*, vol. 10, pp. 762–786; N. Schur, *History of the Karaites* (Frankfurt, 1992) and the bibliography there.

4

THE MESSIAH OF AMADIA
David Alroy

Four centuries after the Persian messiahs had waged their struggles, David Alroy, another localist, militant messiah, led an armed insurrection bent on the redemption of the Jews in Persia's borderlands. He was better educated in Islamic culture, philosophy, and law than were his predecessors and shared their syncretist tendencies; his facility in science perhaps helped him perform deeds that others took as evidence of his magical powers. Unlike the rural eighth-century Persian messiahs, there is no evidence in the accounts of Alroy that he followed ascetic practices. Alroy gravitated toward the urban center of power; he was the first of several Jewish messiahs after Jesus who confronted the ruler—in this case, the sultan, face to face.

The messiah who became known as David Alroy lived in the first decades of the twelfth century. He was from Kurdistan, from the mountain country known as Daghestan, beside the Black Sea. His name was originally Menahem ben Shlomo al-Duji. His choice of the name David—Menahem is a messianic name, according to the Mishna and the Book of Zerubbabel—is unique and daring in itself. The last name, al-Ro'i/al-Ruḥi, is probably the result of an orthographic error in Arabic. (Ibn Verga calls him David al-David because of a similar error.) He has been known in English as David Alroy since the time of Disraeli's novel *The Wondrous Tale of Alroy* (1839) (Figure 4.1). Disraeli knew of Alroy from the account in the eighteenth-century English translation of *The Travels of Rabbi Benjamin*, which had been published in England in 1784.

Alroy's father and another man, Efraim, a speechwriter or "man of language," as he is called, had created a turmoil in "Khazaria," the land of the Khazars, a

81

Figure 4.1: Disraeli's tale establishes its own reality for Alroy, fitted to its own needs, no less than does the depiction of Alroy in this engraving (which accompanies the Dunne edition of Disraeli's fiction of 1904). The Near East was becoming the subject of commercial attention of a new sort for Great Britain as the Ottoman Empire's grip slipped away, and its economic desirability was accompanied by romance. The combination made its contribution to the atmosphere in which the Balfour Declaration was inscribed. Disraeli's own idealization of Judaism, his ancestral faith, led him to take an interest in this heroic Jew; but any similarity between the Alroy of this very bad novel and a real Alroy is quite accidental.

famous central Asian nation of converts to Judaism. There, it seems, these two men conspired to initiate a campaign to conquer the Holy Land. Support for their plan was easily obtained among the Jews of the mountains, no less fierce and independent-minded than their non-Jewish neighbors. Some time elapsed between the start of his father's campaign and the beginning of Alroy's career. Alroy spent the intervening years studying in the yeshiva of Baghdad, under the tutelage of the gaon (headmaster) himself. According to our sources, he excelled in his Jewish studies and in studies of Arabic and science, and he mastered the arts including the mastery of magic.

Following the decline of the Crusader kingdoms and the reinvigoration of Moslem forces, the competition between Moslems and Christians for the control of trade routes rose sharply. The chaos and violence that marked the struggle between these two great powers inspired Jews to look upon this time as the moment of the apocalyptic war. The ruler of Mosul, Imad al-Din Zangi, habitually incited discord between local Jews and foreign Christians, so he looked contentedly upon Alroy's movement. In any case, the Jews were happy to cooperate with the Moslems against the Christian invaders. Alroy himself is said to have been a handsome young man, and the propaganda distributed about him, advertising not only his program of penitence and fasting but also his promise of conquest, encouraged Jewish support. Both elements of Alroy's movement echoed the programs of the earlier Persian messiahs.

As the Christians gained headway, Alroy was initially defeated, and Zangi himself was killed. The city of Amadia, Alroy's hometown and a center of sectarian Moslem intrigue, became the prime target of his attacks. Its fortress controlled a route that might in fact have led a victorious Alroy on to Edessa and Jerusalem. Alroy summoned Jews from all over the region to sneak into Amadia with their weapons hidden beneath their cloaks, and he did achieve control of the city for a time. When he was eventually captured, he escaped by means of his magic. The Persian powers soon located him and either killed him themselves or had him assassinated by Jews who feared reprisals (see the accounts below). Following Alroy's disappearance, a pair of swindlers in Baghdad promised the faithful a miraculous nocturnal flight to Jerusalem. Themes that appeared in the prospectus of Alroy or Efraim no doubt inspired the fraud. The idea of flying was persuasive as a way to cover the great and dangerous distance back to Israel miraculously, a necessity since the time of the exile. It gained new strength from the legend of the miraculous night flight of Mohammed. Other individuals and groups in this same period also believed that they would fly, either on their own power or carried by celestial beings. (Recall the Jewish messiah of Lyon's attempted flight, discussed in chapter 3.)

Alroy's movement remained alive in Amadia and elsewhere after his death. He was never condemned for his efforts, not even by Maimonides, and when Kurdish Jews were finally able to settle in modern Israel, they named a village for him in the Jezreel Valley, behind the Carmel range, near the ancient seat of the scholars of the Mishna. In 1958, the Israel Defense Force, for its own purposes, issued a pamphlet about the life of Alroy. In it, he is praised as "a statesman of great [geopolitical] vision and great deeds, in whom were combined a talent for daring strategy and a capacity for clear thought in weighing the odds, [and for] caution and executive strength. He had no peer among the leaders of messianic movements in the Middle Ages."

Account by Benjamin of Tudela

Benjamin of Tudela (in what is now Spain) was a Jewish traveler who wandered the Jewish world between 1160 and 1173 and kept a journal, which remains as one of the most important historical documents of the period. As a journalist, he was curious, impartial, and as precise as possible, although he accepted the word of legends when he had no other sources. His purposes in traveling probably had to do with commercial possibilities. No doubt, the popular hope of finding the Ten Lost Tribes also played some role in his motivation. Benjamin's account of Alroy was the one upon which almost all other accounts rested. He must have heard the story in the territory of Iraq, probably in Baghdad itself, since he never visited Kurdistan or any of the other sites mentioned in the account.

Ten years ago today there rose up a man and his name was David Alro'i, of the city of Amadia. And he studied before the exilarch, Hasda'i, and before the head of the yeshiva, the gaon Yakov, in the city of Baghdad. He was quick in the teachings of Israel, in the law and in the Talmud, in all the wisdom of Ishmael, and in the secular books, and the books of magicians and mediums. It came to his mind to raise his hand against the king of Persia and to gather the Jews who live in the mountains of Haftoun and go out and make war against all the other nations and go and take Jerusalem. And he gave signs to the Jews by false wonders and said that "The Holy One blessed is he has sent me to conquer Jerusalem and bring you out from beneath the yoke of the other nations," and some few Jews believed him and called him, "Our messiah." And the king of Persia heard the report and sent to him to come speak with him, and he went to see the king, without fear, and when the two of them were together, he [the king] asked him, "Are you the king of the Jews?" He answered him, "I am." The king was angered and gave orders to seize him and put him in the prison, there where the prisoners of the king were kept until the day of their death, in the city of Tabristan which is on the banks of the great river, the Gozan. And at the end of three days the king was seated to speak with his ministers about the matter of the Jews, that they had raised their hand against him. And then David came before them, for he had freed himself from the prison with the permission of no man. And at the moment the king saw him, he said to him, "Who has brought you here? Who has set you free?" He said to him, "My art and my skills have, for I fear not you nor all your servants." At once the king called out to his servants, "Catch him!" And his servants replied, "We see no man but hear his voice." The king and all his ministers were all astonished at his art. And he said to the king, "Now I am going on my way." And he went and the king after him and his ministers and servants coming after their king until they came to the bank of the river, and he took his kerchief and spread it out on the surface of the water and crossed the river upon it. Right then the servants of the king saw him, that he was crossing the water upon his kerchief, and they took off after him in little fishing boats, to bring him back. But they could not catch him, and they said, "There is no magician in the world such as this one." And on that same day he went on to Amadiya, ten days away, by the [power of the] Explicit Name, and he told the Jews what had happened to him and they were all astonished at his art.

Then the king of Persia sent a letter to the emir al-Mu'minin, the caliph in Baghdad, the lord of the Ishmaelites, asking him to speak with the Exilarch and the Headmaster of the yeshiva, Gaon Yakov, to stop David Alro'i from doing this thing. "And if not, I will kill all the Jews in my kingdom," and all the Jewish communities of Persia sat in great distress. And the Exilarch and the Headmaster of the yeshiva Gaon Yakov sent to him: "Know that the time of the Redemption has not come, nor have we 'seen our signs.' [Ps. 74:9]. 'For man shall not triumph by power,' [1 Sam. 2:9], and we decree that you cease from doing such a thing and if not, you are cast out from all Israel." They sent to Zakkai, the prince, who was in the land of Asshur [Mosul], and to R. Yosef the Seer, known as Burhan al-Mulk, to dispatch the letter to him as well. They themselves wrote to him to warn him, and he did not receive the letters. At last one king, Zun al-Din, king of the Turks, a servant of the king of Persia, arose. And he sent for the father-in-law of David Alro'i and gave him a bribe of ten thousand gold pieces to kill him in secret. And he came to his house and he was asleep upon his bed and he killed him and his idea came to nothing. And the king raised his hand against the Jews dwelling in the hills. And they sent to the Exilarch to come to their aid and appease the king. And the king was appeased by one hundred talents of gold that they gave him—"and the land was quiet" [Jud. 3:11] thereafter. (From M. N. Adler, ed., *The Travels of Benjamin of Tudela* [in Hebrew; London, 1907])

A central issue in Alroy's campaign finds expression in his promise to capture Jerusalem and "bring you out from beneath the yoke of the other nations." Maimonides, following Babylonian Talmud Ber. 34b, sees Jewish liberty as representing the only distinctive difference between the days of the messiah and the present, though he might have other, more supernatural, differences in mind after this change has come to pass. The response of the exilarch and the headmaster to Alroy's movement was due to their fear of reprisal by the Moslem authorities against the Jewish community, but the response itself obscures their motive and stresses the fact that no *supernatural* evidence that could support Alroy's claim has been produced. The buildup of tales about Alroy's magic deeds and talents is, to some degree, a reaction to this. The swindlers of Baghdad in the Ibn Abbas account (and the slightly different account published by Mann in *ha-tekufa*, cited here) relied on the reputation of Alroy's magic powers, and so does the mockery his followers suffer at the hands of the Gentiles. The resolve of the Kurdish Jewish community to see Alroy as a learned and courageous freedom fighter prevailed over the whole question of his magic deeds.

Account by Ha-Cohen

R. Yosef Ha-Cohen (1496–1578) was an Italian physician, of Spanish descent, who resided in papal France. He was a historian and wrote the work from which the following passage comes, *The Vale of Weeping* [emek ha-bakha], in 1558. The purpose of the work was to provide a history of Jewish sufferings (in Hebrew) that would match an earlier one (in Portuguese) by Samuel Usque, *The Consolation for the Tribulations of Israel*. Both of these very early works of Jewish historiography sought to detail and justify the history of the sufferings of the Jews and were stimulated by the forced conversions, trials, tortures, and executions in Spain and Portugal, and the expulsions from the two countries.

There was a Jew in Persia, in the city of Amadia, which is in the mountains of Haftoun. His name was David al-Ro'i. . . . There were about one thousand Jewish householders in Amadia at the time, speakers of Aramaic. David studied with

Rav Hasdai and with R. Yakov in Baghdad and became skilled in the Talmud and sciences and magic and got to be proud of himself. He gathered a large number of Jews from the settlements around the mountains of Haftoun to go wage war for Jerusalem. He said to them, "I am the messiah." Many of them believed him and said, "Indeed, he is our messiah." They revolted against the king of Persia and slew many of his men by the sword.

The king saw that he might not be able to conquer him. He sent to David who then came in on [the promise of] safe conduct. The king of Persia spoke with him about his dreams. David said to him, "I am God's messiah, so pay me honor this day." The king became angry with him and ordered him lowered into a pit in Daghestan on the river Gozan. His feet were laid in iron.

Three days later, the king was speaking with his ministers and servants about the Jews who had transgressed against him, and along came David, for he had by his art smashed the doors of bronze. They were astonished, and the king said to him, "Who brought you here?" He said, "I came here by my art for I fear neither you nor your servants this day." The king said to his servants, "Catch him!" They said to him, "And where is he?" David spoke to them but they did not see him. . . .

David went to the palace and spoke with the king again. He said, "You cannot overcome me. See it with your own eyes: I'll go as I please." And he left him. He took the scarf off his head and spread it out on the Gozan and crossed the river on it. The king and his ministers saw it and were very astonished.

The king ordered many men to pursue him in boats, and they couldn't catch him. On that same day [Alroy] traveled a journey of ten days with the aid of the Explicit Name. He told his brothers in Amadia what had happened to him and they were very astonished. . . . (*The Vale of Weeping*, ed. M. Letteris [Vienna, 1852], pp. 48–49)

This account (and its parallel in Usque's history) shows a certain sympathy for Alroy. The Persian king's punishment of Alroy is associated with the evil and unavailing attempts of Joseph's brothers and Nebuchadnezzar to do away with righteous prophets by lowering them into pits. The psalm in which the line "His feet were laid in iron" appears (Ps. 105:18) speaks of Egypt and the Exodus, and verse 15 has God ordering kings "not to touch my anointed ones [*meshihai*]." Ps. 107:16 contains the line about the smashing of the doors of bronze, referring to God liberating his faithful from prison. Ha-Cohen accepts Alroy as a member of the household of Israel in good standing, suffering for no fault of his own. He sees Alroy and his warriors as "brothers."

Account by Ibn Verga

R. Shlomo Ibn Verga (1450–1525) was a Spanish Jewish historian. He moved to Portugal after 1492 and then to Italy. The work from which the following passage is excerpted (in English, *The Tribe of Judah*), is an account of the persecutions of the Jews during his own life. (Its title means equally, "The rod of the Spanish Jew.") The differences in style and emphasis between his account and the others—his defamation of Alroy, his description of the wealth and happiness of the Jewish community of Amadia, his addition of the king's threats of mass murder and torture—reflect his own experiences with expulsion and forced conversion in Spain and Portugal. He despaired of the spiritual meaning of suffering and of the redemption of the Jews. His treatment of the messiahs is particularly derisive:

About seven years before [the catastrophe mentioned previously], Israel suffered mightily due to the deeds of a worthless man who claimed to be the messiah. The king and his ministers were enraged at the Jews, for they thought that the Jews were attempting to bring down their reign through the messiah. This cursed man was named David al-David and was from Amadia. A great community of Jews lived there, about one thousand households, wealthy, replete, well thought-of and successful. This community was the most important of those settled in the environs of the river Sambation. . . . They lived in the realm of the king of Persia. And this man, David al-David, studied under the exilarch Hasdai. . . .

Those who joined in his company called him the messiah and praised him and extolled him. When the king of Persia heard about the man . . . he became very fearful and sent for him . . . to display his signs, and if they really were signs, he would know that he was the messiah in truth and would understand that God had made him king and would acknowledge him and be obedient in his service since it was the will of God that made him king. And David al-David came along fearlessly. . . . The king asked him, "Is it true that you are the messiah?" David al-David answered, "I am the messiah. God has sent me to redeem the people of Israel." The king responded, "I will imprison you, and if you free yourself, I will know that you are the messiah, and if not, it will be your punishment, on account of your foolishness, to remain there forever. I will not kill you since you are a fool."

After David al-David had been captured, the king summoned his ministers . . . to determine what should be done to the Jews who had committed a crime against the realm and revolted. And while they were sitting in council, they heard that David al-David had freed himself from the prison . . . and that it was not known where he had gone. The king sent his knights and ministers after him . . . but they returned and said to the king, "We heard his voice near the river, but did not see him at all." . . . And then the king and his servants took horse and pursued him . . . but did not see him. They called to him and he answered, "O fools! I am off on my way. If you have the strength, come take me." And he stretched out his scarf over the Gozan and crossed the river. . . . Then the king said, "An act such as this no man has the power to carry out but only the King who has made him king. I mean, the Eternal King. And thus has this man been crowned, and we must acknowledge it." His servants and ministers said to him, "What we have seen are deeds done by magic and legerdemain alone." Then the king ordered boats and they crossed the river . . . but did not catch him. . . .

And when the king saw that he had no success that way . . . he sent to the leaders of the Jews in Exile to catch the man and bring him in to court, and if they failed to do so, he would kill all of them, the young and the old both, and would torture the leaders of the Jews and then burn them one by one. He sent to the emir al-Mu'adin, who was in Baghdad, to act with appropriate diligence in the matter, especially as concerned the leaders.

Then the leaders of the Jews in Exile sent to David al-David to give up his foolishness, so that it might be well for him and all the flock of Israel who were in great danger. If he didn't repent, he would be excommunicated for eternity in this world and in the next. They also sent a letter to Zakkai, the president . . . and to R. Yosef the Seer . . . asking them to write on their own part that it was a time of trial for Israel and that the many mercies of Heaven [alone] could save them. And all of them sent letters to David al-David to warn him that he should turn back from his evil way. He received all the letters and read them and made fun of them and laughed and neither attended to them nor feared them.

And merciful God set it in the heart of one of the kings of Turkey, whose name was Zeyd al-Din and who was a vassal of the king of Persia and one who loved Jews deeply and who knew David al-David's father-in-law, to say to him: "You know your people well and that it is in deep distress . . . therefore, it is your duty to save yourself and your people. The Jews will give you ten thousand pieces of gold—I promise this—if you kill this man. . . . You will be rewarded by God as well. . . ." And the man set himself to finish the matter in order to save his people and for the love of reward. That night he summoned David al-David to a feast and made him drunk. And at midnight, when he was drunk and sound asleep, he sprang upon him and cut off his head. . . . And he brought it to the king, Zeyd al-Din. . . . And the king, Zeyd al-Din, sent the head to the king of Persia with faithful witnesses to testify that it was the messiah he had been concerned about. And the wrath of the king over David al-David was quieted, but he was determined in any case to seek vengeance upon the Jews who had followed him. He required of every community that it transfer to him all those who had followed the cursed man. They responded that they did not know who they were and how should they seek them? Then the king ordered them held captive. They had people negotiate for them and compromised with the king on a huge sum of money, one thousand plaques of gold. (*shevet yehuda*, ed. M. Wiener [Hamburg, 1855], pp. 50–51.)

Anonymous Account

The anonymous account that follows was first published by Mann in the 1926 *Revue des Etudes Juives* (LXXI) and then in 1928 in his two-part article in *ha-tekufa* (23:243–261; 24:335–358). He writes that the (Hebrew) text is part of a longer work that "mentions various contemporary false messiahs."

In the days of the ruler al-Afdal: In those days there arose hotheads from among the people of Israel and they glorified themselves and thought to bring about the vision and they fell [Dan. 11:14] In the mountains of the land of Khazaria, there arose a Jew whose name was Shlomo ben Duji and the name of his son was Menahem and together with them a spokesman whose name was Efraim ben Azariah Ha-Yerushalmi, known as Ben Sahalon. And they wrote messages to all the Jews, near and far, in all the lands around them, and news of them, [along with] their letters, reached a great distance: to all those places on the face of the earth where Jews live among all the peoples who are under all the skies the news of them came. They all said that the time had come when God would gather his people Israel from all the lands into Jerusalem the holy city, and that Shlomo ben Duji was Elijah and his son, the messiah. And when all the Jews of all the lands had heard the words of their letters and greatly rejoiced and then had stayed hoping days and months and neither saw nor heard any word: and many of the Jews . . . [spent] many [days] in fasting and praying and deeds of piety for they were awaiting God's salvation as his servants the prophets had said: and when they saw nothing, their hearts broke to pieces within them and the Jews were ashamed before all the Gentiles: for all the Gentiles and the uncircumcised had heard the news that had come to the Jews and all of them laughed and made fun of the Jews and said, "Behold the Jews seek to fly to their land but have no limb with which to fly." And they added more and new slanders upon the Jews, and the Gentiles said that everything Jewish was lies and nothingness. (J. Mann, "Messianic Movements during the First Crusade" (in Hebrew), *ha-tekufa* 24 [1928]:347–348)

This account, like the others quoted here, except for that of Ibn Verga, is not unsympathetic either to the prophet or to his followers, though it is most tender toward those other Jews who suffered contumely for no reason at all. The quote from Dan. 11:14, "There arose hotheads from among the people of Israel and they glorified themselves and thought to bring about the vision and they fell," indicates the view that the movement is composed of hasty youths, who are attempting to take into their own hands the fulfillment of a prophecy, rather than leaving it to the Lord in his time.

Defamatory testimony by Ibn Abbas of Morocco

Samau'al/Shmuel ben Yehuda Ibn Abbas (ca. 1125–1175) lived in Iraq, Persia, and Syria, was a convert to Islam, and wrote the account that follows in his work *Silencing the Jews* [*ifham al-yahud*]. He argues against Judaism and, particularly, against rabbinic Judaism, declaring it irrational. In this passage about Alroy, Ibn Abbas seeks to defame the Jews, particularly their leadership in Baghdad, by ridiculing their gullibility, which for him is typical of the religion. Ibn Abbas did apparently have access to original documents, including the first epistles authored by a messiah since Bar Kosiba's.

In order to show how [the Jews] are inclined to believe whatever is false and impossible in a great hurry, we will mention an incident that will show as well how weak are the intellectual powers of the Jews of Baghdad. This happened in these our times. A good-looking swindler called Menahem ben Shlomo grew great among the young Jews in the environs of Mosul and became known as Ibn al-Ruhi. He was a greatly honored sage in the religion of the Jews who dwell in the city of al-Amadia, which belongs to the district of Mosul. The commander of the fortress fell for the swindler's tricks and because he thought him an honest man, allowed him to visit. The swindler sought to be near the commander often, and since he knew him to be a man of little discernment, it came to him that he could conquer the fortress so that he might gain a safe and secure haven. So he wrote to the Jews who were wandering through the cities of Azerbaijan and its environs, since he knew that all the Jews of Persia were greater idiots than any others. He told them that he was the one who would save them from the Moslems. He wrote them in all sorts of different subtleties and swindles. This is the text of one of his letters that I have seen: "And if you should say, 'Are we wandering and going about in order to make war?' No. We do not seek that you make war but that you gain Redemption by one who will rise up and he will show you here how to blind the eyes of the king's messengers who serve within [the fortress] gates." And at the end of the letter he demanded, that "every one of you [who comes here must have a sword or weapon hidden beneath your clothes." The Jews of Persia and al-Amadia obeyed him and came running to him with sharpened weapons. Eventually, he had a large force.

The commander of the fortress, who had a good opinion of him, thought at first that the crowd had come to visit his friend since he had become famous in his land for his good reputation. But thereafter, he came to know what were the plans of the crowd. Yet he was one who sought not to kill, and so he killed only the leader of the rebellion, the swindler. Those who remained, when they learned of his death, strayed here and there in woe, wailing and mournful, and understood nothing of the matter, even though it was clear to any person of discernment. In fact, the Jews of al-Amadia praise him until the present in many of their gatherings. And there are those who think he is the expected messiah. And I have seen Persian Jewish communities in Khavai, Salmas, Tabriz, and Maraga who mention his name while taking great oaths. The Jews of al-Amadia are extreme in their dealings with Christians in all matters that touch on the Jews wherever it is possible to oppose them. In that city there is a group that is faithful to a religious practice that comes, according to them, from the above mentioned swindler, Menahem.

When the rumors about him reached Baghdad, two swindling Jews, elders and men of esteem, conspired and wrote letters, in the name of Menahem, to the Jews of Baghdad, to announce to them the Redemption for which they had been long waiting. They set the date for a certain night in which they would all fly to Jerusalem. And the Jews of Baghdad, who glory so in their acuity and their analyses, attended closely to this and trusted in the truthfulness of the two men. And the women brought them their wealth and ornaments so they might give them to whoever needed them. And so the Jews donated a fair part of what they owned. They had clothes made for themselves and gathered on the rooftops that night, in order to wait for the angels who would carry them to Jerusalem on their wings. And the mothers who were there and had babies to nurse worried tearfully, lest they should fly before their children or their children before them, that the children might thus die from lack of nourishment. The Moslems were restrained from pursuing the Jews and were astonished at the whole affair before they came to know of the empty promises that had been made to the Jews. That whole night until the dawn, the Jews tried to fly. Finally, they came to know that they had been misled and had become a laughing matter. The two swindlers fled, taking with them what they had gotten from the Jews. The hoax they had worked became known, but the Jews tried to keep the matter from the public. They called the year "the year of flying" and used it to tell how old someone was. This is the way the people of Baghdad count years, those who continue to be Jews. The whole matter is an eternal and constant shame for them. From what we have mentioned, there is sufficient reason to teach them the right path and to keep them reined in, for the matter shows clearly what their interest is and in what they believe. (*Silencing the Jews*, from the Hebrew translation in Aeshcoly in *Movements*, pp. 188–190)

All five of these accounts of Alroy show clearly the influence of the authors' contexts on their perceptions of this messiah and of messiahs in general. In the case of Ibn Abbas, we are confronted by a polemic, anti-Jewish view; he regards the messiahs as quacks and their followers as dupes. Ibn Verga presents us with the genuine pain and doubt of one who looks back on his own generation's sufferings and finds them senseless. He was a skeptic, despairing of finding truth in religion, but he looks upon his people with compassion and commiserates with them. Benjamin of Tudela depicts Alroy as a stage magician who uses his art to encourage a rebellion. Benjamin sees the act as wrong and its consequences as disastrous but for the intervention of the Jewish authorities. Nevertheless, he notes no self-interest on Alroy's part and judiciously ascribes his fall to the lack of support he received from his own community. Ha-Cohen and the anonymous author quoted by Mann look back from their own tortured times and see Alroy's struggle as one to free his people from helpless subservience and from subjection to murderous whimsy, whether it arises from Islam or Christianity or from having to maintain a position caught between the two.

BIBLIOGRAPHIC NOTE   Aside from the references cited in this chapter, the study of messiahs in S. Baron, *Social and Religious History of the Jews*, vol. 5, includes his description of the Alroy episode on pp. 202–205.

5

THE MESSIAHS OF THE INQUISITION
David Reubeni and Shlomo Molkho

After the twelfth century, the stage of Jewish messianic activity shifted from the Islamic east to the northern Mediterranean to Spain, where Jewish communities experienced freedom and oppression intermittently as the fortunes of the dominant powers of Christianity and Islam rose and fell. The first section of this chapter will trace the rise of Jewish mysticism in this period, the development of crypto-Judaism (converting to Islam or Christianity while secretly maintaining Jewish practices), and the effect both of these had on Jewish messianism and messiahs. David Reubeni and Shlomo Molkho, the two messiahs who are the focus of this chapter, can be seen as figures that bridge the period between the previous localist, militarist Jewish messiahs of the Islamic world and later Jewish messiahs who drive toward cosmic goals, employing the symbols and acts of apocalyptic mysticism. In Reubeni's accounts, we find the motifs of the Ten Tribes, the asceticism that can be traced back to the Mourners of Zion, and militarism; but at the same time, he is focused on a return to Israel rather than local power (he has no locale of his own). He is little influenced by tenets of the newly arisen Kabbalah. Molkho, himself from a crypto-Judaic background, supports Reubeni's military posture and shares his asceticism and pietism but is deeply stirred by the Kabbalah and does cosmic deeds. The Israel of his vision may not be the earthly Israel that is Reubeni's destination but the mystical Israel not on this earth.

THE DIASPORA FROM THE THIRTEENTH TO
THE SIXTEENTH CENTURY

The lifestyle of the Jews of the western part of the Moslem world began to come under attack by different forces during Maimonides' lifetime. From one side, the stricter Moslems of North Africa claiming they could no longer tolerate the easygoing ways of Islamic Iberia, especially the leniency shown to Christian and Jewish inhabitants, invaded it in order to reform it and to contain the expansion of Christian Spain. Within Jewish society itself, many, especially in the Ashkenazic community, rejected Maimonidean rationalism; they had never been partners in the Arabic-Jewish synthesis and viewed both philosophical justifications of Judaism and non-Ashkenazic codifications of the law as acts of arrogant intellectualism that ridiculed them and their own traditions. Out of these tensions rose the Kabbalah, late in thirteenth-century Spain. This Jewish blend of medieval philosophical and mythological ideas shifted the focus of Jewish esotericism toward the rescue of the nation from its constant tribulations in the chaos of its environments, whether Spain during the Christian Reconquest, Germany during the Crusades or all of Europe during the expulsions. Interest in a redemptory figure began to stir throughout Europe's Jewry.

Accounts by Abulafia

On the cutting edge of this trend, the first messiah-candidate of the era, Abraham Abulafia (1240–1292?) appeared in Iberia. He adapted the meditative and individualist practices of Islamic and Hindu circles to Jewish texts (including those of Maimonides), thereby seeking to unify the human with the divine (although this conflicts with the Jewish concept that humans cannot become divine). He was an active promoter of his own ideas and saw himself as a national redeemer, though he lacked any program to regain the land of Israel. He never gained much of a following in his lifetime, but his focus on the mysteries of the Hebrew alphabet and on the world itself, as configurations of the divine names, contributed to all later meditative practices, as well as to theurgical usages in Jewish mysticism and messianic events. Two autobiographical accounts illuminate his desires, intentions, and anguish and delimit his achievements. The first account, quoted here, is from the introduction to his book of commentary on a very early text, the *sefer yetzirah* [*Book of Formation*], the fundamental source of Hebrew alphabetical mysticism:

> It has been my whole intention in all that I have written up to this point in this book, to arrive at that which I will now reveal to you. It is, that I am the man mentioned in the first introduction to this book. I was born in Saragossa in Aragon in the kingdom of Spain. Before I was weaned, that is, while I was yet nursing milk at my mother's breast and was among my brothers and sisters . . . I began to read the Bible with its commentaries and grammar, that is, the whole Written Torah, twenty-four books, with my father, my teacher of blessed memory. I went on to learn some of the Mishna and some of the Talmud with him and the greatest part of my education came from him. I was eighteen years old [Abulafia writes the number eighteen as the Hebrew word for *alive*] when he died. . . . I continued living where I had grown up for two years after my father's death. When I was twenty [Abulafia writes this as the word *yod*, the name of the first letter of the Tetragrammaton] and the spirit of God awoke me and impelled me, I left there and came straight to the Land of Israel, over sea and land. It was my plan to go to the Sambation river

but I was not able to get beyond Acco because of the conflict between Ishmael [the Arabs] and Edom [the Christians]. I left there and came back by way of the kingdom of Greece. There, on my way, I was married, and the spirit of God awoke me and I took my wife with me and set out to find what I sought, to study Torah. I was in Capua, five days' walk from Rome, and found there an admirable man, intelligent and wise, a philosopher and an expert doctor, named R. Hillel, may his memory be blessed, and joined myself to him. I learned a little of the science of philosophy from him and it was erased from my mind at once, completely. I sought with all my strength to learn it and studied it day and night and did not relent until I studied [Maimonides'] *Guide to the Perplexed* many times. I also taught it in many places. . . .

When I was thirty-one [Abulafia writes the number using the Hebrew word *El* = God], in Barcelona, God woke me from my sleep, and I began to study the *sefer yetzirah*, with its commentaries, and the hand of God rested upon me, and I wrote some books of learning and some books of wondrous prophecy, and my spirit was a lively thing within me and the spirit of God came within my mouth and a holy spirit fluttered within me and I saw many wondrous and awesome visions in signs and wonders and among them there were gathered about me jealous spirits and I saw false images and my thoughts took fright for I could find no other like me, none of my sort who might show me the way in which I should walk, and so I became in truth like a blind man at midday for fifteen years and the Adversary stood at my right hand to oppose me and I was maddened by what my eyes beheld and sought to fulfill the words of the Torah and to bring this second curse to an end for fifteen years [Abulafia writes the number this time with the letters of the divine name *Yah*], until God took pity on me and granted me the counsel of wisdom and was beside me and a help to me from 1240 to 1285 and preserved me from all manner of hardship. And at the beginning of the year "Elijah the prophet" [1285], God desired me and brought me to the Holy Palace, and it was during this time that I completed the book that I composed here in Messina, for my dear, pleasant, fine, intelligent, understanding pupil, who longs to learn the truth of the pure Torah, that is Sa'adia [my best student], for I detected that he clung to me so lovingly that he had the capability of remembering that which he learned from me, for forgetfulness is common, and had the capability of grasping what I knew and of being a help to his companions to aid them in intellectual achievement and to aid those who are like them with the mass of that which is written here [in this book]. And I know that if it had not been for those images, they would not have separated from me, and that those images were the cause of their leaving and their going away from me, and that those very images were divine causes whose purpose was to set me firm in my purpose again to lighten my heart and eyes to withstand the trials, for on account of them I kept watch over my mouth and my tongue and restrained them from speaking and my heart from thinking and returned to the appropriate place to which it was correct to return and to keep watch over the covenant that had been made and my comprehension and my mastery, which had been whole until then; and I gave praise to the name of the Lord my God and the God of my fathers, who has never left off his concern and his truth at any time, whose covenant is merciful, and who has granted such a thing to a heart that is dearer than mine in his concern. And so it came to me, when I looked upon these fine things that are coming new into the world, to [write this and] return the hearts of fathers unto their sons and sons unto their fathers. (A. Jellinek, *Bet Ha-Midrash*, vol. 3, pp. xl–xliii [in Hebrew; Jerusalem, 1967])

This book is the fourth book of the explication of Razi'el [Abulafia's name for himself, the numerical equivalent (*gematria*) of his first name, Avraham], the third in composition, for Razi'el wrote the *Book of the Upright* (*sefer ha-yashar*) first and was in the city of Mt. Patros in the land of Greece and wrote it in the year 5039 [1279] of the creation of the world, and he was 39 years old then, in the ninth year since the beginning of his prophecy. But until that year he had not written a book that could at all be called prophecy, even though he had written many other books of art and some of them were of the secrets of the Kabbalah. And in that ninth year God stirred him to go to Great Rome, as he had commanded him in Barcelona in the year of h'lh [*Eloah*, the God] (5041), and on his way he had passed by Trani, where he had been taken captive by Gentiles on account of some slander that the Jews had laid against him, and a miracle was done for him and God took him up from there and he was saved and passed by Capua and there, in the tenth year of his leaving Barcelona, wrote a second book, the *Book of Life* [*sefer hayyim*]. And on the fifth month after Nisan, the eleventh month after Tishrei, that is, the month of *Av, came* [the two words are a palindrome in Hebrew] he to Rome and determined to go, on the day before Rosh Hashana, to the pope; and the pope, who was in Soriano, a certain city a day's walk from Rome, commanded all his gatekeepers that if Razi'el came there to speak with him in the name of all Jewry, that they should take him immediately, and that he should not at all look upon him, but that they should take him outside the city and burn him, and the wood [for the fire] was laid behind the interior gate of the city. And this thing was made known to Razi'el and he paid no attention to the words of those who spoke but went off to be alone and saw visions and wrote them down and began this book then and called it the *Book of Witness*, for it was a witness between him and God that he had given up his soul for dead on account of his love for God's commandment and was a witness as well concerning God, who had saved him from his enemies; for on the day of his going to appear before this pope, two mouths were born unto him, and when he entered the outer gate of the city a messenger came to him and told him that during that night the one who pursued his life [i.e., the pope] had died suddenly of plague; on that very night, he had been killed and died and Razi'el had been saved; and then he was taken captive by the Little Brothers in Rome and stayed in their monastery *koaḥ* ["strength"; the equivalent in Hebrew of the number twenty-eight] days, for he was taken captive on the day of the Fast of Gedaliah in the year h'lh for it is the year of the nation [*om*, the sum of which is the same as the sum of *Eloah*] and he went free on the day of the New Moon of Marheshvan. And I have written this here to speak the praise of the Holy One blessed is he and his signs and miracles and wonders with Razi'el and with his faithful servants. (*sefer ha-edut* [*Book of Witness*], as published in the *Monatsschrift für Geschichte und Wissenschaft des Judenthums* 36 (1887), p. 558)

Messiahs of Inquisition Spain and Portugal

A popular account of the disputation held in Barcelona in 1263, between R. Moshe ben Nahman (Nachmanides) and the apostate Pablo Christiani, mentions the (Jewish) messiah's coming to the pope to demand of him the liberation of Israel; "and only then will the messiah be considered really to have come, but not before that."[1] This debate alone provoked such publicity—attested to in the accounts and commentaries—that afterward, few who engaged in Jewish scholarship could have been ignorant of Christian theology. Certainly, in the West from the thirteenth century on, the influence of Christian ideas can be felt in Jewish doctrine, particularly in works of mysticism. After the expulsion from Spain, the Jewish exiles carried Christian themes with them into the lands of the Ottoman empire.

The public disputations were but one of the phenomena that arose from the struggle between the emerging social ideal of (some degree of) religious freedom and the political hopes of particular Christian or Moslem religious parties. Whichever party rose to power, a cryptofaithful performance, not only among Iberia's Jewish population, was the likely result. Tens of thousands of Jews had been forced to convert to Catholicism in the seventh century, when Judaism was outlawed by the Goths. Repeated attempts to suppress Jewish practices and to deal with the lingering influence of Judaism (and, presumably, Jews) on new converts demonstrate that the policy was unsuccessful. Some degree of secret practice continued among the converts, and when the Arabs and Berbers invaded in the early eighth century, a large number of Jews were present to assist them. Twice more, in the twelfth century, North African Moslem forces crossed into Spain ostensibly to counter the growth of Christian power and the laxity of the Moslem Andalusian regime in matters of religious practice. These puritans renewed the regime's intolerance of Jews and Christians, and while some Jews fled north to seek shelter from the more lenient Christian kingdom, others converted, perhaps insincerely, to Islam. Spanish Moslems also adopted the strictures of their invading coreligionists, then reverted to former, laxer practices and beliefs when they could safely do so. By the time of the Reconquest, the assumption of one confessional posture after another had modulated into a positive adherence to a religious masquerade; a well-defined religious variety established itself for generations to come. Rabbinic authorities in the region held that insincere conversion to Islam under duress could be undone and, contrary to Ashkenazic opinions and deeds during the Crusades, that the ultimate sacrifice—death before conversion—was not called for or even proper. Conversion was conclusively established, justified by an incontrovertible and broad-reaching argument, as the only Jewish option, barring death, during the sequence of events that began in Spain with the massacres of 1391; was followed by mass conversions, the institution of the Inquisition, and the expulsion of all Jews in 1492; and continued in Portugal, with more forced conversions—first, of Jewish children, in 1497, and shortly thereafter, of all the remaining Jews. If a person was a Jew and would be a Jew again, then the period spent posing as a non-Jew was a dimly lit, but still Jewish, time, too.

Those who sought to be Jewish during the period of these events, having been deprived of all original Jewish sources but the Bible (in Latin), were forced to choose their acts and attitudes as Jews from the descriptions of Jews that the Inquisition provided in its edicts and other polemic literature. These descriptions were meant to aid the faithful in recognizing those guilty of Judaizing (as they termed the secret adoption of Jewish practices), or were accounts of the deeds of secret Jews that the Inquisition had condemned. This inversion of the authority of texts and of the meaning of acts advanced the tradition of unreality among western messiahs. The messiah, or his theological amanuensis, could now elevate his intention over any of his acts. Even his conversion to another faith, like his defeat or death, could be transvaluated. The explication of the exigency of pseudofidelity added an additional layer to the "sufferings of the messiah."

The experience of the converts—conversos, or New Christians; or Marranos, as many Spanish Christians called them, or, as the literature more persuasively refers to them, *anusim* (the "coerced")—provided the background for, and the focus of, the later mystic circles of Italy, Turkey, and the land of Israel; many members of these circles were themselves former converts. In Iberia, the role the anusim played in the careers of David Reubeni and Shlomo Molkho was a formative and fateful one, and at least one other messiah appeared among the Jews, in 1542: "After these things [the sequence of events noted above], a new messiah arose among the Jews. He was a cobbler named Ludovico Diaz, born in Setubal. He began to preach and his reputation spread abroad among the Jews. He said that he was the messiah and many believed in him. Among the other believers was the physician to the bishop, Don Alfonso, brother of the archbishop of Portugal. The doctor's name was Francisco Mendes. At the age of thirty-seven he circumcised himself, [obeying] the command of the messiah. The messiah and all his followers were condemned to be burned. So, year after year, twenty, thirty, forty people were burned alive and more than 200 were severely punished." From another account, which confuses the cobbler with Reubeni, it appears that the cobbler confessed, under torture, to having lied in order to elevate himself.[2]

Ines of Herrera was descended from Jews and, after her mother's death in 1499 or 1500, she received a visitation from her in a dream. Her mother ordered her to carry out certain acts—in particular, that of charity. Later, she was visited by a *claridad* ("brightness"), which informed her that Elijah would come to her and that soon after, all the conversos would be carried away to "a certain place of abundance." Many whom she told of the events believed her, and many came to see her. She fasted Mondays and Thursdays and kept the Sabbath, donning clean garments. In his confession before the Inquisition, one of her followers, Juan de Segovia, told Ines' tale of being conducted through Heaven by her mother, as an angel, and by a young boy, who had recently died. There she saw mysteries and heard the roar of those souls who had been tortured and burned here on earth. She was told that Elijah would soon come and preach to the anusim about the messiah, who would appear and escort the believers to the promised land, where young Jewish boys waited to marry the young girls of the anusim. Ines predicted the appearance of signs in the heavens that would announce the coming of the messiah, and adjured her listeners to keep the Sabbath, to fast, to believe in the Torah of Moses, and to give charity to poor anusim. Fasting and keeping the Sabbath exposed believers to risk since the Inquisition warned that failing to work, lighting candles, changing clothing or linens, or cleaning the house on Friday/Saturday were marks of a secret Jew, as was any refusal to eat (especially to eat pork) outside the home. (These warnings served as behavioral guides for the marrano messiah, as they did for all marranos. Reubeni's appearance stirred so much interest among the Portuguese converso community because he observed these practices and made much of them. He seems to have increased his fasts and the stringency of his Sabbath observations, and to have become more scrupulous in his diet, once he arrived in Iberia.)

Ines of Herrera was not a messiah but a prophet; the lines that distinguish the two roles are obscured by the fact that she gained a substantial following and was merited with the appearance of Elijah, the messianic herald. The occurrence of Ines' visions accorded with the doctrine that held that, at the time of redemption, not only men, but also women and children, even in the Diaspora, would be granted the gift of prophecy (this was based on Joel 3:1, and followed by some rabbinic literature and by Maimonides in his *Letter to Yemen*); and her experience stimulated the idea that redemption was near. (Women and children also play an important part in the recognition of the Safed messiahs [see chapter 6], and of Shabtai Zvi [see chapter 7] and the messiahs of his lineage.)

The accounts of Ludovico and Ines give some idea of the messianic beliefs, conduct, and expectations of the population of anusim in Iberia. Some beliefs were commonly held. Elijah's appearance and the appearance of heavenly signs had always been associated with the coming of the messiah; other features were unique to this circumstance. The emphasis on fasting and charity is a crypto-Jewish practice as noted, but it certainly falls within the framework of that doctrine which holds that the messiah's coming depends on human effort. The outstanding contribution of the marrano experience was the inverse construction it placed on reality. The tradition of the military messiah was suppressed for a long time by this way of looking at things; despite the attention given by the anusim to Reubeni and his dream of reconquering the land of Israel, he stands apart from the spirit of his time and place as well as from the next sequence of Jewish messiahs, beginning with Luria and Vital and continuing to the most recent. Certain lines do connect Reubeni to the Persian and the Yemenite messiahs (see chapter 10).

Asher Lemlein and an Anti-Hagiographic Account

At about the same time that Ines was undergoing her ordeal, another prophet-messiah appeared in Istria, near Venice: Asher Lemlein was German, from Reutlingen, and although his activity took place largely in Italy in 1500–1502, his followers' propaganda campaign spread his story across many parts of northern Europe; his fame and influence continued after his death. We hear again the traditional debate: Those who opposed messianism and the calculation of the date of the eschaton asserted that Lemlein's failure to bring about the redemption before he died caused many to convert from Judaism; others credited Lemlein's program with inspiring acts of penitence during his lifetime and thereafter. David Ganz—who, as the student of the great Prague rabbi, Yehuda Löw, was disposed toward the scientific worldview, and was acquainted with the new astronomy and with Kepler himself—was not ashamed to write that his grandfather demolished the oven he had used only for the baking of matzah after Lemlein promised that the next Passover would find the Jews in Israel. The few accounts that remain do not clarify the question of whether Lemlein wished to be perceived as the messiah or only as a prophet. One account says that he pronounced himself king. Another reveals his prophecy that he would gather the dispersed of Israel. He called for repentance, fasting, and the giving of charity and moved large numbers to act along these lines. The time was not inappropriate for a messianic program: Iberian Jewry was in desperate straits and the Turkish success in the naval war against Venice seemed to signal the defeat of Rome and the advent of the apocalyptic war. The year, 1501, had even been previously calculated as one in which the redemption would come. (But then, scarcely a year was not calculated as appropriate, and in no case can it be shown that the prediction of a particular year brought about a messianic appearance, nor that such a prediction predominated in the determination that a given messiah was genuine.)

The following text is one section of a German pamphlet that was written to demand the confiscation and destruction of Hebrew books, in particular the Talmud. Its author, Yosef Pfefferkorn (1469–1522 or 1523), converted to Christianity in 1505 and changed his name to Johannes. From among his many diatribes, *The Jew-glass* (*Der Juden Spiegel*) has remained the best known and studied. In the section presented here, Pfefferkorn holds up Asher Lemlein to ridicule, in order to persuade his "dear brothers" to convert as he had. He uses, as Heiko Oberman writes, "that admixture of argumentation and indictment which by then was routine from centuries of Christain missions to the Jews" (*The Roots of Anti-Semitism* [Philadelphia, 1984] 32). Early Christian anti-Jewish propaganda had attacked the Jews for their refusal to accept Jesus as the messiah; with the polemic compendium by Raymond Martini, *Pugio fidei* (*Boxing for the Faith*, 1278, in Latin), the attack came to focus on the Jewish "false-messiahs": "The third villany in the deeds of the Jews and the greatest insanity of all was that after forty-eight and one-half years had elapsed since the destruction of the temple and the death of their aforementioned false messiah Bar Cosba they produced another no less false one named Ben Cosba" (*Pugio* 3.3.21.9). In *The Friars and the Jews* (Ithaca, 1982), J. Cohen notes that Bar Kosiba (Bar Kokhba) is here said to have lived during the destruction of the second temple (70 CE) and to have lived again, as it were, according to Martini, in 118 or 119 CE. The dates are wrong among other things, but it seems possible that Martini might have conflated the story of an earlier messiah with that of the real Bar Kosiba. The tradition that Martini established, of attacking the Jews for their faith in false messiahs, was continued by other missionaries and was found useful by Pfefferkorn as he, faithful Catholic, fought against humanism and the Protestant Reformation.

My most beloved brothers! You have just heard [in the preceding passage] how your sufferings and the manifold aspects of your faith have been explained and our faith defended with truth from the holy Gospels and from your own scriptures, the Prophets and the Law of Moses [the Pentateuch]. I ask you: If you should take the five books of Moses literally would that not mean that Moses was the greatest man ever to have lived on earth? Consider then: would you not then have been betrayed by him? For where is your messiah? Time is now long past. Consider further and take this to heart: You have in fact not even had a king over you nor any prophet since the birth of Christ. Your temple and your offerings are vanished. You have been scattered all over the wide world and it is impossible that you should be gathered in again. Moreover, I am aware that it is written that in 1502 a Jew called Lemel arose in Italy and preached to you and sat one half year in penance to prepare himself for the arrival of the messiah, and when that half year's penance passed, a fiery pillar together with a dark cloud was to surround all the Jews, as happened at the time of Pharaoh; also then they would return to Jerusalem, rebuild the temple, and offer sacrifices. And he gave you this as a sign: The Christian church would pass away and collapse and a great and hard penance would occur [among the Christians], the like of which your forefathers never saw.

Oh how pitifully you are deceived! Where now are the cloud and pillar? Where are your sacrifices and Solomon's temple? Don't you know what Isaiah wrote, "I am sated with your offerings of rams and fatlings," etc. [Isa. 1:11—"I have no desire for the blood of bulls"]. You see well that our churches stand yet and have not been reduced but rather have markedly increased and you have been left in great distress. Even though God punished your forefathers great and often for their sins, he always left them prophets to comfort them and, when they regretted their sins later and repented, they were redeemed; but now for you there is neither comfort not redemption, as you can well mark by your hard and oppressive penance. (From *The Jew-glass* text in H. Kirn, *The Image of the Jew in Germany in the Early Sixteenth Century* [Tübingen, 1989] [in German] 218–219)

Accounts of Messiahs of the New World

The aftermath of the expulsion from Spain and Portugal can be credited with sparking the first messianic eruptions in the New World. The most significant activity takes place around women of Jewish descent in Mexico—of particular note are Dona Juana Enriquez and Ines Pereira. Enriquez was born in Seville around 1602, of a lineage that had been enmeshed in the nets of the Inquisition for some time. Pereira was born in Mexico. A summary of the relevant Inquisition documents and histories reads, in part:

[Dona Juana Enriquez] is comparable to the most notable Jewesses whose cases are well known in the Tribunals of the Holy Office of the Inquisition. She is the granddaughter, sister, niece, aunt, and cousin of a great many Judaizers who have been penanced, reconciled and relaxed by this Inquisition during the four autos-da-fé that it has dealt with.

She was imprisoned and her property sequestered because she was a Jewess who was observing the law of Moses. She, as well as her sister, had been taught by her mother. However, she, of all of them, was the most observant of Judaism. Her heart was so filled with perfidious Judaism that it was difficult for this Tribunal to convert her to such a state in which, with good conscience, it could extend mercy to her.

She had a grand manner when she fasted. She observed Saturdays with baths and other rites and Jewish ceremonies. Among Christian Catholic people, some people came to be venerated as saints because of the purity of their lives and their perfect observance of the Evangelical laws. Thus also, among the Judaizers of this kingdom, she came to be acclaimed as the perfect and saintly Jewess because they saw her a great faster and reciter of prayers. She was so ceremonious and punctiliously bathed herself and cleaned so much before celebrating the Jewish holidays. [She was also venerated] because of the many charities she dispensed to those who observed her lapsed law or because of their good deeds, or because they agreed that they would fast because of her. [It must not be] omitted that she attended all the funerals and interments of those of her nation. Maybe, because of her false zeal, many died as Jews. She made them give heed to the law of Moses with their last breaths, telling them that it was necessary for their salvation. A woman could not be more daring!

As she was such an exact Jewess, the custom in her house was to cook on Fridays all the food that was to be eaten on Saturdays, including the meat dishes. By Friday eve, she had already sliced the bread, combed and adorned herself, put on clothes . . . and dressed her hair in order to enter the Sabbath purified and not to have any occasions on Saturdays to break the Sabbath.

Because other Judaizers knew of the punctiliousness with which her household was kept, they went to visit her on Saturdays to enjoy the occasion and celebrate the Sabbath festivities.

Among the Jews of this era in this kingdom, there was the belief that the Messiah would be born from either the faction of Simon Vaez Sevilla or from that of Thomas Trevino de Sobremonte. And both [factions] were deluded. She [Enriquez] was one of the women from whom the Messiah might be born. However, all of these women who were potential mothers of the Messiah have come out [from autos-da-fé with *sambenitos* [penal costumes] and one of them [this one] has even been lashed.³

It is hard to resist adding the following description of the worship of Ines Pereira:

> It appears that as soon as she was old enough to use her reason, she began to Judaize because by the time she was seven years of age she was observing the law of Moses. The reason for this was that all her relatives . . . were falsely persuaded that this young Jewess would give birth to the Messiah. [One relative] convinced his sons and daughters of this and thus compelled them to keep the law of Moses. This is also why, in her young years, they dressed her with a tunic of voile. They would place her in the middle of the drawing room and surround her with burning candles. They worshipped her and adored her as a person from whom would be born their redeemer and chief. Without a doubt, they awaited this during her first pregnancy, and when the baby was born all of her relatives fasted [as an expression of thanks to the Lord for good fortune].⁴

These customs—fasting, Sabbath preparations, the deathbed conversion to Judaism, the maintenance of dietary laws, the giving of charity, and so on—gain their pecular strength from the admonitions of Inquisition manuals, as they do in Iberia and throughout Catholic Europe. As in the instance of Ines of Herrera, unique in Spain, the interest in the messiah in the New World adheres to females, because, in these cases, they are expected to mother the messiah. Taking the male role as family head and head of the community, they become messiahs in all but name. One factor that contributes to this development is the loss of male presence, due to frequent sea voyages, and of religious prestige, due to the cessation of circumcision. Another is the Jewish tradition of the heroic mother of the messiah, Hepzibah, cited in the widely distributed *Book of Zerubbabel*.

DAVID REUBENI AND SHLOMO MOLKHO

The activity of David Reubeni (*ha-re'uveni*, of the tribe of Reuben) is difficult to confine to a single category. He acted as a general, a statesman, a prophet, and a messiah. He continues a line of foreign figures—Ethiopians and others—who appear in Europe and in the land of Israel, telling tales of lost tribes of Jews living in various mysterious landscapes beyond the river Sambation. He worked no miracles in public, nor did he ever publicly state that he was the messiah, but said only that he was the leader of the forces of his brother, a Jewish king in the land of Habur. His program was aimed at redemption on a global scale: He proposed to gather the forces of Christianity into a partnership with his brother's troops and to take the land of Israel away from the Turks.

Contemporary documents make it possible for us to know what Reubeni looked like, but not what his name was or his age when he came to be noticed. David is a name that might be taken on one's accession to the messianic position (as it was by David Alroy), while the name Reubeni summons up the legend of the Lost Tribes of Israel. It seems that we learn of the physical characteristics of those messiahs whose physicality is central to their mission (for instance, Bar Kosiba and other warrior messiahs), while the bodies of others (such as Jesus) never receive this kind of attention. Daniel da Pisa, a leading figure of Italian Jewry—a banker, the chosen head of the Jewish community in Rome, and Reubeni's representative at the Vatican—wrote, regarding Reubeni, "He comes from afar—his form and his manner of speech make that clear: His appearance is dark, short, lean; his language is a mixture of Arabic and some Hebrew. He is a man of merit who fasts daily and trusts in the Lord, according to what he says, more than any creature on earth. He is great of spirit, stouthearted, and fearless in the face of multitudes."[5] Giambattista Ramusio, a noted Venetian geographer and traveler of the period, interviewed Reubeni in 1530 in order to write a report on him for the senate of Venice. He concluded that Reubeni was an adventurer and described him as follows: "In truth, he is an Arab, for his build and color show that he is not from one of our lands. He is thin and very spare and like the Jews of Prester John. His appearance gives witness that he is quite wealthy: He is clothed in silks and accompanied by five respectable servants, one of whom is Portuguese, intelligent, and clever."[6] We can assume, since no mention is made of his age in these or later accounts, that he is neither especially young nor old when he appears in Italy (in 1525), or even when he disappears from the stage (around 1538). We also hear something of his character in these accounts—one report stressing his moral and physical hardihood, and the other, his noble display—and his peculiar language. But beyond what is said here, Reubeni's origins remain a mystery. No study of his own journal has conclusively identified his native language. Reubeni spoke a strange Hebrew and was insulted when addressed in Arabic. The language he used, like the figure he cut, was employed by him as part of the exotic, aristocratic, yet Jewish impression he wished to make on others, one that held strong appeal for the converted Jews of Spain and Portugal.

As we can see from these brief descriptions and from the materials of Reubeni's own journal (*The Story of David Ha-Re'uveni*, quoted here), his lineage as a messiah was twofold: He claimed to be the brother of the king of the Jews of

Habur (a land of exile; see 2 Kings 17:6), a descendant of King David, and a member of the tribe of Reuben[7] (Figure 5.1). For Jews, the mystery of the ten northern tribes of Israel, which had "disappeared" following their defeat in the eighth century BCE, held out the hope that Jewish independence, a Jewish kingdom of free Jews, had not been lost. Not only did this possibility soothe the pain of their existence as a subject and despised people, but it excited hopes that the tribes that would come out of unknown lands would retake the land of Israel and lead the way into the messianic age that the Bible had prophesied. Thus it was that great interest was awakened, particularly in Spain, upon the discovery of the Khazar kingdom much later. That case involved the conversion of the king and noble families to Judaism, rather than a lost-and-found tribe, but the Khazar king was asked for any information he had about the messiah's coming. Similar discoveries included the kingdom of Himyar in Arabia and the Beta Yisrael (Falashas) of Ethiopia. As long as there were unknown lands, there was hope for Jewish continuity from the valiant past and for redemption. One land suspected of harboring the Lost Tribes, Yemen, itself became the site of messianic activity (see chapter 10).

For Christians as well as Jews, their belief in the continued existence of the tribes was strong well into the twentieth century. As is evident from the interest shown by the pope and by the king of Portugal, Reubeni's proposal was further enriched for Christians by the identification of the mystery region with Havilah, where "the gold of the land is good" (Gen. 2:12), and perhaps by some guilt, in the face of the apocalypse (believed to be at hand), over the treatment of the Jews. Pope Clement VII and other Christian rulers who accepted Reubeni's embassy, and allowed his presence in the lands of the Inquisition, did so largely for apocalyptic reasons: They hoped for success in the war against the Turks to reclaim Jerusalem, and they associated Reubeni with the mysterious figure of Prester John, whom contemporary legend brought into contact with lost Israelite tribes from Armenia to Arabia and Africa, and who was said to have brought whole African tribes to the Cross.

The "Portuguese servant" mentioned by Ramusio was Diogo Pires. This young man of converso parentage first encountered Reubeni at the court of John III of Portugal, where Pires was serving in an important clerical capacity. Reubeni came there in 1525, carrying letters from the pope to the king in support of his plan to unite the forces of Christian Europe with his brother's army in Habur and then take the Holy Land back from the Turks. Pires credited Reubeni's role as the commander of the forces of the messiah, and was swept up, like other conversos, in apocalyptic passion. Pires changed his name to Shlomo Molkho and circumcised himself. As can be seen in a text quoted below, Reubeni was not entirely pleased: He did not wish to be seen as stirring up the conversos. Their excitation threatened Reubeni's relations with the Christian powers and exposed him to the Inquisition, from which both he and Molkho had only the frail protection of the pope. Reubeni was forced to leave Portugal. For the next three or four years, he wandered through southern Europe, and was imprisoned and ransomed in France; he then returned to Italy, largely unsuccessful in his efforts to gather support from either nervous local Jewish communities or the Christian nobility. Molkho took another path.

After Reubeni left Portugal, Molkho traveled alone along the Mediterranean,

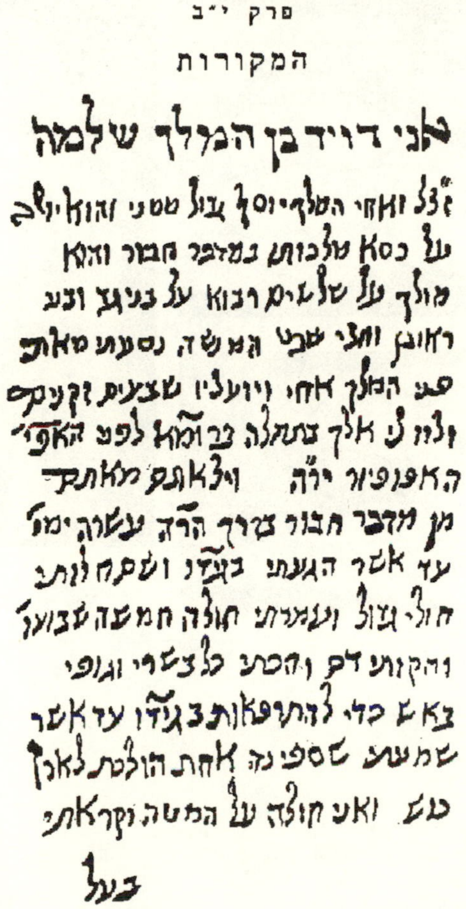

פרק י״ב

המקורות

אני דויד בן המלך שלמה
ז״צל ואחי המלך יוסף גדול ממני והוא יושב
על כסא מלכותו במדבר חבור והוא
מולך על שלשים רבוא על בני גד ובני
ראובן וחצי שבט מנשה, נסעתי מאת
פני המלך אחי ויועציו שבעים זקנים
וצוו לי אלך בתחלה בעיר רומא לפני האפי׳
האפיפיור יר״ה ויצאתי מאתם
מן מדבר חבור בדרך הר״ד עשרה ימים
עד אשר הגעתי בג׳דה ושם חליתי
חולי גדול ועמדתי חולה חמשה שבועות
והקזתי דם והכתי כל בשרי וגופי
באש כדי להתרפאות בג׳דה עד אשר
שמעתי שספינה אחת הולכת לארץ
כוש ואני חולה על המטה וקראתי
בעל

Figure 5.1: The first page of the single manuscript of the *Story* (from Aeshcoly's book, *The Story of David Ha-Reuveni*, p. 218). The manuscript, which was in the collection of Hayyim Michael of Hamburg, disappeared without a trace from the Bodleian Library sometime after 1867. In that year Y. Y. Cohen made a tracing of the manuscript, laying a transparent page over each page of the work. (Cohen also made another copy, not a tracing but a reading which contained an abundant number of errors.) There is sufficient evidence from the facsimile to support the contention that the unicum was written in Reubeni's time, and it is reasonable to assume that he wrote it himself. The material is written in the first person, and the punctuation, like other linguistic features, is quite idiosyncratic. (Reubeni's language has failed to illuminate his origins, though current scholarship disagrees with Aeshcoly's appraisal of an Ashkenazi background.) When new sections are begun, a large, somewhat decorative initial letter is employed. The style, introspections, and interests are those of a diarist, and the additions made by Prato (an accounting of expenses) are in a different hand and cover dates later than the story itself.

Figure 5.2: The flag (*top left*) is probably that carried by Molkho to the fateful meeting with Charles V at Regensburg. It was probably made for Reubeni, perhaps by Benvenida Abravanel, and Molkho was so accustomed to carrying it that it appears as a part of his own aristocratic signature (*bottom*). Banners were important ornaments to Reubeni and Molkho's nobel and military performance. The fine robe of Molkho's (*top right*) remains in the Jewish Museum of Prague. Another garment of his, a silk prayer shawl, contained magic names and conjurations embroidered in symbolic colors. It has been lost but is described in the Idel article, "Shlomo Molkho as a Magician."

preaching and continuing to study the Kabbalah. He was later rumored to have been in many places. His stay in Salonika, among circles that would later have connections to the Safed movement of Luria and Vital (see chapter 6), was to have the greatest impact. In Salonika, he encountered R. Yosef Karo (see chapter 6) and made a strong impression upon him, as he did upon others who attended his sermons and became his followers. His sermons attracted Christians as well. He correctly predicted the sack of Rome and envisioned this as the beginning of the redemption, with himself as the messiah. Betrayed by jealous and fearful Jews in Salonika, he fled to Rome and "suffered" as a beggar for thirty days outside the Vatican to fulfill a talmudic legend concerning the advent of the messiah. As he had for Reubeni, Clement VII became the protector of Molkho, whose star rose still higher when he correctly predicted a flood in Rome and an earthquake that took place in Portugal. Seeking to meet with Reubeni in Venice in 1530, he was forced to flee back to Rome. There he was turned over to the Inquisition and condemned, but was saved from burning by the pope, with another unfortunate taking his place in the flames. He ultimately did meet Reubeni in Italy, and they rode together to meet Charles V at Regensburg, in modern-day Germany (Figure 5.2). The purpose of their meeting with Charles was to promote Reubeni's plan for the Jews and Christians to join in a war against the Turks; it appears that it was Molkho who presented the plan. For reasons that will be cited later, in the letters of the pope's special representative in Germany, Hieronymus Aleander, the emperor was not amenable to their project, which was actually on the agenda of the Reichstag which was meeting in Regensburg at that time. Molkho was sent in chains to Mantua, where he was tried and burned to death in 1532. Reubeni was apparently sent on to Spain, released there by the Holy Office of the Inquisition, and then put to death by its secular arm, the government of Spain, some five years later. He might have converted to Christianity just before his execution. Whatever the actual reasons for their executions, both were probably condemned on charges of having persuaded conversos to return to Judaism and having had a malign influence on Christians during the religious unrest then prevalent in Germany.

The two are alike in significant ways. They both played roles as prophets and messiahs. Both were ascetic in their habits. Reubeni, in particular, seems to have been familiar with that tradition of asceticism that began among the Mourners of Zion and was passed on to the messiahs of Persia and Yemen. The pure life they lived served as a way of heightening their closeness to holiness, and their Jewishness, and of distancing themselves from the material world. Yet both of them were accoutered with the clothing, flags, swords, and outward manners of nobility that served to communicate their power and social positions and to distinguish them from their oppressed and lowly brethren. (In fact, remnants of their clothing and flags endured for some time and were treated respectfully and even as holy objects. Those that still exist exhibit characteristics of magical usage, such as special colors and the embroidered Holy Names, as well as marks of social prestige, as in the choiceness of their fabrics and their embellishments.) Neither of the two were learned in a conventional sense; Reubeni lacked a familiarity with traditional sources and practices, while Molkho's knowledge of traditional and Kabbalistic material, it seems, sprang up full-blown very soon after his conversion. Both had great appeal for Christians and for Jews, conversos, and crypto-Jews. Both met unknown ends, as it turned out. Reubeni's death went unrecorded; his spirit did not outlive him. The will for a military/political redemption clashed with the deeper spirit of Marranoism, which attributed an other-worldly importance to its history of suffering and the concealment of its Jewish identity. What endured was Reubeni's tale of his career, precisely because it offered colorful romance and adventure to the homebound. What Molkho offered was in accordance with the Marrano temperament; and his learning, his preaching, and his devout conduct (including his self-circumcision—an act that was not altogether uncommon among the victims of the Inquisition, though usually carried out just before their execution) continued to inspire the imaginations of those, sensitive to the experience of the Marranos or themselves Marranos, with whom he later met in Turkey. His scholarly ability, gained as if by magic, impressed Kabbalists especially, and his pure death moved many. Accounts of Molkho's immolation in Mantua were challenged by accounts of his later appearances. While such rumors may have sprouted from Molkho's reputation as a magician and his earlier nonexecution in Rome, the narrative of the messiah has its own requisites, as we have seen.

The autobiographical accounts of Reubeni are from a single work, *The Story of David Ha-Re'uveni*. Molkho's memoirs, visions, and a poem come from *The Beast of the Reed*. (The title refers to Rome and its fall; cf. Zohar III 241.) Other accounts and letters are presented in Aeshcoly's edition of *The Story of David Ha-Re'uveni* and are also quoted in his *Movements*. All the accounts tell their story with a natural ease, in their own language, the flavor of which I have tried to preserve here in my own translations. I have arranged them, whenever possible, according to the sequence of events and, within that, to reflect multiple perspectives when they are of interest. The foregoing introduction to the accounts, being drawn from the same documents, should serve to comment upon them without encumbering the words of the participants.

Account by Reubeni: from Habur to Alexandria

I am David, the son of King Shlomo, may the memory of the righteous be a blessing, and my elder brother, Yosef, sits on the throne in the wilderness of Habur and rules over thirty myriads, over the tribes of Gad and Reuben and the half-tribe of Manasseh. I have journeyed away from the presence of the king and his advisors, seventy elders, who commanded me that I should go first to Rome, before His Majesty the pope. . . .

I entered Egypt at the New Moon of Adar [1523], in the evening. . . . We entered the house of R. Avraham, Master of the Mint, the greatest [Jewish] man in Egypt. I said to him, "I am a Jew and I want to stay with you three days or four, and I will reveal a secret to you, and when you see a way to go to Jerusalem—guide me [to it]. And I don't want either silver or gold from you or food, but only the house." And R. Avraham answered me, "I cannot permit you to come into my house—for you came in disguise, as an Ishmaelite—and if you stay in my house you will cause me harm." And R. Avraham would not let me stop at his house at all. And I said to him, "Be merciful to me for the love of God and the elders—for the reward of carrying out a commandment is the deed itself." And he responded to me, "The commandment is a great one upon me and all Israel dwelling in Egypt, that you not come into my house." Then I went out of his house. . . .

And I arrived in Gaza, into a house as big as a camp, and they gave me one of the upper rooms and I was alone [but] in my room a Turkish Jew from Beirut, named Avraham Dunas, was staying. I stayed in that room for two days and said nothing to him, and I was praying all day long and speaking to no one. And after that I called to him and said, "What is your name?" And he said to me, "My name is Avraham. . . ." And I said to this Jew, "Do not be afraid or alarmed, for the end is coming soon for you, and the Holy One blessed is he will bring the evil ones down to earth and uplift the lowly upon high, and the time will come soon when you will see great matters and much confusion and quarrels among kings, and you, Avraham, will do me a great favor if you will find some Turks for me who will direct me to the Temple; and the way should run first through Hebron." And he said to me, "I'll do it all." He went away and saw some Turkish donkey-drivers and came back to me and gave me a donkey and carried out the negotiations between [a driver] and me. And I did not wish to reveal my secret to him until I was on the way, when I told him the main things.

Thereafter, he came to me with a jeweler named Yosef, a store-owner, and he had a brother whose name was Yakov and their aged father was yet alive. And he and Yosef the jeweler stayed with me some two hours, and I hid my matters from them but passed the outline on to them. And the Jews sent me meat and bread in secret, by way of Avraham the Jew. And I stayed in Gaza five days.

Afterward, I traveled from Gaza on the nineteenth of Adar and went on the road to Hebron. I traveled during the day and by night until I came into Hebron, to the place of the cave Machpelah, on the twenty-third of Adar in the afternoon. . . .

Thereafter, I stood praying at the opening of the well. And I watched the opening of the door to the cave on the night of the Sabbath until the dawn and in the morning I stood praying until evening. And at night of the first day of the week, I prayed at the mouth of the cave and did not sleep until the morning. And the seventy elders had told me that on the third day I would find a certain sign, and I stood wondering in silence about what I would see. And in the morning of the third day, before the sun rose, the guards summoned me with great rejoicing and said, "Our lord, the son of our lord the prophet! Arise and rejoice with us, for a great joy has come to us, that the water has risen into the mikveh of this synagogue and has not done so for four years." And I went with them to see the water, lovely and clear, come into the mikveh from a distant land.

Thereafter, I traveled from Hebron on the twenty-fourth of Adar and went to Jerusalem. . . . I entered it on the twenty-fifth of Adar [1523] and that same day entered the House of the Holy of Holies. . . . And I said to the guards, "Since I know all these places you can go on your way for I want to pray, and in the morning I will give you alms." And they went on their way. And I already knew that everything they said was lies and falsity. And I prayed until all the Ishmaelites came to pray, and they came out of the Courtyard after their prayer two hours into the night. They went to their houses and I went under the Foundation Stone [of the Temple]. Afterward, the guards put out all the lamps in the Courtyard but four. Before they closed the doors they came searching, to see if they might find a man asleep in the cave and expel him. They found me and said to me, "Go out from this place, for we are guards and cannot permit any man to sleep here and so we have sworn to the king. So we don't want you to sleep in this place; and if you don't leave, we will go to the governor, and he will have you put out against your will." And when I heard their hard words I went out to the Courtyard and they closed the doors around the Courtyard. And I prayed all night and fasted and this was the night of the fourth day of the week, and in the morning when the Ishmaelites came to pray in the Courtyard I went in with them, and when they had completed their prayer I called out loudly, "Where are the guards?" And all of them came to me, and I said to them, "I am your lord and the son of your lord the prophet. I came from a distant land to this sanctified House and my soul longed to remain within it and pray and not sleep. And thereafter, four guards came and expelled me." And I said to them, "I am your lord and the son of your lord—if you wish peace from me, it will be best, and I will bless you, but if not I will have my revenge upon you, and I will write to the [Great] Turk of your evil doings." And they said back to me, "Pardon us this time, for we do wish to serve you and to be your servants as long as you stay in the Temple, and we will do what you wish." Then I gave them ten ducats for alms, and I stayed in the Temple and fasted in the Holy of Holies five weeks. I ate no bread and drank no water except [during the Sabbath]; and I prayed beneath the Foundation Stone and upon it.

And ten emissaries came to me from my brother, Yosef, the king, and the seventy elders, and they were in disguise and stayed by me in the Temple. . . .

The Ishmaelites have a representation at the top of the Dome of the Courtyard, a half-moon turned to the west. And on the first day of the holiday of Shavuot [1523], it turned to the east. And when the Ishmaelites saw this, they called out loudly. And I said to them, "What are you shouting about?" They responded, "On account of our sins, this image of the half-moon has turned to the east of the sun, and this is an evil sign for the Ishmaelites." Then some of the Ishmaelite craftsmen went up and returned the image to its position as on the first day; and on the second day the image returned again to the eastern inclination, while I was praying, and the Ishmaelites cried and shouted and tried to turn it back and couldn't. And the elders had already informed me, "When you see this sign, go to Rome." I looked at the Gates of Mercy and the Gates of Repentance and went beneath the Temple, and there was a great building like the upper building, and I did beneath the Temple what the elders had ordered me to do, in a place no man could touch me. And the image appeared in the way it did after I carried out the commands of the elders beneath the Temple. . . .

And thereafter, I went from [Mt.] Zion into Jerusalem and went to the house of a Jew named Avraham Hagar, and he was a jeweler and stayed above the synagogue. . . . The third time I went to his house, before I traveled away from the Temple, I said to him, "Draw me Venice and Rome and Portugal," and he drew it all for me. And I said to him, "I want to go to Rome." And he said to me, "What are you going for?" And I said to him, "I am going on a good purpose, and it is secret, I cannot reveal it, and I want you to advise me how I should travel." (Aesh-coly, ed., *The Story of David Ha-Re'uveni* (in Hebrew; Jerusalem, 1994), pp. 7–31)

A letter from Damascus

The following is an anonymous letter.

Pay attention to what I say, and do not ridicule me, for what I have to say is true and firm and established. . . . And I cannot write everything I know; a hint will be enough for a sage. Now, know you that there came here to Damascus a man from the tribe of Reuben, an emissary sent to this area, and I saw him today . . . and before he came here, he was in Egypt, for that was the shortest path on his way from his prince. . . . The name of the prince who sent him was Hananel, known as Armilus, and so called because he was in the war with Armilus, enough said. He is 250 years old, this prince, and from the tribe of Reuben, and [he] has an army of 60 myriad warriors, each of them mighty, and some of these troops are from the tribe of Dan, but a part of them is from the tribe of Reuben, and they crossed the river Sambation. From our side the river is dry as if it never contained water. . . . Before the emissary arrived in Damascus we had already received letters from peo-ple in Egypt . . . to mention and warn us . . . not to ridicule or laugh at the words of the emissary, as the people of Egypt had done, for . . . a letter came to them . . . from the tribe of Reuben, signed at the end by twelve princes and signed besides them as well by the great prince Hananel, called Armilus, the com-mander of the army. And so, when . . . the people of Egypt saw the letter, they made a great repentance for, according to what we have heard, there were no worse sinners and evildoers in the world than the Egyptians, and they repented. And here in Damascus twelve men traveled away to Aleppo for Passover and after Passover went to His Majesty the King. And a lad came to them in Turkey, no more than twelve years old, and he, the one whose name it is forbidden to write [the messiah], enough said. But I have the hope that you will have news of it before this letter ar-rives. Every single day we hear news that there are now peoples as many as the sand of the sea and the stars of the sky on the way. And it is said here . . . that the great people mentioned has come near to Mount Hor, near the grave of Aaron the priest. And my hope is with God that within days they will gather together. I recall to you and seek from you that you not make jest of my words at all.

Now you will know what happened today. Before I finished writing this letter it came about that the owner of this house brought the emissary here to eat and drink with me . . . and while the emissary was at table, another man, a resident of Damascus from a village outside the city, came and on his way back to Damascus found an estimable old man on the road, who said to him, "Go to the city and you will find my companion, whose name is David, and say to him that he should has-ten his deeds and make his words brief, for he has already been there long enough, for the labor is great and the time is short, for he has stayed too long in that city."

And that is what the Damascene, from the country, did; and he found the emissary, David. And when the man but began to say to the emissary what the old man on the road had asked him to say, David said to him, "Don't say a word to me, for I know what has been put in your mouth to speak. This will prove it to you: you came across an old man on the road, who said to you that you should tell me on his behalf, how I must hasten and get on my way, for I have been here too long, for the time is short." And more than forty Jews heard and saw all this. We wait every day and every hour for news. It is not possible and I am not able to write all that I know. Thus, be you wise, and do not doubt or concern yourselves about me. God has recalled us and he will rescue us and redeem us soon, and let us say, Amen. Remember that "repentance and charity annul the evil decree" [from the liturgy for the High Holidays], for thus said the prince's emissary, that many and mighty troubles will happen upon us if we fail to make a great repentance. The emissary of the prince said to me that you may expect to recover all your debts, and so many other things, enough said.

May it be God's will that my words be true and the redeemer come soon and in our days, and let us say, "Amen."

All of this I, Yehuda the Least, son of our honored teacher, R. Shlomo DeBlanis, here in the city of Castillo, have copied letter for letter, word for word. The twenty-eighth of the month of Av, the weekly portion of which is "Righteousness, righteousness you shall pursue so that you may live and inherit the land." [Deut. 16:20]. (From A. Neubauer, "Concerning the Ten Tribes" [in Hebrew] *kovetz al-yad* 4 [1888] pp. 35–37)

Account by Reubeni: David visits Pope Clement VII in Rome

I left Alexandria with my servant, Yosef, in the middle of the month of Kislev, [1524]. I fasted every day and prayed night and day . . . until we arrived at Venice and I went to the home of the head [of the community], that is, the *capitania*, and he gave me a place and I fasted in his home six days and nights, eating no bread, drinking no water, and prayed night and day. . . . R. Shimon ben Asher Meshullam came to me and said, "I have heard that you are an emissary on an errand from the seventy elders [i.e., the Sanhedrin], going to Rome. Tell me why they have sent you and I will send two men with you and cover all the expenses." I said to him, "I am going to the pope, and I can say nothing more except to him, for the good of all Israel. And if you will be kind to me, for the love of the Name and the elders and all Israel, send two men to come to Rome with me, and you will gain merit through the deed, and they will bring you back good news." . . .

I, David, the son of King Shlomo of blessed memory, from the wilderness of Habur, arrived at the entrance of the city of Rome on the fifteenth of the month of Adar I [1525], and a non-Jew from Venice came up to me and spoke Arabic to me and I was angered with him. I went to the courtyard of the pope, mounted on an old white horse, and my servant went before me and [some] Jews came with me. I entered the house of the pope, still riding on the horse, and then entered the presence of the cardinal, Gudio [Egidio di Viterbo], and all the cardinals and officers came to see me. His honor, our teacher, R. Yosef Ashkenazi, who was teaching the cardinal, was in his presence as well, and his honor, R. Yosef Tzarfat, came before the cardinal while I was speaking with him, my translator being the comrade who accompanied me, and the Jews listened to everything I said to the cardinal. I said to him, "I will speak in brief with you and completely with the pope." I stood before the cardinal until night, the night of the Sabbath, and the Jews asked the cardinal that I might come away with them until after the Sabbath, and the cardinal said to me, "If you wish to go with them, go, and if you wish a room here in my home, I will provide you with one. Tomorrow, I will go before the pope and I will send you what the pope says in a message." So I went. . . . I fasted during the Sabbath, and during the whole day men and women, Jews and Christians, came to see me in my house until night. The cardinal mentioned, Gudio, sent a message by his honor, R. Yosef Ashkenazi, and he came back to me and said that the pope had ordered the cardinal that I should absolutely appear before him on the first day of the week at eleven, and that the pope was very happy and desired to see me, and so in the morning before prayers they gave me a horse. . . .

At eight in the morning, I came in to the house of the pope and entered the home of Cardinal Gudio, where there were some twelve honorable elders of the Jews and some boys. And as soon as the cardinal saw me, he arose from his chair, and he and I went to the living quarters of the pope. And I spoke with him, and he listened to what I had to say politely and said, "This matter has come forth from God!" And I told him, "King Yosef and the elders had ordered me to speak with you, [and ordered] that you make peace between the emperor and the king of France, absolutely, for your making such a peace is good for them and for you; and you should write me a letter [to deliver] to the two kings mentioned, that they should be at our aid and we at their aid, and you should write for me as well to Petri [Prester] John." And the pope responded to me, "The two kings that you say I should make peace between them—I cannot do it, and if you need the aid of the king of Portugal—it will suffice you, and I will write to him and he will do everything, and his land is closer to your land, and they are accustomed to go by way of the great sea every year, more so than the two kings you mentioned." And I answered the pope, "Whatever you wish is my desire, and I will turn neither to the right nor to the left from whatever you might command me, for I have come on the service of the Name, and for no other matter, and I am prepared to please you and to do good for you all the days of my life."

[Reubeni meets Daniel da Pisa, a Jew with status in the Vatican, and gains his assistance. Time passes.] Then [da Pisa] wrote me a letter to the pope that day and I sent it to the [registry] by my servant, Hayim. . . . And on the second day of the week I sent Hayim to the registry and as soon as he came in he was told, "Go, summon your master the ambassador to come immediately before the pope, for he calls to him." . . . And I came in with [da Pisa] before the pope and spoke this to him, "I have waited upon you for nearly a year, and my desire is what God and your honor will. Write me the letters that I requested from your honor and to Petri John and to all the Christians through whose lands I may pass, greater and lesser." And his honor, our teacher, R. Daniel spoke with the pope and the pope responded to him with good words and said to him, "I will do what the ambassador wants."

And afterward I left the presence of the pope with R. Daniel da Pisa, rejoicing and happy, and went to my home in peace. And there were then in Rome forty-five scandal-mongers—may God grant them the desire to repent so that they may return from their evil opinion—and there were also mighty Jews in Rome and in the kingdom of Italy, fit for war and knightly, and their heart was like that of a lion in all things. And the Jews who are in Jerusalem and Egypt and in all the lands of Ishmael have weak hearts and are fearful and cowardly and are not fit for war like the Jews of Italy. May the Holy One blessed is he make them strong and multiply them a thousand times and bless them. . . . (Reubeni's journal, from Aeshcoly, *Story*, pp. 31–42)

Memorandum from Clemens

In this year [1526] an embassy of Jews from Arabia appeared before the throne of the pope, led by the brother of the king of Arabia Deserta, of the tribe of Jews, and sought to make a covenant with the Christians for a war against the religion of Mohammed, the Arabs, and the Turks. He likewise sought a letter of recommendation from the pope to the kings, to obtain ballistrae of metal, like those which strengthen the forces of the [Moslems].

Since there are relations only between the Arabs and the Portuguese, who sail abroad to India and travel to the Red Sea and the Persian Gulf, or with the Ethiopians in the east who are separated from Arabia by the Red Sea, Clement sent the Jewish emissary to the kings of Portugal and Ethiopia and besought them that they bestir themselves concerning the whole matter as is fit and make contact with the Arabian Jews in order to enlarge the Christian faith. . . . (Raynaldus, *Annales Ecclesiastici*, from the Hebrew translation in Aeshcoly, *Movements*, p. 380)

Account by Reubeni from Portugal

I came off the ship onto dry land . . . and there came to me immediately Christian officers and converted Jews, babies and women . . . and we came to the city of Tavira to the house of a convert . . . who was honorable, and whose wife was of high character. And the judge of the city came to me and rejoiced greatly concerning us, and said to me, "All that you wish I am prepared to carry out according to your commands." . . . And the judge wrote a letter to the king about our arrival in Tavira and I wrote a letter to the king of Portugal. . . .

And in those days a monk from the land of Spain came and spoke with R. Shlomo [Prato, Reubeni's secretary] . . . and the evil man said that there was no king of the Jews and no kingly line among us; and he stood in front of a large window, and I was jealous of God's reputation, and I stood up in front of him and threw him out the window down to the ground in front of all the non-Jews. . . . And the great judge heard of it and was very happy about the matter.

And we came to a great city called [Albufeira] . . . and we went into the house of a convert. And throughout the whole city, wherever I went, younger and older converts came to me, men and women, and kissed my hand in the presence of Christians. And they became angered at the converts because they kissed my hand and made requirements concerning the matter and said, "Do him great honor, but do not kiss his hand, for [it is only fit to do so] for the king of Portugal." But this made their will strong, for they believed in me with complete faith, as Israel believed in Moses our teacher, may he rest in peace. And I would say to them, wherever I came, that I was the son of King Shlomo, "And I have not come to you with signs and wonders and magic, but as a man of war, which I have been since my youth . . . and we shall see the path upon which the Name will lead me to the Land of Israel. . . ."

[Ultimately, the king of Portugal refuses to give Reubeni ships and weapons but provides him with money and a ship back to Rome.] And I stayed in my house for two days and the king's brother, the cardinal [Don Enrique] summoned me . . . and paid me great honor, and asked about the flags [I had] and about the route I would take. . . . And I answered him that the flags were my symbol, and the route I was on I traveled, with the aid of God, to Rome.

And the cardinal said to me, "If you will convert to my faith, I will make you a prince." And I answered him, "You would make me like the raven that Noah sent out from the ark and that never returned! Would this please the angels?! For I am the son of a king of the progeny of David the son of Jesse. . . . How could you say such a thing to me?!" . . .

And there came before me that night many converts, fearful and weeping. And I said to them, "Trust God forevermore, for you will merit seeing the rebuilding of Jerusalem, and do not be afraid; and I have not come before the king this time to take you and bring you to Jerusalem, for there are great wars to fight in Jerusalem first, before you come. We will make our sacrifices and then we will come to you to bring you to the settled Land."

And a great prince of Ishmael [Islam] came to me as well, and he spoke to me at length and asked me, "Why have you come here from your land? What are you seeking from the Christians?" And he was a great sage . . . and said to me, "The end of the reigns of the Christians and the Ishmaelites has come, and within three years all the kingdom of Edom will be in the hands of the king of the Jews in Jerusalem, and all the nations will come back to the one faith." And he said great and awesome and mighty things to me and I did not want to say anything at all back to him. (Reubeni's journal, from Aeshcoly, *Story*, pp. 62–130)

Account by Molkho, about himself and about Reubeni

When the mighty warrior, the pious one, our teacher, R. David Ha-Re'uveni reached the court of the king of Portugal, in a dream that night I saw awful visions, each different from the other, and I was greatly frightened by them. It will take a long time to tell them all when permission is granted me to do so. The essence of the vision I saw: they commanded me to carry out my circumcision. I would be in contact with our teacher R. David, may the Rock preserve him, daily and tell him what I saw in my dream, in order that I might gain his counsel concerning it, for it seemed to me that these things appeared to me on account of him. But he concealed himself from me and said, "I know nothing of all this; is it really on account of me that these fearful visions you see appear to you?" And I said to myself, "Perhaps he does not wish to reveal the matter to me until I carry out the circumcision." I left him and that night I performed the circumcision by myself; none other was with me. And the Holy One blessed is he aided me and healed me for the sake of his name though I felt great pain and distress and fainted, for the blood flowed

like a surging spring, and the Merciful One, the Healer, healed me in an unbeliev-
ably short time. And afterward I arose from my bed and went to our teacher,
R. David, may the Rock protect him, and said to him, "Speak with me, my lord,
and conceal nothing from me, for I have already carried out the commandment of
my Creator on high and see, I am circumcised as any other Jew." Then he looked at
me with an angry countenance and rebuked me and said, "What have I done that
you should have put me and yourself in such great danger?! If the king comes to
know of it he will say that I enticed you to do this though I knew nothing of it or
even thought about it at all." I was astonished at his words, yet thought to myself
that he continued to conceal these matters from me. And after I was sealed with
the signet of my Creator, awful things appeared to me, great and mighty, and great
secrets, and they made known to me the hidden things of the wisdom of the Holy
Kabbalah and great combinations among the *sefirot* and showed me the treasuries of
wisdom and illuminated my heart with our God's teaching. And then they ordered
me to go to the kingdom of Turkey and permitted me to publicize the reasons, and
in order to diminish the quarrels and questions, investigations and inquiries and responses of the Jews, I put abroad the story that our teacher, R. David, was sending
me on a secret mission to Turkey. But now I will tell the truth before him who made
the sky and the earth, that I neither circumcised myself nor traveled at the direction of flesh and blood but according to the will of the Lord our God. (Molkho, *The
Beast of the Reed,* ed. Aeshcoly [in Hebrew; Paris, 1938], pp. 7–8)

Account by Reubeni about Molkho

The king summoned me . . . and said to me: "How did this happen, that I
should hear that you have carried out a circumcision upon my scribe?" And I responded, "It's not true, Heaven forbid! I have not come to do things like these. Do
not attend to scandal-mongers." . . . And the scribe, who had carried out the circumcision in secret, came to me from where he had been hiding among the converts and spoke with me that same night. I was angry with him, and said, "See what
you have done to us! Now go to Jerusalem and get away from the king—otherwise,
he will execute you or burn you." And he went away from me. This scribe had
come to me at the beginning of my arrival at the king's court and said to me that he
had dreamed that night that he was performing a circumcision and said, "Do me
the mercy and perform the circumcision, or order [that it be done] upon me." And I
was angry with him and said, "You shall not do this thing at this time, otherwise,
you will be in danger and so will I; if the matter becomes known they will say that I
did it." And I advised him, "Keep your position in the court until the Holy One
blessed is he opens the way. He knows man's thoughts. Keep hold of yourself and do
not do this thing at this time for you and I and all the converts will be in great danger." And he went away and carried out the deed of circumcision all by himself. He
was a scribe and esteemed by the king. And the king of Portugal and all his nobles
and the converts and the Christians came to know of it . . . and the scribe fled
and the nobles and the king said . . . that I had caused it that this scribe should
do the circumcision, even if I had not . . . done it myself. (Reubeni's journal,
from Aeshcoly, *Story,* pp. 93–94)

Account by Sambari

This account states that Reubeni was from the land of the Moors (Morocco), and that Molkho said that he was the messiah and Reubeni, his prophet. No other writer makes these statements and they reflect later appraisals of Reubeni's visit to Portugal, in which Molkho's importance is emphasized. Sambari's *divre yosef* is the second half of his history text (the first part, a series of biographies of the sages, was lost). He wrote in the seventeenth century in Egypt and was the source for much that is known of Islamic practices and treatment of Jews at the time.

In the year of Creation 5,284 [1524], a man from the land of the Moors came to Rome. His name was David Ha-Re'uveni, and he postured as a prophet and said that he was the commander of the army of the King Messiah. He went and spoke with the king of Portugal and took with him a translator to speak for him, for he knew only to speak Hebrew and Arabic. He said to the king of Portugal that God had sent him to prophesy to his people, to Israel, that "we will go now by way of Constantinople and wage war against the Sultan Suleiman the Turk and take his land from his possession only so that Jerusalem and all around it may come under the authority of my lord, the messiah of the God of Israel."

The king of Portugal rejoiced and bowed before him and sent him to his chief priest to test him with riddles. The converted Jews believed in what he said. The man wandered to and fro and in every place in which he stayed he was honored and people believed in him. He made some flags, embroidered with the holy names, as well as a shield, on which were inscribed holy names, and told people that it was the shield of David, king of Israel, with which he went forth to fight God's wars. It is said that this is kept yet in the synagogue of the holy community of the city of Polonia. And he fasted six days and nights in a row.

While David Ha-Re'uveni was there [at the court of the king of Portugal] God awoke the spirit of a certain young man who was one of the king's scribes, a leading courtier of the kingdom, a handsome lad, of goodly appearance. He was of the seed of Israel. He determined to return to the faith and circumcised his foreskin and changed his name to Shlomo Molkho. He said that he was the messiah and David Ha-Re'uveni was his prophet. And when he had circumcised himself the spirit of God rested upon him. (R. Yosef Ha-Sambari, *Words of Joseph*, from Aeshcoly, *Movements*, p. 386)

Dream vision by Molkho after his circumcision

I saw a venerable elder, his beard very long and its appearance as snow, white. And he said to me, "Come with me to a ruin amidst the ruins of Jerusalem." And I went there with him. And it seemed to me that amid these things I was a long time on the road. I saw three trees along the way, all of them come forth from a single root, their branches divided toward every direction. And upon their branches I saw many doves, white ones, and among them other doves of the color of ash, and they were more numerous than the white ones. And the color of the ash that was upon them seemed not to be their original color but [it seemed] that they were first white and became the color of ash. And other doves, black ones, among them, and they were fewer than the white ones. And nearby those white ones was a great square field, and through the midst of the field passed a great river, and on the other side of the river was a multitude of people, warriors and knights on horseback, bearing very many weapons, swords and bows and instruments of iron for the hurling of iron and fiery balls. And it was the aim of this force to cut down the trees, and I heard it said, "These trees are from our region, thus let us cut them down and fell them to the earth." And they attacked the doves of ash and the black ones as well, and they would fall at once to the earth. And large birds came and ate their flesh until not one of them remained. And I looked upon this great assault against the black and the ashen doves and then some people came near to me and asked me, "What is this thing?" And I said to them, "This people has struck those doves, which have fallen to the earth, and now they seek to attack as well the white doves, which are very beautiful and which fill the tree that it might not wither." And the people said to me, "Let us make a high wall around them and a barrier to defend them." And I said to them, "Let us do so." And we hastened toward them to make for them a barrier of timber and dirt beside the river. And the warriors did not cease their hand from smiting the doves and killing them, and when they saw the barrier that we had built to save them they destroyed it with weapons of fire and struck some of the people who were with me as well. And the large birds descended to eat their flesh as they had the doves. And then I was struck in my chest by an iron ball, from a weapon of fire. And the ball came out through my back and I struggled mightily and with difficulty not to fall to the ground, but I had not enough strength and I fell down. And as I fell, I said, "Woe is me, for the birds will eat my flesh as they did the flesh of the people who were with me, and I will not be buried among my brothers." And yet I was calm and saw great visions and I said, "It is true what was said to me while I was alive, that man sees greater things after death than in life." And I saw the white doves which had been in the tree, some of them having become the ashen color and some of the ashen ones, white. And the people who remained alive and were standing beside me brought me a woman to heal me. And it was asked, "Who is this woman?" And they answered me, "This is the woman so-and-so, the wife of so-and-so," and I have not yet been given permission to reveal her name. And the woman pleaded to God pitifully, praying that he heal me, and the people mourned for me deeply. And the number of doves diminished and many changed their color. And while the woman was praying I saw an apparition like that of a man and his clothes were white as snow and his appearance was as the appearance of God. And I saw another man facing him, and his appearance was very much more awesome than that of the first man and his clothes were whiter and finer and splendid. And he held large scales in his hand and he sought to set them straight and even, and he began to walk along the way of the first man whom I had seen. The second man, who was bigger than the first, walked toward him through the air until both of them drew near to me. The first man asked the people standing with me, "Has any bird descended upon this one?" And they answered, "We have not allowed the birds to touch him," and at once he sent the people far away so that not even one of them could be seen in the field. And the two of us remained together, I and the great man, and the second stood over us in the air, and the first man fell upon me and put his mouth on my mouth and his eyes on my eyes and his palms against my palms and spoke words to me in the name of God, repeating them several times, and stood me upright and said to me, "Have you understood the appearance of the doves and the changing of their colors, what they are and what they mean, and these Gentiles that attack them and kill them, what that is?" And I said, "My lord, your servant has not yet understood this thing, but I feel pity for the doves and for my companions and I have compassion for them and my heart hurts for them and yet I know not what they are nor do I know their troubles." And he said to me, "Look up at all the armies and you will comprehend their end and you will know what the doves are." And he blew out upon the Gentiles and they became a heap of dust. And the man did not cross over the river to attack the Gentiles, and [he] was on the other side of the river, where the doves were. And he blew out upon the doves that had changed their color and they all became white and there was none among them different from another. And the water in the river increased from what it had been, and trees came up on the two banks of the river and fruits of different kinds. Then I said to the man, "Let my lord tell his servant what these wonders and miracles are, if I please you." And he said to me, "You cannot know the things now but it will not be hidden from you." And I bowed down before him and said to him, "Let my lord speak to his servant so that I may be certain of what all these things mean." And he blessed me. And I awoke from this apparition and I understood nothing. Thereafter, I saw the appearance of the first aged man whom I had seen in the first apparitions. And he explained everything to me. And I do not yet have permission to make public any of what he explained. And when the Holy One blessed is he brings me in peace to the land of Edom [Rome], I will write out at length all that I have seen with a clear explanation and send it from there to those who fear God and esteem his name. (Molkho, *The Beast of the Reed,* ed. Aeshcoly, pp. 8–9)

A Poem of the Endtime, by Molkho

The sealed, revealed/ at least in part:
those writings writ/ of the cut apart:
they'll not be found/ in victory's bound
but put in stocks/ and set to mock.

When done is all/ I will declare
the words select,/ send perfumes perfect:
"From Mount Carmel/ has sent you El
the one to tell/ the stranger farewell."

The nations will fight/ but men of might
will put the stranger to flight.
And then will be the time,/ o of cities the prime,
to flush Rome—Edom's pest—/ from out of the Nest.

Shlomo the Fair/ his sword will wear
its edges both bare/ his folk to spare
more nights of care;
and the nations fear/ till gifts they bear.

Aplenty of shame/ will clear Israel's name.
The Jews will enjoy/ the disgrace of the goy.
More than double consoled/ will Zion behold
the judgment of old/ Rome's fate unfold.

And after that time/ foretold here in this rhyme
God will him vest/ and in charity dressed
the good few who do flee/ through the troubles that be
shall conduct to safety
by the hands of the one/ whose name is Yinon [the messiah figure cited in
Hebrew in Ps. 72:17]. (Molkho, *The Beast of the Reed*, ed. Aeshcoly, p. 14)

Account by Ha-Cohen: A pure offering

Ha-Cohen (the Italian physician and historian mentioned in chapter 4) wrote
about Molkho's meeting with Charles V:

> And Shlomo sought to speak in depth with the emperor about the faiths. He
> went to see him when the emperor was at Regensburg and spoke with him there.
> And the heart of the emperor was hard, and he would not listen to him because of
> his impatience. And he ordered that [Shlomo] be put in a pit with David the
> prince, his companion, and his men. And there they stayed some days.
>
> And the emperor saw after the Turk retreated, that the situation had eased and
> he went away from that place. He returned to Italy and brought them with him in
> chains in wagons to Mantua and set a guard upon them. And the emperor said to
> the sages that it was the order of the king and they found against him for his sin and
> condemned him to die. They said, "Bring him out and let him be burnt." On the
> day they put a strap around his cheeks and led him out, and the whole city was in
> an uproar over him, and the fire was ablaze before him. One of the ministers of the
> emperor said, "Remove the strap from between his teeth for I have something to
> say to him on behalf of the king." They did that. He said to him, "The emperor has
> sent me to you to say that if you return from your ways—he will keep you alive and
> you will be of his court; and if not—the disaster is upon you." And he neither arose
> nor moved from his place. And he responded like a holy one, like an angel of God,
> "My heart storms and rages that I ever walked in that faith—so now, do what seems
> good to you, my soul will return to the house of its father as in the days of its youth,
> for it was happier then than now." And they burned with anger against him and
> threw him upon the wood that was upon the fire and sacrificed him as a burnt offer-
> ing to God, rising up whole in the smoke.
>
> And God smelled the sweet scent and gathered in his pure soul and it became

his darling always at play in his presence. And his servants were brought out from the prison and went on their way. Nothing remained from their corruption but the Prince of the Reubenites alone. They put him under guard.

The emperor went to Bologna and brought him along in bars in a wagon. They brought him to Spain and he stayed there many days and died in prison.

Many in Italy believed in those days that R. Shlomo Molkho was saved by his art from those who sought to extinguish his soul and that the flame had not touched his body, and one witnessed and swore before the congregation and flock that he had stayed in his house for eight days after the fire and from there had gone on his way and not been seen again. God knows. (Yosef Ha-Cohen, *The History of the Kings of France*, from Aeshcoly, *Movements*, pp. 427–428)

Account by Josel: The way to Regensburg

R. Josel (1478–1554) was a German-Jewish lobbyist of the Middle Ages. Despite his vast experience in negotiating for the lives of his fellow Jews—he had dealt with three emperors, electors, princes, dukes, and peasant mobs—he despaired of being able to offer assistance to Molkho (and Reubeni). As Aeshcoly notes, Josel was simply afraid: He chose to write a letter, rather than making direct contact; he fled the vicinity. Josel describes Molkho's acts and thoughts as "dissident" and "strange." His sense of his duty to his community—which constantly forces him to leave his own affairs and go to wait on the emperor—keeps him away from Molkho; nevertheless, his feeling of esteem for Molkho, and perhaps a sense of shame for himself, are revealed in his use of the phrase *nuho eden* ("His soul is secured in the Garden of Eden") at the end of his account, and in his statement that Molkho brought many back from sin. Josel had great admiration for those who underwent torture and were killed for the sanctification of the name of God. Josel's interest in messianism aside, he probably mentions Molkho, and not Reubeni, because he thought Molkho holy and worthy of being remembered.[8] All this emerges in his brief journal entry of Molkho's end:

In the year [1532] I was forced to come back to His Majesty, the emperor, on the day of the Council in the city of Regensburg in order to keep watch over [Jewish affairs]. . . . In those days a foreign man had appeared, a convert to Judaism, who was known as Rabbi Shlomo Molqo (!), may Eden be his rest, one whose ideas were dissident ones, with the intention of inciting the emperor by saying that he had come to summon all the Jews to come out to war against the Turks. When I heard what he intended, I wrote him a letter to warn him not to agitate the emperor so that he might not be consumed in the mighty fire. And I left the city of Regensburg so that the emperor might not say that I was involved in his doings and his strange ideas. And when he came before the emperor he was bound in iron chains and was led to the city of Bologna. There he was burned in the act of sanctifying the Name of the religion of Israel, for he had turned many back from sin. His soul is secured in the Garden of Eden. (R. Josel of Rosheim, memoirs, from Aeshcoly, *Movements*, p. 426)

The end of the story: two letters

[To Giovanni Batista Sanga, adviser and secret agent of the pope, August 21, 1532]:

Now this infidel Portuguese Jew, whom while yet in Rome I advised be burned, has come to the court of His Majesty the emperor, accompanied by Antonio di Leva, and been received and given an audience. As the Jew himself has told me this evening, the emperor listened to him with great interest for more than two hours and asked him many things and heard from him that he was the object of pursuit of all the Christians. And he said that the emperor had ordered that he be given a dwelling in this city, under the protection of Lord Antonio di Leva. He brought with him a flag, shield, and sword, with the aid of which he intended to conquer the Turk, and said that he must be the first of the warriors. I do hope that the emperor, who knows this man well, will not care to listen to his follies. I do not like it that this infidel should bring his Jewish symbols into a place where we must bring the cross, for it is the duty of all Christians to put their entire faith in the cross, and there can only sprout dishonor and damage from the madnesses of this Jew.

He came to visit me, full of beseechments, and it seems that he does not altogether trust me, and surely, if it were in my power, I would not have permitted him to take his leave, for much shame to the Church of God comes from this. Wherever he goes he raises a furor as in Mantua, as was told me by our man in Verona. I am certain that His Majesty, when he knows the truth, will not want to suffer this monster, and I am convinced that, even without any further information, His Majesty, who is quite cautious, has already seen for himself that the thing is no good. But I am certain that when he knows the truth he will take yet more care to see the matter straight.

[To the pope, September 1, 1532]:

This same infidel Portuguese Jew, together with another [Reubeni from Arabia], who came to Rome in the first year [1523] of His Holiness, has come here together with Antonio di Leva, and they have brought with them the Jewish flags, shield, and sword, which, according to his contention, have been sanctified by the names of God in Hebrew. He makes great promises as concerns the Turk and he says that he must be one of the commanders. And he promises certain victory through himself and through his holy instruments and that he will kill the Sultan or take him prisoner. I have known, on the basis of information from our man in Verona . . . that these two were on their way here. At that time I informed His Majesty of it; and again later through others as well, since His Majesty was at Baden at the baths some distance from here and I was here and unfit to travel there or ride at all until the day the two of them reached here. In spite of the fact that the Portuguese, who is their leader, said to me that His Majesty listened closely to him and ordered that he be given a residence in the city, nevertheless all of them were taken prisoner and brought on the next day to the alcalde of His Majesty's court. What happened thereafter is not known. I have today sent a letter that they not hasten to set them free because I hear that there come to him many supporters from various places and there is a great danger that with their appearance and the promises of this arrogant infidel, His Majesty will grant him credence. For if we should be victorious the world will be shaken [because] the victory [would] be credited to him and his Judaism, and if we be humiliated in the war—if God bring upon us disgrace then it will be on account of our sins—the thing will be ascribed to His Majesty and to all the Christians.

But God, in whose hands rests the heart of the emperor as usual inspired His Majesty so that he not only would not err but he would have the understanding to do the holy deed and imprison them. Now we must be very careful that they not escape by way of the supporters they have but that what justice and God's honor demands be done as well as that which the general good of Christianity requires. Therefore and on this account, I have sent today to inform the emperor's men. (Hieronymus Aleander, special representative of Pope Clement VII in Germany, from the translation of the Italian in H. Fraenkel-Goldschmidt, *R. Josel of Rosheim* (in Hebrew; Jerusalem, 1996) pp. 183–184)

In these first-hand accounts, which determine the fate of the mission, we can see clearly the use of magic names, for which Molkho is to be credited, along with military symbols and a military aim—Reubeni's—as they are brought to bear on the emperor at an appropriate time. We can well understand Josel of Rosheim's fear of being caught between the powerful forces of the church and the emperor, the Italian lord, and German burghers. Yet something of the holy awe and admiration the Jewish lobbyist feels, especially in connection with Molkho, dwells within the heart of the emperor as well as in that of the pope as they contemplate his fervor. Only the vigilance of the nuncio turns the trick and halts a plan that could have stormed the quarters of the emperor, the pope, and the Reichstag and led all of them on, hand in hand with their Jewish allies—some of whom were warriors and magicians from distant and legendary lands; some local, well-endowed businessmen and financiers—to win Jerusalem from the hands of the Turks.

BIBLIOGRAPHIC NOTE   Other materials may be found in Molkho's *Glorious Book*, newly reissued. A new edition of Aeshcoly's *The Story of David Ha-Re'uveni* (in Hebrew; Jerusalem, 1993) contains an introductory essay by M. Idel that updates research and focuses on the poem translated here. Idel has written elsewhere about Molkho, particularly in "Sh. Molkho as magician" (in Hebrew; *Sefunot* 18 [1985] and in *Messianism and Mysticism* (in Hebrew; Jerusalem, 1995). On the Lost Tribes, see A. Gross, "The Ten Tribes and the kingdom of Prester John," *pe'amim* 48 (1991). The background to the meeting, between Molkho and Charles V, along with a critical examination of all the reports about it and scholarly treatments of it, and of the reasons for its failure, is presented in H. Fraenkel-Goldschmidt, *R. Josel of Rosheim: Historical Writings* (in Hebrew; Jerusalem, 1996), pp. 177–186.

6

THE MESSIAHS OF SAFED
Isaac Luria and Hayim Vital

While many Jews converted to Catholicism during the repressive periods in Spain and in other European countries, others chose to leave Europe altogether. In 1492, Jews were no longer given the option of conversion in Spain and were simply forced out, with most of them winding up in the Moslem lands of the Ottoman Empire. Thus the center of Jewish life returned to the Middle East, and the mystical theology that had begun in the regions of the northern and western Mediterranean continued to develop back in the land of Israel. This chapter focuses on two major figures in the development of the Kabbalah—Isaac Luria and Hayim Vital—both of whom also assumed the role, one after the other, of messiah. These figures are not militant or ascetic but are oriented toward the Apocalypse, adhering to a mystic worldview that seeks the repair of the world in a cosmic sense. An insistence on a higher truth, different from sensory or logical truth and often its opposite—the hallmark of mysticism—typifies their vision. Their localism coincides with the fact that they have actually reached the land of Israel. They stressed, if they did not actually introduce, the idea of the transmigration of the messiah soul.

THE RETURN TO ISRAEL AND THE RISE
OF THE SAFED COMMUNITY

The Jews who were forced to flee from Catholic Europe into the welcoming arms of the Ottoman Empire, in the first decades of the sixteenth century, suddenly found themselves within reach of the land of Israel, and many did settle within this territory. Tiberias became a Jewish grant; Safed became a center for Jewish trade and manufacturing; Jerusalem found itself repopulated by Jews. Other aspects of redemption followed this return to the land; ancient Jewish institutions like rabbinic ordination were restored. The very graves of ancestors, long lost, were repopulated.

Safed, a town in the Galilee, was one of four major Jewish communities in the region. Damascus was a larger and wealthier community while Jerusalem, where the ruins of the temple stood, was more significant in terms of its history and prestige. Still, Safed was quite an important town in this period, not only due to its role in the textile trade and its proximity to the district capital of Tiberias; the town was also distinguished by its scholarly groups with mystic and pietistic interests. A large number of scholars from the sanctified period of the Mishna and the Talmud were associated with the region by history and legend. Situated in the environs of Safed was the site of the cave where R. Shimon bar Yohai hid for seventeen years from the Romans and, according to a legend, wrote the Zohar, the basic work of the Kabbalah. His cave and grave at Mount Meron became a pilgrimage spot where many came seeking the blessings of fertility. The very topography of Safed, high in the Galilee, offering startlingly clear air and vistas into vast distances, encouraged its equivalent in the mystic perspective. One important tradition, reinforced by the Zohar, held that the messiah would first appear in the upper Galilee, presumably in Safed. The disasters that Jews had experienced in the Catholic countries of the Mediterranean received theological interpretations that inflamed messianic passions; the expulsions, forced conversions, and general sufferings of these Jews were seen as omens of the final days preceding the coming of the messiah. Jews who had been expelled from Spain and Portugal now congregated in Safed in order to be on hand when the messiah appeared, and to be near Bar Yohai's tomb. They brought with them, from Spain, Portugal, and Italy, an industry—textile manufacturing— that quickly made Safed an important economic center. Immigrants continued to settle there throughout the sixteenth century. The scholars and students who came to Safed created its second most important source of revenue: Charitable support for schools, scholars, and synagogues flowed in from Jewish communities all over the world, who wished thereby to contribute to the bringing of the messiah.

Under the aegis of Isaac Luria (1534–1572), active and detailed programs through which cognoscenti could influence cosmic conduct, and lead the way to salvation, quickened the imaginations of Jews worldwide. Luria expanded upon the concept of soul rebirth and developed methods to reach the dead, who were said to be eagerly waiting to communicate with the living. He identified historical disasters as messianic birth pangs rather than as punishment for Jewish failings; he pronounced the cosmic rejection of Israel all but requited. The Lurianic theory of the messiah is one piece of an entire cosmology that he introduced. Luria held (or so his students reported; he himself didn't write very much) that the universe had been broken at its creation, and that it could be repaired by restoring—among other things, and as a scene that opened the final act—the soul of the messiah to its proper place or operation. Luria lived in Safed only two and a half years before his death. Near the end, he saw that he would not in fact be the victorious messiah, the result on which his whole theology had been based, and he reintroduced the figure of the messiah of the lineage of Joseph. He put himself in this role and was accepted as such by his students, particularly after his death. Luria was not the only member of the Safed community to picture himself as the messiah. Before him, R. Yosef Karo, author of the most important code of Jewish law, the *Shulhan Arukh*, said he had been receiving visits from the spirit of the Mishna, assuring him of his cosmic role. One moving passage in his spiritual journal expresses Karo's desire to die the holy death—as a burnt offering—of which Shlomo Molkho previously had been found worthy. Luria identified his most important disciple, R. Hayim Vital, as the messiah that would follow him. Vital accepted his role, but he suffered recurring doubts and misgivings throughout his life.

ISAAC LURIA (ASHKENAZI)

Luria was born in Jerusalem in 1534. His father died when he was eight, and he and his mother moved to his uncle's household in Egypt. His uncle, a wealthy man and an important bureaucrat in the Ottoman administration, arranged for him to study traditional subjects with leading teachers. Luria then married his uncle's daughter and worked as a merchant. While in his twenties, he began to study mysticism, principally the Zohar and its explication by the greatest authority of the age, R. Moshe Cordovero. Eventually, he moved to an island in the Nile, where he studied alone for some seven years. He made a pilgrimage to Israel and later, in 1570, return to settle in the town of Safed.

Cordovero, the famous exegete of the Zohar, had taught briefly in Safed. As he lay dying, Cordovero told his students that his successor would be the one who saw a pillar of cloud preceding his coffin on its way to the graveyard; it was Isaac Luria who beheld it. During the two and a half years that Luria spent in Safed, the most talented students gathered around him, drawn by his personality and the practices he instituted. He occasionally spoke in the Ashkenazi synagogue in Safed, but more often, he lectured while walking or seated with his followers outdoors under trees, pointing out the resting places of great figures from the Mishnaic and Talmudic periods. (His perceptive soul revealed the unmarked graves to him.) According to Luria's teachings, a person's soul was composed of bits and pieces of various older souls. These fragments influenced the person's conduct and he had to achieve full unity with them in order to achieve the repair of the self and the cosmos. Parts of Luria's own soul, he revealed, came to him from biblical figures and great scholars, near-divine men of superior attainments and cosmic significance. These past-and-present psyches knew the secrets of the present and the future as well. Luria taught his followers how to unite themselves with the life of higher spheres and to partake of the infinite in their daily lives. All of his students had flaws to repair, and the older souls that made up their composite souls also sought atonement and the completion of tasks appropriate to them and their places in the cosmic order. Though his character was that of a charismatic and a revolutionary, Luria lived a pious life and preferred seclusion. He never wrote down his mystic teachings. Ultimately, he concentrated his instruction on one student, Hayim Vital, whose education he regarded as his most important task. Luria thought of himself as the messiah of the lineage of Joseph, and of Vital as his heir.

Luria's messianism modified the role of the messiah and tied his success to the efforts of the individual as well as of the community. His cosmology was based on the universe of the Zohar, in which the divine descended into creation through ten attributes, known as *sefirot*. Luria connected the human and divine poles of the imperfect result: The universe, he said, was broken (the *shevirah*) as a result of God's initial withdrawal (*tzimtzum*) from it, which was followed by his return to it as an uncontrollable ray of light, shattering the vessels that were intended to serve as reflectors. It required focused and aware human beings to repair it (*tikkun*) so that it could operate properly. The removal or defeat of the shards (*klippot*) of the broken vessels beneath which the world lies would release the entrapped sparks of light and allow them to flow upward again. The inner world of the individual—the microcosmos—was one with the macrocosmos, and the repair was largely a matter of performing traditional prayers and observances in an inward and aware manner, reuniting (*yihud*) that which was separated through mystical concentrations (*kavvanot*). The role of each individual was determined by the nature of his own soul and deeds and by his soul's history and the deeds of each of its component souls. The messiah's success—indeed, his very life—depended upon each individual Jew's doing his part. Luria died young, his task having been unfulfilled by him or by his children, who predeceased him. His work was regathered by his students. The tales of his life and the inner meaning of his acts and visions became the first hagiographa in Judaism, a pattern for other sacred-tale collections that followed and that, like it, carried the potential within themselves to achieve the repair of the cosmos. Luria is known as *Ha-Ari ha-kadosh* ("the holy lion"). Ha-Ari is an acronym for the Hebrew words "The Ashkenazi, R. Isaac," or "Our master, R. Isaac," or "The divine R. Isaac."

When his teacher died, Vital appointed himself the accurate transmitter of his master's thoughts and the keeper of the written recollections. Some of those who studied with Luria consented to Vital's domination; others retained their notes and wrote their own accounts; still others wrote their renditions of Luria's theology on the basis of second-hand accounts, having had minimal contact with the milieu of Safed or even none at all. Luria's thinking, to begin with, had been unsystematic, the overflowings of a splendidly creative personality; and the transmission of his perceptions produced versions rich in contradictions. All of the accounts, including Vital's, contradict themselves and each other. This is not simply a result of the non-denotative, allusory nature of the language of instruction. Luria insisted on oral transmission, his teachings having arisen from transitory stimuli—a site or a passing wind or other natural phenomena. Mental and physical stresses provided separate stimuli for confusion. The daily lives of the people involved were filled with pain; the frequent sickness and untimely deaths of mates, children, and companions tested the philosophy of a rational, meaningful cosmos. The people of Safed often resorted to acts of magic, seers, dream-communications, and spirit possession. This may seem out of character with the pietistic quality of the Lurianic theology and the contemplative, learned focus of its enactment, but magic practices had accompanied theosophical speculation and the performance of the *mitzvot* for as long as Jewish esotericism had existed and were common resources in critical circumstances. The mystic narrative itself arose from disaster. It envisioned an absent, exiled, suffering God, somehow ensnared in evil, desiring, yet unable, to manage the universe, suffering from his own lack. Luria saw Jewish history and his own life in this image. He showed it to other Jews, illuminating their history and their own lives, and they all strove desperately to achieve the repair of themselves/God through adherence to his theology and its urgings for self-condemnation, confession, and piety. Daily encounters with disaster were repaired by daily encounters with visions and visitors from the other world. Everything had a meaning; every mishap had its source in some misdeed, which could be revealed and repaired by contemplating and penetrating Luria's formidably elaborate construct or, more directly, through magic. This coupling of belief and conduct emerged under the high, blue skies of Safed—in the thin air of loss and lonely anguish, where divine personae enacted a sacred drama. The sacred biography itself was the product of the popular traditions of Safed, the sum of the experiences and reflections of Luria's students and companions (Figure 6.1).

All of the texts from which the accounts of Luria, quoted here, are compiled come from versions of the hagiographa generally identified as *The History of the Ari*, in the collection of the same name, edited by Meir Benayahu (in Hebrew; Jerusalem, 1968). Benayahu's masterly presentations and studies have guided my own compilation, translation, and comments throughout, but the interpretations are, finally, my own. The history of these texts is still controversial, but the variants all shed light on one another and on the image of the Ari as it has taken shape and influenced its successive messiahs and accounts.

There once lived a man in Israel, the land of the gazelle, the glorious land, and his name was Rabbi Solomon, may his memory be blessed. He was whole-hearted, upright, God-fearing, and shunned evil. One day, as he was in the synagogue, praying, weeping, and beseeching God, after everyone else had left, Elijah the prophet appeared to him and said, "I am come from God to tell you that your wife will conceive and bear you a son and you shall call him Isaac. And he will begin to release Israel from the *klippot* and through him many souls now in a shattered state and wandering will be made whole. He will reveal the hidden mysteries of the Torah and the meaning of the Zohar. Nothing in the world will lie outside his knowledge. Be very careful, therefore, not to circumcise him until I myself come and circumcise the child."

And then he disappeared. Rabbi Solomon stayed behind and prayed, "Please God, bring about what you have promised. Let no sin of mine restrain it. Even though I am not worthy, do it for your own sake." At night he returned home but said nothing. And as he watched his wife's belly swell he wept from great joy. And when the time came she gave birth to a son and the whole house was filled with light.

On the eighth day the child was brought to the synagogue to be circumcised. The father looked all around to see whether Elijah had come. But he didn't see him. He was distressed because everyone there was urging him, saying, "Come on; take your son and circumcise him." He put them off by saying that not all his relatives had come yet. This went on for about an hour. The father's soul was in great pain. He wept aloud and thought to himself, "If Elijah has not come, this child

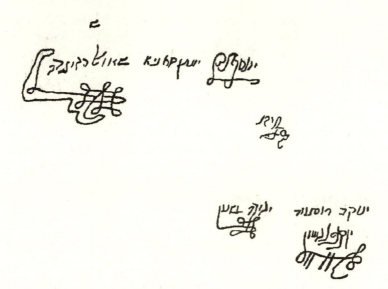

Figure 6.1: Signatures appended to the convenant made by several of the students of Luria and Vital in the month of Av, 1575, at Vital's demand, shortly after the death of Luria. In it, those signing their names—Yehosef Arazin, Yonatan Sagis, Shmuel de Uceda (*top line, right to left*); Gedalyahu Halevi (*middle*); Yakov Massoud, Ya'uda Mishan (*next to last line, right to left*), and Yosef Latun—agree to learn from Vital, to keep secret whatever they learn with him, as well as whatever they learned from Luria or from Vital while Luria was alive. They agree that they are not to reveal anything without Vital's permission since they would have understood nothing without him. Their oath is to last ten years.

Their signatures reflect something of magic in the way they are formed. They represent some psychic essence of the signatories—having to do with their roles as students and coactivists in the Lurianic myth—which is pertinent to the covenant they sign. Molkho's signature had more to do with his actual messianic role, referring to the banner he bore with Reubeni, but also to the banners of the Israelite tribes.

Vital's effort to retain control over Luria—actually, over his thoughts and his own notes of them—by keeping the knowledge secret, as secret as is his own signature, which is lacking here, failed well before the ten-year period expired.

must not be the one he foretold. It must be that my own sins have held back this good thing." And even while he was weeping Elijah appeared to him and said, "Cease your weeping, O servant of the lord. Come near the altar and make your offering. Sit and hold your son. That's what everyone will see. I will sit in your lap and I will circumcise the child. I only delayed my arrival to test you, to see whether you would keep my command and do what I asked."

The father sat down happily, then Elijah sat down as he had said and no one saw him. The boy was circumcised and brought home. But before the child arrived home, he was healed as though he had been circumcised days before. People were astonished.

The child grew and was weaned [Gen. 21:8] and was brought to school and learned more and faster than any child his own age. By his eighth year he was learning the Talmud like a veteran student and no master could stand before his questioning.

And then his father died. His mother said to him, "Let us go to Egypt, where my uncle can help you." They went to Egypt, where his uncle welcomed Isaac with honor and treated him as his own son and even found him a teacher, who agreed to take Isaac as a pupil because he had heard of him and his wisdom. Isaac studied with him until he was fifteen and his knowledge went beyond that of all the sages of Egypt. His uncle gave him his daughter in marriage.

This tale has a profound influence on the genre of tales that serves thereafter to begin collections of hagiographa. It gathers motifs and plot constituents from biblical tales that have themselves brought together motifs and plot constituents from tales that preceded them (like the divine messenger mentioned in the tale of the childless couple) and from rabbinic tales (*midrashim*) that build on the biblical readings of these components, drawing from later or more exotic literary treasuries. The Lurianic tale seeks to gain the strength of tradition by fulfilling expectations. It also seeks to individuate itself, to be appropriate for its particular focus, through a lexicon that is unique to the vision it declares (such as the prediction that the child will "begin to release Israel from the *klippot*"). Fragments of the literature of ideas— philosophy, ethics, theology—are incorporated in it to serve a narrative purpose. Among all the accounts of Jewish messiahs, the tale of Luria's birth and childhood is the most complete of its kind, deriving from the biblical tradition. The previous tale that most nearly resembles this one is the birth-and-youth tale of Jesus in Matthew's Gospel.

In the tale of Luria's birth, a miracle connects the parents and the child; a vision of Elijah, harbinger of the messiah, appears to the deserving father and informs him that Elijah himself will perform Luria's circumcision while sitting in the chair traditionally reserved for him at the initiation ritual of every Jewish male. The child arrives in a glow of light (as does Moses). The father faces a trial that pits him against those who lack his faith and vision (as in Abraham's trial with Isaac) and is rewarded as he brings his son forward for circumcision on an altar (again recalling the binding of Isaac in Gen. 22). The altar image refers to the sacrificial life that Molkho led and Karo longed for, joining the martyrdoms and exile in Spain with the Crusader period, and assures the infant Luria of the fulfillment of his duty as the messiah of the lineage of Ephraim. The details of Luria's biography also come together in this image, interpreting the historic moment in terms of the mythic pattern of the sacrificed messiah. (The expiatory human sacrifice, perhaps the central image of Christianity, is generally anathema to Jews, often viewed, from disputation to blood-libel, as an invidious misreading of its Bible, but it seems to have fully entered into Judaism in this account and in the one of Luria's death (quoted below). The tale insists that the time after the expulsion from Spain is that of the apocalypse, but the theme of a generation unfit for the fulfillment of messianic expectations arises when the father doubts his own worthiness and thus also places his son's ability in doubt. This doubt requires the passage of the father from the scene. The miraculous healing of the circumcision has a history of its own in other accounts that suggest the separation of the heroic flesh from the world of mere matter, but the time and place of this tale recall the denial of circumcision to crypto-Jews during the time of the Inquisition. The account of Molkho's self-circumcision stands out from several other tales of circumcisions performed by suspected crypto-Jews who had fallen into the relentless grasp of the Holy Office. Like Molkho, but unlike the others, Luria's circumcision wound is quickly cured, leaving him well and free from complications. The motif of the quick healing echoes the crypto-Jew's fervent wish to be circumcised, but safe from prying spies.

It is not at all unusual at this time for a scholar or trader, unattached to any particular local employment, to travel between the distinguished Jewish communities of Egypt, Syria, and Israel; within this tale's framework, the pattern of a safe passage into Egypt and a safe return from there recalls the tale of Jesus. The revelation of the prodigious mastery of the child Luria occurs before his flight but immediately after his weaning, retracing the steps of Isaac on the way to Moriah. Luria's marriage contrasts the ascetic, even Gnostic portrayal of Jesus with a Jewish success; but marriage for him only begins a more tragic pattern that leaves him bereft of children and leads to the failure of his attempt at cosmic salvation.

The Master attained [knowledge] of all the sorts of art that exist—the art of physiognomy and of cheiromancy, the speech of the palm trees and of birds, of flames and of the ministering angels. He could read a man's sins in his forehead and what soul was his, as well as what he had come to this world to repair. He also knew if the soul was composed of one or more previous souls or was one that had been of a scholar of the first, second, third, or fourth generation or of one of the prophets. And he could distinguish the souls of evildoers that had been reborn as trees or stones, wild animals, worms and insects, unclean birds and clean ones. He could tell what had happened to a man and what was yet to happen to him. And all this in the blink of an eye. He knew what transgressions a person had committed from his youth until the present moment. He could tell what soul abided with a man, to help him in performing the religious duties (*mitzvot*). He knew people's thoughts and could release their souls from their bodies and speak with them.

He knew how to make mystical unitings (*yihudim*) at the graves of the righteous ones and would lay himself down upon their graves with his arms and legs spread out and bring down the soul, spirit, and psyche of that righteous one and speak with him. And that righteous one would reveal secrets and Elevated Mysteries to him that had been discussed in the Seminars of High Heaven. His face would glow like the sun and no creature could bear to look upon his face. No fly ever lit on his table, the fragrance of the Garden of Eden rose from his couch as it was with Elisha, as is written in the Zohar. He could hear decrees concerning what was to happen in the world as they were announced in Heaven. He could take a sick person's pulse and determine what spiritual aspect he had damaged and give him the proper repair. He could hear the chirping of birds at the passing of the Day of Atonement and know who would die and who would live through that year.

Luria and Vital and their students performed acts of uniting with the holy dead in their graves in order to establish communication between their world and the dead in paradise. The manner of uniting imitates the way Elisha resuscitated the dead son of the great woman of Shunem (2 Kings 4): face to face, mouth to mouth, eyes to eyes, hands to hands (but outstretched). The dead man may thereafter speak words through the mouth of the living man with whom he is coupled; the living may see through the eyes of the dead. The Zohar (II 44a) puts Elisha's achievements above those of all other prophets except Moses. Three couples stand behind the communicative acts of uniting: Elijah and Elisha, Moses and Joshua, Cordovero and Luria. Also invoked here is the relationship between teacher and student in life and in death, the one becoming part of the other, the model of Luria as Vital's master. Elijah anointed Elisha; at their final meeting before Elijah's departure, Elisha begged to be united with him as a double soul. He replaced him as prophet when Elijah passed away in the cloud that Elisha alone saw, which assured him of his fitness for his task. Luria, likewise, gained acceptance when he saw the cloud at Cordovero's passing. It is Moses' glowing face that had to be concealed so that ordinary mortals could look upon him after his close encounters with God; he consecrated Joshua to replace him. The unitings at Safed (and in those forms of Judaism—such as Hasidism [see chapter 8]—that continue the act of stretching out on the grave or standing about it to pray and seek responses) bring about further unities, as do other meditative acts, opening channels among all levels of creation to achieve certain repairs. Luria's table is the altar of temple sacrifice upon which no fly ever lit (cf. Mishna Avot 5:5).

> There was a woman who was having great difficulty giving birth and was in great danger. Her relatives came to the house of the Master [to ask] that he find the appropriate repair for her, to save her. That same day there appeared before the Master other men and women, calling out to him, "May the king deliver!" concerning the woman who was in travail for three days, seeking that he deliver her. The Master responded, "It is true that she is in danger. She has two sons in her belly. There is a repair, if it can be found." They said to him, "Master, tell us." He said to them, "The repair is that a man who has never looked upon a drop of semen in his life come and put his *brit* (covenant; i.e., circumcised organ) in her mouth and she will give birth right away and be saved." They asked him, "Who is this man? We will go to him." He said, "I know, but I do not have permission to reveal him to you for fear of spreading tales concerning others. But do this: put it about the whole town that you are seeking a man who knows of himself that he has never seen a drop of semen and that he should come and save three Jewish souls." They did so. And when the gaon, our teacher, R. Moshe Galanti the elder, heard the announcement he went with them straightaway and put his *brit* in her mouth and she gave birth immediately.

Saying more than they know, the people call upon Luria in the language of 2 Sam. 14:4, in which the woman from Tekoah calls upon King David to save her two sons. Luria is thereby equated with the king-messiah and, like David, accomplishes what is asked of him. (Luria will not name the man they must seek because in doing so he would declare others less pure.) The tenth Sefira of the Kabbalah is considered a female emanation from God, the Shekhina, and is represented, in the anthropomorphic design of the Sefirotic structure, as the mouth; the ninth Sefira is a male emanation and is represented as the *brit*. Joining the two is an act of uniting at every level. The procedure is known in another guise from Vital's own book of magic, which discusses the threat posed to infants by the demon Lillith, Eve's enemy and the enemy of her children. Lillith gains progeny by gathering the semen spilled in masturbation or in nocturnal emissions. The tale rests upon the historically high number of infant deaths in Safed; the phenomenon is rationalized in the explanation that Lillith's power over infants comes through an inversion of the appropriate use of semen. The fear of accidental emission still retains its power in some Jewish groups today and probably lies behind the Great Tikkun ritual of R. Nahman, of Bratslav (see chapter 9).

> The companions once asked him why the Master did not write a book of his knowledge. He said to them, "Know this, that when I wish to make some explanation to you, I try to find some very narrow conduit so that you might be able to receive the explanation and not lose it all, like an infant who is strangled by too much milk. That is just how it is when I open my mouth to tell you something. The abundance swells up like a flowing river, and every secret is attached to another. How could I write a book? Rather, each of you must write what you hear."
>
> Nevertheless, he only gave permission to R. Hayim Vital to write, for only he could descend to the depths of [Luria's] knowledge. In spite of this, [the companions] did not heed him and everyone wrote. Finally, [when he caught R. Moshe Meshullam writing and lying about it], everyone was frightened and ceased writing.

> One day the Master noticed a boy studying at the yeshiva, and said to his father, "Your son is possessed. You are wasting your money on medicines and cures." The father said, "Sometimes he has heart pains. This has been going on for ten years. The medicines cure him and it goes away, then comes back." The Master said, "I assure you that it is a spirit." And he ordered the spirit to speak. It told this story: "I was a pauper in Rome and this boy was then in charge of funds for the poor. He gave me nothing and I died of hunger. Now I have returned, by order of Heaven, to bring him death in this time. I will leave the boy alone if you command it and on the single condition that he look upon no woman for three full days."
>
> The father asked his son how he felt and he replied that he felt better even than when he was taking all the medicines. The Master ordered the father to keep watch over him, alone in the house, for the three days. He warned the father that the spirit was full of malice and cunning.
>
> On the third of the days the father went to the synagogue to pray and the boy's mother and aunt came to visit him and kissed him. At that instant the spirit rushed back into him and choked him to death.
>
> The Master could only see to it that none but the family heard of the death, so that people might not say, "The prayers of the Jews are of no help; they kill their own children."

> One day the companions were studying about God calling forth the snake to bite the womb of the gazelle so that she can bear her young. The Master said to the

companions, "There is a secret here that is very deep and it is dangerous for me to tell it to you. The master of the Zohar has advised: 'Seek it not. Do not try the will of the Holy Blessed One.' Even he was afraid of the danger." But [Vital] pressed him and urged him until he interpreted the passage. And the Ari said, "I have always told you I would answer every question you have and fulfill every request you make." And when he had finished, he cried out, "Blessed is the true Judge!"— which is what one says when hearing the decree of death. "I told you many times how dangerous this was; now I have heard the decree that my son Moshe will die within eight days."

When they heard this the students were very disturbed. The Master got up and went home and asked his wife how his son was and she said, "He came home from school only an hour ago. He said his head hurt him. He went to bed." The Master went up to his room and saw that the boy was burning like fire and at once he realized that the boy would die. Even before the eight days had passed the boy died. The disciples grieved. When the *shiv'a* [seven-day mourning period] was over the Master sent for them; they were too ashamed to come to him. He told them, "Don't be afraid that because of my son's death I will hold back anything from you. Even if I knew that all my children and you and I as well would, God forbid, die, I would hold nothing back from you, none of the Exalted Mysteries or the Secrets of the Torah, so that you might be repaired and so that the whole world might be lit up by your art." And the students rejoiced. They had thought that they would be reproved on account of the death of his son. They fell at his feet and said, "May the king live forever, he and his sons in the midst of all Israel!"

Six months later, when they had forgotten this whole episode, they passed by the marker at the graves of Shemaiah and Avtalyon. The Master said to the companions in the name of these two sages, that they should pray on behalf of the messiah of the lineage of Ephraim, that he might not die in their days. The companions did not know that these two scholars had said to do so in order to save the Master himself. The Master, in his great humility, did not explain the thing to the companions. When the Master departed this world, then they knew that he had in fact been the messiah of the lineage of Ephraim and had only come to the world in order to bring about the Redemption and to make the world complete for the King Messiah.

The terrible "secret" referred to here begins with a talmudic passage praising God's miraculous timing and giving examples (TB Baba Bathra 16). In this particular miracle, the womb of the gazelle must be softened at exactly the right moment so that she may give birth, and God appoints a snake to do the job. The Zohar expands on this in two places (II, 52b, 119b): The gazelle is the Shekhina; the snake is The Snake; the child being born is, if the moment is right, the messiah of the lineage of David, but otherwise, just another messiah of the lineage of Joseph, doomed himself and not yet capable of returning Israel from its exile. The Snake, who is Evil, must be employed but, thereby, gains power—too much power if it is used in the wrong way or at the wrong moment, which may cause the death of the messiah and his lineage. Luria's revelation to his disciples attracts the Snake's attention, wakes him early, and dooms Luria, his son, and his task.

On the Sabbath eve the Master would take us out into the fields of Safed, dressed in white clothes and singing to greet the Sabbath Queen, the Shekhina, our wife, their mother, their sister. The Ari would have us close our eyes, he said, because we would only be confused by the mingling of the souls of the righteous rising at that moment from the graveyard and the souls that were descending to be extra souls for Israel on the Sabbath, like flocks of birds going up and down through each other. While we sang, "Come my beloved, to greet the bride," the Master asked us, "Friends, would you like to go with me to Jerusalem before the Sabbath so that we may celebrate it there? Now we can be made pure. Now Jerusalem can be restored. Now is the moment of Redemption." Now, Jerusalem was more than two days walk from Safed, and some of the other students replied, "Let us first tell our wives, so they won't worry about us." And then the Master wept, "Oh, how well the Adversary labors to delay the Redemption of Israel. There was never a better moment for the Redemption and if all of you had cried out in one glad voice, "Yes! Now!" then the Temple would have been built straight-away and all Israel would have entered Jerusalem. But that moment has passed now and Israel is exiled once more." And when the companions heard this, they were sorry for what they had done. But it was no help.

The song, "Come my beloved" (*lekha dodi*), written by Sh. Alkabetz, one of the companions of the group, was introduced to Judaism in Safed as members of the community gathered to greet the Shekhina, the Sabbath Queen, in the fields. It is sung today inside synagogues everywhere.

Once he saw a raven passing and calling out, "You as well as your king are doomed." All at once, that same week, he fell ill, for he was stricken with a plague, and he, of blessed memory, was the first to die. And it was a great plague among the people and most of the companions of the group who had been studying with him died.

Samuel warns the people (1 Sam. 12:25): "If you do wickedly, you and your king too are doomed." In another version of the above tale, the raven is identified as Samael, King of Demons, who is enabled, by a quarrel among the students, to attack Luria (cf. the quarrels among Jesus' disciples). Luria and Cordovero were both thought to have descended to the most secret depths of wisdom and to have died young as the result of the work of some evildoer or of an evil act in their time. The idea was very popular, but Vital, who lived a long life, said it came from people who wanted to spread scandal about the secret Torah and its students.

HAYIM VITAL (CALABRESE)

Vital was born in the land of Israel, probably in Safed itself in 1542 or 1543. His father, Yosef, is recorded as living there and as practicing as a scribe; the *tefillins* ("phylacteries") he wrote were executed with great diligence (and were expensive). Vital writes that his father's soul was that of Ezra the scribe and of Rabbi Me'ir, as well as of the scribe Yeshbav. Vital studied with R. Moshe Alsheikh and received rabbinic ordination from him in Jerusalem in 1590. Ordination had just been renewed due to the feeling that the messiah's coming was imminent, and that the rabbis of Israel had the right and responsibility to renew the lost tradition. (R. Alsheikh had received his ordination from R. Yosef Karo.) Vital made a living from his several teaching and rabbinic positions in Damascus, Safed, and Jerusalem. This income was augmented by donations from abroad, as were the livings of most members of the community of Jews who resided in the land of Israel in this period and for a long time afterwards. Vital merited the particular support of Yehoshua ben Nun, a wealthy resident of Safed and the principal of a yeshiva there. He must have been well reimbursed, as well, for his occasional preaching in Damascus, Egypt, Safed, and Jerusalem.

In addition to learning traditional subjects, Vital began to study the Kabbalah when he was quite young. His initial explorations into it, like those of Luria, were guided by Cordovero's writings. But Vital also became quite interested in the magical Kabbalah and in alchemy. The integration of these two radically different approaches to the world of mystery—the speculative and the experiential Kabbalah— is typical of the period. Vital, in fact, after more than two years of devoted study, wrote a compendium on alchemy and practical magic, which he later came to look upon as an error, if not a transgression. Nevertheless, he remained quite close to seers of different kinds (those who looked into mirrors or oil or water; those who asked dream questions and received answers; chiromancers) in both the Jewish and Moslem communities and often turned to them with questions for them to ask heavenly authorities. He reverted to magic practices, perhaps in order to make a living, after the time he had spent with Luria in Safed. Some money also came in from his writings. His brother, Moshe, taking advantage of Vital when he was in the throes of a serious illness, received a bribe of 500 gold pieces from Yehoshua ben Nun in return for allowing one hundred scribes to copy Vital's compilation of the Lurianic material, together with Vital's expansion of it, some 600 pages, according to the tale. Like Karo, Vital lived a long life; and he saw two wives and all but one of his children die. His relations with his first wife were apparently poor. He resided intermittently in Jerusalem, Safed, and Damascus. He was seriously ill several times and intermittently blind from 1604 until his death in 1620. His son Shmu'el took over the preparation of his materials for publication. Ultimately, Shmu'el's rearrangement and editing of the *Eight Gates* became the best-known presentation of the thoughts of both Vital and Luria.

Vital is undoubtedly the most important kabbalist after Luria. The main stream of Jewish mysticism from the end of the sixteenth century to the present flows from the explications and expansions of the Zohar made by these two men and then presented by Vital. The Zohar itself has come to be read as Luria and Vital interpreted it. Contradictory and varying viewpoints appear frequently in Vital's own work as well as in his compilation of Luria's teachings. It is quite difficult to know, at this point, how much of what is attributed to Luria is actually the work of Vital. The two studied together from 1570 to 1572 and certainly influenced each other. Luria felt that his teaching was all for Vital and for no one else. Each recognized the other as the messiah; each recognized himself in the role of the messiah of the lineage of Joseph. Vital had no peers, though he organized study groups. He must have been a good preacher, specializing in sermons urging repentance in the face of the coming time, but he was also capable of inspiring dislike in others, and he cut nothing like Luria's charismatic figure. He ceased his public preaching for long periods and might have given it up altogether following Luria's death. He was even jealous of others in the Safed community who were more charismatic than he was—particularly the poet Najara—and was filled with doubts about his own messianic role. His long, bitter struggle with Yakov Abulafia, an important rabbi in Damascus, came down to a mere quarrel over prestige, though Vital's claim to messiahship was a serious threat to the independence and validity of any lesser claim. He sought absolute control over the propagation of Luria's theology. Though he was initially unsuccessful in gaining this, his prolific writings have assured him a place equal to that of his teacher. His spiritual journal, *The Book of Visions* (*sefer ha-hezyonot*), gives frank insight into a complex spirit, at times arrogant, at times utterly lacking in self-confidence; at times intellectual, at times given over to rank superstition and magic. The journal has four parts: (1) the events of his life; (2) the dreams he had and "can remember"; (3) dreams others had about him; (4) the words of his master, the Ari, about him and his soul.

All the accounts quoted here are from Vital's *Book of Visions*, edited from the autograph by Aeshcoly (Jerusalem, 1954). There were some previous, ill-prepared editions of the work that had quite a bit of influence on later kabbalists, especially on the Hasidic master, R. Yitzhak Eizik Safrin, of Komarno (see chapter 9). Aeshcoly died before he finished the annotations to his edition of the text. A new edition and a new translation by R. Morris Faierstein are in press.

> 1.2. 5,314 ("Hand") [years] since the creation. I was twelve, and a great sage in the art of palmistry looked at the lines of my palms and said to me, "Know that when you are 24 years old, many thoughts will come into your heart [urging you to] give up studying the Torah against your will for two and a half years, and thereafter two ways will appear before you, one toward the Garden of Eden and the second toward Gehenna. And the choice will be yours to make then—and if you choose the way to Gehenna there will be no man more wicked than you in your generation; and if you choose the way to the Garden of Eden you will transcend beyond measure all those of your generation in wisdom and the fear of sin." And none of what he said failed to come to pass.

"Two and a half years" refers to the time Vital devoted to the study of the arts of magic and alchemy, rather than preaching repentance and studying the speculative theology of the Kabbalah. He abandoned this "way" but continued to resort to it and attend to it, while worrying that he had harmed himself irreparably. "Gehenna" is used here to mean utter perdition, rather than in its technical, Lurianic, sense as a place of purification for the souls of those who have sinned.

> 1.9. 5334. R. Mass'oud Cohen of Der'a came to Safed and told me that when he was leaving he went to say farewell to R. Abraham Avshalom, a great sage and

knowledgeable in future events. He [Avshalom] said to him, "To life [le-hayyim] and health." And he said to him, "The meaning is that he [Cohen] should come to [me], Hayim." And he gave him greetings in my name. And he told [him] all my characteristics and that I was a certain young man living in Safed. And he said to him, "Say to him in my name, that he is the messiah of the lineage of Joseph and that he absolutely must go to Jerusalem and live there for two years, but in the third year the choice is his to make, whether he will live there. And after the first year the spirit of the Lord will begin to move in him. And from then on there will be argument concerning him between the men of Jerusalem and the men of the Galilee. And the men of Egypt will aid Jerusalem but those of the Galilee will prevail and bring him back to live there in the Galilee and there thousands and myriads of Israel will gather to him. And he will reign over them and he will teach them Torah. And then I will go there and I will be the messiah of the lineage of David and he will be the messiah of the lineage of Joseph, [my] aide. And that he must be careful when he goes to Jerusalem as mentioned, not to gather men around him, for great harm will be drawn to him on this account, and that he will be brought into prison for this reason. And that which our rabbis of blessed memory said concerning the messiah of the lineage of Joseph, that he will be killed, I will struggle with all my might to rescue him from that decree, for it is said of him, 'He asked life of you / You gave it to him.' [Ps. 21:5]. Of which the explanation is, that the messiah of the lineage of David will seek of the Name may he be blessed that he give life to the messiah of the lineage of Joseph who is named Hayim, and the Name may he be blessed will grant him life."

Among the four holy cities of the land of Israel—Tiberias, Hebron, Jerusalem, and Safed—the struggle for primacy in this period was between Safed and Jerusalem. The move of the messiah to Jerusalem in order to take up residence there, after his appearance in the Galilee, had eschatological implications. Vital's uncertainty regarding the right time for him to move to Jerusalem, as reflected in his many reports of others' assertions, displays his self-doubts. He never did stay in Jerusalem for any length of time. Perhaps the competition among Jerusalem scholars and authorities did not suit him. He was never a legal authority of any consequence, while many of the Jerusalem personalities were. In the above account, moreover, the mention of imprisonment refers to the close attention paid by Ottoman authorities to mass disturbances among the populace, particularly in the sphere of religion. The conjunction of religious support for a political insurrection in a messianic event and governmental repression is a constant theme in the accounts, regularly expected and brought about by the acts of both parties involved.

1.24. Now, in section 22, I wrote what happened in the matter of the spirit itself which was in the daughter of Rafael Anav, that which I saw with my own eyes and that which Rafael and R. Yakov Ashkenazi told me, and this all took place on the Sabbath of the New Moon of Av, and on the morning of the first day of the week [the spirit] came out, without doubt, and ascended to its place. Thereafter, other things happened which were not through the agency of the spirit mentioned while it was yet clothed in her, for it had already left, and the girl was left completely healthy, but occasionally saying that she saw visions awake and in dreams by the agency of angels and, infrequently, of the spirit mentioned as well. And therefore I had doubts about her words, whether they were true or mixed of good and evil for the reason mentioned and for another reason as well: because I did not see this with my eyes as I saw in the first case. But what I marveled at was that her words were nothing but [concerning] repentance and the fear of the Lord and words of reproof. So I won't refrain from writing them, as they have been reported by trustworthy people who were present.

The night of the seventh of Av, they said to her that she should say to me that at first the soul of a particular *tanna* [scholar of the Mishna] was revealed to me by means of the *yihud* [act of mystical union] with which I joined myself to him, and that it had been a long time, actually two and a half years, since he had been revealed to me. For two reasons: one, that I had abandoned the *yihudim* mentioned; and two, that I had abandoned my preaching and reproving the people to call them to repent as I had at first. And on account of these two reasons themselves, my daughter had died in that plague. The night of the eighth of Av, Elijah of blessed memory said to her while she was awake at the time of the Sabbath *kiddush*, "Say to R. Hayim and the other sages of the city that they are failing to carry out everything that they have heard and a great evil will fall upon the dwellers of Damascus therefore, and in particular to R. Hayim. Say to him also, Why did you sin on the sixth of Av and bring down an angel in a cup to ask him, 'Should I believe all of the things that we have said to him [me] by way of the spirit mentioned?' And see, his master, of blessed memory in his life also said to him that he had only come to the world to call the people to repentance and that the angel he brought down also said all this to him and still he hesitates and is indecisive and does not altogether believe! I fear for him that there might come upon him, may it not happen, many troubles because of his entreaty."

The tenth of Av I asked her through her father, "Why has the righteous one known to me ceased speaking with me and what is his name and is there any hope to bring him back?" And she answered me that on the night of the eleventh of Av she had seen my teacher of blessed memory and he had said to her, "Say to him on my behalf that he should stop asking these questions so many times. And I am not able to give him an answer except for this, these three words: *ashrei metei beytekha* 'Happy are those who die in your house' and he will understand the meaning of the words on his own."

The night of the twelfth of Av she saw my teacher of blessed memory in a dream, in a cave, and he said to her, "What answer has R. Hayim given you?" She said to him, "He said to me that he didn't understand those three words." He said to her, "There could be nothing simpler. Has his mind stopped working so that he doesn't understand? Where is the art that I taught him? Let him remember that evil spirit which I brought forth from him. Now it is four years that he has not seen me in a dream, and now I thought I would return to him, but since he hasn't understood the words of my response I don't want to return to him."

And here, in my humble opinion, is the meaning of the evil spirit mentioned, a matter of the resurrection of the dead, in that he revived me on our walk to the village of Akhbara, because the spirit that was in the grave of the goy had caused me harm, or perhaps it was how my mouth had become twisted in the first *yihud* that I had learned.

Vital's friends, as well as the visionaries and magicians he consulted, must have grown weary of his constant demands for proof of his role. In the account above, the subject of the most famous case of possession (in Damascus) puts that emotion into the words of her contact. By recording the criticism of his teacher, Vital himself acknowledges that he has been conducting himself poorly, and he testifies to his own inability to believe in himself when he fails to understand what his teacher has hinted at. The "twisted" mouth indicates that their communication has been at fault and that Vital has failed; the words from the other side come out of his mouth in the wrong way.

2.5. 5326, the night of the Sabbath of the eighth of Tevet. I said *kiddush* and sat down at the table to eat. My eyes were flowing with tears; I was sorrowful and moaning for on the tenth of Heshvan past I had married my wife Hannah and a spell had been put on me. I said to the Name, blessed is he, "I took her back as the result of a dream question. How can such distress as this have befallen me? Especially for now there is against me the transgression of wasted seed when I examine myself [after being] with her?" I also wept on account of the two years I wasted, away from the study of the Torah, as I wrote in the pamphlet concerning the matters of my soul, section 2. And as a result of my great anxiety I ate nothing and went to bed weeping until I fell asleep from crying.

And I saw myself seated in the house of the master Shem Tov Halevi of blessed memory praying the *minha* [afternoon] prayer that is called *et-ratson* on the Sabbath. And after the prayer there stood facing me an old man who looked like the master Hayim Halevi my neighbor of blessed memory, and he called my name and said to me, "Rabbi Hayim, do you want to go out with me now to the field to accompany the Sabbath Queen as she goes away as you are accustomed to as she enters, and there I will show you awesome things?" I said to him, "I am ready." We went out and walked to the wall of the old tower on the west of Safed in front of the khan, where the opening in the wall once stood.

I looked and there was a high mountain, its top in the sky. He said to me, "Come up the mountain with me and there I will tell you the words of the mission upon which I have been sent to you." And in the blink of an eye I saw him standing on the top of the mountain, and I was still sitting at the bottom, for I could not go up at all for it was as steep as a wall, not sloped like other mountains. I said to him, "I am astonished, for I am a young man and I could not climb up at all and you are an old man and went all the way up in the blink of an eye." He said to me, "You, Hayim, don't know that I go up and down this mountain a thousand times a day to carry out the missions of the Place [i.e., God], so why should you be astonished at me?" When I noticed that at first he had called me "R. Hayim" and now he called me "Hayim," and not "Rabbi," and when I heard the frightening things he said to me, I knew that he was certainly Elijah of blessed memory of the tribe of Levi and my eyes flowed with tears and I, I took my leave in great fear. Then, in tears, I pleaded with him and said, "Let my soul be worthy in your sight and raise me up with you." He said to me, "Do not be afraid, for this is why I was sent to you." And he took hold of my arm and raised me up to the top of the mountain with him in the blink of an eye. I looked and saw on the summit of that mountain a ladder standing on the ground with its top reaching in to the sky; and there were only three rungs on it and between each rung and the next the distance was the height of a man. He said to me, "They have given me permission to help you this far; from here on see what you can do yourself." He went away and disappeared and I wept from great sorrow.

And then a woman of refinement, as beautiful as the sun, was standing at the top of the ladder and I thought to myself that she was my mother. She said, "Why are you weeping here, Hayim? I heard your tears and have come to help you." And she extended her right hand and raised me up to the top of the ladder. I looked and there was a large round window from which a great flame of fire came forth, back and forth like lightning, with great force, and it burned all that was present there. I knew in my soul that this was the flame of the turning sword at the entrance to the Garden of Eden. I called out to the woman from the bitterness of my soul and said to her, "Mother, Mother, help me or this flame will burn me up." She said, "There is none who can help you with this flame but yourself alone. So I will advise you what you can do: Put your hand on your head and you will find a woolen thread there, white as snow. Take it and put it in the window of the flame and it will close and you can pass quickly by."

And it seems to me in my humble opinion that the thread signified that my black hair—which was Din [Strict Judgment]—had turned white by some merit found in the mystery of "and the hair of his head was like clean wool." [Dan. 7:9]. So I did it and passed by quickly and immediately the flame began to come forth again as it had [before]. Then the woman disappeared.

And Elijah, of blessed memory, returned and appeared to me as before and took hold of my right hand and said to me, "Come with me to the place to which they sent me at first to bring you." And he brought me to a great and measureless courtyard. Inside it were flowing great rivers of sweet water watering that garden. And on both banks of the rivers were fruit trees, pleasant to look at and endlessly fresh and rich. And most of them were apple trees, whose fragrance was like that of myrrh and aloes. And the trees were very tall and the branches that extended from them were bent down almost to the ground so that they formed a sort of shelter. And in that garden were birds without number that looked like white geese walking about the length and breadth of the garden and studying the Mishna tractate of Shabbat, for it was then the night of the Sabbath as mentioned at the beginning of the dream. And while they walked they read a [passage of] Mishna or a chapter and stretched up their necks and ate apples from the tree itself, then drank water from the rivers. And this was what they did constantly. And I understood immediately that they were the souls of the righteous, those who composed the Mishna, but I didn't know why they had the forms of geese or other birds and not the forms of humans. And they conducted me on farther inside, until I saw a great and high platform inside the garden as if on top of a high hill and no house was beneath it. And it was the height of a man above the ground of the garden, and its entrance was to the west, and there was a ladder of three stone steps from the ground to the entrance to the platform. And Elijah of blessed memory disappeared from my view. And I went up the ladder by myself and went in the entrance of the platform and saw the Name, blessed is he, seated on a chair along the southern wall in the middle, and his appearance was as the Ancient of Days, old and his beard as white as snow, utterly splendid, and there were righteous sitting there on the floor before him on beautiful new carpets and tapestries learning Torah from his mouth. And I knew in my soul that these were the righteous called the Ones of the Ascent and they were in the form of humans, looking constantly upon the countenance of the Presence and learning Torah from his own mouth and that this was not so for those who composed the Mishna, for they were in the form of birds and geese for it is said of them, "One who sees a goose in a dream may look forward to wisdom." And they were standing in the courtyard and in the garden and did not receive the countenance of the Presence constantly as did the Ones of the Ascent and did not learn Torah from his own mouth.

And when I entered and I saw his face, I was alarmed, and trembling seized me, and I fell on my face to the earth at my feet and could not gather my strength at all. And he extended his hand and took hold of me by my right hand and said, "Hayim, my son, arise, why have you fallen upon your face? Do not be afraid." I said to him, "My Lord, I have no strength, and all my glory has become my destroyer from the great fear I have of you, and I do not have the power to arise." And he said to me, "Look, I have sustained you, and I have made you strong. Stand up, and sit to my right in this space that is vacant, right beside me." I said to him, "How shall I sit by your right hand in this place which is already prepared for the master R. Yosef Karo to sit?" And he said to me, "That was my intention at first, and then I gave him another place, and I have given you this place, and I have made it ready for you." I said to him, "But this is the place of Samuel of Ramah [the prophet] of blessed memory." And he said to me, "It is true that this is his place, but when the Temple was destroyed, he took it upon himself not to sit in this place until the Temple of the time to come is built. And ever since, he has gone away to Jerusalem to the destroyed Temple and waits there always, mourning over it, until the time of the end when it will be built, and therefore his place is vacant, and I have assigned it for you to be seated in it." Then I seated myself at his right, just beside him, on tapestries upon the ground like the rest of the righteous who were there.

He said to me, "Is this a goodly place in your eyes?" I said to him, "Who is there who could recount the praise of this Place of Ascent? Surely you will make clear to me, why do those who composed the Mishna differ from these Ones of the Ascent so that there is such a difference between them as I have seen with my own eyes?" And he said, "Have you indeed forgotten what the sages said, that in the time to come the Holy One, blessed is he, will make wings for the righteous, and they will float upon the water; and they said this concerning [the men of] this group who are called those who composed the Mishna, who appear in the form of birds with wings and float upon the water of the rivers of the Garden of Eden, as you have seen with your own eyes?" And then I said to him, "My Lord, I have recalled what is written in the introduction to the Book of Repairs [of the Zohar] concerning the verse, "If he calls . . . ." and "the mother broods upon the fledglings . . . and the children you may take for yourself"—that the fledglings are those who composed the Mishna, the children are those who composed the Kabbalah, and those are the Ones of the Ascent and are in human form."

I said to him again, "My Lord, let my soul be worthy in your sight, leave me in this place and do not send me back down to the lowly world for it is known to you that my intention is to do your will, and I fear that the leaven that is in the dough will cause me to sin and I will lose this holy place." And he said to me, "You are still a young man, and you have yet time to engage yourself in my Torah and my commandments, and you must return there to perfect your soul and at the end of your days you will come here to this place. And if you are afraid that you will sin if you descend, extend the palm of your right hand to me and swear to me that you will not leave off engaging in the Torah on account of any other matter at all, and I too will swear to you that if thus you do, I will not change or exchange this place of yours for any other person under any circumstances, and this will be your place, to my right, eternally established." Then I raised my hand and swore to fulfill all that was said and he swore to me to fulfill his word as said and said to me, "Go in peace and remember and do not forget any of these things." Then I descended from the Ascent there, I by myself, and found myself standing in this lowly world while in the dream itself and saw nothing of what I had seen when I first ascended.

This account and the following one reveal quite a lot about the intermingling of Vital's daily life with his cosmic visions of himself and his teacher and their missions. In later material, particularly that of the Hasidic messiahs, this intermingling will be intentionally brought forward; here, it is unself-conscious. Vital's difficulties with his wife, which he speaks of in more than one place, lead to his encounter with a kinder woman, his mother, and to her symbolization as the Sabbath Queen. The time is at the end of the Sabbath, as the prayer setting tells us. Vital doubts himself fit for the attention of his mother/the Shekhina, a theme that recurs, when he sees that he is less physically capable than his guide, an older man, and he reacts to the change in the way the guide addresses him. At the beginning of the episode, Vital writes that he feels his punishment (the distress he suffers with his wife, including the spilled semen) is his own fault, and due, in part at least, to his involvement with magic. The punishment has come from the cosmic aspect of divine strict judgment (Din). In his mother's forgiving presence, the punishment for his deeds has been rescinded. Left to himself at the crucial point of his journey, he gains a token from his mother. The thread, he writes, is his hair, a symbol of the emanation of the divine into this world. It has been black (contrasting his youth and folly with Elijah's age and holiness) and now turns white as it passes into the realm of Hesed, the aspect of mercy, Din's counterpart. He passes through, his guide returns, and he views paradise in some conventional symbols. The apple trees, drawn from the Zohar, are a symbol of the Shekhina, which became central in the teachings of Luria and in his hymns. The apples themselves unite the colors red, white, and green, which symbolize, respectively, the merciful, judgmental and perfectly balanced aspects of the cosmos. He encounters the "Ancient of Days" (as Daniel describes the God of the Apocalypse), again an elder. Vital's self-doubt arises again, but this fatherly figure extends help to him and takes him by his right hand, restoring his strength. Vital confirms God's opinion of him as the right man for the place he has been given when he produces the correct interpretation of what he has seen in the Garden, supporting the validity of his school and his absorption in mysticism. God then assures him of his place in spite of what may come. But Vital has fallen into uncertainty again in the next account.

2.6. And three months later, on the night of the Great Sabbath [the Sabbath before Passover], I dreamed and saw myself going about in a large field, and I passed through the entrance of the Ascent mentioned and remembered that that was where I had gone up and made the oath to the Lord of all, as mentioned. Then I went up the same ladder and entered the opening. What had happened to me the first time happened again: I fell on my face in fear, everything as was mentioned, and after I arose I sat in the same place mentioned.

Then he said to me, "Why have you forgotten what you promised me in this place?" I said to him, "I have been engaged in study, but it is true that I have not worked as is well and fit at your Torah. With all this, tell me if, Heaven forbid, your oath is annulled?" And he said to me, "Don't be afraid. Your place is still where it was and prepared for you, and our oaths are yet in good standing. So go back and fulfill your oath as is fit, and I too will fulfill my covenant with you and give you this place which I have promised you." And he went on, "Hayim my son, go now to the congregation of the Ashkenazim, for they are bringing in a new Torah scroll, and sing and play before it as is your custom in honoring a Torah scroll. And take your father-in-law, R. Moshe Sa'adia, with you, and say to him that he must not be careless in carrying out this commandment, for it is his custom as well, for it is a great commandment." Then I departed from his presence and bid him farewell and he too bade me farewell.

I left through the entrance to the Ascent and found myself in this world and ran into my father-in-law who was searching for me as well. He said to me, "I've been looking for you for a long time so that we could go together to pay honor to a Torah scroll." I said to him, "They commanded me too in a certain place to come look for you for the same purpose." We went to the Safed road, and there were a lot of people conducting a Torah scroll finely decorated with garments and apples of gold and going before it with burning candles and oil lamps and singing before it until we came into the Ashkenazi synagogue where the congregation was already praying the *yotser* [prayer] of Sabbath, for this dream was on the Sabbath, as mentioned, and we prayed the *yotser* with them together with the *shema'* and the *amidah* and the cantor's repetition [of those prayers]. Then we opened that Torah scroll and seven men read the portion of the week from it, as is the practice on the Sabbath. Then we prayed the *musaf* [additional] prayers and when the praying was over I wanted to leave the synagogue. But my teacher R. Moshe Alsheikh and my father and master, of blessed memory and my father-in-law caught hold of me and asked, "Where are you in such a hurry to go? Stay, for a circumcision will be done here now." I sat down and they brought in an infant to be circumcised. They gave me the child to sit as his *sandak* [godfather], and they circumcised him and said to me, "See, this is your son." Then they themselves brought a great and splendid feast to the synagogue, and all of us ate the feast of the circumcision there. And I awoke.

Two years later my teacher the Ashkenazi of blessed memory came to Safed, and I studied with him. Near the time of his death, he said to me, "A son will be born to you now, your wife is already pregnant with him, and he is five hundred levels above your own level, but there is some doubt as to whether he will survive," and so on. My teacher of blessed memory died and the son mentioned died too after a year and a half. I named him Yosef, and he was perfect in knowledge. One week before he died, he spoke words that were near-prophecy.

And I think that my teacher of blessed memory was the scroll of the Torah of the Ashkenazim, and his soul migrated to my son, Yosef, who was the child I circumcised in the dream.

Once more in despair, Vital has another vision of himself being reassured by God on the Sabbath before Passover. In his dream, he returns to this world, encounters three older male figures (though, significantly, not his father), and celebrates the installation of a new scroll of the Torah in the synagogue associated with Luria, Ashkenazi synagogue. The Sabbath is the Shekhina, among the days of the week; a total of ten men, representing all the ten *sefirot* now in working order, participate with Vital in an unexpected celebration of the circumcision of a child who turns out to be his son. Vital sees that his son is the new Torah, is Luria, the expected messiah. Since the account is certainly transcribed in this form a good deal later than the time of the event, Vital knows that Luria has not redeemed the world. Sadly, he knows too that this son, Yosef, has died. His son Shmu'el has the next vision that Vital records.

3.33 On the 24th of Shevat my son Shmu'el dreamed that two Turks came to my home, and I closed the door. Then one of the sides of the door opened on its own, and they came into the house that way and sat down beside me and said to me, "Don't be afraid. We are righteous Jews and have come in the form of Turks so that you will receive our words with joy and carry them out." One of them wore a white turban and the other a green one. I saw that they had come to hear words of Torah from me, and I spoke to them. During the speech, I explained to them the degree of the first-born male and his importance to the Blessed One. My son said to me, "What is this degree?" I said to him, "Look. The messiah is a first-born. On his father's side he is from the tribe of Judah while his mother's family is from the tribe of Reuben, the first-born, even though some part of the birthright was given to Joseph. All this concerns his body. But his soul is from Joseph who took the main part of Reuben's birthright, and he is also the first-born of his mother, Rachel." Then my son turned his face towards the one wearing the green turban and said to him as if jesting, "See, I am my mother's first-born; is it possible that the messiah will be one of my children?" He said to me, "It is possible that you will be or that one of your seed will be." Afterwards he spoke with me and said, "You must know that we have come to you on a mission from the wise old man who dwells forever in Jerusalem and who is your ardent friend. Now take this message that has been sent to you." I said, "I know him well and that he is my great friend. Is it possible that he lives yet?" And he said to me, "Why should you be surprised? Why shouldn't he be alive?" I took the message and read it. Many matters, some very lengthy, were written in it, but what he [Shmu'el] remembered was only: "You, R. Hayim, already know how wondrously esteemed you are in Heaven. You also know that the Redemption can come only through your power and that it is therefore in your interest to make haste on your own part to bring the Redemption nigh; you will receive a great reward. If you delay, Heaven will force you to do the work in the end. Since you will be forced to do it you will not receive a great reward. Certain it is that the Redemption can come only through your power, whether you do it willingly or are forced to do it." This was what was written in the message.

After I read the message, the one wearing the green turban repeated the terms of his mission, as it had been written. His companion said to him, "Why are you relating all this? Does he not know it all very well?" Then I gave them something to eat and drink. Then [Shmu'el] awoke.

On the fourteenth of Adar II, R. Caleb saw my son Shmu'el in a dream. He had a long red beard. R. Caleb was astonished. I said to him, "But look, my son is the reincarnation of my teacher, the Ashkenazi of blessed memory. He has been reborn in him now so that I might teach him this [mystic] art, to perfect him and compensate him for that which he taught me."

Shmu'el is Vital's firstborn, whom he had with his second wife, the one he liked. Shmu'el is the reborn Luria and will be the successful messiah. Vital's account of his son's dream (there are many of these in the third part of his journal) brightens the passages that have shown him in error and in despair, in sickness and near death. All this has been caused by his own doubt. He has not felt himself worthy and has not taken on his assigned task with full confidence. Vital associated his lack of success, his lack of charisma, especially as compared with his teacher, and his jealousy of other more successful preachers and teachers with his unwillingness to assume the burden. Here, he is reassured that, willy-nilly, he has his job to do. The unwillingness of the candidate is a constant in the account he gives to others or even, as here, to himself. He shows that he has no interest in putting himself forward and risking the damage he must perforce suffer, but this is no pose or rhetorical device—Vital knows himself and has real doubts.

BIBLIOGRAPHIC NOTE   One can read about Safed in S. Schechter "Safed in the Sixteenth Century," *Studies in Judaism*, 2d ser. (Philadelphia, 1908); in the introduction to R. J. Z. Werblowsky, *Joseph Karo: Lawyer and Mystic* (Philadelphia, 1977); and in H. Ben Sasson, "The Jewish Image of Erez Israel," in M. Ma'oz, ed., *Studies on Palestine during the Ottoman Period* (Jerusalem, 1975). A work (in Hebrew) with an extensive bibliography is N. Schur, *The History of Safed* (Tel Aviv, 1983). The *Encyclopaedia Judaica* articles on Luria, Vital, Karo et al. were written by Gershom Scholem and contain bibliographies as well. Some of this material was updated in Scholem, *Kabbalah* (New York, 1975). *Jerusalem Studies in Jewish Thought* 10 (1992) is entirely devoted to the Lurianic Kabbalah, with important contributions from J. Dan, Y. Liebes, M. Idel, B. Sack, and M. Pachter.

7

THE MESSIAH OF IZMIR
Shabtai Zvi

In the seventeenth century, outside the land of Israel, Jewish messianic contenders again began to proliferate. This chapter focuses on the first and foremost of these, Shabtai Zvi, who attained a higher level of fame and influence than had any Jewish messiah since Jesus. Zvi was a student of the Lurianic Kabbalah; his own revolutionary view of cosmic repair turned legal and normative behavior on its head. Others, seeking to abide by his teachings engaged in acts that ranged from ascetic to antinomian. Zvi saw himself as a sultan rather than a military leader, but this posture was real only in his imagination. His conversion to Islam was interpeted as if it echoed the conversions of the Jews of Iberia to Catholicism, but in his case it would come to be seen not as forgivable in one facing death but as required for the messiah, who had to reach the lowest depths of baseness in order to gather there the sparks of light that, once raised up, would complete the repair of the cosmic order.

At this time, the fire of the Lurianic Kabbalah, with its assurance of the repair of the universe and the messiah soon to come if only true support and belief could be won, continued to warm Jewish communities around the world. It was transmitted through an elite and made palatable for a broad public. In the mid-seventeenth century, Jewish communities throughout the world trembled on the brink of a strange future. Among other pressures, the ascent of the wealthy, enfranchised Amsterdam community, on the one hand, and the Cossack massacres of Ukrainian Jews, on the other, provided new hopes and fears, and the usual evidence that the apocalyptic cataclysm was close at hand. The messiah who would return all Jews to Israel was awaited daily. When the Jews of Holland, many of them refugees from Catholic persecutions and converts who had reconverted, were given quasi citizenship, their new freedom and their old doubts and liberal ideas brought them to confront new liberal schools of thought. They and other Jews considered Zvi's messianic candidacy a legitimate one and rose passionately to his support. Some followers later fell away for a very interesting reason: The idea of the "messiah of the lineage of Joseph" had come into existence in the early first century CE as a response to the parousia, the "second coming" of Jesus. Both these ideas, among others, provided explanations for the failure—particularly, the death—of a messiah that allowed his believers to continue to believe in the propriety of his mission and of the missions of others after him. The idea of two messiahs having begun in this way became, by the time of Shabtai Zvi, a necessary feature of a messiah event. Shabtai Zvi was the "messiah of the lineage of David"—that is, the second of the two messiahs and the victorious one. Several attempts were made to find the individual who had preceded him, the messiah of the lineage of Joseph who had fought and died and prepared the way for him, but a convincing candidate was never found. For not a few followers, the absence of a preliminary messiah cast the status of Shabtai Zvi as the messiah of the lineage of David into such doubt that they abandoned their support of him.

The most important factor that afforded Zvi credibility after the height of the movement was probably the parallel drawn between his own life and the crypto-Jewish experience that followed his conversion to Islam under duress (in 1666). Nathan of Gaza, a resident of the land of Israel and a brilliant student of the Lurianic Kabbalah, prophesied the advent and nature of the messiah and then found him in Zvi. He explained the conversion as a further step the messiah had to take to achieve the redemption of the broken bits of the universe; Zvi had descended into the ultimate darkness in order to reclaim the energy that had fallen there, sunken in the mire. This theology granted absolution, and more, to the reconverted conversos; it sanctified their initial conversions. Shabbateanism (as the movement associated with Shabtai is known) retained followers until the early twentieth century and spawned messiah after messiah, not only in the Ottoman Empire but also deep in central Europe and in Poland, each one claiming the temporary possession or the inheritance of the soul of Zvi.

Shabtai was a handsome figure. His mother doted on him. He studied Jewish law and mysticism, conducted himself as a pure and lonely penitent, and eventually taught the Lurianic system of the Zohar to a few students in Izmir. He emitted a sweet fragrance, had a lovely complexion, a fine voice, and he loved to sing both Jewish and local favorites, particularly the *romanceros*, ballads of Iberia that had come to Turkey with the exiles. He developed odd practices, such as swimming in the sea at night and wearing white robes, that attracted attention and amplified his reputation. He revealed himself as the messiah in 1648 and pronounced the explicit name of God to indicate that the time of the redemption of Israel had come. This early proclamation was not met favorably; he was excommunicated and banished from Izmir. In Salonika, Zvi again carried out ceremonies intended to indicate his messiahship and divinity. In one of these, he married the Torah. Again he was banished. After spending some time wandering, he came to Jerusalem and to the attention of Nathan of Gaza. Nathan convinced Zvi that despite his apparent rejection—or, rather, given the evidence of his suffering—he *was* the messiah.

In March of 1664, as Zvi's illumination reached its pinnacle, he wedded a woman called Sarah. His first two marriages had been annulled because they had never been consummated, but this marriage was apparently successful. Sarah was an orphan from central Europe, her parents having been killed in anti-Jewish riots. She had found work in a Christian hospice but had left it to wander in madness through Italy. She conducted herself licentiously, read futures in cards, and performed magic. The tragedy of her origins, her contact with, and escape from, Christianity, and her strangeness drew Zvi to her. In his perception, her sexual experience was reborn as true virginity. When they married, she became both "Queen Sarah" and "Rebecca" for Zvi and his followers. Zvi had no children with Sarah but may have sired children in a much later marriage following Sarah's death.

By the time Zvi returned to Izmir in 1665, a flood of letters and legends had preceded him and effectively reversed his ban. The excitement that greeted him spread throughout the Turkish empire and, from there, throughout the Jewish world, making a special impact on descendants of Marranos in Italy, and the Netherlands and on Christians in England. Zvi and many of his followers abandoned many traditional practices, including the dietary code and sexual restrictions, and some discarded rational economic conduct. The old code of law was reinterpreted as it was made to suit a redeemed age. The new law involved the remission, and even the reversal, of the practices of the previous dispensation. Meanwhile, many of his followers inside and outside Turkey turned to penitential practices.

Such an uproar surrounded Zvi that the government decided to imprison him, in Constantinople at first; from there he was transferred to Gallipoli. He lived there in what would become known in his movement as the Tower of Strength. This was actually a prison for nobles who were awaiting trial; a Jew had never before been so honorably and importantly treated. Shabbatean theology saw Zvi's imprisonment as further evidence of the end of the current dispensation, marking the stage just prior to the messiah's kingship; the prison was nothing other than a palace.

In the summer of 1666, Shabtai Zvi, threatened with execution by the sultan, who had taken alarm at the size and temper of his following—converted to Islam. As a convert, he received an honorary post and a salary from the sultan's purse. His conversion stunned many who had believed that he would ascend to the messianic throne, and that the Jews would rise ever higher, dominate the world, and return to the land of Israel. Others understood it as an act of necessity, which would further the redemption of the lost sparks of light hidden within the shards of darkness. Nathan promoted this view against the plethora of alternative explanations. The movement splintered into many rival camps, several of which were led by messianic heirs who emphasized different aspects of the theology and practices of Zvi and Nathan. Zvi died in Dulcigno (now Ulcinj, Yugoslavia) on September 17, 1676.

There is no need here to delve deeply into the marvelously varied and creative ideas that appear in the Shabbatean theology developed by Nathan, Shabtai, and others; Gershom Scholem, an explicator of genius and devotion who gained an understanding of the Shabbatean religion that surpassed that of any believer, has done that in his great work, *Sabbatai Sevi: The Mystical Messiah*. Though the theology continued to develop during the final years of Zvi's life, focusing especially on the meaning of his conversion and exile, the necessity of evil, and of evil acts that transform themselves and become good, is a constant of the faith. The theology made strange sense, was not entirely new, and was, to a degree, independent of the history of Zvi himself and his own times. It became especially compelling, however, when it explained Zvi's life, incidents within the Jewish world, and the affairs of the sect and world events. Scholem claims that Zvi was a manic-depressive. However the facts may seem to fit current psychological models, this is no easy matter to verify. Zvi did undergo moods of depression and exaltation, perform "strange acts," and achieve illuminated states (Figure 7.1).

Account by Ben Ozer

The passages here are from the account written by Leib ben Ozer, in Yiddish, and are taken here from Sh. Zucker and R. Plesser, eds., Zalman Shazar, *The Story of Shabbetay Zevi by R. Leib ben Ozer (Amsterdam, 1711–1718)*, from the original Yiddish ms. with Hebrew translation, introduction and notes (Jerusalem, 1978). He wrote the account in Amsterdam not long after Zvi died in 1676 in Dulcigno, ten years after his apostasy. Having been neither a follower nor a fervent opponent of Zvi, Leib is relatively objective and fairly complete. He sought information assiduously and notes its authenticity when he reports it. He cites letters and other documents and refers to having used oral accounts. He remarks on his failure to establish certain facts.

After Shabtai Zvi had been living in Izmir a month or three, he made it known that the Holy Spirit had said to him that he should have intercourse with [Sarah] the wife he had married in Egypt since, according to what he said, he had not touched her until then, just as he had not touched his two previous wives; but that now it had been told him in the Holy Spirit that he should conduct normal relations with her. And the woman too revealed that it had been told her in a prophecy how she must cleave to her husband, and so that is what they did on the seventh of Tevet, in the fifth thousand and four-hundred and twenty-sixth year of creation (1665). And on the next day she displayed the evidence of her virginity as is the bride's custom, which stirred great rejoicing among the Jews of Izmir who believed in him. That same morning Shabtai Zvi walked to the synagogue. He ordered that a great silver bowl be borne before him, filled with fragrant spices, as much as one man could carry. Behind that man walked two other men with two vases filled with roses and other flowers in water and behind them, a sage carrying a comb in its sheath. Then Shabtai Zvi was seen, striding between two sages, carrying the large fan plated with silver which he had with him always and with which he would on occasion touch the head of whomever he wished to honor, and to such a man it would seem as if he had been assured great honor and importance, and there were men who would not exchange such honor for great riches. And thus he walked to the synagogue and hundreds of people walked in his train to honor him, and more came out singing psalms that were only sung on the holy Sabbath day. Then they prayed and he ordered that the Tetragrammaton be pronounced as it is written,

Figure 7.1: Engraving of Shabtai Zvi, purportedly made from life. There are many others more or less contemporary with it, though the portrait did not assume holy status as a mantra or an icon (as did the official portraits of Yakov Frank and his daughter Ewa; see chapter 8). (Yet, seeking to quiet Jewish disruptions in 1666 the Polish monarch, Jan Casimir, issued an edict against the public display of portraits of Zvi.) All such depictions of Zvi's face are quite similar to this one from Thomas Coenen, *Ydele Verwachtinge der Joden getoont in der Persoon van Sabethai Zevi* (Amsterdam, 1669).

which disturbed many people, but they dared not interfere and were forced to listen with a heavy heart; and when the prayer had been finished he ordered prayers to be said [on behalf of the congregation] and everyone made donations of charity to the poor as his heart led him and a great sum of money was gathered for no one wished to hold back, on account of the honor of Shabtai Zvi, even though there were those who gave against their will. And when he came forth from the synagogue hundreds ran after him and kissed his hands—young and old, boys and elders, women and men—to pay him honor. (Shazar, *The Story of Shabbetay Zevi*, pp. 19–20)

Nathan the prophet wrote a letter to the master of the port of Alexandria, a very wealthy man named Rafael ben Yosef, after he heard that the noble Rafael had become a believer in Shabtai Zvi. . . . The noble responded and asked Nathan to write him more concerning the root of the matter and the whole truth concerning Shabtai Zvi and what would befall him. Nathan wrote back and said that what he wrote was a prophecy delivered to him in the Holy Spirit from God. Nathan [wrote him instructions for prayer] and said that they were ordained by R. Isaac Luria and that no one but his pupil R. Hayim Vital could understand them, and that R. Isaac Luria had been destined to be the messiah and that his generation would have attained Redemption had it been deserving and if there had not been so many non-believers, as, on account of our many sins, there are those today who do not wish to believe in Shabtai Zvi. But in the days of R. Luria, the non-believers had held off the Redemption, while in this moment they cannot do so any longer; but woe to them and their souls for they do evil to their souls and will not merit seeing the consolations of Zion and Jerusalem, but the Redemption they cannot hinder any longer for the heavenly host is complete and the Shekhina has risen up out of the Exile. Nor need you be astonished that we in our generation should merit the Redemption despite our being unworthy in our doings, for our messiah Shabtai Zvi has suffered the pain of exile in our behalf, and he atones for all of Israel by being forced to suffer the agony of exile for such a long time, since for eighteen years he has been driven from one city to another and decreed an outlaw. Such things are an atonement for all the sins of Israel. Nor is this all. There is no end to relating the tortures and sufferings Shabtai Zvi has endured; no man can grasp with his intelligence what has happened to him from the very beginning. Thus it is within his power to treat any Jew as seems fit to him, and if he judges someone fit for mercy or for the whip, that is what will happen, for he will slay the evil man by the breath of his mouth, but he is pious and humble and seeks out righteousness in the most evil man, if he only wishes to improve. . . . Every Jew must believe that Shabtai Zvi is the true redeemer, he and no other, without seeking any sign or wonder from him, even though he has the power to do signs and wonders in multitudes as he has already, but it is forbidden to doubt him. By his merit has this generation earned the right to see the beginning of the Redemption, which we have looked forward to for one thousand six hundred years and which no generation has merited until ours, therefore shall there be no mercy for the nonbelievers and infidels in whatever comes upon them, neither for them nor for their flesh and blood.

And now I will reveal to you as well how the reign of our lord and messiah Shabtai Zvi will be revealed, soon and in our days, as was said to me in the Holy Spirit: In another year and some months Shabtai Zvi will take the kingship from the ruler of Turkey, without war, only by way of songs and hymns and by praise and gratitude to God, may he be blessed, and the Turkish ruler will place himself in his hands and go along with him as his servant throughout his kingdom and pass everything on to Shabtai Zvi. And he will conquer all the nations of the earth in this fashion and all the kings of the world will be the servants of the Turkish king and the Turkish king himself will be the servant of Shabtai Zvi. Nor will there be any bloodshed among the Christians, especially not in Germany or Poland, rather all the nations will give themselves up by their own good will and without any force at all, but only by the breath of his mouth will he catch the earth. But at that time Israel will not have come forth from the Exile nor will the Temple yet be rebuilt and all the Jews will yet be in the places where they are now, in the lands of their dwelling, and will be considered to be lords, and whatever they order, the nations will be obliged to carry out, and every one of the uncircumcised will stand before a Jew like a slave before his master and tremble and be filled with fear and terror of what the Jew will command.

But the Temple will not yet be built at that time. Shabtai Zvi will erect an altar in Jerusalem and discover the ashes of the red heifer hidden away at the time of the destruction and will sprinkle the waters of purification from sin over all Israel, for all Israel is defiled by corpses and must atone by the sprinklings of the third day and of the seventh day and then may Israel make sacrifices in Jerusalem, and this will last four or five years. And then the messiah Shabtai Zvi will cross the river Sambation. And meanwhile he will hand the reign of the earth over to the great ruler of the Turks who will be king meanwhile, and he will set him to command all the Jews, whom he will protect and leave in the places of their abode. But three months later the Turkish king will rebel against the Jews on the advice of his counselors and will torture them and cause them great distress wherever they live, by sword and famine and plague, until the prophecy of the prophet Jeremiah be fulfilled upon them: "He that is for the sword, to the sword, and he who is for the famine, to the famine" [Jer. 16:2], for they will be required to suffer the birth pangs of the messiah and "only one will remain in a city and only two of a family" [Jer. 3:14], and none of all the Jews in the world will be spared these troubles except for the Jews of Gaza for the city of Gaza is the first of the kingdom of our messiah, and just as King David was shown honor in Hebron so was Shabtai Zvi greatly honored in Gaza. . . . And this will go on six years as is written in the Zohar, that in the days of the messiah there will be troubles for Israel and in the seventh year, the fallow year, the land will rest. It will be a jubilee and all will go out free, which is hinted in the name of our redeemer Shabtai, that is Sabbath, which is the seventh year, in which complete Redemption will be brought us by Shabtai. And at that time which is the seventh year, the king Shabtai Zvi will return from over the Sambation river and will bring with him the wife he took there, the daughter of Moses our teacher, for Moses our teacher will already have risen in the resurrection of the dead 15 years previous and is on the other shore of the Sambation, and there has been born to him a daughter named Rebecca, born for Shabtai Zvi, and he will bring her with him, and the wife he now has will be Rebecca's handmaid, and Rebecca will be fourteen years old when she marries Shabtai Zvi. And know furthermore that only a few of this Exile will merit coming to Jerusalem, only those who are completely righteous and stand the test of the six years of plague and sword and famine and throughout all the tribulations remain absolutely faithful to God and his servant, Shabtai Zvi. And they will be very few and will merit coming to Jerusalem when the reign of Shabtai Zvi is revealed. And Shabtai Zvi will come from across the Sambation river, riding the Great Lion bridled by a fiery seven-headed snake from whose mouth come forth consuming flames. And thereby Shabtai Zvi will humble all the kings of the earth and all of them will bow and prostrate themselves before him—kings, princes, dukes. And in Jerusalem the Temple will descend, rebuilt in Heaven and perfect, and will stand erect in a moment as if it grew there. And then Shabtai Zvi and Moses our teacher and the Jews from across the Sambation will come to Jerusalem in great glory, and there will be no more than seven thousand pious Jews left in the Land of Israel who have remained strong in their faith throughout the great and terrible decrees. These will be the remnant of all the lands of Ishmael and Edom, from all the places where there were Jews, excluding those across the Sambation who have come to Jerusalem with Shabtai Zvi. And immediately thereafter the resurrection of the dead will take place in the Land of Israel for the righteous buried there, and the evil will be cast out of the land and will not rise until the general resurrection, after forty years, when all the dead outside the Land of Israel will rise. Attend to what I write you, a true prophecy which will come to pass, and you may believe it completely. (Pp. 22–30)

Since many still refused to believe in Shabtai Zvi, there was a great hatred between his supporters and his opponents, whom the masses called infidels and whose refusal to believe in Shabtai Zvi was, in the eyes of the masses, as if they had betrayed the God of Israel and were unfit to be considered Jews. And even when, on account of their fear of the multitude, they said nothing, they were accounted infidels because they did not associate with the believers; and if the believers had been able to take the life of such a one who did not believe the matter it would not even have been considered a transgression but rather a great good deed, and he [the victim] an outlaw.

This happened once. The multitude picked up its feet and raced in great force to the house of an important man in Izmir whose name was Hayim Peña, a rich man, and cast stones at the door and windows of his house until not a single window remained whole; and they tried to break down the door and to stone him as well. It was his good fortune that it was the eve of the Sabbath near dark and the time for the beginning of the Sabbath so that everyone was forced to cease the stone-throwing and leave the house alone in order not to profane the Sabbath. Otherwise, they would have stoned Hayim Peña and plundered his house. This Hayim Peña used to pray at the Portuguese synagogue. That Sabbath morning Shabtai Zvi and his men entered and sent a message to the heads of the synagogue that Hayim Peña should be driven out of the synagogue, and they put a writ of excommunication upon him; since he didn't believe in Shabtai Zvi, he was not fit to enter the synagogue. But the directors of the Portuguese synagogue did not wish to do such a thing to such an important man and disgrace such a fine man without reason. When Shabtai Zvi saw that they did nothing to Hayim Peña, he himself went to the Portuguese synagogue with five hundred of his men behind him. When the Portuguese saw them coming, they locked up the synagogue and Shabtai Zvi commanded his men to break down the door at the height of the Sabbath day, and this was done immediately since whatever Shabtai Zvi said to his men was in their eyes as if spoken at Sinai and they were quick to carry it out, as they did then in breaking the door down during the Sabbath. And when Hayim Peña saw it he understood that it was him they were after and fled by way of a secret hole in the roof and so saved himself. And he did act wisely, for they surely would have killed him, on the Sabbath day itself, for they continued to seek through the whole synagogue for him, but they couldn't find him since he'd escaped and their design came to naught. Then Shabtai Zvi ordered which psalms to sing and what acts to do at that time and that was done. And he came up to speak and became so enraged that his color changed. . . . And when he'd finished speaking, he came up to the Holy Ark and took a Torah scroll into his arms and sang verses from the Song of Songs and explained them according to the Kabbalah, revealing great secrets, and it all worked very well, and he said explicitly that he was the messiah and he would redeem Israel from the Exile. (Pp. 44–47)

Now I must write you concerning another matter so that you will not be so astonished at what Shabtai Zvi managed to do. How was it possible for so many people, great sages and defenders of the law among them, to permit him to mislead them so. See, there is no generation that has not within itself Abraham, Isaac, Jacob, Moses and Aaron, so how is it possible that everyone became so confused? As long as I've lived this remains a great astonishment to me and I have discussed it with many great rabbis. . . .

And this is one of the greatest occurrences, clearly supernatural, that came to pass in those days and a reason for the great belief in Shabtai Zvi, for in the year five thousand four hundred and twenty-six of the creation [1665], in the month of Tevet, it happened in many places, in Izmir and in Constantinople and in Adrianople and in Salonika, that prophets arose in hundreds and thousands, women and men, boys and girls and even little children; all of them prophesied in the holy tongue and in the language of the Zohar as well, and none of them knew a letter of Hebrew and all the less so of the language of the Zohar. And this is how it would be: they would fall to the ground like someone struck with epilepsy, foam would come forth from their mouths and they would have convulsions and speak secrets of the Kabbalah in the holy tongue concerning many matters, and what they said, each in his own way, was this: The reign of Shabtai Zvi, our lord, our king, our messiah, has been revealed in Heaven and Earth and he has received the crown of kingship from Heaven. . . . And wherever you went you heard nothing but that Mr. So-and-so had become a prophet and that Miss So-and-so had become a prophetess; and here there was a company of prophets, some prophesying in one way and others in another way, but the sum of the matter was always that Shabtai Zvi was the messiah and our righteous redeemer. Now, a man might think that all this was trickery and some people created themselves prophets. Not so! You must believe that this was how it was. Hayim Peña, whom Shabtai Zvi searched for in the synagogue and sought to kill because he didn't believe in him . . . and who thereafter made peace with Shabtai Zvi and believed in him on account of his fear, came home one day and found a crowd there and did not know why so many people were standing in front of his door. He asked why there were so many people standing by his door, and they told him that his two daughters had become prophetesses and were prophesying like the other prophets. When this man Hayim went inside, he saw that his daughters were shaking and having convulsions and speaking great things. They said that they saw the sage, Shabtai Zvi, seated upon a throne in Heaven and the crown of kingship upon his head, and many other things. And when they had finished their words, they called out several times in succession: "Crown, crown." . . . People said that Shabtai Zvi had spoken with Hayim Pegna a few days previous and said that his daughters must remove their mourning costumes, which they were wearing on account of their mother's death, and wear their best clothes, and that is what they did. When his daughters sought to prophesy, they would remove their mourning dress and put on their finest clothes and would prophesy. (Pp. 53–56)

On the third of Nisan in [1666] the four hundred and twenty-sixth year of the sixth millennium [after two different missions from the Grand Vizier had come to take him from his home but only did him homage and allowed him to remain], Shabtai Zvi went to the Grand Vizier but he wouldn't let him enter and instead sent a pasha with one hundred janissaries to seize him and imprison him. When the pasha saw Shabtai Zvi, he bowed before him and kissed his hand and paid him great honor and then went back to his master, to the Grand Vizier, and said: "My lord, why do you wish to imprison such a splendid person as he? In all my life I have never seen such a man, his appearance is like that of an angel. If you do not believe me, permit him to come before you and you yourself will be astonished at the sort of being this is." The Grand Vizier immediately ordered that Shabtai Zvi be brought before him. Shabtai Zvi came before the Grand Vizier and blessed him and the two began to speak. Shabtai Zvi's brother served as the translator.

I have not been able to establish what happened there. In any case he remained there several days. Some say he was imprisoned. Some say that he was not imprisoned in Constantinople but remained by the Vizier in great honor. Finally, the Grand Vizier sent him to a place called the Dardanelles . . . a great and mighty fortress where important people are jailed or settled, given a whole palace like that of a king's son and treated as great lords, all their requests are met and they are only guarded so that they do not flee until their case is judged, and then they are moved away. This is what was done for Shabtai Zvi. They settled him in the fortress . . . in Nisan and he stayed imprisoned there until Elul, over five months, all at the expense of the Turkish ruler, which greatly rejoiced the hearts of Jews everywhere who thought this a great matter. . . . People came to speak with him in this fortress from all quarters of the world and brought him fine gifts and paid him honor with large donations. The guard who kept watch over him made a lot of money from what he was paid to let people in to see Shabtai Zvi. Everyone who came to see him left his presence requited and completely faithful to the belief that Shabtai Zvi would gain great things from the Turkish ruler. He was dressed in red clothes and the scroll of the Torah that he had with him was clothed in red and set by his right side always, in a red cover with gold decorations. The room he sat in was a king's chamber. The walls were covered in golden Turkish textiles of fine quality and great worth. On the floor lay the most precious carpets and before him stood a pure silver table and in its center was a gilded tray. His inkstand was made of pure gold inset with precious stones and all the vessels that stood upon the table were made of silver or gold inset with precious stones. To his right was a bed of gold and at its head a silver scarf and on his left he had a fan with a handle of gilded silver. And so he dwelt in the fortress like a king in his court. And there were many rooms and a beautiful garden with a little house for his entertainments and it was all for his use. The courtyard was enclosed from outside and Turkish guards kept watch over it from outside and as an important man is held in prison, so was he held, which was a matter for wonder. But in my opinion he was wise to do so, so that all who might see him would admire him. All the more so since his appearance, his stature and his presence, was truly very handsome; so much so that it would be hard to find his like. I spoke with people who ate and drank and were near him in the fortress where he was imprisoned and who were not his proponents and they told me that there was none like him in stature and in the way his face looked, like that of one of God's angels. His cheeks were always ruddy. And they testified that when he sang Sabbath hymns to God, may he be blessed, which he did several times a day, it was not possible to look into his face, for one who looked at it, it was as if he looked into fire. (Pp. 65–73)

Guided by Scholem's work (and that of his students, I. Tishby, M. Benayahu, Y. Liebes, and many others), we are able to understand, at least in part, the significance Nathan attributed to Zvi's activities, in the context of Leib's report of the image of the "birth pangs." That passage in Leib's account brings together the dynamics of cosmic history, world history, the history of Zvi's sect, and his own biography through the manipulation of a single hoary image.

The high points in the history of this image in Hebrew literature begin with Isa. 13, a chapter that described the Day of God's Judgment over Babylon. The judgment is made upon Babylon's sins and is described as frightening, as painful as childbirth, and of cosmic extent. This day is followed by the redemption of Israel (the birth): the return of the Jews to the land of Israel and to peace (Isa. 14:1–3) and the submission of non-Jews to Israel's rule. In the Apocrypha, Pseudepigrapha and early rabbinic works, the Day of Judgment is expanded—it becomes a week of seven years typified by elaborate natural calamities and warfare. At this point, it is generally agreed, only a few righteous ones will be spared the suffering due to their deeds of penitence and piety. This period also comes to contain acts that reject the traditional community and law (cf. the Syriac Book of Baruch; Mishna Sotah, 9; and TB Sot 97–98). The next major enhancement of the image occurs in the description of cosmic paroxysms in the Zohar (II, 8–10), where each lovingly detailed stage of the messiah's advance is followed by a retreat. Passages from the Zohar (chiefly, II, 8–10, 52b, 119b, and III, 249–250) that attract attention in later messianic texts and traditions treat of the figure of the hind and her birthings. These all elaborate a Talmudic passage (TB Baba Bathra 16–17) that describes the mysteries of God's creation and, in particular, the hind's birth shrieks and the actions of a serpent, summoned to bite open her closed womb. The hind symbolizes the people of Israel, compressed into the image of the presence of God, the female presence known as the Shekhina. (See Luria's interpretation, in chapter 5). The hind bears the flow of redemption into this world from above. Her head is lowered to a point between her legs so that she can shriek as she, carrying the messiah within her womb, calls out at the only possible moment that redemption can begin. The serpent bites her to nourish itself on her blood and, being appeased, its evil sanctified, bites her again to open the wellsprings of cosmic love and salvation/repair.

The opposition of some Jews (and other nations) to Zvi is thus necessary in this world, paralleling the role antagonistic cosmic forces play in restraining perfection, thereby enabling it to come about. The enemy does battle, then ceases, bringing the whole cosmos to rest. The Turkish emperor assists Zvi by helping him, then by opposing him. The "only possible moment" comes in 1648, which, when this number (5,408 years after the Creation) is transcribed in Hebrew letters, is equivalent to the phrase "end of days." But the Jews who looked for redemption that year found disaster instead as the Ukrainians massacred tens of thousands of them in their uprisings. (The year 1096 had also been designated as the year of redemption; it was instead the year of the First Crusade and of the destruction of Jewish communities along the Rhine.) The Ukrainian calamity was interpreted as establishing the year when "the birth pangs" of the messiah's nativity began. Shabtai Zvi reveals himself as the messiah in that year, initiating advances and reverses that would recur in both his career and his emotions. These culminate in his crossing the river into glory, accompanied by Moses' daughter, on the seventh day (Zvi is named for the Sabbath, Shabtai; his family name is the Hebrew word for a sort of deer, the hind or roe, the symbol of the land of Israel) of the seventh seven of the years of rest, the Great Jubilee.

Letters from the Shabbatean period

The two letters excerpted here come from a collection of letters that forms the correspondence that took place, during the Shabbatean period, between R. Yakov Sasportas and proponents and opponents of the movement from all over the Jewish world. Sasportas was a refugee in Hamburg from the Great Plague in London and tried to ascertain the facts concerning the movement and its events from all those who were involved or had information on it. (London saw many contemporary accounts of the movement, in addition to collections of documents such as Sasportas's; the London accounts included lengthy ones by interested spectators like Sir Paul Rycaut, Robert Boulter, and John Evelyn, as well as brief mentions by such observers of the popular scene as Samuel Pepys. Evelyn's account was translated immediately and printed in Hamburg. Amsterdam saw Thomas Coenen's full report; Venice saw Jacob Becherand's. It is difficult to overstate the international Christian and Jewish interest, scholarly and popular, in the movement at the time.) Sasportas was dubious about the movements, though cautious about saying so at the time. In editing his letters later (after 1666), he chose to portray himself as having been a staunch opponent of it. Many rabbinical figures did support Zvi's claim; among those who did not, most hesitated to attack him openly.

O Light of Israel, Right Pillar, Mighty Hammer, Excellent Judge, Complete Sage, Beloved, Honored Teacher, Rabbi Yakov Sasportas, may his light shine.

(Ships have ceased coming from Turkey because of the war, and the believers here have no sure news of the matter.) Several schools have arisen among them concerning Shabtai Zvi.

One school holds that Shabtai Zvi did not change his religion and [that he] has been libeled. This is what actually happened: Shabtai Zvi went to the king singing hymns and without a sword, as was prophesied. When the king beheld him, he embraced him and kissed him. He set the crown of the kingdom upon his head, as was prophesied, and wound a green scarf about it. One who caught a glimpse of this thought he had converted to Islam. . .

A second school holds that if he converted, there is a deep purpose in it: that he wished to explore all the treasuries of the king of Turkey and his ancestors, so that when his kingdom came to be, he would be expert in all the ways of kingship.

A third school has it that there are numberless secrets [involved] in his conversion. God has ordered it. Shabtai Zvi must go into the world of the shards to subdue them. Therefore he has dressed himself in them.

A fourth school says simply that if he converted, it was not he himself, but a shadow. He himself rose into the sky and has disappeared.

The story has it that when Shabtai Zvi came into his presence, the king fell to the earth and prostrated himself before him. The king ordered that he be taken to the baths. The king laid out new robes for him, in which he could dress himself after coming up from the baths. And when he came forth 50,000 men gathered about him to look upon him. And he slid his hand into his pocket and brought forth gold coins. And he cast the coins before them, though there had been nothing in his pocket. And there was so much gold that the 50,000 men could not carry it all and had to hire beasts to haul it away. (Y. Sasportas, *The Faded Flower of Zvi* [*tzizat novel tzvi*], ed. I. Tishby [in Hebrew; Jerusalem, 1968], pp. 247–248, 250)

After Zvi's conversion, Nathan of Gaza wrote the following letter to a believer near Corfu. It makes clear, at the outset (and for the first time in the movement), the doctrine of the necessity of the messiah's conversion and the impossibility of communicating it to those who are not believers; it closes with words of comfort that promise the coming of the kingdom to those alive and faithful:

The reason for all this cannot be revealed, and certainly cannot be written except for those who have entered the Field [of the Shekina] and ascended and returned, and soon everything will be revealed, with God's help, nor is the time spoken of at all distant but a near time, with God's help, and he who is patient will attain it. Therefore, my brother and all those who are companions in the full faith of Israel, who await and expect and tremble at these words, be strong and of good courage, fear not nor be dismayed, return to the Lord your God with all your hearts and souls and give thanks to his great name, for surely we are destined to see that which neither our fathers nor their fathers saw. And even if some should say that these are nothing other than empty words of consolation since I have not the power at present to display their truth in a deed, nevertheless I will not allow myself to deny you, saddened and fearful about this thing, who seek of me righteous judgments and long for closeness to God, for my sake and [yours] God will be honored and for the sake of all Israel, impoverished and needy, awaiting in anguish and distress the sanctification of his name, may it be blessed, and for the sake of his Torah. We shall soon and joyously behold it.

The word of Nathan Benyamin. (Sasaportas, *The Faded Flower*, p. 262)

The provenance and interpretation of the following letter are discussed by Scholem. It is the last letter we have from Shabtai himself. He was in a state of radiant spirituality, moving from verse to verse in the Bible, finding, in every one of them, proof and assurance of his mission and its success. He erected a serpent, not of copper—cf. Num. 21:4–9—but of silver (that is, not red, the color of judgment, but white, the color of mercy), at the end of the festive re-creation of the redemption from slavery in Egypt and set it up on a standard. Scholem points out that Zvi "assumed the role of a Moses redevivus" and notes that the name "Zvi" is read, through a well-known code, as "Moshe." (The analogy between the first redemption [in the springtime, from Egypt] and the first redeemer [Moses] and the last redemption and its redeemer was a common one, as we have seen.) Zvi never repented of either his conversion or his belief in its purpose. Up to the end, he signs himself with his Hebrew and Moslem names. Whatever may have motivated his choice at the time he converted, it suited him down to the ground.

[In Dulcigno, on the night of the termination of the Passover festival, 1676,] Shabtai made a serpent of silver and put it upon a pole [and said to his followers]:

My brethren and dearly beloved, all men of faith in the city of Sofia, who shall merit seeing the salvation of the Lord and see with their own eyes the Lord's return to Zion, behold: I bring an angelic messenger to you to make proclamation to you of my glory here in Egypt and some little of what he has beheld. Take heed of him and attend his word, do not try him concerning any matter he utters to you in my name, for I will not forgive you this when God comes to make judgment, and the Lord shall certainly be upraised to judge, and there is no God who can deliver you from my judgment for there is no other God but me. If you do obey the voice of the angel and do whatever I order you then I will rise and make your treasuries full. This is the word of the man who has gone up to the cloudy heights of the Father, the Supernal Lion and Celestial Stag, Anointed by God over Judah and Israel, Shabtai Mehmet Zvi. (From Scholem, *Sabbatai Sevi*, p. 915)

In the following section I have brought together six poems that relate to each other as a dialogue between hagiography and anti-hagiography. The collection shows how anti-hagiography responds to claims that a hagiographic account has laid to symbols, events, and personalities in its literary formulations. The claims set forth in the accounts by proponents stimulate counterclaims by opponents who employ the very same materials; both sorts of literary creation are out to establish their hold on the exclusive truth.

The first poem is actually the first document that has come down to us, betiding Zvi's messiahship to Europe. It was written in Italy by an unknown poet.

The king in his splendor will now appear
wreathed in the crown of kingship,
to give the righteous justice and, without fear,
the eastern kingdoms subdue and grip.
For the poorest of folk he'll bring the truth near,
for the holy seed who to the Law adhere.
O God, grant Shabtai Zvi grandeur.
Return, rebuild your dwelling pure.

(*Sabbatai Sevi, the Mystical Messiah* (Scholem, Princeton, 1972) 331, the original version of this work in Hebrew contains the full poem: (*Shabbetai Zevi and the Shabbetaian Movement during His Lifetime* (Tel-Aviv, 1967) vol. 1, p. 265)

The poem elaborates the theme of a Jewish king who will reverse the unjust treatment of the Jews in the Christian (Italy) and Ottoman Empires and turn the Lost Ten Tribes loose on the kings of the east (Persia), the latter an ancient theme in messianic literature and accounts of messiahs. This Zvi and God will do on behalf of "those who to the Law adhere." The process will end with God returning to his temple and rebuilding it. The poem is carefully dated—October 5, 1665. Perhaps it was stimulated by reports reaching the poet that day; perhaps the date calendars the countdown to triumph.

The brothers Jacob and Emanuel Frances, in the later years of their lives, were residing at this time in Florence and Livorno. Though highly educated in the Jewish religio-legal tradition and adhering to its customs, they were quite enlightened and tended to deprecate the Jewish mystical tendency in general, preferring a legal and ethical Judaism. When it began to be announced that Zvi was the messiah, the proofs of his righteousness were drawn from new mystic readings (those of Nathan of Gaza) of older mystic texts (such as the Zohar or the works of the Lurianic circle). Zvi's "strange acts" (particularly the verbal ones among them: his pronouncing the Explicit Name of God and his singing secular songs of romance) were, moreover, a radical departure from the brothers' views of the Jewish tradition. The brothers burst into parodic poetry.

Speak truly of all Zvi's done evil
and blow the whistle, call his mind feeble.
His head's in the sky, his bed's in Hell.
He'll help the sinner? He's likely to approve the devil.
. . . .
If it were mine, I'd hoist this Hind, if only things could but be level.
(Quoted in the Hebrew version, vol. 2, p. 425)

The poems of the Frances brothers are replete with biblical cues and plays on words of the Bible and the religio-legal literature that are difficult to translate, but the main point of Emanuel's agreement to go hunting the Zvi ("the Hind," "the Roe," "the Deer," all plays on the meaning of his name in Hebrew) with his brother lies in the view they shared, that Zvi—and his followers—were mentally incompetent. The brothers are of a single mind that Zvi's program of redeeming sinners by abandoning the strictures of the Torah could only promote bad behavior.

> Golden calves from the holy dust of cherubim his hand have made.
> Prideful fools of the Law and Yoke to waste have laid.
> Of wantons' parts I see a shambles made,
> and my voice cries out at all my sense does see betrayed.
> (From Scholem, vol. II, p. 426)

As opposed to the anonymous Italian poet of the first poem, the brothers foresee doom as a result of Nathan's new law for the new age: bodies dismembered as they take the law to pieces. They do not believe the process will result in a rebuilt temple but, instead, that its fragments—the golden-plated cherubim—will be remade as idols.

This attitude did not sit well with their compatriots. The Frances brothers wrote their lampoons during the height of the movement when the religious passions of Zvi's proponents were running strong.

> Cords of evil wrapped all around me
> blaze then break like wicks, you see.
> Tongues now drawn sharp no more than lashes be,
> though my blood and age they never cease to seek from me.
> They'd grind me into grits without God's power shielding me.
> (p. 426)

The poet is sought out by Zvi's followers. His work—his account of things—attacks their accounts and so he must be silenced. (The fierce, even murderous force Frances imputes to the enemies of his account of things does not seem to be exaggerated within the context of this apocalyptic verbal battle.) But he relies on his own sense of propriety for security.

The next poem was written after accounts of Zvi's being crowned by the Sultan have reached Italy. Of course, it is only in the accounts of proponents that this event occurred. Jacob's counteraccount denies the event. The defeat of the Christian empire by the Moslems continued to be a sign that Jewish messianists looked for, when not looking for its opposite. The ridiculous idea of a Moslem crowning the messiah of the Jews becomes more ridiculous as we read of the two working hand-in-hand for the redemption of the world and of the princes (or ministers) of Turkey kneeling before Zvi. The poem ends with Jacob speaking in the voice of his fellows. They lament his unwillingness to accept the mystic messiah and his surrender of a place in the redeemed land of Israel (in Hebrew, *eretz ha-zvi*, "the land of the Hind").

> Distant sounds of righteous Zvi come close to hear:
> Your own messiah's crowned by Mehmet's hand
> to work with him. Princes kneel now to a man.

Believe it not. We must our minds keep to us.
Not our anointed one is he; he's not the king for us.
On God's mercy wait; to save you can no man
but he who comes from God can bring us to our land.
I hear many say of me: Oh him none can save.
He has no faith. For him what can it mean
to have no part in the blessed Land of Zvi?
I laugh at them. How you do rant and rave.
How? Should I believe you? whatever can you mean
when your every point's no more than horns upon a Zvi?

(p. 426)

In the next poem—there's one more charming one that R. J. Z. Werblowsky, the translator of Scholem's work, made a splendid effort to catch (p. 404)—Jacob Frances may be directing himself against the illegal and unrighteous conduct of Shabbateans dominating the Jewish life of the community of Florence.

Let them kneel to Bel! crouch to Nebo! crown Milkom! seek Peor!
Woe are they who release God's people and even force them to his law
    abhor.
Favors they hand out to profaners, and faithful ones with fines belabor.
The Talmud, head and corner of the faith of yore
drools from their lips like spittle sinking to the floor.
Against Gemara they've built a city, and within it raised a tower;
faith's fort torn down, divorced the wife of youth, they've taken to a whore.
They've shoved away the gems that blocked them; rocks and stones they
    value more.
The ways of truth they've left behind. We will call them wise no more.

(p. 427)

Again, the theme of idol worship predominates. The elders of Florence (or of Jewry) have abandoned their tradition, erected a Tower of Babel, left behind the faithful wives of their youth and the precious pearls of wisdom in favor of a man, an idol. They deserve to lose their power for their perversions of justice. The pointed attack on misrule suggests that Frances is writing about something happening in Florence, while the biblical imagery in his poem strives against the biblical imagery in the anonymous poem.

BIBLIOGRAPHIC NOTE   In addition to Yehuda Liebes whose articles have been appearing regularly since the late 1970s in various Israeli journals, some translated in one collection, *Studies in Jewish Myth and Jewish Messianism* (Albany, 1993), scholars who continue to do new work and make new contributions include most importantly Yakov Barnai and Avraham Elqayam.

8

THE POLISH MESSIAHS
Yakov Frank and His Daughter Ewa

In the century after Shabtai Zvi's death, many continued to adhere to Shabbateanism, and many figures claimed to have inherited Zvi's messianic soul. This chapter first summarizes the careers of Zvi's successors. It then focuses on one of these, Yakov Frank, concerning whom we have more primary material by far than is available for any other Jewish messiah. Frank's antinomianism encompassed his conversions to both Islam and Catholicism and his elevation of himself, a fearless and physically powerful figure but uneducated and disdainful of religious traditions, above the Jewish rabbinic elite. His messianic activities were at the local level, in Poland and Moravia for the most part, but were imbued, as had been those of Luria and Zvi, with cosmic significance and the mystic vision. He was a militarist and supplied military training to his followers, but his maneuvers were aimed at gaining entry into the highest reaches of European society, rather than at making war on it. Frank first emerges, in a period of instability, within the society of Eastern and Central Europe, and within the Jewish society inside that. After his lengthy imprisonment, his movement successfully undergoes routinization and reenters both societies, changing them by bringing them together. It opens up assimilation to the Jews as a means of gaining power in the dominant, non-Jewish society; it enriches the resources of that larger society in Poland, Hungary, and Bohemia for generations to come. (It is said that, by the middle of the nineteenth century, over half of Prague's lawyers were from Frankist families.) The movement is anathematized in both societies until today: Non-Jewish Poles consistently attack liberal politicians as being not true Poles, not true Catholics but of Frankist-Jewish essence; Jewish Poles gleefully claim that the Polish national poet Adam Mickiewicz was a secret

Jew, from a Frankist family. Jewish scholars view the movement as the ultimate stage in Shabbatean degradation and as the abandonment of all Jewish ethical and religious values.

IN THE AFTERMATH OF SHABTAI ZVI

All messiahs after Zvi were influenced by him. From Zvi's death until the present, no new possibilities or themes have been added to the menu of messianic features. The most important messiahs after Shabtai Zvi present themselves in two styles: Some have doubts and recant and some don't. Those who had doubts about themselves, and were weak in asserting their claims, tended to defend their failures by accusing the Jewish people of lacking faith and righteousness, and of failing to support them. These figures or their followers conclude in retrospect, like Luria, that they are the messiah of the lineage of Joseph, destined to fail: Avraham Cardozo and Moshe Hayim Luzzatto fall into this category. Others did not give up and maintained their messiahship to the death: Yakov Querido (Filosof), Yehoshua Heshel Tzoref, Yehuda Leib Prossnitz, Barukhia Russo, and Yakov Frank. Of the several figures who played the role of prophet rather than that of messiah, Hayim Malakh is the most consequential one. The prophet of Hasidism and several other leaders of that movement returned to the ambivalent style of previous messiahs.

Shabtai Zvi had married his third, and last, wife, Yocheved, in order to establish an alliance with an important Izmir family—the Filosofs. When Zvi died, Yocheved announced that her brother, Yakov Filosof, had inherited his soul. The idea that a claimant is the psychic heir of his immediate predecessor strengthens his claim, and also provides consolation for the predecessor's failure by giving his soul another chance. It deviates a bit from the reigning (Lurianic) myth: A particular individual's unique soul has been transferred in this case, rather than the soul in question being the original unindividuated master-soul of the messiah. Partisans of Yakov and Yocheved followed Zvi into Islam. (Yocheved's Moslem name was that of Mohammed's wife, Aisha.) Two group conversions occurred in 1683 and 1686 in Salonika. Yakov, known as Querido ("the beloved"), died in 1690.

Avraham Miguel Cardozo (1626–1706) was born into a crypto-Jewish family in Spain, returned to Judaism in Leghorn in 1649, moved to Tripoli while in his late twenties, and remained there for some ten years. The education he had received in Christian and Jewish theologies and as a physician—a configuration not atypical of crypto-Jews—informed the visions and dreams that led him to Shabbateanism. He did not convert to Islam, considering this an act prescribed for the messiah alone, and yet, arriving in sacred Izmir after his expulsion from Tripoli, and then from Tunis, by anti-Shabbatean forces, he did announce that he was the messiah of the lineage of Joseph. He claimed that Yocheved had recognized him as the leader of the believers (the Dönme, literally "those who turn," in Turkish) and had wished to marry him. He was an antagonist to Christianity and, in particular, opposed its doctrine of the incarnation of the messiah. After much more traveling (to Bursa, Istanbul, Israel, and Egypt), also occasioned by expulsions, Cardozo recanted his messiahship but remained active in Shabbatean circles. He was in correspondence with the messiahs and prophets Tzoref and Malakh and met Hayon while in Safed.

Yehoshua Heshel Tzoref (1633–ca. 1700) concentrated his endeavors in Lithuania and Poland. He was a jeweler (as his cognomen, "silversmith," indicates), and largely uneducated. When Zvi converted, Tzoref was inspired; he ultimately became the most important proponent of Zvi's doctrine in Poland. Moving from Vilna to Cracow, in the heartland of Shabbatean territory, he took himself to be the messiah of the lineage of Joseph, who would manage affairs in the interregnum between Zvi's seeming death and his return and final reign as the messiah of the house of David. (This is yet another variation on the messiahs-of-two-lineages theme. Shabbateanism renewed all the old renditions of this theme and introduced not a few.) Tzoref lived an ascetic life. Many Polish Jews made pilgrimages to see him and to hear his tales and prophecies on current events. His connections with Malakh involved him in the Society of the Pious and its voyage to Jerusalem, though he did not make the trip. Tzoref's conduct closely resembles that of the rebbes/tzaddikim of later Hasidism. His writings and character directly influenced the development of the cult centered on the Ba'al Shem Tov, his theology, and his traditions.

Hayim ben Shlomo (between 1650 and 1660–1716 or 1717), known as Malakh ("the angel"), was Polish but studied with Zoref in Vilna, briefly returning to Poland after spending some time with Shabbateans in Italy, and before leaving again for Turkey for further study. When he returned to Poland once again, he met Yehuda Hasid and cooperated with him in founding the Society of the Pious and arranging its millennial journey to Israel in 1700. When Yehuda died, many of the Shabbateans of his group took Malakh as their leader. He was expelled from the land of Israel, and went to Istanbul and then to Salonika, the center of the most radical form of Shabbateanism, one which continued to produce messiahs; in Salonika he met Barukhia Russo. Driven out of Turkish territory, he returned to Podolia (southern Poland) and established Shabbatean practices there, laying the groundwork for the rise of Yakov Frank. It is not clear whether he proclaimed himself the messiah while awaiting Shabtai Zvi's return.

Yehuda Leib Prossnitz (Leibele Prossnitz, or Prostitz; 1670–1730), as might be assumed, spent significant time in the southern Moravian city of the same name. Like Tzoref, he was uneducated. He made his living as a peddler until he reportedly began to receive visitations from, and have dreams of, Luria and Zvi. He, too, was an ascetic; gathered followers; taught children; preached Shabbateanism; was persecuted and banished; and then found himself to be the messiah of the lineage of Joseph (in 1724, after encountering Shabbatean missionaries from the Salonika group). Though excommunicated and banned from several Jewish communities, including that of Frankfurt, his teachings were passed down through his student, Meir Eisenstadt, to Yonatan Eybeschuetz. The latter, a popular and trend-setting legalist, was involved in Shabbateanism and faced accusations of secret adherence to the movement throughout his life, especially after the discovery of majic amulets he had written employing the name of Shabtai Zvi.

Barukhia Russo (b. Salonika; d. 1720 or 1721) became the messiah, and divine as well (in 1716). Some of the group that had held Zvi to be divine took Russo as his inheritor. Russo was known as the Holy Lord (Señor Santo), and as (like

Zvi), the God of Israel (Elohei Israel), and, after his conversion to Islam, as Osman Baba (a common name among the dervish fraternities). His teachings included the idea that the Supreme God had no concern or responsibility for this world, and that the highest Torah (the *torah di-atzilut*, of Emanation, the highest of the four worlds of the *sefirot*), positively commanded those acts that were most stringently prohibited in the Torah (the Torah of *beriah*, of creating) that governs the lowest realm. The idea that a new Torah permitted some things that had been prohibited was a vital one in Zvi's teachings, developing hand in hand with the peculiarities of his psyche and conduct. With Russo, these prohibitions/commandments came to include forbidden sexual activities—incest, adultery, orgiastic practices—as well as forbidden foods and new festivals. Russo died young; his grave became a pilgrimage site. Adherents of the Russo sect of the Shabbateans would profoundly influence the careers of both Malakh and Yakov Frank, during their stays in Salonika and in their own regions.

Moshe Hayim Luzzatto (1707–1747) was born in Padua. He studied the humanities, languages, and science as well as receiving a traditional Jewish education. He was a brilliant poet and dramatist. As a young man, he was swept up by the Kabbalah, particularly that of Luria and his successors. He was not part of the Shabbatean circles in Italy but did, it seems, declare to his Holy Society that he was the messiah. This group of adoring fellow students and followers was formed in order to emulate the fictitious fellowship created by R. Shimon bar Yohai (described in the Zohar) and of the genuine associations formed around Luria and others. Luzatto's compositions in the language of the Zohar, including one work he called the Second Zohar, and his authorship of 150 psalms, which were to replace those of the Bible in the time of the messiah, convinced authorities (still engaged in the war against Zvi and Nathan of Gaza and the later Shabbatean prophets) that he was dangerous. He endured a series of bans and excommunications, trials and recantations, but continued his activities. Apart from his role as a messiah figure, Luzzatto, like Frank, was present at the awakening of the modern age in Judaism. Luzzatto was the most important single figure in the rebirth of Hebrew poetry and drama and wrote one of the most important and well-received books on Jewish ethics, the *Path of the Upright* (*mesillat yesharim*). After residing for some time in Amsterdam, he died tragically in the land of Israel.[1]

YAKOV FRANK

Yakov ben Lev was born in 1726, in a village near Husiatyn in the south of what was then Poland, the land known as Podolia. He died as Baron Jakob Jozef Frank in Offenbach in 1791. His father was an itinerant peddler and perhaps a bookbinder or a preacher, who often took his son with him on his travels west across the Dniester River, and south through the Balkans into the realm of the Ottoman Turks. In Turkish territory, Frank's father, and later he himself, were in contact with members of some of the sects that still regarded Zvi as the messiah. Frank became a trader himself and a caravaneer, conducting other traders. He mentions his dealings in gray goods and other fabrics, leather, coins, and jewels, and he makes many references to his work as guide/wagon master. He spent most of his early adult life in Walachia.

While acquiring the customs, languages, and habits of his suppliers and customers, Frank seems to have been urged, or to have decided on his own, to take up what has been called "the leadership of the Shabbatean movement in Poland." In fact, there was no such unified movement at the time, only cells scattered throughout Central and Eastern Europe; one of Frank's goals was to create unity among them. He crossed the Dniester into Poland in 1755 and succeeded in attracting some followers. All of southern Poland was in a state of flux at that time; the Cossack uprisings within Poland and the rapacity of her neighbors were partly to blame, along with economic stagnation and political fecklessness. The integrity and autonomy of the Jewish community itself had collapsed.

The Jewish authorities of southern Poland were in a particularly bellicose mood in the wake of the mass disturbances caused by Shabtai Zvi. They issued a complaint against Frank on the basis of a tale told by a young boy who said he had witnessed orgiastic conduct. At their instigation, Frank's followers became the objects of pursuit by the Polish government; Frank was captured but was released, after claiming to be a subject of the Ottoman Empire and protected by it; he then crossed back into Turkish territory by himself. Throughout his life, Frank demonstrated a remarkably fluid identity, ready to be, say, do, wear whatever was expedient. In this first instance of official metamorphosis, he abandoned his own followers—his theology stressed the importance and rectitude of such an act.

Frank eventually returned to Poland, after another arrest and flight in Turkey and a conversion to Islam, which he undertook in accordance with the teachings of Barukhia Russo. Upon his return, Frank came to command a substantial following. Several of the group had been attached to one antinomian set or another in Salonika. After further inquiries into the nature of Frankist activities at a rabbinic proceeding in Satanow (reported in a work of R. Yakov Emden, the great adversary of all forms of Shabbateanism), Frank and his group were excommunicated. Frank sought and received the support of the Catholic Church of southern Poland—which had its own agenda—and through it, that of the Crown. He had convinced the church of his movement's "Zoharic" and "anti-Talmudist" stance, and that it would accept baptism. He was granted a couple of indulgences: some time to prepare for baptism and permission to retain a few trivial customs of Jewish tradition. In return, Frank agreed to conduct a public disputation against recognized Jewish positions and authorities. (Jewish converts to Catholicism were not unknown in southern Poland in this period, and a public disputation in which the blood libel was a subject of debate was common. A case of 1712, that of one Jan Serafinowicz, parallels Frank's in many ways.) Two disputations followed, in 1756–1757 in Kaminiec-Podolsk and in 1759 in Lwów.

Nine propositions were disputed in the first of these debates. The most important feature of the Frankist position was the ambiguity and outright misdirection of its statements and argument, concealing Frank's own theology. Still, item 3: that the Talmud was anti-Torah; item 6: that God has appeared in human form but sinless; item 8: that Jews were not going to be elevated above all other peoples when the messiah came; and item 9: that God himself would appear and make atonement and cleanse the world of sin—clearly stand outside Jewish positions. (The first six Frankist theses in the second disputation were also heretical; all seemed to proclaim the veracity of specifically Christian dogma. The seventh—that the Talmud teaches the use of Christian blood in rituals—while it is a uniquely Christian idea, is not a Jewish heresy, just a lie particularly dear to the heart and institutions of the Catholic church of the region.) The bishop decided in favor of the Frankists in 1757, and Talmud burnings soon followed. The sudden death of the bishop inflamed the non-Frankist Jewish community's pursuit of the sect, in the face of which Frank once again fled.

Having gained the support of the Crown, Frank returned to Poland shortly afterward, to his followers' settlement at Iwanie. When he requested the second disputation, the church was pleased to comply but insisted that Frank's group abandon all Jewish customs and proceed toward baptism. Though Frank and many of his followers did convert to Catholicism (Frank's conversion took place in Lwów in 1759 and again in Warsaw that same year, as the king's godson), the church remained suspicious. After a zealous priest extracted confessions from six of his followers concerning their belief, the second disputation was interrupted and Frank was arrested. The church was particularly disturbed to find that Frank had been speaking of himself, and not Jesus, in the debate over the messiah's incarnation. Frank was kept in jail in Czestochowa as a Christian nobleman, the Baron Jakob Jozef Frank. His first two names are combined in Frank's mythic rendering of the patriarchal legend (he is "Jacob" and "Joseph," too); his surname recalls his Turkish background. It's noteworthy that the appellative "fra/enk" is a multivocal one; Turkish Jews use it to refer to a European Jew while European Jews use it to refer to an oriental Jew. Frank employed both these meanings. He appears to be straightforward with himself, but nothing is what it seems to others. As an adjective, "frank" incorporates all this in an old meaning, "free from restriction."

Frank stayed in the royal fortress adjacent to the Bright Hill shrine of Poland's national icon, the Black Virgin, for thirteen years, directing his sect from within its walls. He was impressed by the intensity of Polish Catholic worship of Jesus' mother there and added a new flavor to his image of the Maiden—the Shekhina, the Matronita. Emissaries from his "Fortress of Strength" (so termed after the prison that had housed Shabtai Zvi) were in touch with the Russian court, and when the area was conquered by Russia, he was set free (in 1773). His wife had died (in 1770) and his daughter, Ewa (Awatchka, or Awatchunja, née Rachel), inherited her role as the incarnate Matronita in his teaching and in the eyes of the sect. (Zvi's wife had been known as the Matronita, as was Russo's after her.) Frank never remarried. He moved to Brünn (Moravia), where his cousin Shendl Dobrushka lived, and stayed on there as a wealthy and respected noble. He conducted a court that included a military-and-manners academy, to which the children of followers were sent to be educated in the ways of aristocrats, to prepare for the coming times. He strove to realize those times. He attempted to meddle in the state affairs of Turkey, Russia, and Austro-Hungary; he was granted an audience with Maria Theresa; he even claimed that Ewa was the daughter of Catherine the Great of Russia. In 1786, having bankrupted Brünn, he moved to Offenbach and carried on in the same manner, appearing rarely in public, but always in a state of pomp and ceremony, and in an exotic costume; he was a pet of the Prince of Ysenburg. During the years in Brünn and Offenbach Frank was closely tied to the founders of the Freemasonic lodge known as the Asiatic Brothers, contributing ideas to their constitution and adopting some of the practices, garb and style of Freemasonry. He died in the throes of a seizure in 1791 and a grandiose funeral was held. His daughter replaced him as head of the sect; he had prepared her for the role. She was known as "the Lady," as Frank had been known as "the Lord." She continued in the role of the Matronita, the female aspect of the deity, and was the center of the temple, the *Gottes Haus*, at Offenbach, to which the believers continued coming until her death in 1816 (Figure 8.1).

Frank's theology changed over his lifetime. Although he was attached to Shabbatean circles, and their antinomian belief and practice undoubtedly inspired his own exaggerated version of Shabbateanism, he soon began to develop his own mythology. He certainly seems to have known some traditional rabbinic sources in spite of what some scholars have written; but it's possible that he simply picked up stray bits and pieces of traditions from various mystic circles. He makes references to the Zohar, the Lurianic Kabbalah, and Shabbateanism, as well as to prayers, the Bible, and other traditional rabbinic sources. The Kabbalistic system of ten emanations (*sefirot*), five configurations (*partzufim*), and four worlds is entirely absent from his theology, though the ideas of disaster (*shevirat ha-kelim*) and repair (*tikkun*) are present. Frank's own mythic composition is based in doubleness;[2] he refers to his own double as the Big Brother, and his inner circle, called the Brothers and Sisters, has its match in the Big Brother's court. This court is made up of benign demiurges; its personae are opposed by a collection of evil demiurges. There are, for example, two maidens in this upper sphere—one kindly, one malevolent—and this idea too has resemblance to Kabbalistic theology where such figures, however, lack substance. All the beings in Frank's universe are actually in touch with Frank and his court. Far above both spheres dwells the ineffable True God, whose match is the God of this lower world. Natural affairs—the weather, illness, the lives of animals, and the like—are controlled by appointees of this lower God, a concept that emerged during the beginnings of Jewish mystical texts, remained present in the practice of magic, and is now reinserted in this theology. Every detail of our world is doubled in that upper world, and there are signs within our world that indicate that this is so. Nothing here is only what it seems; the surface hides its duplicate or triplicate. If Frank has a strong and obedient following here, the repairing of Jacob's failure to reach the home of his brother Esau can be achieved, resulting in "wholeness" (in Polish, *całości*), integration. If one possesses *stałości* ("stability") here, "help" will begin to come from the other world. The discipline that is appropriate to such a mythology involves submission to the leader's orders at every turn. Frank stresses the rejection of all old traditions and patterns of behavior but retains those—including bits and pieces of traditional literature when they are useful—necessary for his group's affective identification with its historical community. He ascribes current failures and disasters to a lack of faith and proper behavior among of his followers, but sometimes he upbraids them for failing to ask him questions or argue with him.

In Brünn and Offenbach, Frank recited his dicta in their canonic form. It seems likely that the language of his recitation was Yiddish. The dicta might then have been translated, first into Hebrew and then from Hebrew into Polish, and later assembled, edited into Polish manuscripts (passages of which are translated below), and kept as sacred literature by his followers. Today, the *Zbiór Słów Panskich* ("Collection of the Words of the Lord") forms the single best source we have for understanding Jewish messiahs. We are certain Frank spoke them to his followers; in that context, they are unself-conscious self-revelations. These dicta establish several sets of beliefs, biographies, and ideas with which, we can be sure, Frank identified, and which changed along with him. The copies I have translated are all from the last extant Frank manuscripts (6968, 6969/1/2/3) in the Jagiellonian University Library (in Kraków), except for the dicta numbered 2189, 2213, 2248 and 2253, which are from a manuscript in the Public Library of Lublin. (My numbering corrects the errors in all the manuscripts.) In the translations here every attempt has been made to be faithful to the manuscripts. Words from foreign languages and from Polish, when they seem to be loan translations, appear in italics when they are first used; anachronisms have been left unaltered, as have clumsy syntaxes, verb-tense discords, sudden shifts in personal pronouns, and editorial insertions. The process of performance, stenography, translation, and editing may thereby be observed in the way the dicta appear here in English.

The oral/literary genres employed by Frank all contribute to the character he constructs for himself and for his attentive followers. The call vision establishes Frank in his role as the chosen one. His autohagiographa (my term) tell the story of Frank as they reveal the cosmic drama and the history of his following. The threefold tales substitute a character—a prince or noble, for example—for Frank and tell of his adventures in quest of a princess. The other genres—dreams that either he has or others have about him, homilies, theological statements, disciplinary instruc-

Figure 8.1: (facing page) The sacred portraits of Yakov Frank (*top*) and of his daughter, the Matronita, Ewa (*bottom*), of heightened importance in the movement after Frank's lengthy encounter with the icon of the Black Virgin of Czestochowa, were kept by descendants of Frankist families for generations. The most famous instance was Justice Louis Brandeis's copy of the portrait of Ewa. It had no doubt been given to him by his mother, Alice Goldmark, the descendant of one of the Prague Frankist families, very many of whom, whether converted to Christianity or not, were engaged in the practice of law.

The scene at Frank's bier gives a visual image that compares with the description of the court's parades that was written from Offenbach by Bettina von Arnim, in a letter to Goethe: ". . . Since you left, the life-style of the town's population has playfully changed over into the miraculous. . . . A mystic nation walks among us in wonderfully colored costumes: long-bearded men, young and old, in purple, green, and yellow gowns, handsome youths in close-fitting, gold-trimmed clothes, one leg green, the other yellow or red, galloping on fiery steeds with silver bells around their necks or playing guitars and flutes as they stroll through the evening streets, [and] the silver-haired prince of this people, attired in white and seated in front of his palace on a pile of magnificent rugs and pillows, surrounded by his entourage. . . . Little boys [are] bringing golden bowls, while music resounds through the open windows." (From Mandel, *The Militant Messiah*, p. 107)

tions—relate Frank to his following; the followers appear in them as he determines, either facilitating his plans or frustrating them.

The call vision

A call vision—a narration of the divine summoning of a prophet or similar figure—appropriate in hagiographic collections, appears in Frank's dicta in not one but two complete versions. The first version, in which the Islamic air predominates, is the earlier one. The problem term *frenk/frank* in this version probably signifies a member of the European Jewish community living in Turkey. The non-European clothing and the presence of women in this version testify to the Islamic influence (women are a feature of the Islamic paradise but not of the Jewish one). Likewise, in this version Frank may be awarded the title of a Jewish religious leader in the Ottoman Empire (*hakham*, though this is obscured by the Polish and has been translated as the adjective "wise"). The relatively more important role of Zvi in the first version also belongs to the Turkish background of Frank's sect of that time. Though the sweet odor of paradise is an image shared by Judaism, Islam, and Christianity, it is reminiscent of descriptions of Zvi's fragrant odor. The rose given to Frank is a symbol of the Shekhina in the Zohar and is identified with Rebecca, who was destined to be Zvi's wife, according to some Shabbatean texts; the soul of Zvi is said to be rooted in the *sefira* of the Shekhina. The rhetorical object of the first version, then, is to replace Zvi with Frank.

The second version was updated, probably at Brünn. A follower must have pointed out the incongruity of the first rendition in the present circumstances, far from the Islamic context; otherwise, Frank would not have given room to uncertainty and mitigated his authority by issuing a second account that conflicts with the first. The presence of women in paradisical chambers goes unmentioned in the second version, as does Zvi's peculiar clothing; kings and patriarchs are added, and the authority of Zvi ("the First") seems to depend on theirs. The term Frank uses for himself in the second version, *prostak* ("simpleton, boor"), is Polish and Yiddish. It identifies Frank with the disenfranchised, unlearned class of Jews he strives to engage. Frank uses it as a term of self-praise, rejecting traditional social stratification and the image of the elite scholar class by emphasizing the need for physical hardiness and heedless courage.

In both versions the theme of the messiah's unwillingness to serve can be identified with a messianic tradition that stems from the Gospels, but the descent of Frank into the depths, followed by his reascent through his own powers recalls a core tenet of Shabbatean theology. This call vision departs from the traditions of the genre as well, in that Frank receives no details of the heavenly world, but, on arriving at the summit, begins his quest in a world that awaits his discovery.

Version A
1. I had a vision in Salonika, as though the following words were said to somebody: Go lead Yakov the wise into the rooms and when you and he come to the first room, I admonish you that all the doors and gates be opened to him. When I entered the first room, a rose was given to me as a sign by which I could go on to the next and so

on *consequenter* from one room to the next. And so I flew in the air accompanied by two maidens whose beauty the world has never seen. In these rooms I saw, for the most part, women and young ladies. In some, however, there were assembled only groups of students and teachers, and wherever just the first word was spoken to me, I immediately grasped the whole matter from it and the full meaning. There was an innumerable number of these chambers and in the last one of them I saw the First [Shabtai Zvi], who also sat as a teacher with his students, dressed in *frenk* clothing. This one immediately asked me: Are you Yakov the wise? I have heard that you are strong and brave-hearted; to this point have I come, but from here further I have not the strength of proceeding; if you want [to proceed], strengthen yourself and may God help you, for very many ancestors took that burden upon themselves, went on this road, but fell; with that he showed me through the window of this chamber an abyss which was like a black sea, hidden in extraordinary darkness, and on the other side of this abyss I saw a mountain whose height seemed to touch the clouds, at that I shouted Be what may, I will go with God's help. And so I began to fly on a slant through the air into the precipice until I reached its very bottom, where, having felt the ground, I stopped. Walking in the dark, I came upon the edge of the mountain and seeing that because of the steep flatness of the mountain, I had difficulty getting up on it, I was forced to clamber up with my hands and nails and using all my strength until I reached the top. As soon as I stopped there, an extraordinary scent reached me, and there were many Truebelievers [Shabbateans] there. Seized by great joy, I did not want to go up onto the mountain with my whole body, saying to myself: I will rest awhile here, for sweat poured from my head like a river in flood on account of the tortures which I had bore to climb this mountain; but when I am well rested then I will come up on the mountain toward all the good that is found there. And that is what I did, I let my feet hang and sat with my body and hands at rest on the mountain. Then I went up on the mountain.

Version B

33. Just as I told you before when I was led to those rooms in which were found all the kings of Israel and the Patriarch, they said to me: Yakov, we have come this far, from here you must go on alone. I am a *prostak*, I answered, and have no understanding, by what means will I go there? Don't worry about that, they answered, none of that matters, wisdom is hidden in the lowest of places; nevertheless I still held back; at that the First, having put me on a table and having opened the window, showed me a precipice, saying: look, this is an impassable place, we cannot go there, but you, if you just would not hold back so, would have less difficulty in passing over your road, but since you delay you must pass through all the tight places. And at that time I saw all the burdens, which I would have to take upon myself. And so I was pushed into that abyss.

Autohagiographa

In these tales, Frank is the lead character in the drama of the world's repair, and everything that happens to him is of cosmic proportions. His strange acts do not provide a model for his followers to emulate; he alone can do what he does.

3. Rabbi Mardocheusz, being a teacher of Jewish children in Prague, had the same dream thrice night after night. In it he was told: Go away from here and reveal the secret religion to Yakov. He saw the same thing once, twice, and three times but paid no attention to it. Then one day, an ordinary man came to him and said to him: Run away from here because here they want to beat you up for adultery and accuse you of various other things; at that he became extraordinarily frightened and ran away, and, since he had a nephew by the name of Yakov, he thought that he should tell him the mysteries of the secret religion. He did so when he came to Lwów. Then it happened that he, having left everything behind, came to my wedding in Nikopolis and, having found me there under the canopy according to their customs, he not knowing me at all, it came to him to reveal absolutely everything to me. Hearing all this I asked: And where is the messiah? He answered: in Salonika. If this is so, I said, then I'll go to him right away. I want to serve him with all my heart. If there is need to chop wood, I will; if they order me to carry water, I'll do it gladly; if they need somebody for war, I will stand in the front line; having heard this, he became very frightened.

The Shabbatean faith was often revealed to the bridegroom by an emissary since a human couple's wedding night also stimulates the sexual mating (*zivug*) of the lower and higher worlds. R. Mardocheusz doesn't understand what his role entails; he first reveals the dream message to the wrong Yakov and tells Frank only by chance, or by destiny. Frank must have said the words "it happened that he . . . came to my wedding" with deep irony. R. Mardocheusz has opened the door to the one destined to walk through it, and he is afraid because the dream has been fulfilled, and because the *correct* Yakov—Frank—says that the way lies through rough deeds, not through study or meditation but through war itself.

8. To the question asked in Rohatyn, Why did the Lord return to Salonika for the second time? the Lord gave this reply: When a householder moves from one house to another, even though he has gathered up all his vessels, implements, and moveable goods, he nevertheless still returns a second time to his already empty house, lights a candle, looks and looks from corner to corner [to see] whether he hasn't forgotten something; so do I.

This tale takes the form of a parable, although Frank is relating a true deed that he did. Frank is not instructing the questioner. His answer is very much in the Jewish tradition of Talmudic debates, in which the argument proceeds and an answer is reached on the basis of certain agreed premises, and then someone questions the premises. The answer Frank gives is a paradoxical one and goes to the heart of the very reasonable problem raised by the questioner, "If you're perfect, why do you have problems? Why do you have to do things more than once?" The question threatens Frank's claims, but he is able to provide a homey kind of answer that can yet be taken as quite deep.

10. Once in Nikopolis the Lord came into the room very worriedly with heavy steps; Osman, who was then present, asked him: Wise Yakov! Why are you so dis-

tressed? The one who has the power to send plague into the world /:answered the Lord:/ came to me and I was obliged to determine the limit to which he could spread his plague; this has greatly worried me.

Waves of plague swept Poland in the seventeenth and eighteenth centuries. In the world of the Kabbalah, especially as it was developed in Poland, nature is controlled by Powers; some administer the winds; others, the waters; still others, animals; and so on. Frank is the master of all these Powers and is forced to make a decision that will cause some people to die. Again, he doesn't want the role he has been assigned. He doesn't want to be harsh or dictatorial. But he has no choice, and this causes him anguish.

11. When I was in Salonika for the first time, I was awakened abruptly one midnight and told: Yakov, go outside the city to the seaport and perform there a certain act. How can that be I said when the gate of the city is locked and [it takes] the strength of 30 Turks to open it? Don't worry about it, [just] go. And soon the keys were brought to me and the heavy gate opened as easily as if it were a simple door. I went to the sea and performed the deed of union *etc. etc* and came back having closed the gate behind me; the keys were taken from me and carried to their place.

In this dictum, Frank reports performing a *yihud* (see the tales of Luria in chapter 5), joining himself to another soul. Some have suggested that the deed was a *zivug*, a sexual act intended to stimulate more supernal matings and joinings. The text of the episode follows the word "union" with "etc., etc.," but there is no evidence that a sexual act, rather than some sort of magic, is being concealed. Frank doesn't mention that anyone else is on the beach. The beach scene itself recalls an episode in Zvi's life when he nearly drowned, and it is perhaps with his soul that Frank unites his own. A miracle occurs when the heavy gates become common (in Polish, *proste*) doors and Frank, trusting always in his own physical power, has the strength to open them, for he too is *prost*.

15. When I was in Salonika the second time I received an order to perform contrary deeds and so when I met a Turk on a Greek street I drew [my] *yatygan* [a Turkish sword] and forced him to speak the names of the First and the Second [Barukhia Russo] and to make the sign of the cross, and then I did not let him go until willynilly he did it; similarly having met a Greek in a Turkish street I forced him to say the words: *Mahomet surullah*, i.e., Mahomet is the true prophet, and also the names of the first Two and ordered him to lift one finger upward according to the Mahometan custom. And again when I met a Jew he had to make the sign of the cross for me and also pronounce those two names when this happened in a Greek street, while when I met him in a Turkish street he had to raise one finger upward and name those two names. And I was performing these deeds daily.

The "contrary deeds," recalling the strange acts attached to the legend of Shabtai Zvi, refer to the inverting, antinomian principle Frank preached and practiced: Nothing is what it seems; that which is held to be holy is deadly, and the awe must be stripped from it in order to expose what is real. This achieves the repair of the holy.

23. [I] seeking then to leave the town, the ones left from the [followers of the] Second did not want to help me with anything, fearing that I, having a few grosz [small coins], would not go away, I succeeded with Rabbi Isohar, who gave me 5 [gold pieces] for the road. With that I hired a horse from the wagoneers who, according to custom, were traveling in 2 companies. The Jews bribed the Turks to kill me on the way. The Turks posted themselves on the road. My horse became lame as soon as I started out. I exchanged it then with my wagonmaster and at the same time borrowed a blanket from him, in which I wrapped myself, and rode up to the front [of the caravan]. The Turks thinking that I was on the lame horse in the back, as they had seen me at the beginning of the trip, killed the wagonmaster and took him to the Jews, who recognized the futility of their plot.

24. Likewise, when for the second time I was leaving Poland for Salonika, the Jews incited the Turks to kill me. The Turks pursuing after me encountered an extraordinarily beautiful woman on a horse. Burning with desire to get her, they rushed away after her. She fled and led them after her further and further away, and I rode on my way.

Devoted to his enterprise, Frank is repeatedly saved from harm by (apparent) accidents. In the dictum above, the apparition of a beautiful woman saves him. The Turks are blinded by their lust; Frank knows it is the Maiden.

35. Traveling once with my partner through [some] villages, my partner ran into peasants to whom he owed money; wanting to go on, several peasants, having come to us, stopped us. I wanted to jump on them, but they said: We don't have any business with you, that other one owes us 900 *levs*; and my partner knew that I had 600 *levs* with me; the peasants tied the debtor up and he began to lament, saying: Yakov, for God's sake, do this, give me 400 *levs*, this will settle my whole debt to them and I will get free, as soon as I get home I'll take my wife's corals, worth 100 *złóty*, and I will give them to you. I agreed to it: gave him [the money]. Having returned I asked for the corals. My wife is sleeping now, replied my partner, tomorrow morning I'll give it to you, and for the kindness you did me, I will give you an iron-covered cart, which is at my father's. In the morning my partner, with his wife and everything he had in the house, had fled. I ran to his father with the note, which he had given me to take the cart, but it wasn't given me; his father told me that his son owed him more money, and for security he put that wagon in his yard, which was surrounded with a high fence. At midnight I came there with two ladders which, after having tied [them] together, I put against the fence, took the cart weighing 100 *ok* [ca. 1200 lbs.] on my back, carried it over [the fence], and having descended the ladder with it I carried it on myself for half a mile to Roman. The father ran after me but everybody denied him the cart [by] proving that his son had done me greater damage by taking the 400 *levs*. This is a second display of my prostak-ness.

This dictum, like many others, contains much local language—terms for coins and a unit of measure. The term *prostak* that appears in it indicates someone not only ignorant of rabbinic literature (an *am ha-aretz* at least knows prayers and some Torah) but utterly ignorant and simple and crude. The exaltation of the simpleton and the use of local terminology were features of early Hasidism as well; Hasidism arose in the same area, and during the same period, as did the Frankist movement (see chapter 9).

Frank's passage over the wall into the father's courtyard and his theft of the wagon repeat the image of the treasure that is kept away from mankind by a jealous Creator, a cruel or errant demiurge, but that may be taken by one who is prepared to pass different sorts of tests. (Similar imagery appears in the Zohar and in other Kabbalistic literature that came before him and, after him, in Hasidic tales as well, and it recurs in his own dicta.) Frank shows that the path to the treasure lies through resolute, fearless action and physical strength. There is no miracle here. The tale is of a simple deed carried out by crude means in a non-Jewish milieu. The tale takes place on a cosmic level too. The father-king; the treasure unrighteously held back; the effort to penetrate the treasury; the possession of the treasure; the discomfiture of the father-king; and the reversal of the son's intention (which is to return evil for the good his partner has shown him) into an abundant reward all have to do with the repair (*tikkun*) of a good plan (for the universe) that has been broken. On the third level, it is Frank who carries out the repair using determination, courage, and strength as his only tools. Some followers very likely understood the wagon to be the *merkabah*, the chariot of Heaven.

36. Having come to the river Totorozh, I found there 150 wagons, standing on the shore, afraid to go further because of the high water. Without saying anything, I took my robe, put it and my bundles on my head, and despite the most terrible danger, I swam across the river with my horse. From the other shore, people shouted at me, what was I doing? for God's sake why was I taking such a risk? Listening to none of it, I swam across and that same day I managed 6 miles to Roman. Those people had to wait there 11 days, after which [when] they got there, they asked about me and were surprised at seeing me alive. And my prostak-ness did this.

In this dictum, all of Frank's uncommon abilities come together to set him apart from his community's way of life; he swims, owns and rides a horse, and neither fears the river in a flood nor cares for advice. He says nothing, keeps his clothes dry, and then covers a good day's distance to the village of Roman. None of this is common behavior in the Jewish world, yet it is not sufficiently uncommon to be impossible. If Frank sees it as possible, he can do it, if guided by his vision. Guided by Frank, his listeners can envision it as well. All the rest are left waiting on the far shore.

37. In the village of Faraon in Walachia there is a fearful pit whose depth is bottomless and is terribly wide. I jumped over it constantly on my horse, at which the Turks constantly marveled. From this consider, how crude and unconsidered my deeds were, and as well that I was chosen, for I was very upright and God-fearing.

38. Some robbers were hiding in a certain forest. They had all the comforts of life in their cave, even their own musical instruments. When I was passing by, I went in and, having found nobody, I noticed the drums, flutes, *tolumbas* [Turkish drums] *etc.* Having taken up a drum I began to beat it on purpose with all my strength, so that they would come to meet with me. Note that this is not a deed that anybody in the world would consider wise. Yet I was chosen, and that's why I have selected such people. Even though they won't be wise, but with wholeheartedness toward God they will deduce their part.

Frank alludes to his Turkish background to show his listeners that he is associated with the home of Shabbateanism, and that he is a world-traveler and has been places they've only heard about—in the East, in the mountains, in caves, among robbers. He enters the underworld by accident, out of mere curiosity, while the demons who guard the treasure are all gone. By coincidence, Frank finds himself in the right place at the right time, but instead of taking the treasure, he announces his presence and summons the enemy to show them something. In recalling this adventure, his summons goes out to his listeners as well.

41. After coming to Poland, the Lord said to Mrs. Matuszewski, O.B.M., What is in the heart of the merchant who, having come to the *Jarmark* [German, market-fair] with a very precious stone, and in spite of the great number of people [there], not even one was there who could understand the value of the stone?

In this dictum, Frank is communicating his unhappiness at not being accepted and obeyed. The fair of his parable represents a liminal place and time; nothing is fixed, everything is in flux. Everyone there is trading one thing for something else, exchanging themselves. Any jewel transaction, depending as it does on an agreement that the stone really is a jewel, demands the buyer's faith in the seller. The stone is itself liminal and becomes a precious object through the transaction. The merchant and his stone in the parable arrive at the fair from Frank's own experience as a dealer, but stones of parabolic value appear with regularity from the Bible to Frank. The Zohar's precious stones include one from which the world itself derives; one that rises from the lower realms to become a jewel in the highest diadem of the sefirot, Keter; and one that tries the love of the righteous man through pain. Frank's parable here inverts the one in Matthew (13:45–46) in which a merchant seeks to buy jewels and finds one for which he exchanges all his worth; Frank can't find a fit buyer for his stone.

Frank also tells some miracle stories, in which the context, plot, and characters are supernatural ones. The following is his birth/circumcision tale:

44. My grandmother, my mother's mother, was a very learned astrologer. When I was born, all the witches assembled around our home and surrounded it, even their queen was there at their head. There was a dog in our house—a cross between a wolf and a [canine] bitch, this [dog] did not sleep at all, but barked all the time, for if he had fallen asleep even for a moment, then they would have seen to it that he would have never awakened, but he kept watch vigilantly. Then on the 8th day at

the circumcision, they surrounded our home as before and wanted to do something evil, but were unable to, because that dog kept guard again, and the old grandmother with her craft fought against the evil also, saying: Watch him carefully, bring him up properly, for a new thing will come to the world through him.

47. Traveling with Jakubowski from Salonika to Poland, there prevailed at that time a pestilence in Podolia, we came to one township where the plague was felling the people, and we lacked food, wine, bread, cheese *etc.* then remembering that from those contaminated with plague one does not take money, I told him the opposite: You go there, purchase everything but don't give them money. He did just that. He came to the baker, bargained for bread, put it in his sack, but when he had to pay, the baker fell down and died. He went to the shopkeeper where he bargained for cheese. He put the cheese away and the shopkeeper died. He went on to the store to buy vodka. The same happened with the owner. In a word, just wherever he went he bought everything without money, because the plague was sweeping the sellers away. Coming [back] then to me, where I was waiting for him, a rider on horseback knocked him down with his horse. What are you doing? shouted Jakubowski? Are you going to ride right over me! He didn't even finish saying it when the rider toppled over and fell to the ground; this is how it is. I did all this because it was promised to me, that no plague, nothing at all could get at me, therefore all my orders were carried out successfully by the hand of the one whom I assigned, and so should you be.

This is a tale of the miraculous protection that Frank can extend to those who are in his company, whether on the journey or hearing the tale of it. It contains the theme of inversion: The rich become poor; the poor come into the possession of goods; the powerful are defeated by the weak. Logical reality is all turned upsidedown. Frank's ironic expression is hard at work here. His theology allows for taking advice but taking it literally, i.e., against its meaning. If it's dangerous to take money from the pestilence-ridden, it is, *a fortiori*, more dangerous to take food from them. Frank's literal understanding wipes out the middle term and thereby wipes out the owners and wipes the food and the road clean for his use and that of his followers.

50. In Podolia, when I was traveling with Jakubowski and Nathan, I was very careful about my deeds. Once when staying overnight in a certain town I heard lamenting in a certain house. I went there. I found a Jewish girl who was already dying and over whom the whole household was lamenting. Be quiet, I shouted at everyone, and leave me alone with her. They all went out, and I spoke these words: I command you to be well. And then I did a deed with her; she woke up, she became well, I ordered that she be dressed in a white blouse. Then when I was leaving I ordered them all that it should remain secret. This woman is alive to this day, has children and is healthy in every way and is rich.

51. A similar deed happened in Czestochowa with the daughter of Henryk Wolowski, who was almost dead and her mother, having come to the Lord, began to plead hard about the child, the Lord told her to laugh two times and to plead

while laughing, saying to her: Go home, your daughter will be well. and it happened just so. This child lives to the present.

These two miracle cures show Frank in a circumstance more typical of the *ba'al shem*, the folk doctor of Jewish country life—a circumstance built upon the miracle stories of Elijah and Elisha and of Jesus. There is no implication of sexual activity in the first tale; the phrase "And then I did a deed" typically signifies a magic act. The second tale matches that of Jesus' cure of the daughter of Jairus, inverting the laughter of those who did not believe in Jesus' power, so that now the laughter itself bespeaks Mrs. Wolowski's faith. As in the tale from Mark (5:35–43), Frank requires (in dictum 50) that his observers keep the matter to themselves. Again, the tale's wish is to be told, and it gets its way. One must assume that the tale-teller also wishes, even intends, that the tale of his power be told, and that the tale of his modesty, a coy claim to leadership, be told, too.

Siḥot ("homilies")

The topic of the following six dicta is the part the Company has to perform in order to achieve its goal. Frank tells the members of the Company that they rise or fall together (dictum 6); that they need to be alike in their purpose and their very being (14); that they must understand him properly and act in perfect faith, or they will fail (30); that he treats them with leniency and finds them lacking virtue (129); that a way to safety is provided for them (193); but that without unity, they will never reach his goal for them: "life" (130), by which he means unbounded physical strength, vigor, and power—youth as well as immortality:

6. While yet in Iwanie, a certain lame Rafal asked the Lord: If someone in particular of the Company should be guilty [of something], will you punish all of them for it? The Lord answered: If someone should drill a hole in a ship, will not all be endangered? Just so all of you sit in one ship.

14. When still in Iwanie the Lord was saying: I shall beg the Holy Lord not to let me be pockmarked and you, if you will be good and entire, then, we shall all sit together at a round table and you will all be completely similar to me in every way so that it will be impossible to differentiate you even by a single hair, and whenever one of you goes out then [people] will always say that this one is the Holy Lord himself.

30. While yet in Dziurdziów [Giurgiu] the Lord said: In the very first town I come to in Poland, there I will be put in prison. In Iwanie the Lord said this verse, which Jacob said to his children *Vide: Gen: Cap. 48.22*. Since you will carry out my burial [cf. the commentary of Rashi to this verse] I will give you a bigger part, or a better one than the other brothers; so when in Dziurdziów I revealed to you about the prison and in Iwanie indicated to you that you would have to carry out the ritual of my burial, then you should have right away guessed that I was giving you a sign that the grave should have been understood as the prison, and you should have said that

We won't let you go alone, that We want to go together with you, just like Ruth said: Wherever you will go, there I will go, where you will stay overnight, there will I spend the night; your people is my people, your God is my God [Ruth 1:16–17]. And since I did go to prison then you should have known that I would not go there in vain and that I [was] seeking and pursuing a very great thing, having [great] value, I, seeing and recognizing your wholeheartedness and desire towards me, would have taken two from among you, and would have revealed what it is that I am seeking, but since you went to Warsaw and in spite of my wish made an open disclosure, therefore I read this verse [as applying] to you: Since you were hasty *etc.* the one Jacob said to Reuben in *Gen: C. 49. v. 4. Paches Kamaim al tausar ki aliso misch kewe owicho os chilalto iezui olo.* He runs there as quick as water. You will not be the elder. Because you rose up on the bed of your father you have shamed my bed by that ascension.

Frank mentions the common goal of the movement—"What . . . I am seeking"—which must remain unrevealed until the Company is ready for it. But the followers have demonstrated their lack of faith by exposing Frank to the inquiry in Warsaw, which led to Frank's long stay in prison. As doctrine, it speaks to the listeners negatively—"You should have (but didn't)," then "I would have (but couldn't)"—but the dictum positively intends for the listeners to be perceptive, faithful, and obedient.

193. In Iwanie I told you the parable of a rifleman who pursued a bird through a forest. The bird sang and the hunter followed its voice. The bird flew in front of him from tree to tree, until it fled inside the palace of the king. The hunter pursued it even there. What did the bird do? It perched behind the portrait of the king and was no longer afraid of the hunter. So we must take shelter beneath her wings, for she is the portrait of the king himself.

The Shekhina is in fact "the portrait of the king himself," and she will give shelter to her devotees. Many of the ascriptions of time and of place of utterance that are found in the dicta, especially the reference to "Iwanie," are not what they seem. Frank employs this one to return with his listeners to the time of the initial settlement of their community. Although both Zvi's wife and Barukhia's were called the Matronita, as were Frank's wife and daughter, the Shekhina doctrine developed more fully after Frank's exposure to the national mariolatry at the shrine near his jail in Czestochowa. By the time of the canonic delivery of the dicta in Brünn and Offenbach, Frank was struggling to elevate his daughter's role, and he identifies her with the female divinity. Portraits of Zvi were an integral part of his cult in Poland. The sanctified portrait of Ewa may issue from this tradition but gains an enhanced role as a result of contact with iconolatry at Czestochowa.

129. When fishermen catch whales, it is their custom to tie a rope around the neck and, when it gets too tight, to loosen it a little, until the fisherman gets to the shore with his boat, then he jerks it and pulls it to the shore; it is similar with you, I have

you tied by a rope which I have loosened on you intentionally, to see if you possess virtue, steadfastness, but I did not find that in you.

130. Only to wipe out all laws, all religions, did I come to Poland, and it is my desire to bring life forth into this world—if you had gone in wholeness and one of you had not departed. But when I saw your trespasses and not one of you remained to whom I might give life, I had to let that power slip from my hands.

Drushim ("lessons drawn from the Scriptures")

185. Neither you nor the whole world knows anything of Esau: who he is and what he is. It was not in vain that Jacob bowed down to him 7 times; and concerning the 400 men who were with him, we know nothing of who they are. Pay heed: when those wondrous garments were put into his [Jacob's] hands he was entrusted with that which we pursue. But just because the robes are of a certain nature, should we assume that the one who wears them is of that nature as well? For a fool looks only at the costume; but one who is wise, at the one who wears the costume. Jacob could not receive the blessing except by being dressed incognito in those robes. The proof of which is that Isaac smelled the odor of the clothing and blessed him. I want you to merit coming to Esau and seeing him, so that my children might be like Esau.

All the biblical allusions here are from Genesis, chapters 32 and 33. Many of the interpretations suggested by Frank come from the Zohar: For example, Zohar I, 171b, has Jacob bowing to the Shekhina. Zohar III, 152a, discusses the clothes and the person wearing them, in order to explain how the soul is clothed in the body; likewise, the secret Torah is disguised in dress appropriate for this world but can be known in its real meaning to one who will look beneath the garb. Zohar I, 142b, draws on the midrash of Genesis Rabbah for the tale of the descent of the miraculous robes of Adam to Nimrod (the great hunter) and goes on to explain how, once the clothes have been returned to Jacob, the elect patriarch, their miraculous odor returns, and Isaac, having smelled it, knows that it is proper to bless Jacob.[3] In Genesis Rabbah 75:12, the 400 men (Gen. 32:6) are either kings wearing crowns or commanders of 400 divisions. Through all this Frank tells another story: that Jacob has the robes only temporarily and that they really belong to Esau. The Zohar explains that Esau fought and killed Nimrod for them. In Frank's language, "coming to Esau" (or "to Seir" or "to Edom"; these are bynames for Esau, and "Edom," especially, refers to Christianity) means coming back to the way things should be, to the secret faith, to the world of power and physical prowess. When Frank refers to the Big Brother elsewhere, by that name, (his older brother), he, being Jacob, is referring to Esau, with whom he wishes to achieve unity. The religion of Edom is not simply Christianity, nor is baptism more than a necessary layer, a necessary passage and a disguise through which Christianity may be conquered.

186. Our fathers labored, walked, and designed those ways along which we now walk but they surely never trod them. We now must go and really tread them, just as one treads out wine in the vineyard.

This reference is to Isaiah 63:1–6, especially verse 3, where God's vengeance is compared to treading out the grapes of wrath, crushing them, and squeezing from them the good wine, leaving the skins and seeds behind. The laws (the ways the fathers prepared) must be utterly crushed beneath the feet of Frank and the Company so that the juice can be gotten out of the fruit, free from dregs.

187. Who can speak of Isaac, Jacob, Esau, who can penetrate them? For they are the beginning and end of the world. In particular, from the place where I am now staying in Brünn, I certainly cannot speak of them. But you must know this: Esau is a true man; Seir is likewise a man; Edom, too, is just such a man; the father of Edom is also a true man. And all of them are the leaders of the world.

188. From what place did Isaac take the blessing which he gave to Jacob and Esau? Surely from a high and precious place. Isaac knew that Jacob was a whole man and would dwell in both tents. But Esau was the sort of man who knew only hunting, and was a man of the fields; then why did Isaac love him more than Jacob? Likewise, when Isaac had nothing to eat, he asked only Esau to take his weapon and hunt and cook for him a dish from his hunting, so that he would bless him, and did not say that to Jacob. And thereafter, when Jacob stood before him, dressed in Esau's clothing, Isaac asked him, Is it you that is my son Esau? He smelled the odor of his clothing, then blessed him. From this, you can see how deep was his love for Esau. If Isaac was so great a man, one who could grant blessings, how could he be so mistaken then and give the blessing to Jacob? And when Jacob received that blessing and was told, You will be lord over your brothers, why was that not fulfilled? What is more, Jacob is now living under his rule, even though Esau said, What do I care about the birthright? *etc.* But you must know that at the palaces of great lords a curtain is always hung in front of the door, and before the door is opened the curtain must be drawn aside; and likewise, precious stones are generally hidden in little caskets; and such is the case here, Is there only one Esau? You must know that there is Esau and there is a second in front of him, and there are two at every place, one to help and a second to harm. The herb of life is hidden within the herb of death. But I wish that we might be worthy to see the Esau to whom we go as soon as possible, for he who is worthy to see him will receive eternal life; but not that Esau who is in front of Esau.

The layering of disguise over disguise in his homily repeats Frank's doctrine of doubleness. Nothing is only what it seems, but the external appearance does hint at what lies beneath it. Frequently, the hint is inverse, what lies outside is the opposite of that which it covers. The "herb of life" reference is drawn from the Talmud (TB Yoma 72b) and shows that Frank was able to make use of the literature he was condemning, and that his followers were sufficiently well versed to recognize the source.

That Jacob would "dwell in both tents" (Gen. 25:27) is interpreted in the Zohar (II, 175b) to mean that Jacob was the perfectly balanced patriarch containing full measures of both love (known as Hesed in the Sefirotic system and judgment (Gevurah or Din). And yet, in Frank's reading of his type-story—the story of Jacob, Esau, and then Joseph—Jacob is imperfect; and the blessing of Isaac, "Be lord over your brothers" (Gen. 27:29), is not only ineffective, but also, by disdaining his own right to the blessing, Esau has assured his own possession of it and his supremacy over Jacob. Again, the Torah, as the Patriarchs would have it, or as the rabbinic authorities would have it, is only right in Frank's assessment in that it is predictably the reverse of the higher truth, the Torah of Emanation.

190. The Maiden may hide herself when one alone sees her, but when several become worthy to see her and look upon her, she can no longer hide or conceal herself. Even though she might be able to keep out of sight for a short time, in the end she must stand revealed to all. Recall the parable of the servant-girl who inherited her lady's property. How often do people try to paint her so that she might never disappear and the whole world might look upon her? But that only comes from the side of death. But we, when we are worthy to see her and shelter ourselves beneath her wings, be they invisible, will attain life; and she will reveal herself more charming every day; and each will see her according to his degree: the more worthy one is, the more beautiful he will see her; and each will look upon her in accord with his own heart.

Prov. 30:23 provides the figures of the lady and the servant/thief, whom Zohar III, 69a, interprets, respectively, as the true Shekhina and her evil image ("the female of the great depth"). Frank also sees the lady as the Shekhina, the Maiden, picturing an all-encompassing persona of purity and love and a powerful representative of humanity in the upper world (like Mary). Ps. 36:8 provides Zohar I, 57b, with the image of the Shekhina as the shelter from physical death, which is only brought about by sin. Frank uses this image to promise, as had preceding messiahs, an end to sin and an end to death—monstrous eminences of the domain of the servant-girl who now rules—but where the others mean that righteousness, as defined by tradition, will displace sin and so there will be no death, Frank means that when the Maiden repossesses her world, no act that is committed will be sinful, and thus death will have no dominion.

192. I came to Edom with only a small handful of people. I sent not nor sought permission from any king to enter that country. No one prohibited me when I entered there. Moses had 600,000 men with him and had to seek permission [and,] having sent to the king of Edom that he be permitted to cross through his country, (but) the king refused him, saying, I'll come out against you with arms.

Edom is here equated with Poland and its state religion, Catholicism. Frank recasts the history of his entry into Poland—his crossing of the Dniester in 1755—as a heroic feat. He contrasts it to Moses' failure to cross into Edom on the way to the land of Israel. Frank says that Moses failed because he was insufficiently courageous, ensnarled in the Torah of fear and restriction. The king of Edom, under no such restraints, was a true king (a reference to Num. 21:14–18).

Theology

Frank's theology constitutes something so new that it alters the substance of the Kabbalah itself to the same degree that Luria's put a new face on the Zohar. Frank's lacks the fineness of Luria's because his access to the resources of the literature is so limited; but while it is crude, it is striking, going beyond Shabbateanism, particularly in Frank's celebration of his own sturdy character.

578. No man in the world has yet had a soul, not even the First or the Second. Not any of the Patriarchs, the pillars of the world, have had souls. For a soul cannot come from any other than God himself and from no other place. At that time the worlds will be stable, and he who possesses a soul then will also be eternally stable and will be able to see from one end of the world to the other and more and more and higher, as was said above. For at the creation of Adam three things were missing and where there is lack there can be no stability and that is precisely what is written [Gen. 2:3], *Eiszer boro Elohim laisos*—God created so that he could make which means, in order that he might make man without a flaw thereafter. We can see it clearly, when children ask their father for bread, does he give them a stone instead? Just so you see that there exist honest, God-fearing men and we see that even though they ask God for bread yet they get none. Where is the love of the father for his own children? And further, how is it proper for a father to kill his children? from which it follows that the true God himself has had no part in the present creation. Therefore, all the vessels have been broken until now, for he who created them broke them himself so that they might come out purer and finer, and that, that is what stands [Gen. 6:4]: *Wehanfilim houi beorez*—There were *nefilim* in the world. And they were already called *nefilim* because of their falling and being cast down from greatness. Therefore it cannot be that there has been a soul in such a coarse and lowly flesh as is now. I wanted to lead you to a certain place where you could first bathe and cleanse yourself so that you might have the strength to receive a soul. And now you cannot reach that degree, so that you might be worthy to come to Esau. I wanted to say only one word to you and immediately your eyes would have been opened, but it would have been necessary to speak to you from the beginning and not from the middle, for when the beginning is not known then one may not understand things well. How could you fail to understand when I wrote it to you in a letter? If I had given you one word you would have put your hands beneath my feet so that I might not tread upon the earth. It is a sign that I have something to say. You would have had to come forth in humbleness and she would have taken pity on you; and now that she will reveal herself to the world it must be the way that she pass through my house; and you would have been prepared to serve her; and the King would have come to take her from your hands, as it clearly stands [Zech. 9:9]: *Hine Malkech owau loch*—Behold your king will come to you. If you had endured those 13 years, just as I said to you in the parable, about that master who left the building for 13 years, that is precisely to come to her as the Psalmist said, *Ani haiom ieladticho*—I bore you today. Now I will suffer in Brünn another 13 years for you. You must now stand apart and be beneath

the heels of the sheep so that you not be hurt, for your own good, until you come to Esau.

Departing from the Kabbalah of the Zohar and of Luria, in which all parts of the soul were to be found in the first Adam, the Shabbatean Kabbalah stressed the idea that some of the soul was lacking altogether at the creation of this world and remains distant from it. Frank collapses the soul's parts into a single soul and insists that this soul resides with the "true God himself"—perhaps the super-Sefira, the infinite Eyn Sof—and was not deposited in the "present creation" by its creating deity. He says that when this world becomes "stable," the soul will come to reside in this world, in the Adam of that time, the messiah. The time will be that of changelessness because change betokens defect and decomposition, just as desire entails lack and fear implies ignorance. Adam lacked godly stature and the vantage from which to see everything at once. Shabtai Zvi (the First) and Barukhia Russo (the Second) both failed to overcome death and change; thus they could not receive a soul. Frank infers, from the Hebrew text of Gen. 2:3, that something was left unmade on the first six days, and that the Sabbath was to be the perfecting of that work, the repaired world of the messiah.

Opposing the rabbinic doctrine that disaster indicates the presence of sin, Frank proves his point that this world is not the perfected world, when he observes that those without sin do go hungry, suffer, and die. Frank utterly rejects the idea of secret sin or its punishment and, on this basis, he spurns guilt. He nonetheless believes that the destroyed nature of this world is purposeful, and he follows a line of the Kabbalah (and of Shabbatean doctrines) that maintains that God encompasses evil (as well as good) and seeks to purge himself of the evil by creating this world. Frank refers to this world as that of the broken vessels (see chapter 6, on the Lurianic myth) and in this tradition he interprets the *nefilim* of Gen. 6:4 (elsewhere understood only as giants), through its Hebrew root, as "the fallen." At this point, Frank's new religion, the *das/da'as edom* (the faith/knowledge of Esau, Edom) appears again by name, and Frank laments that if his followers had only shed their attachments to traditional Judaism, its texts and its psychology of submission, they could have reached Esau/Edom.

Frank makes reference to a letter (known as the "red letter" for it was written in red ink [in Hebrew, the consonants *'dm* are the root of both the word for Edom and that for red]), which he dispatched widely throughout the Jewish world from his prison-cathedra in Czestochowa (where he was housed from 1770 to 1783); more letters were sent later by his daughter. The "she" in the letters is the Shekhina, daughter/wife of the Unknowable, Ineffable "King," the True God himself, who will come to them (cf. Zech. 9:9), Frank's followers, the only true congregation, to receive her from their hands. This reunion between God and the Shekhina signifies the completion of the perfect world. On that day the faithful would be born as they were to remain eternally, unchanging and perfect, as in the perfect creation, with souls. Having failed so far to achieve stability (wholeness), the Frankists are insufficiently prepared for the struggle and must bide their time, meekly, in subservience to Frank, and must continue to learn ("beneath the heel of the sheep/ beside the footsteps of the flock," Song of Songs 1:8, as read in the *Zohar hadash, midrash shir ha-shirim*, 70d).

Dreams

Frank's dreams are striking in their forthright and revealing character; only occasionally do they seem polemical and artificial. Interpreting one follower's dream of having sat with others around him and eaten pieces of candy, Frank says the meaning of it is, "*May my help come soon!*"—a pun on the name of the candy, *halvah*, and on the Hebrew/Yiddish optative interjection "if only," "may" (*halavai*, in Hebrew). Frank seems to show here an awareness of the principles of image-to-word symbolism in the dream process, and a sensitivity to his own overbearing role as the interpreter of others' dreams, which he makes light of in the pun. His dreams divulge his emotions with as little restraint as those of Vital. The dreams of his followers and, pitifully, those of his daughter, too, are much poorer; they are imitative of his and are told to him in order to please him.

> 2251. The 13th of July [17]84. I went to a *szkol*. Another one followed me and said to me: Yakov! wait for me and I will go to the *szkol*. I answered: I will not wait, because the road runs toward me.—Exposition: Some road is prepared for me.—I saw myself then in the court of the Prussian king. In one room sat the king of Prussia, Friedrich, but on lower benches there sat 12 or 13 lords; all were as if dumb and none opened his mouth. I was the cupbearer. I brought a flask of old, very powerful Tokaj wine. The king gestured to me that I give him some of that wine to drink. I had thick glasses in my hand; I mixed half a glass of fine sand with half a glass of wine, and mixed the sand with water and gave it to him myself to drink and he drank. The king gestured that I give some to those lords to drink. Again I mixed sand and wine and gave all of them to drink. I also brought wine with sand again and gave them to drink a second time.

A playful quality appears here, in the pun on the word "runs" and in the *prostak*-trick Frank plays on the foolish nobles and the great king. A hint of an autohagiographic quality emerges as well in the number of the nobles—which recalls the number of brothers in Frank's court, the number of tribes of Israel, the number of Jesus' Apostles, the number of paladins at Charlemagne's court, and the tradition descended from that—and their humble relationship to the king. The type of wine mentioned creates verisimilitude through its familiar exoticism; the other local touch—the name and nation of the king—elevates the tale to global significance, given Friedrich's importance. Frank, the mere cupbearer, makes fools of the great and they ask for more.

> 2189. In the month of October, 1775 the 13th day in Brünn the Lord saw a dream like this: I came to one inn in which I was given kasha with milk. Having tasted it, I experienced a great sweetness and I recognized by the taste that it was mare's milk. Then I saw that that kasha was from horse dung. I also saw that I rode on (short) [narrow] bridges, everywhere with fear, but I crossed them luckily.

According to the most famous of the Hebrew dream-interpretation manuals, Almoli's *Interpretation of Dreams*: "One who sees himself drinking mare's milk will find wealth." Grasses and grains are, in general, likewise regarded as harbingers of wealth in Almoli's work. Excreta are symbols of concealed wealth or, otherwise, harbingers of fortune. The "sweetness" Frank feels appears elsewhere in the *Collection* in connection with the access to power: In dictum 48, for example, questioning a proponent of a contending Shabbatean sect, Frank asks, If he came to taste the bitterness of death, why did he not taste the sweetness of power? This dream may thus be the most artificial and self-conscious of the visions found in the Lublin manuscript. Still, the inn and the animal imagery, the oral-anal/intake-output motif, and the inverted vision itself are characteristic of an easily identifiable worldview that is uniquely, commonly, and guilelessly Frank's.

Of the several sayings of Rabbi Nahman of Bratslav, one of the most famous—now commonly sung—is, "This whole world is a very narrow bridge, and the most important thing is not to be afraid." (The Polish word that describes bridges in the Frank dream actually means "short," but that makes no sense in the parable and is probably an error of mis-specification for a more general term like "little," or there may have been an error in transcribing *tzarim* (in Hebrew/Yiddish, "narrow") as *ktzarim* (in Hebrew/Yiddish, "short"). Comparing the tales R. Nahman told with Frank's, and keeping in mind that he began to tell them after making an initiatory journey to Kaminiec-Podolsk—Frankism's earliest home—it seems incredible that R. Nahman did so in ignorance of Frank's earlier efforts. The parallel here draws the two messiahs close together and gives even more support to the thesis that R. Nahman learned from Frank's dicta or his followers.

2213. I saw myself in a Jewish szkol, in which Truebelievers also sat. The Jews jumped at them and beat them bloody; the Truebelievers also beat the Jews bloody. But I left that szkol so they would not beat me too.

The Truebelievers are followers of Shabtai Zvi; the Jews, normative, rabbinic Jews. Frank sees himself as a force independent of either group and achieves victory by allowing them to destroy each other.

2246. The 22nd of June [17]84. Two maidens from Poland, daughters, were leaving and wanted to lie down on the bed. I wanted to have intercourse with them; at that one nun came, undressed and also lay on the bed. I lay on the bed. The nun says to me: Lord Franek, what are you doing? indeed I am married. I reply: What of it?— Exposition: That thing with the nuns was prepared for you, that you do that with them in squares, towns and streets, and that would have been an eternal praise for you, also that the priests would become your servants. But you did not want it.

2212. The 21st of October 1783: I saw as if I had on my hand a gold ring, it fell from my hand on a mirror and broke it into small pieces. Then I turned the mirror over on the other side; it also shone and a ring also fell from my hand and broke it.—The Lord interpreted: My assistance hastens to come.

This dream is so revealing and so unself-conscious it dazzles. There can be no simpler expression of Frank's awareness of his own duplicity and his own desires than the mirror, the clearest image of self-alienation, and the symbol of the golden ring. Frank steadfastly refuses to look at himself with a question in mind; he has the golden ring and the power to destroy self-doubt at every turn.

Threefold tales

Frank's threefold tales are constructed just like his autohagiographa. On one fold these tales are simply stories; on the second, they tell the Kabbalistic myth of the creation, shattering and repair of the cosmos; on the third, the details of the history of the Jews appear, ending with that of the Shabbateans, Frank and his following, and almost, but not quite, reaching as far as the repair of the broken world. The tales and the autohagiographa have the power to repair by being told. In the auto-hagiographa, Frank plays the role of the hero-messiah, while in the tales, a fictional character plays the role of the hero-messiah Frank. The setting of the autohagio-graphic tale is the consensual world of the average observer, with all its local color markings; another world, well known but known to be fantastic, presents itself in the threefold tale. The tales often contain elements from the domain of the fairy tale, but they, like the autohagiographa, are true.

It's just as difficult—more so, in fact, since there is absolutely no continuous tradition of the interpretation of Frank's tales—to identify all the elements of the Frank threefold tale as it is to identify those of R. Nahman's more famous tales, the *sippure ma'asiyot* (see chapter 9). In both cases, all the elements in the tales should operate on all three folds. Frank provides some help when he elucidates the discipline/moral of the tale in a coda, stepping outside the tale to address his follow-ers/listeners directly. In the first tale presented below, on the second fold, the king is the ruler of this broken universe—not the true God, who is far away, but the one re-sponsible for all the wretchedness. His son functions as Yesod (foundation, the ninth Sefira); and Iwan, as the male aspect of the tenth Sefira, Malkhut (kingdom). When Iwan goes on his dangerous quest for the prince's quiver, the plot on the sec-ond fold is the (future) history of the messiah's descent into evil, which he makes in order to release the lights that fell when the vessels broke in the cosmic cataclysm that began the universe. By doing this, he begins a process of *tikkun*—coupling and reknitting—that will reverberate upward so that the ninth Sefira (Yesod) mates with the sixth (Tiferet) and so on, until the universe is perfect and stable and ruled by the "true God himself" (the Eyn Sof, that which is above the Sefirot). The quiver, now returned from its distant location, mates the sun and the moon, sym-bols for Yesod and Tiferet, that are carved on it. On the third fold, the tale inscribes Frank's journey through this world as a mere servant, rough and tough and crafty, magically endowed and accompanied by his loyal helpers—the Company and all the animal kingdom—who are girded at his command for war against the forces of all religions and their fearsome (but not to him) restrictiveness.

In the passage of the tale that he labels the parable (the moral of the tale on the third fold), Frank cites the "burden of silence," as the phrase is traditionally in-terpreted, from Isa. 21:11 (cf. TB Sanh. 94a; Zohar II, 130b–131a; and H. Vital, *shaar hagilgulim*, introduction, 26, end; contrast the common interpretation, "the burden of Duma"). Frank wants to require his followers to keep their activities and beliefs secret, particularly after the confessions of 1760 that led to his imprisonment. The telling of the tale itself, its performance, by Frank transformed its threefold nature into a live unity, all of it modified by the interactions of the circumstances and especially by the dependence of the tale-teller on his listeners.

138. There was once a prince to whom a dream appeared three times. He was carrying a quiver carved with the sun on one side and the moon on the other. When he awoke he begged his father to have that quiver brought to him, at any cost. His father summoned his most important nobles and sent them off to many countries, over seas, to find the quiver of the sun and moon. They went, but came back having gained nothing and lost everything. Next he selected his greatest senators. But these too returned, likewise unsuccessful, tired to death and worn out as well. It so chanced that a certain prostak named Iwan Iwaniewicz, a Russian prince, happened by. He began making fun of the gentlemen, laughing at them. They, being completely worn out, were on their way back. He repeated his acts several times until he had aroused their anger and they began to beat him. But he, in his turn, thrashed them all. The gentlemen, greatly offended, went to the king and reported that, A vile man has appeared here laughing at us and several times making fun of us. The king had him summoned. When asked why he had made light of the gentlemen he answered, Why shouldn't I have a little fun with people who set out to search for something without knowing the path or way that leads to it? And the king asked him, And do you know the place? He answered, I know there are three bridges: one of brass, the second of copper and the third of iron. I must first cross them and only then will I be able to find that thing the king seeks. /:Here the Lord added, The Truebelievers know nothing. There are black, red, copper, iron, silver and golden people, and mountains likewise.:/After a long ride, they came to the first bridge, the one of brass. Iwan said to his two men, Stay here on this side of the bridge, but do not fall asleep during the whole of the night. Amuse yourselves however you choose, play cards or anything else, but do not sleep. He stretched a white towel above their heads and said, As soon as you notice this towel begin to turn red, come to me straight away. So, having told them this, Iwan went beneath the bridge. On the other side of the bridge he saw a horse with a three-headed rider upon him. When Three-heads approached the edge of the bridge his horse became frightened. The man noticed and said to his horse, What do you fear? Is Iwan Iwaniewicz trying to scare you? Well then, I'll lop off his head! Then Iwan leaped out from beneath the bridge and called out, I have come here not to lose but to take! The battle commenced. Iwan's men, left behind, saw that the towel had turned blood-red. They came running to his aid and began to fight, horse against horse, hound against hound, bird against bird and so cut off all three heads of Three-heads. They went on until they came to the bridge of copper. Things happened as before. Iwan gave his companions the same orders, with this difference: that they were to come to his aid when blood had begun to drip from the towel. Iwan squeezed under the bridge again. A seven-headed man rode up on the other side. His horse, frightened, leaped back nearly a league. The knight asked his horse the same questions, and Iwan called out, here too, Not to lose have I come but to

take! Soon they began to battle with each other and immediately the blood began to drip from the towel. At this sign his comrades ran out and again, as before, fought until they had cut off all seven heads. They went on until they came to the bridge of iron. The same instructions were given as had been before, with this change: that they were to hasten to his aid when blood began to pour from the towel. Agreement. Iwan went off under the bridge. A nine-headed knight rode up on his horse. The horse sprang back a league and a half. The nine-headed one asked him, Why fear Iwan? Iwan rushed out from under the bridge and made the threat, Not to lose but to take! and began the battle. Blood began flowing from the towel. His companions came and joined the fray. All nine heads were cut off. After the three knights had been beaten, our victors glimpsed a great castle. Iwan said, Wait here and let me go ahead of you into the palace. He transformed himself into a pretty kitten and ran into the palace. A lady sat there, the wife of the three-headed knight. She caught the kitten and petted it while saying to herself, Iwan Iwaniewicz has killed my husband, but I will avenge myself tomorrow. I will lead the sun down lower than usual so that it might burn very hot, and I will transform myself into a well and a tree spreading over it, green and leafy. As soon as he gets to it, he will want to rest. Then shall I have my vengeance upon him and on them. Having heard this, the kitten ran off. When he'd gotten back to his companions, he reminded them to do nothing without asking him first. The next day the sun began to heat up extraordinarily. His comrades saw the well and the tree and, delighted, wanted nothing more than to rest beneath the tree and sip water from the well. God forbid! Iwan shouted, Don't you dare! I'll go first. When he'd come close to the well, he bent himself over it, very carefully and craftily, so that his sword just happened to fall from its sheath. He picked it up casually and then shoved it into the well with all his strength. The well turned to blood and released all its slain power. And then he said to his companions, Now let's go to the palace. We'll have some rest there. We'll meet many princesses and ladies who've been locked up there for a long time. There is [found] the sun-and-moon we will take back to the king. When I told you that tale you should have known that if I were Iwan, you should be sons of Iwan and there was no need to weigh yourselves down with teaching, but only to bear the burden of silence. By my parable you see that the king sent important noblemen out and all returned empty-handed. You should have understood that the thing was not given to the wise and the learned but to a prostak such as I am, because the wise look to Heaven, though they see nothing there. But all nourishment springs from the dirt and so it is to the dirt we should look. In the end, both his companions heeded him alone. They turned aside neither left nor right, but only followed his advice. Therefore, what they sought and desired they found, whole. From this you should have understood that the parable applies wholly to you.

EWA FRANK

Ewa Frank's court at Offenbach tumbled into financial collapse when followers from the cities ceased bringing contributions to her. We have to mark her accession to her father's reign as the Jewish equivalent to the general rise of simple charlatanry in the period. Something of the jumble of her father's teachings remained, along with a few of the Believers, so that rituals and meetings, intermarriages and christenings, were features of the court conducted for her, along with the humiliations and rapacious alms-gathering borne by all who visited.

An account of the court was written by Moses Porges in his memoirs. His parents sent him there from Prague, which had become the most important center of activity of the sect. He managed to escape, but with his faith destroyed and his wallet empty.

I got to Offenbach—an open city—just after nightfall. It was dark and rainy. I asked, "Where is the Polish court?" I was directed toward another part of the city. A magnificent building. Tears of religious ardor gushed from my eyes as I stood before the holy house. The door was opened for me; a young man, dressed in Turkish garb, greeted me, embraced me, kissed me, called me "Brother" and said that I was awaited. A group of Believers was assembled, I discerned among them an elderly, honorable and stately man with a snow-white beard. He was wearing the uniform of a colonel. His name was Czynski. This man led me to a room on the second floor. There he promised me that he would always help me with advice, like my own father, and that he would instruct me how to behave in the presence of the Holy Mother. Afterwards I was led to another chamber where there were seated three men in Polish garb and with long beards looking into large folio volumes, sunk deep in thought. I was shocked and dumbfounded to see various emblems of the Catholic church, a painting of the *Gevira* [The Lady, Ewa Frank] in the adornments of the Holy Mother [the Virgin Mary], and yet other paintings of various men and all kinds of figures with Hebrew inscriptions on them. On one painting were inscribed ten words which I recognized from the High Holiday prayers: Keter, Hokhma, Binah, Gedulah, Gevurah, Tiferet, Netzach, Hod, Yesod, Malkhut, all connected among themselves by lines and all of them connected to the word Eyn Sof. One of the people sitting there turned to me and said, "My son, the Shekinah is in need, *shekhinta begaluta* [the Shekina is in exile], Edom and Ishmael [Rome and Islam] have captured her. Her children must free her and suffer together with her. When the three Sefirot are joined together properly in trinity, like the triple-thread, then redemption will come. Two of them have already appeared in the form of human beings. We must wait for the third to come. Fortunate is he who is chosen to be joined with Tiferet for from him will be born the redeemer of the world. Do your service and remain on guard at all times so that you may merit being the chosen one." And thereafter I was given a card on which was drawn the picture with the ten words.

Later in that same night many believers, old and young, visited me. On the next day I was summoned to appear before the Gevira. She inhabited the first floor. A chambermaid met me in the anteroom and had me wait a little while. How excited I was and how my heart beat! At last the door opened and I crossed the threshold. I dared not look the Gevira in the face, but fell to my knees before her and kissed her feet, for so had I been instructed. She spoke a few friendly words to me, praised my father and my decision to come here. When I withdrew, I deposited my wallet with the sixty guldens of silver and gold upon a table and left the room with my face towards the Gevira. The impression she made upon me was of grace and nobility. She had a friendly face which expressed kindness, delicate modesty, and gentleness and her eyes, a saintly dreaminess. She was no longer young but created an effect of charm. Her hands and feet were splendid and beautiful. As I later learned I had pleased her. (N. M. Gelber, ed., "The Memoirs of Moses Porges," *Yivo Historishe Shriftn*, 1 [1929] 272–274)

BIBLIOGRAPHIC NOTE   Guidance to most of the important monographs and articles written prior to 1971 can be found in G. Scholem "Frank, Jacob, and the Frankists," in the *Encyclopaedia Judaica*. My own work—short articles in the *Proceedings of the World Congress of Jewish Studies* and elsewhere and *The Collection of the Words of the Lord (Jacob Frank)*, (New Haven, forthcoming)—adds to this and updates it. At the end of his life, Professor Chone Shmeruk, of the Hebrew University, turned his attention to some aspects of the dicta, including their language and the practices that are mentioned in them. Editions of the Polish text of the Lublin manuscript and the Kraków manuscripts appeared in 1996 and 1997 (Warsaw), edited by Jan Doktór.

9

THE TZADDIK OF HASIDISM

The multiplication of messiahs stirred by or associated with Shabbateanism is at least partially responsible for the proliferation of messiahs and prophets in Hasidism, which first arose in the eighteenth century in eastern Europe and has continued until the present, its followers still wearing the clothing of that period, and thought of today as members of ultraorthodox Jewry. This chapter examines the connection between Shabbateanism/Frankism and Hasidism and then focuses on four important hasidic figures who either were considered to be the messiah or closely resembled messianic figures. The accounts of these four—the Baal Shem Tov; Rabbi Nahman of Bratslav; Rabbi Itzhak Eizik of Komarno; and the Lubavitcher rebbe, Menachem Mendel Schneerson—show clear similarities to the accounts of Jewish messiahs presented in previous chapters. The hasidic rebbe is a quasi-divine being. His figure is characterized by tales of miracles and cosmic repair; claims of embodying the soul of a previous messiah figure; in some cases, asceticism and, in others, its antithesis. Antinomianism has been rejected by Hasidism. Militarism also does not appear except symbolically, in some holy tunes, among other things. Localism becomes a primary feature as each hasidic group is classified according to its locale and its rebbe controls followers who came from that region.

FROM LURIANISM TO SHABBATEANISM TO HASIDISM

Frankism was the last variation in the version of the messiah that was imprinted with its essential nature in the school of Luria and Vital and then elaborated by Zvi

199

and his immediate successors. The task of this messiah was nothing less than to repair the cosmos and bring about the end of time. Many former duties of the messiah, including traditional study and observance of legal and ethical principles, disappeared in favor of this larger role and a divine character. These messiahs, too, failed to produce either political or transcendental success, but the desire to achieve both access to Heaven and political freedom remained strong in the heart of the individual Jew. The miseries suffered at this time by traditional Jewish society, in southern Poland particularly, were grotesque. Not only the Polish economy, but the polity itself, was collapsing. Messianic movements arose outside Judaism to enact the passion of Polish non-Jewish society. In order to escape even worse economic and political circumstances in other parts of Poland, the Jewish population shifted toward Podolia, draining the Jewish economy there and causing Jewish self-government to crumble. All this had faced Frankism as well as the nascent movements of Hasidism, and Hasidism was obliged to mitigate the centrifugal force of Shabbatean, and then Frankist, theology. Hasidism's historical moment forced a sort of messianism upon it, as it shared with its predecessors the feature of a semidivine central figure. But from the beginning, the disintegrating society offered little important resistance to its program, and what might have been a full-blown, self-immolating messianic movement suddenly found itself in a position of power and obliged to address daily concerns of governance, economics, and community relations. The peculiar messiah of Hasidism, the tzaddik (righteous one, rebbe), emerged, the familiar autocrat of the spirit, who was surrounded by a management team, a board of directors, a cabinet with more power over him than any previous group of followers had had over its messiah. This latter-day quasimessianism has proven itself sufficiently stable to endure even the lack of a central figure altogether, or, more frequently, both his weakness and his cosmic egocentrism.

There are two major schools of thought concerning the affiliation of Hasidism with Shabbateanism—one holding that Hasidism, in revulsion, moved away from messianic fervor; the other viewing tzaddikism as one of a number of strong links between Hasidism and Shabbateanism. In my view, Hasidism lowered the tone, and scattered the messianic focus, of Shabbateanism and thereby made it legitimate. No longer was attention concentrated exclusively on a single figure, nor was the apocalyptic passion so inflamed. Hasidism localized Shabbateanism, affording each shtetl (Jewish village or quarter) a messiah of its own, the tzaddik. This localism was erected on the Shabbatean deemphasis of what had been the prime goal of messianism: the return of the Jews to the land of Israel and the reestablishment of the messianic movements there. The shtetl locale became the Jerusalem of the Hasidic following, the primary pilgrimage site; there, the faithful brought their offerings, heard prophecies, gazed upon, ate at the table with, and actually had audiences with, the rebbe or tzaddik.

Hasidism was not that far removed from some forms of Shabbateanism. Frankism, which was the movement most proximate in time and territory to the rise of Hasidism, replaced Jerusalem with Poland as the "place of the Ascent." Judaism had not seen such an abundance of messiahs as Shabbateanism produced since the messianic flare-up during the struggles against Rome, and Hasidism continued this plurality in its maintenance, ultimately, of dozens of tzaddikim. Shabbateanism itself may be seen as an extension of Luria's theology and of the practices that emerged from the overheated mystic groups and atmosphere of Safed. Both Shabbateanism and Hasidism continued to emphasize the miracle-working that was so characteristic of the conduct of Luria and Vital. Lurianic society also promoted multiple messiah candidates by positing world salvation through the intermediation of whoever was most spiritually qualified for it. The chain that joins Lurianism to Shabbateanism and then to Hasidism includes, in particular, a somewhat disreputable belief in various forms of metensomatosis: reincarnation, metempsychosis, polypsychism, soul-wandering. The Shabbatean candidates after Zvi were, for the most part, alleged reincarnations of his soul; as noted previously, Zvi's third wife, Yocheved, was responsible for electing her brother, Yakov Querido (Filosof), as the new possessor of Zvi's soul. Furthermore, the dynasticism and internal political struggles in Hasidism find their roots in Shabbateanism, as does one of its common solutions to the (less disastrous in Hasidism than in more typical messianic cults) lack of a direct descendant—turning to the family of the wife of the messiah for a messianic heir.

Hasidism emphasized the cosmic importance of the individual Jew and his acts and held at bay an interest in political and economic liberation, in favor of a hierarchically organized, sectarian mode of life. (Nevertheless, local governments looked on with alarm and were sometimes moved to interfere with, restrain or even confine the leaderships.) The tzaddikim attained entry to the courts and secrets of Heaven at the urgent, faithful behest of their followers (hasidim). In a role that began with the founder of the movement, Israel ben Eliezer, and was continued by the most important contemporary hasidic figure, R. Menachem Mendel Schneerson, the late leader of the Lubavitch (Chabad) sect, the tzaddik has acted as intermediary between his hasidim and the divine. The cosmic character of the tzaddik lies beyond the aspirations and abilities of the hasid, but the tzaddik only rarely or only partially aspires to outright acknowledgment as the messiah. By declaring that worldly affairs (i.e., politics) possess cosmic relevance, the tzaddik directs the individual process of salvation toward national redemption—the traditional interest of Jewish messianism. The tzaddik is a charismatic leader, and he does combine the roles of the messiah-king, prophet, and priest. While Hasidism appears to grant virtually unlimited authority to the passion of the individual, it in fact operates as a hierarchy headed by the tzaddik and his staff. The head is rarely moved by the voice of individual hasidim. This arrangement was introduced and routinized quickly, in response to the messianic-vacuum that followed the collapse of the Shabbatean successors, including Yakov Frank. Once again, the salvation of this world and others depended on individuals acting collectively. The tzaddik was the prime individual, symbolically, and thus had the power to lead others—to the degree *they wished.*

THE BA'AL SHEM TOV

Israel ben Eliezer (ca. 1700–1760) was a *ba'al shem* (literally, "master of the name," a folk healer) in the Ukraine and Podolia (Russia). His character and reputation caused him to be known as the Ba'al Shem Tov, the "good" one (known traditionally by an acronym, the "Besht"). He was from a country background and, at first, barely made a living as a woodcutter and a children's teacher in Jewish schools. Relatively uneducated in regard to traditional texts and approaches, he came to preach worship of God through joy and meditation, rejecting study and ascetic practices as the only means through which to reach the divine. He had visions and worked cures, and attracted followers who believed in the efficacy of his cures and in the truth of his visions and, therefore, in his message and his natural/supernatural status. It is unclear whether he or his followers ever claimed that he was the messiah, but his message and activities were taken to be transcendent, beyond the capacity of other humans, and his advice was sought and followed. He served as a lens through which the needs of Heaven—the repair of the broken cosmos—could be met on Earth through human devotion, and through which the needs of his followers, the blessings of work, health, children, and so forth, could be seen to in Heaven.

In the preface written for the collection of sacred legends about him, titled *In Praise of the Baal Shem Tov*, and originally assembled after his death by his follower and scribe, R. Dov Ber ben Shmuel, we find the following story; it establishes the dual identity of the Besht.

I heard from the son of Rabbi Jacob from Medzhibozh, who is called Rabbi Yakil, that once his father led him to the *bet-hamidrash* ["house of study and prayer"], and the Besht was praying before the ark. His father said to him in these words: "My son, observe him closely. There will not be one like him in the world until the coming of the Messiah, as he is the spark of Rabbi Simeon Ben Yohai and his companions." There is also a story . . . concerning his brother-in-law, Rabbi Gershon of Kuty and the Besht, who brought about an ascension of his soul during [afternoon prayers] in order to raise many other souls. And as it is written in the book [*The Tree of Life* (one rendition of Luria's teachings as presented by R. Hayim Vital)]. . . . "Moses our teacher, may he rest in peace, was quick to raise the souls of the living and dead every holy Sabbath eve." From this story it is evident that he was also the likeness of the soul of Moses our teacher, may he rest in peace. (From the collection of legends edited by J. Mintz and D. Ben-Amos [Northvale, 1993])

The first part of the story connects the Besht with the messiah; he is a forerunner of the messiah, and the last of these before the messiah himself appears. The Besht is therefore not the messiah, nor Elijah, but an anomalous figure in the legend of the messiah's coming. His "spark"/soul is identified with the ostensible author and messiah of the Zohar, R. Simeon Ben Yohai, whose teachings were transformed by Luria and Vital into the Lurianic Kabbalah and reduced by Hasidism to a popular program of conduct.

The second part of the story compares the Besht to Moses. Again, the Besht is not proclaimed the messiah, but the association with Moses draws him closer to that status. (The Moses-messiah tradition is mentioned in chapters 2 and 3.) The ambiguous character of the first tzaddik is developed from these two associations.

He is neither the messiah nor not the messiah. He does possess an aspect of divinity and he is charged with a cosmic destiny.

A second tale from this collection is titled "The Besht in the Messiah's Heavenly Palace," and affirms the role of the Besht, who is of the lineage of the messiah, as a model for later tzaddikim. Here, the Besht is praying before the ark on the Day of Atonement and relates his journey to Heaven to his anxious comrades in the *bet midrash*:

"I had but one more gate to pass through to appear before God, blessed be he. In that palace I found all the prayers of the past fifty years that had not ascended. Each prayer shone as bright as the bright dawn. I said to those prayers: 'Why did you not ascend before?'

"And they said: 'We were instructed to wait for you, sir, to lead us.'

"I told them: 'Come along with me.' And the gate was open."

He told the people of his town that the gate was as large as the whole world.

"When we started to accompany the prayers, one angel came and closed the door, and he put a lock on the gate."

He told them that the lock was as big as all of [the town of] Medzhibozh. "And I began to turn the lock to open it, but I could not do it. So I ran to my rabbi . . . and I said: 'The people of Israel are in great trouble and now they will not let me in. At another time I would not have forced my way in.'"

"My rabbi said: 'I shall go with you and if there is a possibility to open the gate for you I shall open it.' And when he came he turned the lock, but he could not open it either. Then he said to me: 'What can I do for you?'

"I began to complain to my rabbi. 'Why have you forsaken me at such a troubled time?'

"And he answered: 'I do not know what to do for you, but you and I will go to the palace of the Messiah. Perhaps there will be some help there.'

"With a great outcry I went to the palace of the Messiah. When our righteous Messiah saw me from afar he said to me, 'Don't shout.' He gave me two holy letters of the alphabet.

"I went to the gate. Thank God, I turned the lock and opened the gate, and I led in all the prayers. Because of the great joy when all the prayers ascended, the Accuser [who prosecutes sinful souls] became silent, and I did not need to argue. The decree [barring entry] was canceled and nothing remained of it but an impression of the decree."

The narrator goes on to relate, in the following tale:

"Once the rabbi, the hasid, our rabbi and teacher Menahem Nahum of Chernobyl, was in our town, and he told this story to the people. I came in the middle of the story, and I heard his version which contained some changes and something new—that the Messiah said to the Besht, 'I do not know whether you will open the gate, but if you do Redemption will certainly come to Israel.' He said further that this was the gate of the palace of the Bird's Nest through which no one has ever passed save the Messiah, as it is said in the holy Zohar. He said that he heard God's voice saying to him: 'What can I do with you since I must fulfill your will?'" (Mintz, Ben-Amos)

RABBI NAHMAN OF BRATSLAV

If the Besht did not advance himself as the messiah or as a claimant to any of the traditional roles in the messianic sequence, he certainly left the position of tzaddik open to an extension into those roles. The Besht's granddaughter, Feige, was noted for her own spiritual attainments. Her son Nahman stands as the least equivocal messiah in Hasidism, a peer of Zvi and of Frank, from whom he learned much.

Nahman (1772–1811) was born in the sacred geography of early Hasidism, Podolia and the Ukraine. He was raised and educated in the most traditional of hasidic households and married into another that was scarcely less so. By the time he reached his early twenties, he had gained a following in Medvedevka, in the Ukraine, to which he had moved from Medzhibozh. He journeyed to Israel, then returned home, but controversy over him and his beliefs, teachings, and behavior forced him out of village after village. He had little support from other hasidic leaders, but he gained such a hold over his following that his movement continues to adore him as its tzaddik until today. (His followers are known as Bratslavers, from his residence in Bratslav, and as the "dead" Hasidim, since their tzaddik is not alive.) Whatever one might say about Nahman's determination to arouse controversy and to teach in puzzles, two elements emerge clearly: He lived according to what he believed, and his doctrine remains the most original and impressive in Judaism since that of Luria. He never achieved his dream for himself or his progeny: the fulfillment of the messianic role according to traditional expectations. No school of Judaism outside his own sect has contended successfully with his doctrines or managed to incorporate them without altering them drastically. The tales he told have attracted attention and admiration, especially in the modern period, among people struggling with the feeling that reason is inadequate to grasp meaning in the universe or even to identify appropriate conduct.

What follows is from the autobiography of Nathan Sternharz, Nahman's scribe, which is titled *The Life of our Teacher, R. Nathan*. Sternharz assumed the role of manager of the sect after Nahman's death and orchestrated the publishing activities that saw to the dissemination of his master's teachings. His own autobiography concentrates on Nahman's life during the years after the two formed their relationship. His faith in Nahman and his professed inability to understand what Nahman tells him are molded from Nahman's own perceptions of himself. Nahman's tales and lectures are woven in and out of Nathan's account, allowing us a glimpse of how Nahman and his followers understood the tales. These tales work in the same way that Frank's tales and autohagiographic memoirs do. Every detail in the life of this tzaddik rang through the worlds-within-worlds of the universe, charged with intense meaning, echoing the history of the breakdown and repair of the cosmos. Since they are stories told by him, when they are heard by the proper ears they actually effect the repair. Nathan's recounting of the tales in their context sweeps the reader up in the pathos of a messianic impulse.

From the day he was stricken [by tuberculosis], three years before he passed away, he immediately announced that he was obliged to depart on its account, and immediately began speaking of his departure. . . . It saddened me greatly and it seemed to me that the world had been turned upside down and destroyed, Heaven forbid. . . . He remained in Bratslav over the summer and all of [1809 and 1810] until the end of Passover and then left here for Uman. There is a great deal to tell about all this and I will tell the little which I can remember, which God recalls to me.

Those three whole years he spoke about his departure a great deal. After he'd returned to Bratslav from Lemberg he would always tell us about how he was prepared to depart while he was in Lemberg and was ready and waiting and had no fear. And he was very proud of how he was strong in this matter and had been ready to depart without any fear or panic. But it had not seemed proper to him to lie there, even though great men, famous tzaddikim, lay at rest there, even so it did not seem fit to him because it was so far away from his followers and none would come to his grave or have any involvement with it. . . . And he was always telling us about his grave so that it was clear he sought and researched and considered how to choose the place where he would lie but had not found a place which suited him. [Neither Lemberg nor Bratslav suited him,] but Uman did, for, he said, in Uman it would be good to die since many holy ones rested there. . . . No one knew that it had been his intention to move there. . . . The people of Teflik traveled there a lot and he asked them to find him a place to live in Uman. They knew he would be well received there and honored, [but he changed his mind again and again].

He began to tell the "Tale of the Seven Beggars" as Passover drew near, and the story went on for two weeks. He began on the Sabbath of the 25th of Adar, [1810] while I was away. He told the beginning of the tale, of the king who had an only son and wished to pass the kingdom on to him while he was alive, and so forth, until the end of the first day [of the story] which tells of the blind man who boasted of his memory and so on, but no more. The next week R. Naftali came home to Nemirov and told me the whole great and awesome matter. I stood all trembling and dumbstruck. For even though I had already merited hearing matters from his holy mouth which no ear had ever caught, teachings and awesome tales, I had never heard such a tale as this. I was ready at once to travel to him, of blessed memory, to Bratslav and left right away and arrived early on Wednesday, near the beginning of the month of Nisan. The next day I came to see him, of blessed memory, after the morning prayer and spoke with him a great deal as was his custom. Then I spoke with him about the awesome tale that he had told the previous holy Sabbath as I had heard it from R. Naftali. He corrected me from his memory, of which he was very proud, in everything I had wrong and rearranged the events of the story as they were supposed to be. He told me that each of the seven days of the feast one of the beggars appeared and gave [the son and his bride] a wedding present, and so on. And he said that he longed to hear the end, what happened on each of the seven days . . . and the end of the tale he had begun, of the king and so on (for that was always his way, that he would say that he longed to hear and to know the matter that he himself had to reveal). I expected that he would tell me the end because I saw that he wanted to tell it. But his servant came then and said that the time had come for him to eat, and he arranged the table and we left him and thereafter he slept a little.

I came back and spoke with him a great deal, and he spoke with me at length about those things which everyone in the world lacked, [since I had told him about the troubles people were having in Berditchev]. Then I told him in response that Rashi [had explained that no one knows everything, that a person does not know the day of his death and that God has a purpose in concealing this knowledge,] and as soon as I had finished reciting the whole passage he said, "This is our tale." And then he asked where we were in the tale and I was taken aback and said in astonishment, "In the deeds of the second day," and he took it up, "On the second day," and so on, and told the whole tale of the second day, the tale of the man who was deaf, and so on, and finished the story of the second day and no more. There were some few others of our group who heard it, too. Whoever heard these tales from his holy mouth certainly beheld the endless wonders of God [and so it is with any who reads them truly now]. I waited for him to tell more, but he told no more until the night of the Sabbath of the third of Nisan. He was deeply troubled on account of his grandson, the son of his daughter Eidel, for he lay very ill and in great danger and he, of blessed memory, was in great pain on this account, for his daughter had terrible difficulty with her children and had already lost several daughters. He told of his great and terrible sorrow . . . and then stopped and asked, "Where were we in the tale?" I said, "On the story of the third day." He responded, "On the third day the one who stuttered came" and so on, and told the rest of the story of the third day which deals with the pursuit of the heart which has two pursuits and so on (and this was connected somewhat to what he had been telling us earlier of his sorrow) and after he said that they became happy he said [in Yiddish], "They made a party." And right away he told the story of the fourth day, about the two birds and so on, and completed it. Then he got up and left the table. . . .

On Sunday he told the story of the fifth day, about that which is small yet holds a lot. On Tuesday he told the story of the sixth day, about the cure of the princess. The story would always begin from something which he had been told which was connected to it. When he had finished the story of the sixth day, they told him some popular stories and he said that they were about the seventh day. But even so he didn't tell [the story of the seventh day] and we never merited hearing it. After Passover, when I traveled to Uman with him he said that we would not merit hearing it until the messiah came. . . . We stayed with him from that Tuesday until the Sabbath before Passover and he told no more. On that Sabbath eve, the eve of the Great Sabbath, his grandson, his daughter's son, died. What happened in the matter of his holy offspring is impossible to explain.

After the Sabbath had passed, some men from Teflik came and asked him if they should go to Uman and find him a place to live and he agreed. During that Passover there were several fires in Bratslav. . . . I was at his house on the night following the Sabbath and he was saying that he knew nothing at all, as was his way sometimes, when the noise of a fire which was burning in the street next to his house reached us. And he said [in Yiddish], "Already, already." For he was already prepared that there should be a fire and had spoken of it a great deal previously. The people around the table were confused and he got up and went outside in a great hurry and all of us went too, and that very night his house burned down, but we saved everything that was in the house, thank God, down to the last shoestring. He sat that whole night on the side of the hill outside town, across from the synagogue and his house, and watched the city and his house. I sat beside him during the fire and he sat there, rejoicing. Around morning I came back and the fire had burnt out and his house was destroyed and he said that we ought to go back into town. I walked along with him on the other side of the river which ran there. He never went back to his house since it was already burned down, but just walked on the other side of the river to get to the bridge which was there and I followed him. He asked me as I was walking along behind him, "Who would have said that we would be walking along this way on the night following the Sabbath, toward morning?"

We got to the town and he went into R. Shimon's house at the edge of the other side of town, on the road to Uman, and he stayed there the rest of the Sabbath until Sunday. We put all his things in another house which was at the other end of town, far from R. Shimon's. He went there later. On Sunday after midnight he summoned one of his creditors and was speaking with him when one of the men from Teflik arrived with an indication from Uman that they wanted him there and that the house had been arranged. As soon as the man had said this, his holy face grew very red (and at that time I did not know why but later I understood clearly that it was because this was a summons to his passing away for he passed away there in Uman). I always wanted to travel with him. But I understood from him that he didn't plan to take me. . . . [But because of R. Naftali's having to be away] when I saw that he wanted to go to Uman I began to prepare things for the journey so that he would take me. He didn't say a word to me about taking me or someone else, but I went and summoned a wagoner and got everything ready, so that I had the merit of his taking me on the journey to Uman.

If I had lived for no other purpose than to accompany him on this trip it would have been plenty for me, for I had the merit of hearing great things, teachings and awesome discourses which have given me life and will give life to all Israel for generations . . . for on our way what he told me served to make many great repairs, thousands and myriads of damaged souls which could never have repaired themselves and could only be helped by his passing away, as I heard clearly and in hints from his holy mouth. Moreover, several eternal boons for Israel grew out of this. He had already revealed that anyone who came to his grave and recited the [ritual he had decreed, the Great Tikkun] would be aided, forever, whoever he might be, as is well known, and the journey to Uman was the beginning and the preparation for all the mending to be done through eternity, for the place of his grave had already been selected as Uman and it was there that he had to engage in all the repairs to be made. . . . Thus every single turn and each and every movement which the Blessed Name directed in the matter of this journey, how great was God's work in them! How very deep his thoughts! For everything attained its proper end, forever and evermore. And so on that Sunday I began to take charge of the arrangements for the trip, but there were no wagoners to be found. . . . And his daughter, Madame Eidel, may she be well, who was in Bratslav, made an objection and was not at all pleased that he should go to Uman, and he, may his memory be blessed, would not insist on anything. But I saw and understood that his will was indeed firm and I went and hired a wagon for a fee larger than usual, and traveled with him from Bratslav to Uman.

We left on Tuesday morning, the fourth of Iyyar, [1810]. He had prayed the morning prayers and drunk coffee but I had not prayed yet and had to do so on the wagon. We all sat together with him, the man from Teflik and the rabbi's servant and I. As soon as we had left he began to speak with me. He said that it was a good thing that his house had burned so that he might leave Bratslav and so on. Later we came on a man from Teflik [who had just come from Uman and told us how everyone longed to see him there]. And he responded, "All is done for us; everyone is obliged to say, 'The world was created for me.' See we are all on a journey here," and so on. . . . He went on to speak at length, brilliant words. . . . He said that he had grasped these matters as soon as we had left Bratslav and had been greatly astonished at the magnificent wonders of God's conduct of the world, may he be blessed, but that he didn't want to talk about any of it until the man from Teflik came along, by whose presence it became possible to bring the matter forth from potential to performance, speaking these thoughts, thus does God conduct this world, and so on. From [the spot] where we had picked the man up, [until we reached] Uman, we were accompanied by [a group of] people, and he said, "Even so, no generation is left an orphan," and explained [that telling how the Torah can never be forgotten keeps it from being forgotten]. . . . Toward evening we arrived in Teflik and most of the townspeople, especially those of our group, came out to meet us and beseeched him to stay there overnight, but he didn't want to. Even though the rain had begun to fall while we were going through Teflik toward evening, he didn't want to pull off there. We went on and stopped to spend the night in a village near there and many of the people of Teflik came there. . . .

We left for Uman on Wednesday after prayers. As we left the village where we had passed the night he spoke at length with me concerning the doctrine of the departure of the true tzaddik, [who was the beauty, splendor, and grandeur of the world, whose disappearance could lead to disaster unless he left behind him children or disciples to take his place]. And he went on to speak about the recent death of the great rabbi of Berditchev, may the memory of the righteous be a blessing, and then as we were entering Uman he told the tale of the Besht, when he, of blessed memory, once came to a certain town where souls had been waiting for the last three hundred years to be mended [and ascend to the next world]. . . . The whole time of the journey of this Wednesday he sat there troubled and as if threatened. I came to understand this clearly later: . . . that as he came into Uman he was occupied with the matter of his departure and the many souls he had to mend there. More than this I could not grasp for his thoughts were as far above mine as the sky the earth beneath. On Wednesday he arrived in Uman . . . and all the things that happened there cannot be told. . . . On Shavuot all our group gathered around him as always. He didn't want to address us and said that he certainly would not under any circumstances address us. [He moved from that house to another and said that in this, as in the other wondrous things which happened in Uman, were doings about which we would tell ever after for] it was in this second house that he passed peacefully away. (*The Life of Our Teacher, R. Nathan*, pp. 67–69)

Nowhere does Nahman's teaching reach such tragic heights as it does in this account of his telling of the story of "The Seven Beggars," his most famous three-fold tale. Nahman has realized that he will not fulfill his role as the messiah but will die of tuberculosis. He had thought his daughter's son would inherit him and be the redeemer, but the child's death has left him with no descendant at all. His house in Bratslav has burned down, and he has been forced to move to Uman, there to be buried. All this comes about within an implacable, obscurely purposeful plot in which he and the other characters, including the Creator, carry out their terrible destiny. (The death of his own son was the stimulus for the first of his tales.) His followers in Uman work hard to get him to come there and settle; the faithful Nathan struggles mightily to have the wagon made ready to carry him to his end. The story Nahman tells, in this time of inexorable, sad fate, is the story of the world's salvation, but since the story is a true one, it will remain incomplete and imperfect.

Nahman's tales are assembled from common folktales that he has repaired, reordered, to the point that they influence the repair of the cosmos. Just as a crystal in a supersaturated solution teaches the molecules throughout the solution to conglomerate in crystals of like structure, the story informs the cosmos. The teller of such a tale is a cosmic chemist, and his materials include his listeners, who must understand their own roles in what is happening. It is crucial that they listen and be repaired; the storyteller cannot do his work without them. He himself must attain the proper spirit to tell the story. Nahman tells the tales of the first two days of the story before his grandson dies and before the move to Uman. The child's death, the destruction of his house, his daughter's opposition to his move, and the move to Uman itself all intervene. The story of the third day of the wedding festivities, tells of the appearance of the third beggar. This beggar, who stutters, represents Moses, the teller of riddles and the giver of the Torah. His function is the equivalent of Nahman's, and Nahman discovers that he can still tell tales, that his spirit and his power have survived this disastrous sequence of events. When he says to his listeners, joyously, "They made a party," he means that the listeners have played their part along with him and this has all saved him from despair. Their belief in his power and the power of the tale has made the tale work and rescued him. They have all found themselves through their devotion. The cosmos is indeed under repair. It is difficult to imagine a more profound alienation from the consensual world than that of Nahman in this moment.

THE ROLE OF THE TZADDIK: ISRAEL OF RUZHIN

Each tzaddik of a local group could play a role in the realized myth of the history of the universe and the life of God; the size of his role was determined by the willingness of his hasidim to see themselves playing key parts. If they had faith in him, he could guide their steps toward holiness even as they faced the modern world. Poverty and simplicity were not considered barriers to holiness. Intensity of devotion could overcome any fault; even sinful conduct was holy when committed wholeheartedly. Nevertheless, the wealthier supporter generally had more direct and frequent contact with the tzaddik. As Hasidism made common cause with its old opponents, the *misnagdim*, against assimilation, logical positivism, and other modernizing tendencies, these two large segments of Eastern European Jewry formed new alliances through marriage between important families: The wealthy coupled with the scholarly. Women and the poor and the unlearned kept their important places in the legends, but on the ground, wealth and power became the hallmark of the court of the successful tzaddik, himself sometimes now a scholar, and and always accompanied, or even replaced, by males involved in scholarship.

Israel of Ruzhin (1797–1850) thought of himself as the messiah and was accepted as such to an extent greater than usual for tzaddikim. A great-grandson of Dov Ber of Mezeritch (who became the leading figure in Hasidism after the death of the Besht), this tzaddik inherited the wealth, power, and noble manner of his father, Shalom Shakhna, who died when the boy was six. Even before that age, the stories tell, Israel had been noticed to possess superior qualities. His uncle, also a tzaddik, declared that Israel had inherited the soul of the Besht himself. Israel had thousands of followers and a splendid court with all the trappings of nobility. He was imprisoned by the Russians for nearly two years for his alleged involvement in the murder of two men suspected of betraying him, and even after his release, local and national governments kept close watch on him; he was suspected of plotting to become king of the Jews. His successes, his courts, and his grand style made an impression not only on his children and their courts but on tzaddikim throughout the region. From characters such as his and Rabbi Nahman's and the Besht's, the ambivalent nature of the tzaddik, the nexus of two worlds, emerges strongly. The attraction of a powerful, charismatic, and divinely endowed leader, and the equal and opposite attraction of individual communion with God and individual influence over the cosmos, establish one of the tensions that characterizes Hasidism.

THE KOMARNO REBBE, EIZIKEL

R. Yitzhak Eizik Yehuda Yehiel Safrin (1806–1874) grew up in the hasidic movement. Known as R. Eizikel, he succeeded his father, Alexander Sender, who had founded the Komarno site of the hasidic dynasty of Zhidachov, in his role as the tzaddik of the Komarno hasidim. While serving as the tzaddik and as the chief Jewish judge in Komarno, Eizikel made his living by renting concessions for toll collection, and by working as a tavern-keeper, a bookkeeper, and a stonecutter as well. He also wrote legal opinions, commentaries on legal works, and an exegesis of the Zohar, along with his own works on the Kabbalah. He told tales and was a collector and an editor of several books of tales told by or about other Hasidic masters. His collection of remembrances (*megillat setarim*, [*The Scroll of Secret Things*]; ed. N. Ben-Menahem; in Hebrew; Jerusalem, 1944) includes a journal that is named after R. Hayim Vital's *Book of Visions* and is, in fact, quite similar to it. His teachings follow those of Vital and Luria in addition to those of the Ba'al Shem Tov.

I will tell my brothers some few of the ways of God: who I am and what I am and why I have come to this lowly world. In the year 5566 [1806] on the twenty-fifth of Shevat in the sign of Jupiter was I born, in the year *mashiah ben yosef* [the

Hebrew is the alphabetic equivalent of the number]. Today being the eleventh of the month of Adar II in the year 5605 [1845], I have been in this world 14,281 days. I have celebrated 2,040 Sabbaths in this world. By the end of this year, the year *halakha lemoshe misinai* [a law to Moses from Sinai], the year *betov yerushalayim* [that which is good for Jerusalem], the year *Hesed, Emet, Pahad* [a reference to the second triad of the ten sefirot of the Kabbalah: Mercy, Truth and Fear] I will be 14,476 days old. And Sabbaths—two thousand and *hayyim* [life, 68]. And on the twenty-fifth of Shevat 606 [1846], when I will have gained the merit of the age of *Binah* [a reference to the third sefira, Understanding; and to what is said in *The Ethics of the Fathers* 5:21: "at the age of forty, one is fit for understanding"], the day that makes me forty, I will be 14,619 days old and will merit the *Keter* [Crown, the highest of the sefirot] of Torah.

Now I will speak of the greatness of my soul: who and what I am and why I came to this world. And where I was and to which place in the Stature of Primordial Adam [the universe of the sefirot pictured as a man] [my soul] is attached, I have not yet received permission [to speak].

I was my father's first-born son and would not have come to this world [were it not for the evil part of my soul yet requiring purification] and this world would already have been redeemed. And even so, I would not have had to be in this world for any more than a year in order to achieve the purification were it not for changes and switches worked upon my father. And thereafter our two sisters, righteous women, were born and my father did not have a male child and I didn't want to come into this world since the struggle [with evil] was still ongoing. And when my father the tzaddik was at the home of our teacher and rabbi, the holy and divine Israel of Lublin, and beseeched him that he seek mercy on his behalf that he might have a male child, he answered him, "If I decree that you will have a male child it will be so but it will mean that you will not have a long life for there will not be room for both of you in the world." My father took the responsibility upon himself and [the Seer of Lublin] passed on to him [one of the] Awesome Names which would bring down my soul, and said to him that he would have a son, a great light. And as soon as I came from the upper world to my mother I said to her, "Mother, keep me here with you, for so it has been decreed." And I was born in the year *mashiah ben yosef* on the twenty-fifth of Shevat and until this very day . . . 14,281 days later, I have not yet made the necessary [cosmic] repair but have wasted my time and failed to do the work of the King.

Three days after my circumcision one of the disciples of our master, the divine Besht, came to lodge in Sambor, the city of my birth. He had many visitants, men and women of the city with their children, as it was the custom among the tzaddikim of our time to bless both the young and old of Israel from the love the Holy One had for the souls of Israel; and among those who came were my mother and I so that the tzaddik might bless me, and when he laid his hand upon my head he shouted very loudly and proclaimed, in Yiddish, *Hoy, hat der kleiner ein moaḥ godol uneshomo niflo'o!* ["Oh, the little one has such a great brain and wondrous soul!"] And my mother was shaken by the sound of the shout and he said to her, "Don't be afraid, for this child will be a great light."

From the day I was two until I was five I received wondrous visions and I received the Holy Spirit and I spoke prophecies when a person asked something about the future and I saw from one end of the world to the other, really. And my teacher, my uncle, the man of God, the awesome one, our teacher and master R. Zvi of Zhiditchov, gave me two coins every week to answer him concerning anything he asked. And I spoke out clearly concerning whatever he asked me, and I gave the coins to charity.

The soul of my teacher, my uncle, the holy one, was from the root of the soul of R. Hayim Vital, from a root that was near that of R. Akiba, as has been explained in the *Book of Visions* of R. Hayim Vital. . . . Moreover, he later ascended several degrees higher through his wondrous deeds. And so also the soul of the holy master, our teacher and rabbi, Levi Yitzhak of Berditchev, was from there, from the root of the soul of R. Hayim Vital. And beside these roots and their like, which did the work of the High King with fervor and through unitings and self-sacrifice, there were almost none like them in the days of the *tannaim* [the scholars of the earliest period]. There were many praises with which our master, the divine Ari, spoke of the soul of R. Hayim Vital, whose root was very precious, made up of the souls of many righteous and pious ones; and the Redemption depended upon this soul, and that is enough said. . . . And in addition to all these our master, the divine one, light of the seven days, the charm of Israel, our holy master Israel Besht, may his rest be in Eden, was from there, from the root mentioned . . . and was himself a great oak and awesome and the finest of the fine of the soul of R. Hayim Vital. . . .

My father, may his soul be in Eden, was . . . a disciple of [the Seer] of Lublin, the root of whose soul was from one end of the world to the other, the root of our master Moses and our master the Ari, and he merited the Holy Spirit. . . . I had the merit of seeing him during the Passover holiday. . . . And during the seder of the second night after relating the legend, he took the lamb shank [*zero'a*] out of his plate and extended it to me, pulling back his holy hand three times until he looked with the holy spirit into the root of my soul and gave it to me with fear and awe as was his holy way. And I understood that he meant that the secret of the root of my soul was, "to whom is the arm [*zero'a*] of the Lord revealed" [Isa. 53:1] . . . and that I, Yitzhak Yehuda Yehiel, my soul's root and essence was drawn from the spirit of life which was made to be an instrument to awaken the female [i.e., the Shekhina] to the mating [with God], from the root of the Ari very near this holy one . . . and from the root of Benayahu and Rav Hamnuna Sava and his son. And my teacher, my uncle, was from the root of R. Hayim Vital and his spirit has come over to me since I learned from him. And thus great was the love between our souls. And if I hadn't lived in such a horrid generation as this, when I was forced to repair many souls with a broken and heavy heart, I would have had the merit of several degrees of the Ari's [attainment], and I neglected much, for my only desire was to give pleasure to the Creator truly and with a pure heart.

When I was seven a burning fire blazed in me for the teaching of our master the divine Ari, and I studied his writings with fear and awe and with great passion and whatever was too hard for me I asked my father. And I studied in distress and poverty and earned several wonderful matters and degrees of holiness. Once I had nothing to eat except occasionally and my father was walking about here and there in a tallit and tefillin . . . and teaching me . . . and I was ravenous and my father said to me, "Go to the neighbor lady and get something to eat." And I was very surprised because I knew that that neighbor lady would not give me anything even against a good pawn, but I believed in him and went there and stood at the entrance and a non-Jew was sitting there and said to me, "My son, do you want bread and liquor?" And he gave me everything. And everyone who saw was quite astonished. And I, on account of my huge hunger, had no opportunity to grasp what all this was. And afterward my father said to me, "Do you see, my son, the great quantity of your sins [brought it to pass] that you should only have merited seeing Elijah in such a garb."

And when I was twelve my father went to Hungary and I wept seven days and seven nights and almost went mad, for I begged him not to go, for I saw him passing away there. And he would reply to me, "Thus has his wisdom, may he be blessed, decreed." And he taught me some practices and traveled away and died on the twenty-first of Av in the year *rav shalom* [great peace; i.e., 1818]. I was raised thereafter by my holy uncle and teacher, my father's brother, may he rest in Eden, and learned Torah there under harsh conditions and great poverty and my only joy was the great sweetness of the marvelous explanations that my holy uncle and teacher revealed to me, and he revealed wondrous things to me. And this was all because once he saw our master [R. Yosef Karo] together with my father and asked him to bring me near to the revealed and to the hidden Torah and so he brought me near and put his hands upon me and passed on to me all the paths of Torah that he had attained. Afterwards I went through a short time when Samael, may his name be obliterated, overcame me and I failed to pay attention to what my eyes would look at, and there were two paths before me, one toward Gehenna and one toward the Garden of Eden, and the good stirred [me], and I went into the synagogue one day, all alone, and wept tears like a flowing fountain before the Creator, that he forgive me, until I fainted and heard it proclaimed, "I will restore comforts to him" [Isa. 57:18], etc. And from that day to this, twenty-five years, I have neither looked nor taken a passing glance at another's wife and am protected by Heaven that this might not happen even by accident. And I returned to the work of the Creator, to Torah and prayer.

I married at sixteen, the perfect mate of my spirit. And since I had no spirit in me there were several antagonists to this union, and on account of the quantity of my repentance and my diligent study of Torah no alien came between us. And thereafter I achieved several great and high degrees of the Holy Spirit through diligence in the Torah and prayer and yet, really, I failed to understand that this was not for me, that I was yet distant from the essence of my work. And thereafter I meditated upon this and separated myself entirely from anything of this world. And this was in the year [1823], at the beginning of the winter. I had a special room, very cold, which never warmed up, not even once all winter. It was my custom to sleep a couple of hours every once in a while and spend the rest of my time studying Torah, Gemara, legal decisions and Zohar, the writings of [R. Yosef Karo], the writings of R. Moshe Cordovero, and I fell from all that and was in a state of exceeding littleness for more than three months and many hard and evil shards rose up against me to seduce me to leave my Torah [study]. Worst of all was the sadness that they flung down upon me. And I, my heart was like a rock and I took nothing for pleasure in those days but a little water and bread every day and I had no pleasure from Torah or prayer. And the cold was very hard and the shards mighty powerful and I was at the crossroads, completely free to choose which way to go. And many were the bitter moments that passed over me on account of those seductions, more bitter than a thousand deaths, in truth. And after I had overcome the seductions, suddenly, in the middle of the day, studying the tractate dealing with levirate marriage for the glory of Eternal God, to bejewel the Shekhina with all my strength, there fell upon me a great light and the whole house was filled with a wondrous light as the Shekhina settled upon it. And this was the first time I tasted some little of his light, may he be blessed, truly and with no mistake or admixture, with a wonderful pleasure and a light so very sweet that the intellect cannot grasp it. And from then on I entered in upon the work of the Creator in this wonderful light, not by stages nor did the seductions ever again overwhelm me. Thereafter I fell again for some time and I understood that I must travel to tzaddikim, that they might draw out to me his light, may he be blessed, for I was already in possession of a vessel that had been purged. And I traveled to Medzhibozh to my teacher and my master, the holy rabbi, the man of God, our rabbi, Avraham Yehoshua-Heshel. And during that time my righteous and modest and pious daughter Madame Hinda-Sarah, may she live, was born to me. And I returned home and had good days, shining with wondrous lights. And during that time, my teacher, my father-in-law of blessed memory, passed away and I was left behind, dumbfounded, for my teacher, my father-in-law, was a completely holy and righteous man, my instructor in piety and the awe of God. And I traveled to my teacher, my uncle, at the end of the year [1825], and stayed with him three years and he decreed that I must move from Pintshov and settle near him. So I went back home and my holy uncle and teacher illumined me with a wondrous and brilliant light for days, which shone bright with such a wonderful light that the intellect could not grasp it. And on this account I took it upon myself to live by this tzaddik, come what may. Once, I was staying with him and he said to me that our master, the Besht, was in this world once again and that he was greater by several degrees as a result of the light of the unities he had made than he had been, and that he [my uncle] did not know where he was in the world, and I was astonished. (R. Eizikel, *Book of Visions*)

In the third paragraph of this account, when R. Eizikel intimates that he was just short of divinity, saying he would not have come into this world *were it not for the evil part of [his] soul yet requiring purification*, I have actually replaced, due to the difficulty of translating it, a passage in which he identifies his soul with that of the Ba'al Shem Tov. He explains that the failure of the Besht to bring redemption to the world can be traced to a cosmic source that is identified with the ancient sins of Jeroboam (the calf idolatry of 1 Kings) and with the generation that caused the destruction of the Second Temple. He avers that the soul of the messiah of the lineage of Joseph would not have had to be reincarnated in him if the Besht had overcome this evil aspect. While the passage above displays R. Eizikel's overweening self-adulation, it gives insight into the struggle of such a figure to accommodate his own failings and doubts and periods of despair and depression (*katnut*, "littleness").

THE LUBAVITCHER REBBE, MENACHEM
MENDEL SCHNEERSON

The most powerful hasidic figure to emerge since the end of World War II was the Rebbe, Menachem Mendel Schneerso(h)n, leader of the Lubavitch hasidim, the largest and most dynamic of the hasidic movements. Menachem Mendel was born in Nikolayev, Russia, in 1902 and moved to Yekaterinoslav (Dnieperpetrovsk) in 1907. Both his mother and his father, in many respects the most important teachers of his youth, were scions of important Lubavitch families. After marrying the daughter of the reigning Lubavitcher rebbe, Yosef Yitzhak Schneersohn, and pursuing a scientific education at the Sorbonne, Menachem Mendel became the all-but-designated heir to the leadership. Both he and his father-in-law went through a number of adventures while fleeing from Soviet and then Nazi persecution, before arriving safely in Brooklyn, New York. Menachem Mendel then undertook the preparation and annotation of basic documents of Chabad (a name by which the Lubavitch movement is known—an acronym formed from the Hebrew words for wisdom, discernment, and knowledge) for publication and was put in charge of Chabad's extensive, worldwide system of educational institutions. The system flourished under his management. When his father-in-law died, he assumed the leadership of the movement after a brief delay of demurral (1950–1951). Once in power, he initiated two major innovations: actively making proselytes—a technique shunned by other hasidic groups—among Jews, particularly among those who are uneducated, distant, or even troubled (including drug addicts, the indigent, the homeless, and the criminal); and the "*moshiach*-now" activity.

This last movement-within-a-movement has an antecedent in the teaching of his father-in-law, which, though not particularly strong or enduring in its character, presented its historical moment as cataclysmic. The "*moshiach*-now" movement began in April of 1991, when Schneerson transferred the responsibility, as it were, of bringing about the coming of the messiah and the Redemption of the Jews to the hasidim of Lubavitch, declaring that it was "out of his hands." Since then, "bringing about the coming of the messiah" has involved, for the most part, concentrated and heightened endeavors along lines already developed in the movement, stressing the practical commandments and *teshuvah* ("return to the faith"). Since Schneerson made it clear that he was the messiah, it would seem that his success, rather than the coming of a "new" messiah, depended on the labors of his followers.

More than a little dissention arose within Lubavitch concerning the Rebbe's messiahship. The Rebbe's own participation in the controversy largely involved the maintenance of an ambiguous position; his loss of speech and the gradual decline of other physical capacities increased the tension. He intimated, however (since 1957), that the coincidence of his coming to the forefront of the movement as the seventh Lubavitcher rebbe (just as there were seven generations from Jacob to Moses), along with the fact that there was no direct male descendant who could inherit his role, pointed to the imminent Redemption of the Jews and the terminus of history. The lack of a successor combined with the phenomenal success of the movement under Schneerson's leadership to drive the crisis to a head. Why should

Chabad's success be limited rather than cosmic? Why shouldn't the messiah come now? The Rebbe's long period of hospitalization and near-paralysis intensified these questions. Although some groups within the following argued that it was inappropriate for Chabad or any Chabad hasidim to declare and advertise the Rebbe's messiah nature, all but a few Chabad hasidim believed that he would in fact be revealed as the messiah; he was thus the messiah-to-be. The Rebbe's death in June 1994 received several responses among adherents of the "moshiach-now" movement. The most common of these followed the line developed in basic Chabad documents, finding its authority in Maimonides' theory that each generation may have a potential messiah who becomes the messiah if the generation is worthy—and holding that this generation did not prove to be so; but two substantial groups held (and continue to do so at this writing) that the Rebbe was not dead and/or that he would return.

The current internecine struggle within Lubavitch, like the struggle against Lubavitch by orthodox, non-Lubavitch forces, is a bitter one. One faction, led by R. Sh. Sh. Deutsch, has broken away. But the struggle has largely to do with the missionary program's presentation of the doctrine, that the Rebbe will be resurrected and is yet the messiah. The missionaries—who hold to this belief like almost all Lubavitch hasidim do—only wish to refrain from public discussion of it since they view it as counterproductive. Of course, non-Lubavitch orthodoxy, as represented by the Rabbinic Council of America, condemns Lubavitchers and their belief. Though no non-Lubavitch orthodox authorities support the Lubavitch claim as fiercely as does R. Moshe Butman of Lubavitch, some, like R. Aharon Soloveichik, defend it.

Chabad had exposed its official position on messianic matters through various channels, prior to the Rebbe's death. Schneerson's addresses on the topic of the "Imminence of Redemption," delivered over the last two years of his life, were adapted and published in English (as Sound the Great Shofar: Essays on the Imminence of the Redemption, ed. U. Kaploun [Brooklyn, 1992]). Briefly, the evidence Schneerson put forth for the approach of the end of the present order of the comos included historical events given cosmic interpretation—such as the release of the Jews from the Soviet Union, the fall of Communism, and the events of the Gulf War. These were understood as miracles belonging to the time of redemption. Theologically, the Rebbe's contention was that the messiah is human and is present in every generation, but that his generation was the one most ready to be redeemed since it possessed the merit of all the good deeds of preceding generations. On the practical side, the Rebbe urged everyone to fulfill their part in the redemption by living in constant awareness of its character and in the certainty that the messiah would be made manifest instantly.

Schneerson's addresses were supported by another popular work from the movement, R. Jacob Immanuel Schochet's Mashiach (Brooklyn, 1992), which contains a summary of the traditional rabbinic ideas that provide the theological basis for the definition of the messiah. For this, Schochet turned primarily to Maimonides' Mishne Torah, Laws Concerning Kings, chapters 11 and 12, where he develops his two-stage recognition process for the messiah (see chapter 3). The two-stage process fitted Lubavitch needs, but Maimonides went beyond this, and was still followed by Lubavitchers, in the requirement that the king be of Davidic lineage. There had been no such descendant since the time of the building of the Second Temple. It is a bit odd that Lubavitchers should have chosen to follow, or assert that they were following, Maimonides in the matter. His "law" here is not law. It does not have support from traditional sources or beliefs, and Maimonides himself does not require adherence to what he freely concedes is merely his opinion.

Schochet actually lays out a full menu of messianic possibilities without insisting on one position over any other. In his work, he most commonly reconciles two texts of equal authority that contradict each other, by interpreting them as two stages of a single process and by reading one text, if not both, metaphorically. For instance, if one authority says that the temple will be rebuilt by humans and another says that it will descend, in unearthly perfection, from Heaven, then the two statements might be reconciled by a third—already present or proposed for the purpose—which holds that the human rebuilding is the preparation, through repentance and charity, for the descent of the temple from Heaven.

The concept of the messiah in Lubavitch Hasidism is defined in the writings of the founder of the sect, Shneour Zalman of Liady. In his view, the messiah is no more than a successful tzaddik. The tzaddik is the head of the body of his followers. These are average people, striving to increase their knowledge and to live their lives more righteously. The tzaddik helps them in this struggle and is dependent upon their performance. He differs from them only by having been born into his role. Only he is fit by cosmic fortune to connect them with Heaven, and he demonstrates this through prophecies and miracles, persuasive evidence for a tzaddik's supporters, as we have seen elsewhere.

A single volume of Schneerson's hagiographa already exists in English, titled *Wonders and Miracles* (Kfar Habad, 1993) (Figure 9.1). It is edited anonymously and, while not published by the official Lubavitch publisher, Kehot, appears under its aegis. The book's cover shows the Rebbe, within an ark, against the background of the western wall of the temple. Just as the ark where the Torah scrolls are kept is a place where Heaven and Earth meet, so the Rebbe, within the ark, is a cosmic nexus. (Tzaddikim are known conventionally in Hasidism as "arks for the Torah.") The land of Israel is a meeting ground of the same sort, and the remaining wall of the temple is all that is left of the ancient sacred camp. The cover's design is replete with symbols of intermediation, including the Hebrew letter *vav* below the ark that, not incidentally, connects the ark and the image of the Rebbe with the emblem of a book and the name of this publisher. The publisher is named *ufaratsta*, a reference to Gen. 28:14, in which the word is part of God's promise to Jacob that he shall multiply and spread blessedness throughout the world. This biblical verse is also found in the text of a popular Lubavitch hymn. The letter *vav* links the lower and higher worlds in the Kabbalistic reading of the Tetragrammaton and stands for the ninth sefira Yesod (foundation), of the Kabbalistic arrangement of the worlds-as-aspects-of-God. This central point, through which the upper and lower worlds communicate, next to the tenth and last sefira, is also known as tzaddik—from Proverbs 10:25, "the righteous one (*tzaddik*) is the foundation (*yesod*) of the world," as interpreted in the Kabbalah. The cover inevitably reveals the dual, human-and-divine

Figure 9.1: The Rebbe Menachem Mendel Schneerson on the front cover of *Wonders and Miracles*.

status of the Rebbe and suggests that addressing him will assure the delivery of Heaven-bound supplications and other communications.

In the first paragraph of the book's introduction, this question is asked, followed by the correct answer, "Did anyone know the future that awaited this tiny infant?":

> This would appear to be a strange question. How could anyone prophesy the future of a newborn baby? Nevertheless, the facts speak for themselves. On the day the baby was born, Rebbe Sholom Dov Ber, the fifth [leader] of the Habad dynasty, sent no less than six telegrams with detailed instructions regarding the infant. According to these instructions, his mother was to wash the baby's hands before he ate; she even washed his hands before nursing him. Indeed, he never ate in his life without first washing his hands! (*Wonders and Miracles*, p. 7)

The remainder of the book's introduction is characteristic of the holy tales of a messiah's childhood, demonstrating his brilliance in learning and his longing to engage in holy acts. It also contains two stories of greater interest. One of these shows the young messiah's genius at extracting deep meaning from daily life ("How did you manage to climb that tree so quickly when the others couldn't climb it at all, Mendel?" "They look down, so they are afraid of falling, but I look up so I am not afraid"); the other reveals his unselfish heroism ("The boy's mother was emotionally telling the people around her what had happened: 'My son fell into the water, and he was drowning, but at the last moment [Mendel] jumped into the [raging] river and pulled him out!'"). Physical courage is a hoary attribute of the king-messiah, and both these tales are more than a little reminiscent of the autohagiographa of Yakov Frank.

The stories in the rest of the book are mostly of cures from barrenness and dread mortal diseases. The supplicants are cured at the moment they do what the Rebbe ordains. His pronouncement usually involves a close adherence to the dietary laws, the correction or repair of an inscription, or the placement of mezuzahs or tefillin, or the like; he knows that something is wrong and directs that it be repaired. Occasionally, he knows something is wrong with people who have some influence over the afflicted—for example, a thieving beadle, or a German nurse, feeding poison to her patient. He relies on medical doctors as well, but he may know more than they do; something from the Rebbe's scientific education and inclinations lingers on. As the Rebbe performs miracles, he exhibits some of the attributes expected of the tzaddik, such as the following.

Far-Off Vision
"I don't understand. The Rebbe of Lubavitch was never in my house, but he knows what is in its every corner. I lived in this house for twenty years and didn't know what he was talking about," said the man after he realized what the Rebbe meant. The stubborn man merited a revealed miracle.

The following account was related by N. G. in the name of Rabbi Gershon Mendel Garelick.

A resident of Boro Park, who regularly attended the local *tanya* [the basic text of the Lubavitch, the teachings of their first rebbe] class, wrote the Rebbe about the slow development of his ten-year-old daughter: she spoke at the level of a four-year-old. He wrote the Rebbe many times, but received no answer.

Finally, he decided to travel to 770 [Eastern Parkway, Brooklyn] to personally speak to the Rebbe. In the secretaries' office, he pressured them for a response to his letters. The secretaries assured him that there was no reason to exert pressure. "Every letter that arrives is given to the Rebbe. Only he decides when and how to respond."

"If so," said the man, "tell the Rebbe that I am not leaving this room until I receive his blessing for our daughter." Sitting himself down, the man proceeded to write a new letter. He described in dark colors the conditions in his house, and added that if his daughter recovered, it would bring great light and joy to his home.

After [the afternoon prayers]. Rabbi Leibel Groner [the Habad chief-of-staff] approached the man. "The Rebbe asked me to ask you, 'What about the mezuzos?'"

The man raced home to check his mezuzos.

"What's going on here?" The man asked himself, after finding that all his mezuzos were 100% kosher. Not sure of what to do next, he set out again for 770.

The secretary brought another note from the man into the Rebbe. Again the Rebbe asked, "What about the mezuzos?" The man thought he was going crazy. He went home again to check his mezuzos.

"All your mezuzos are kosher," the [scribe] reassured him.

He returned to the Rebbe's secretary and asked that the Rebbe be informed that all his mezuzos were kosher, and that he did not understand what was expected of him. When the secretary came out of the room, he told the man, "The Rebbe asks, 'What about the mezuzah that is *missing*.'"

The man was shocked. It had never occurred to him that this was what the Rebbe had in mind. He definitely remembered that there was a mezuzah in every doorway of his home.

Taking no chances, the man checked every doorway in his house. At the end of his inspection, at the last doorway, he almost fainted. He suddenly remembered: "The storeroom . . . where all the children's toys are kept. There is no mezuzah there." He ran to the scribe, purchased a new mezuzah and affixed it to the doorpost. Then he sat down and awaited a miracle.

From that day on his daughter showed signs of improvement. A few weeks later, she began to talk like a normal ten-year-old.

"I don't understand," the man concluded. "I lived in this house for twenty years and never paid any attention to that door, but the Rebbe of Lubavitch, who never visited my home, knew what was in every corner." (*Wonders and Miracles*, pp. 48–49)

The Rebbe, of course, also exhibits foreknowledge—in one tale, he blesses a young man called up for duty in the Korean War, and warns him, "Be careful to fulfill the commandment to wash your hands." The soldier, dehydrated at one point, crawls away from his dry encampment, finds a well, and drinks, pausing first to wash his hands. He returns to his camp to discover that it has been destroyed and his comrades slain in a bombing attack. He was saved by carrying out an apparently unimportant commandment (though we know how important it was in the life of the Rebbe himself), reinforced by the Rebbe's benediction.

In one marvelous tale, the Rebbe stresses the holiness of the holy tale itself. Along with R. Nahman's whole theology of holy narrative, a famous hasidic tale lies beneath this one, in which simply recalling the previous performance of a deed is sufficient to revive the salvational effect of the deed itself, now forgotten.

The Rebbe and Kiddush Levanah

The Rebbe had just finished praying the evening prayer in the shul and gone out to the street with his *chassidim* to recite the prayer over the new moon—*kiddush levanah*. Their chances of being able to do so were slim indeed.

"Once," the Rebbe began, "in the city of Lubavitch in White Russia, in the days of the [leader] Rebbe Menachem Mendel, of blessed memory [the Rebbe's great-great-grandfather, after whom the Rebbe is named, who is known by the title of his work *Tzemach Tzedek*], when the last day to recite *kiddush levanah* arrived, the moon was hidden. Concerned over the probability of being deprived of the [opportunity], the worried *chassidim* wrote letters [for help] to the Tzemach Tzedek.

"The Rebbe went out to the courtyard with a cloth handkerchief in his hand. To the crowd of *chassidim* around him, he told a story. 'The chassidim of the *tzaddik* Rebbe Meir of Premyshlyn once brought him a note asking for his help when the moon was hidden by clouds. Rebbe Meir'l went outside with a handkerchief in his hand and said, "When the Jewish people were in the desert and the clouds of glory surrounded them on all sides, how did they recite *kiddush levanah?* We must say that Moshe Rabbeinu [Moses, our rabbi] went out with the congregation of Israel, waved a handkerchief to and fro, and the clouds dispersed." Rabbi Meir'l then showed them with his handkerchief how Moshe Rabbeinu did this, and, wonder of wonders, the clouds immediately dispersed and the moon became visible!'

"This is what the Tzemach Tzedek told his *chassidim.* Then he took out his own handkerchief to show them what Rebbe Meir'l had done. Once again, the clouds dispersed."

When the Rebbe finished his story, he turned to the crowd of *chassidim* and said, "If there are any Jews here who can do what they did, we, perhaps, will also be able to recite *kiddush levanah* this evening."

Rabbi Y. G., one of the *chassidim* present shouted out: *"Der Rebbe!"*

The Rebbe, may he live a good, long time, responded, a wide smile forming on his holy face: "My job is only to tell you the story . . ." Then he quickly added, "I'll be right back!" He went home to recite [the prayers marking the end of the Sabbath] for his mother, Rebbetzin Chanah, who lived nearby.

Unlike Moshe Rabbeinu, Rebbe Meir of Premyshlyn, and the Tzemach Tzedek, this time there was not even any need to wave a handkerchief, for, a short time later, when the Rebbe returned, the skies were already clear. The Rebbe and his *chassidim* recited *kiddush levanah* together. (*Wonders and Miracles*, pp. 188–189)

The irony that emerges here, lightly, is but a reflection of the deeply ironic stance of the tzaddik of Hasidism. Schneerson's expressions of ambivalence concerning his messiahship appear not only in his teachings and in others' tales about him, but also in his initial reluctance to accept the leadership of the Lubavitcher hasidim and in his constant reference to his deceased father-in-law as the current, continuing leader. His father-in-law's gravesite was, for the Rebbe, the juncture of this world and the other, and he went there twice weekly to pray on behalf of his followers (once with unfortunate results—the so-called Crown Heights incident). His attitude toward the state of Israel as a Jewish state, when considered in this respect, reveals, even more, his ambivalent stance toward this world and a higher one. Schneerson prayed for, and showed faith in, the ability of the Israelis to withstand their enemies, but he said that Israel represents neither the promised redemption of the Jews nor even the beginning of that redemption, and was critical of the state's secular governance. He never visited Israel himself, but he saw to the establishment of villages, yeshivas, and other institutions there (including the village publishing the hasidic texts here, Kfar Habad) and sent his followers to Israel to live and work. He played an important role in Israeli elections by directing the votes of his following. Others also attended to what he said, and he was consulted by governmental and community leaders from all over the world. He took a strict traditionalist position on the Israeli political issue of Who is a Jew?, requiring maternal lineage or conversion under the auspices of a strictly traditional authority. He expressed himself firmly on this issue, which involves the religious and civil status of Israelis and immigrants, and had his opinion widely diffused. Amid all this ambivalence, one can see a certain trepidation at work. Perhaps Schneerson was unwilling, finally, to gamble the very real gains he had made for orthodoxy. While the messiah idea stirs up passionate hope and faith, betrayal and failure lie at its roots. The Rebbe moved just one step back from other messiahs who had guarded and lost themselves in gestures of denial and refusal, responding to the hesitancies of their followings and provoking the very response they sought to hold at bay.

This ambivalence typifies hasidic messianism. Hasidism was organized, with permanent institutions, by the late eighteenth century, very shortly after the death of its founder. Followings are often required to find replacements when rebbes die; meanwhile, they may continue to function for relatively long periods with no central figure. This is the situation now in Lubavitch Hasidism. With its permanent bureaucratic organization and functions, international political and economic ties, and organized communities, it must be said that the messianism of the Lubavitch sect is quite different from that of others, not precisely a messianic event, exhibiting no central figure, well routinized and accommodated in several other societies and intent on its continuity. It is the peculiarity of hasidic messianism, in general, that this pivotal concept of Judaism—the messiah and the messianic event—has retained little more than a referential function, recalling theologies and figures that provoked the most critical challenges to Jewish self-perception.

A final note here: Spending some time in Israel, in the winter of 1995–1996, I came into contact with the continuing manifestation of the Lubavitch belief in the messiah-nature of the Rebbe. I was startled—in spite of everything I have come to understand about the maintenance of belief in these cases—by large billboards that had the Rebbe's countenance on them surrounded by lights, and identified him as the "Messiah-King." One night, while coming down a steep hill west of Safed, I almost drove off the road at the sight of seven large posters, that were pasted on the concrete guard and were shining in my headlights. Those posters were replaced in the spring of 1996 by campaign posters for the nationalist prime-ministerial candidate B. Netanyahu (and there are exaggerated tales of planeloads of Lubavitch Hasidim winging into Israel to vote in the elections). Another time, on a long bus ride, I listened intently as two young religious men, neither of them Lubavitchers, one of them a Yemenite, discussed the Rebbe's nature. They agreed that there was, in principle, no reason to reject him as the messiah, even though he might be dead, and that if the Lubavitchers should continue to believe that their leader was the messiah, they were in no way affronted or diminished by that. It was not out of concord with their own beliefs. At the end of the trip, the three of us, each carrying his briefcase and computer, got down from the bus. Outside this moment and place, the controversy continues into the present. Op-ed pieces have appeared in Israeli and American Jewish publications promoting the Rebbe as messiah and demanding that all Jews recognize him as such. In response have come condemnations of the Lubavitch, particularly of the most radical wings that hold that position, as idolaters, fit only to be excommunicated. Almost all of these latter have emanated from Orthodox, non-hasidic, circles. One critical and reasoned response, written by Rabbi J. I. Schochet, a leading Lubavitch authority, stated that the Rebbe had made no explicit claims to be the messiah and argued that such a belief threatens a Jew's concentration on learning and living the Torah and mitzvot. At the same time, R. Schochet wrote that, "I have no problem with anyone assuming that the Rebbe is Mashiach, even now, nor with interpreting his words [to say so], . . . provided that they acknowledge that these are personal beliefs and personal interpretations." (Most of the opinions that have been exchanged are to be found in the Israeli newspaper, *Ha'aretz*, from January, 1998 to the present. R. Schochet's words are from a letter written to *Ha'aretz* on April 21, 1998, responding to an op-ed piece written by Rabbi M. Butman, another leader of Lubavitch.)

BIBLIOGRAPHIC NOTE   The tale of the seven beggars and other tales appear in *The Tales of Rabbi Nahman of Bratslav*, ed. A. Band (New York, 1978). The history of Hasidism is, in general, well covered in the relevant *Encyclopaedia Judaica* articles. We lack authoritative studies in English. (The best single work in Hebrew is Y. Dan, I. Tishby's article "*hasidut,*" in the *intziklopedia ivrit* 17, 756–821.) B. Safran, *Hasidism: Continuity or Innovation* (Cambridge, 1988); and S. Dresner, *The Zaddik* (New York, 1960) are two monographs in English that are of interest. Joseph Dan, *The Teachings of Hasidism* (New York, 1983) is an excellent introduction to this topic and contains a bibliography. G. Hundert, *Essential Papers on Hasidism* (New York, 1991) contains seminal studies. A. Green, *Tormented Master: A Life of Rabbi Nahman of Bratslav* (Tuscaloosa, 1979) is a penetrating study of this tzaddik. M. Rosman, *Founder of Hasidism* (Berkeley, 1996) proposes a revision of our view of the Baal Shem Tov based on the author's historical inquiry. For the modern period, two interesting studies in English are W. Shaffir, *Life in a Religious Community* (Toronto, 1974), and J. Mintz, *Hasidic Peoples* (Cambridge, 1992).

10

THE YEMENITE MESSIAHS
Reprise

I have covered the appearances of Jewish messiahs from biblical times to the present, from the land of Israel to New York City, and I have noted the continuities between messiah events throughout history and across continents, as well as the unique or innovative features of these events in each period and place. There remains one set of Jewish messiahs that I have not yet discussed—those who made their appearance in the tiny and remote land of Yemen (on the southern tip of the Arabian peninsula), from late in the twelfth century to the end of the nineteenth. The history of the Yemenite messiahs stands somewhat apart from the rest, due to the geographic isolation of Yemen and the peripheral nature of the Jewish community there. There was certainly contact, primarily letters, between Jews in Yemen and Jews in other parts; thus the accounts of Yemenite Jewish messiahs do show the influence of previous Jewish messiah events elsewhere. Yet later messiah events elsewhere show no influence from events in Yemen. Although Maimonides took the time to address himself to the appearance of one Jewish messiah in Yemen, the impact of such attention was felt quite differently in Yemen than in the rest of the Jewish world that came to read the letter. The Yemenite community was simply too insignificant (or entirely legendary) in the eyes of most Jews, and its messiah events were too locally directed and contained, to be incorporated into the main line of Jewish messiahs.

For my purposes, however, the Jewish messiahs of Yemen hold a place of unique significance, perhaps due to the very isolation that set them apart from the mainstream of Jewish messianic activity. A large part of this book has been devoted to the accounts written by or about Jewish messiahs, and I have emphasized the im-

225

portance of the accounts of a messiah in shaping the way later messiahs present themselves and the way they are presented by others in their accounts. In the case of the Yemenite messiahs, the importance of these accounts is magnified even beyond its normal dimensions. For one thing, there is such a large number and variety of accounts; it seems probable that the Yemenite Jewish community, in contact through letters with the larger Jewish world, including the most important Jewish rabbinic authorities, was accustomed to seeing itself through the words written to and about it by these outsiders and attributed real importance to these words, its primary link with the centers of Judaism. The evidence supporting this assertion is found throughout this chapter but is particularly strong in the section on Shukr Kuḥayl II, who not only made striking use of accounts of the preceding messiah and distributed his own accounts in a deliberate, far-flung publicity campaign, but even made his own body a text.

I have labeled this chapter a reprise and put it at the end of the book out of the chronological order of the other chapters because I intend it to highlight my major theme, the importance of the accounts of messiahs, and to demonstrate once again how all of the common characteristics of messiah events are present even in this most isolated locale. In order to provide background for the messiah events, the chapter will first summarize the particular common themes present among Yemenite Jewish messiahs—the Lost Tribes, asceticism, the call for communal repentance, localism. The chapter will then focus on the six Jewish messiahs of Yemen:[1] the twelfth-century messiah that Maimonides wrote about; the messiah of Bayhan (who appeared around 1495); Suleiman Jamal (ca. 1667); Shukr Kuḥayl I (1861–1865); Yehuda bar Shalom (Shukr Kuḥayl II, 1868); and Yusuf Abdallah (1893).

JEWISH MESSIAHS IN YEMEN: BACKGROUND AND COMMON CHARACTERISTICS

According to B.-Z. Klorman,[2] all of Yemenite messianism (including that involved in the first Yemenite immigrations to Israel) comprises a single strand of messianic outbursts. The Yemenites were constant and active in their messianism, employing calculations, apocalyptic visions, searches for the Lost Tribes, and communal repentance. This last feature served the nineteenth-century messiahs and incapacitated the opposition of the rabbinic leadership since the rabbis supported such conduct, if not the messiahs themselves who preached it. The histories and legends of the Jewish messiahs of Yemen resemble, and probably show the influence of, those of the messiahs of the eastern Jewish tradition, their near neighbors—Abu-Isa and his inheritors (see chapter 3), Alroy (see chapter 4), and Reubeni (see chapter 5).

The legend of the Lost Tribes (the Ten Tribes, or parts of them, and the Bnei Moshe, the tribe of Moses) epitomizes the way the Yemenite Jews think of themselves. The history of the Jewish community of Yemen retains a distant and legendary character for all Jews, including Yemenite Jews themselves. Reposed in its isolation, this community claimed the oldest continuous tradition of all the Jewries, one dating back to the tenth century BCE. The Lost Tribes were commonly believed, even by the Yemenites, to be somewhere in Yemen or nearby. Likewise, the tradition of the Mourners of Zion, in a way the last Temple servers, remained active among Yemenites until well into the twentieth century, reinforced by contacts with Karaites.[3] Karaite influence appears also in the traditional Yemenite belief that God sits in judgment over Jewish deeds, having decreed the destruction of the temple and the exile as punishment for bad faith; national and individual repentance is the only way to effect his appeasement and the renewal of his beneficence. All the Yemenite messiahs emphasize righteous conduct, prayers and dirges, repentance and fasting. This explains the weak opposition to Yemenite messiahs shown by local Jewish authorities.

The Jewish messiahs of Yemen concentrate on the redemption of their own locale, overcoming the repressions of Yemenite governors and episodes of strict Islamic rule. Beginning in the middle of the nineteenth century, the Ottomans repeatedly sought to conquer Yemen, which had exposed itself to such treatment by its utter failure to erect a sustained political structure throughout its lands. Local imamates rose and fell in bloody battles from day to day. The imam who controlled the capital of San'a' put the first Shukr Kuhayl to death in the same year that he executed the Jewish master of the mint there, leveling a false charge of counterfeiting against him to cover the real irritant—that the man refused to convert to Islam. If the wars and battles and international invasions, and the droughts and blights and plagues, were not enough to keep the country unsettled, this last event, displaying the untrustworthiness of the Moslem government in the anciently kept covenant of noninterference, shook the Jews deeply. Nor did matters improve with the Ottoman conquest, since Ottoman rule brought with it an Ottoman-trained chief rabbi, one who understood the language and procedures of the conquerors but failed to communicate with the local Jews.[4]

Enlightened opponents of the Yemenite messiahs attribute their success to the desperation and gullibility of the people after their hopes to escape virtual enslavement, suppression, and suffering at the hands of the government and their zealous Moslem neighbors were not realized. The adherence of Moslems to the Jewish movements and Moslem messianism itself also played an important role. Klorman demonstrates how Islamic messianism (Mahdism) and Jewish messianism stimulated each other in Yemen, developing shared ideas, images, and political ideals, and associates three Mahdist uprisings—those of Ali ibn Mahdi and his son Abd al-Nabi, in the twelfth century; of Faqih Sa'id in 1840; and of Sharif Ismail in 1846—with contemporary Jewish messianic events. The apocalyptic literature of Jews and Moslems shared motifs—most interestingly, that of an antichrist episode—while differing in their interpretations in accordance with their distinct traditions.[5]

THE YEMENITE MESSIAH IN MAIMONIDES'
LETTER TO YEMEN AND *LETTER TO MARSEILLES*

The account of the first Yemenite messiah which is contained in Maimonides' letters to Yemen (1192) and to Marseilles (1194), differs in its emphasis from his theoretical definition of the messiah in the *Mishne Torah* (see chapter 3). As there, Maimonides displays his antipathy to miracles and social or religious innovations, but he takes into account the anonymous Yemenite messiah's lack of education and does not condemn his call for repentance and righteousness. The account of the Yemenite messiah in the two *Letters* is based on questions and information presented to him by R. Yakov b. Netan'el of Yemen. Maimonides' response reveals his determination that the followers of the messiah and the messiah himself are less to blame for the disturbance of the social and religious order than are R. Yakov and his colleagues. Maimonides is ambivalent in his presentation of the errors of the messiah or his followers; they can be excused for their simplicity and longing, "but I am astonished by your own words—that you, a learned student of rabbinics and faithful to the Torah, should have any doubt about the truth of the claim." The account of the messiah that Maimonides presents is shaped by his insistence on clear-headed, forceful rabbinic leadership. Learning and righteousness are emphasized, and innovation in religious conduct and irrational behavior rejected, whether it be excessive charity (in fact, a communal purse) or a faith driven by belief in wondrous deeds. The weight of his reply is firmly settled on this point, and he adduces no information that might disturb it.

Maimonides, Letter to Yemen

> As to what you recalled, concerning the man who is saying in the cities of Yemen that he is the messiah—know that I was not surprised to hear of it or of those who believe in him. He is certainly mad and one who is ill incurs neither guilt nor sin if he is not himself the cause of his disease; and likewise I am not surprised at those who believe in him; they think so on account of their impatience and their ignorance of the place of the messiah and his high degree. . . . One of the proofs against him is his lack of education, for he has commanded people to strew their money about and to give it to the poor. Any that heed him are fools and he is a sinner for doing the opposite of what the Torah instructs, for one is not to give away all one's money to charity but only a part of it . . . one fifth. . . . Doubtless his heart and mind which have led him to say that he is the messiah have led him to command people to abandon their possessions. If they give their money to the poor they will be impoverished and the poor enriched, and then the latter will be required to return their money to the formerly rich and the wealth will just go on thus, back and forth forever. (I. Twersky, ed., *A Maimonides Reader* [New York, 1972] pp. 460–461)

Themes that appear for the first time in Maimonides' *Letter* are long-lived ones and resound in the later Yemenite messiah events. The fame the Yemenite community achieved by being the subject of one of Maimonides' more important writings—brief yet central to Jewish theology, community self-consciousness, and politics—seems to have shaped the attacks of antagonists, such as Yakov Sapir and the rabbis and sages of Jerusalem and Israel, who followed Maimonides' line of thought. It also lent power to the very patterns the messiahs and their proponents followed. Guided by the *Letter* of Maimonides, later Yemenite messiahs would all preach virtue and seemed to refrain from antinomian practices, while promoting virtuous behavior (even the last and most dubious of them, Yusuf Abdallah, did so, though he did institute a rain ceremony with its own innovative special prayers and acts). Their actions would recall the deeds of the first one that were reported in the *Letter* (even Shukr Kuḥayl II's tithing and communal treasury are reminiscent of the scheme the Yemenite messiah proposed, which kindled the wrath of Maimonides). The leaders of the Yemenite Jewish community would continue to play the role in which they appear in the *Letter*: they were indecisive; they were noncondemnatory; they were swayed by their own longings; they understood and sympathized with their people; and they could not but respect the messiahs for the conduct they preached, even while fearing the outcome of their claims and the threat their movements made to the peaceful, if lowly, life of the Jews of Yemen under Moslem despotism. The local Jewish communities—San'a', in particular—would also play the part outlined for them in the *Letter*; the repression and the occasional instability in the society would recur; and Yemen, finally, comes to present a strikingly unified messiah history that spans a period of over 600 years.

Maimonides, Letter to Marseilles

In his letter to the sages of Marseilles in 1194, Maimonides adds some particulars to the episode of the Yemenite messiah. He describes him as God-fearing, though ignorant, and (pretending to be) a miracle worker. He says that Moslems as well as Jews believed in him:

> After a year [the Yemenite messiah] was seized, and all who had joined with him fled. The king of the Arabs who had seized him asked him: "What is this that you have done?" He replied: "What I have done, I have indeed done, and according to God's word." Then he said: "What is your authenticating wonder?" He replied: "Chop off my head and I shall revive at once." He said to him: "You (can) have no greater sign than this. Certainly I—and the whole world—shall trust and know that my forefathers have bequeathed a falsehood [i.e., the faith of Islam]." At once they killed the poor fellow. May his death be an atonement for him and for all Israel. The Jews in most places were punished by fines, and even now there are some ignoramuses there who maintain that presently he will come to life and rise. (Twersky, p. 473)

THE MESSIAH OF BAYHAN

Relatively little is known of the anonymous messiah who appeared about 1495 in Bayhan (southeastern Yemen). Ḥayim b. Yaḥya Ḥabshush (d. 1899), in his *History of the Jews of Yemen* (written ca. 1893), mentions him, and there is one other account of him in an Arabic chronicle. Ḥabshush's *History* is written in prose with occasional rhymes and literary figures. In his account of this messiah, the author puns darkly on the Hebrew—*hadrei-mavet*, "chambers of death"—for the Hadramaut (the region along the southern Arabian coast), where Bayhan is found. He mentions the peoples of Yemen as Zimran, Jokshan, Medan, and Midian—biblical names of non-Jewish tribes descended from Abraham and from Keturah, his eastern wife (Gen. 25:2)—more than a mere rhetorical flourish. The author draws a connection to the people of the queen of Sheba as well and thus to the history of Solomon and the legendary antiquity of the Jews of Yemen:

> We are the crippled remnant, residents of the Hadramaut, the land of the Sheba'ites, dwellers of the Hadramaut of old, whose neighbors are the wolves of Arabia, the people of the king of San'a', Amar ben Abed al-Wahab, [who] killed the Jews living there on the day of the wrath of their rulers in the year 1495, over the matter of the false messiah who had come forth from there to [reach] as far away as the city of Bayhan and a great multitude with him. By the power of his many troops he angered and incensed Zimran and Jokshan and Medan and Midian along with the rest of their brothers who dwell throughout Yemen. After terrible wars the false messiah was conquered and pursued by the tribes of the area; they left behind neither remnant nor refugee, and until this day no Jew's foot passes through there. (Ḥ. Ḥabshush, *History of the Jews of Yemen*, ed. Y. Kafaḥ, quoted in *sefunot*, 2 [1950] 246–286)

Ḥabshush became an "enlightened Jew" (*maskil*) as a result of his experience as a guide for the French orientalist, Joseph Halévy, who had been sent by the Alliance Israélite to investigate the matter of the Ten Tribes. Whatever ideas Ḥabshush might have held before this journey, he absorbed Halévy's opinions willingly, despairing of the ways of his own countrymen. Ḥabshush's accounts of this and other Yemenite messiahs are contemptuous of them and their followers (and sometimes touchingly self-critical and woeful). The oppression of the Jews at the hands of pious Moslem rulers, and the endangerment (and extinction) of the whole Jewish community as the result of the plot of a few messianists, are common themes in the history of the Yemenite Jews, presented here by an "enlightened" Yemenite.

Well into the twentieth century, the antique literary traditions of the Yemenite Jews continued to determine the flowery, learned style in which even enlightened authors such as Ḥabshush wrote. Memorization of Jewish religious texts—the Bible in Hebrew (and at least the Pentateuch in Aramaic), the Mishna, the prayer books, some of the Talmudic and Midrashic literature and the Zohar—provided a common language that was heavily referential. Reports of current events were often cloaked in language drawn from these prestigious sources, providing a context of commentary. In the account quoted above, mention was made of the names of the tribes descended from Keturah, for example; the non-Jewish groups that are labeled her children in the account are then understood by the Jews of Yemen as somehow related to them. The Hebrew phrase *ze'evei erev*, translated as "wolves of Arabia," comes from Zeph. 3:3. Ḥabshush uses it as more than an amusing pun. In the biblical passage, the phrase means "wolves of evening," and the prophet's criticism of the community of Jerusalem and the impending judgment of God provides the context. The passage in the Ḥabshush text could be understood as a complaint against the Moslem rulers, a lament over the situation of the Jews, and a condemnation of the Jewish community for continuing to display laxity in its religious duties. The

Jews continue to deserve their punishment, in short, though as Ḥabshush sees it, their crime here is folly—crediting and supporting a messiah.

The other Arabic account of the messiah of Bayhan was written by B'a-faqia al-Shihri in the early 16th century.

> . . . the covenant-breaking Jew who was in Bayhan who rebelled against Sheikh Amr and betrayed the agreement and spoke slander against Islam and rode horses whose fittings were decorated with silver and gold; and a great many Jews followed him, in particular those who returned to Judaism after they had converted to Islam. (B'a-faqia al-Shihri, *Chronicle* from S. D. Goitein, *The Yemenites* (in Hebrew; Jerusalem, 1983), pp. 135–138)

Goitein adds (in n. 9), "Additional material in this *Chronicle* tells how the rebels were overcome. A large number of Yemenites went out into the desert pretending to hunt. At the moment when the Jews imagined themselves to be safely settled down, the armies of hunters turned against them and wreaked judgment on them." He comments that such stories of cunning military tactics are common, yet this one appears to emphasize the difficulty the Arabs had in overcoming the rebels. As to the "betrayal" and the reconversions mentioned by al-Shihri, there were many occasions on which the Jews of Yemen converted to Islam in order to save their lives; they returned to Judaism when it was safe. The more religious Moslem rulers liked to regard such a reconversion as particularly treacherous and as a capital crime that they were honor-bound to punish. Riding horses, especially richly caparisoned ones, and other arrogant acts were not permitted to Jews under the covenant of Omar, which governed the conduct of Jews as a protected people (*dhimmi*) under Islamic rule. (This collection of anti-Jewish regulations began in the seventh century in Yemen, with additions and variations occurring until the end of the nineteenth century.)

SHABBATEANISM IN YEMEN:
SULEIMAN JAMAL (AL-AQT'A)

Shabbateanism, as it appeared in Yemen, presents a by-now familiar face: the assurance of a successful uprising and the obligation of penitential conduct. The religious antinomianism that marked Shabbateanism in Turkey and elsewhere was lacking in Yemen. The Jews of Yemen expected the coming of the messiah to bring them together into Israel, but they as well as the Moslems (some of whom joined the Jewish movement) understood that the first steps would reverse the local order of things.

The Yemenite Jews got wind of the messiah Shabtai Zvi (see chapter 7) by mail and by word of mouth just before his conversion to Islam in 1666. Convinced by correspondence circulating throughout Yemen, coming from Jerusalem, in particular, the rabbis of San'a' lent their learned support to the Shabbatean movement. The Jews sold all their goods, preparing for their trip to Israel; some sold their real estate, too, and many ceased working, lent their money, or gave it away in offerings. When the expected signs and deeds failed to materialize in 1667, Moslems launched pogroms in reaction to the scare the Jews had given them (many Moslems having believed Jewish predictions of their ascendancy); these outbreaks were followed by the decree of the imam, Isma'il al-Mutawakkil: that the Jews, as rebels who had been faithless to the terms of their religious and legal standing as a dhimmi, should be put to death. A councilor convinced the imam that harm would befall the state if the decree were to be carried out. He then relented but required that the males go about in public with heads naked of turbans; thus the haughty would be brought low in shame. Jewish expectations were unaffected; the movement looked forward to that year's Passover and "forbade all meat but that which was roasted and wine even on the nights of the festival; ordered the women to shave their heads and the men to cease from sexual intercourse; required all to eat their food humbly, without salt and upon the earth, not to wear their leather coats, nor to sleep in them, nor to wear their [customary] garments of black wool, and to go and pray, to cover their faces and other things."[6] This marked the end of the overture to the messiah event itself.

At the height of these preparations, there appeared in San'a' a man to whom a "great thing had happened"; he was known as Suleiman Jamal and as Suleiman al-Aqt'a. (Both surnames have the quality of epithets—the first alluding to beauty, charm, splendor, and the second, to decapitation. It is impossible to say what his real surname was.) The first accounts of the Suleiman event, the work of much later chroniclers, Jews and Arabs, have recently been amplified and clarified by an examination of the unique *Chronicle* of Ahmad ibn Nasr al-Zayidi.[7] This historian, though anti-Jewish, presents throughout his account—which is contemporary with the events—an unparalleled objectivity. In the section of his work covering the period before 1667, Ibn Nasr writes of the haste with which the Jews prepared to leave San'a' (though Ibn Nasr does not make clear where they intended to go). He recounts one typical incident of their arrogance that demonstrates the fear they spread as they prepared for the victory of their messiah: "A Jew offered to sell an iron axe to a Moslem; the two negotiated the price until the Jew said, 'Pay me whatever you like, for today it will be your possession but tomorrow it will return to me and I will chop off your head with it.'" Ibn Nasr mentions the Jews' expectation of a "voice" or a "sound" that would be heard on the awaited day by all the world—perhaps the sound of the shofar, perhaps an angelic call, perhaps the weeping of Rachel—and their despair in the face of the imam's threatened death sentence. For economic reasons, the punishment decreed upon the Jews, after the death of Suleiman, was gradually reduced until they returned to their previous economic, if not social, status. This moment marks the departure, by and large, of the Yemenite Jews from the field of agriculture and their turn to other trades and occupations in the cities.

> This is what happened then [after the imam's decree against turbans]: the Jews collected around one of their sages, Suleiman al-Aqt'a, praised him, extolled him, and elevated him to such a height that they looked upon him as almost a prophet. They served him the whole time in the midst of their synagogue and considered

themselves blessed on his account. According to their words he was the man who was destined to overcome the Moslems in San'a' and to take into his own hands the rule of the city. The Satan enticed them and gave strength to their aspirations in this direction. Matters arrived at the point that on the Sabbath [or more likely, during one of the intermediate days of Passover] the Jews assembled in their synagogue, surrounding that man. His hair was shaven [from the front and center of his head] and combed straight. The Jews anointed him with expensive perfume and dressed him in fine, rich clothes, clothes of delicate white cloth and silk, like those which rulers wear. They claimed that before the day had passed, the Moslem reign would fall into the hands of this Jew and the Jews with him and that they would rule San'a' and its surroundings.

Finally, that Jew left the synagogue and proceeded toward the palace [of the governor of San'a']—our lord, Splendor [*jamal*] of Islam and Moslems, Ali, son of the commander of the believers, al-Ma'id B'allah, may God be pleased with him—in order to expel him from it and take his place. Most of the Jews came forth to accompany the man and he was like a bride being led to her wedding. The farther they progressed into the city, street after street, the greater grew the number of those accompanying him who turned back to the synagogue, until when he reached the gate of the palace only two Jews were left in his train. They marched on together and came to the fortified entry into the palace, which serves as a passage to the square of the palace opposite the gate of the mosque al-Mur'adia. At that moment our lord [Ali] was engaged there in giving audience to public petitioners. When the two Jews accompanying al-Aqt'a arrived at the aforementioned entry they sneaked away and fled at a run toward the synagogue. Thus the Satan left him alone, by himself. Al-Aqt'a continued on his way, without paying any attention to all this and without fear, toward [Ali] and finally stood erect before him. Then he spoke to [Ali]. No one understood his words, for they were spoken in Aramaic, except for one man who understood that language. He translated his words: Arise from your place for your [the Moslems'] time has come to its end, your days are over and now the reign will pass into our [the Jews'] hands.

When [Ali] understood his words with the help of the translator he ordered that the man be interrogated to determine if he was in possession of his senses or hampered from having drunk wine or the like. They examined him and found the man in possession of his senses and capable of making decisions. [Ali] therefore ordered that the man be dragged off to jail; there he was imprisoned and the account of the affair was sent to Imam al-Mutawakkil. [He] replied ordering that the Jew mentioned should be put to death.

When the response came, the news spread that the imam had ordered him put to death and the Jews were terribly distressed. They offered a great deal of money in order to ransom his life, but they were refused. When they saw that their ransom was refused, they claimed that the man who executed him would be afflicted. They earnestly spread this rumor abroad and many of the weaker Moslems were inclined to believe it. Then [Ali] ordered the man brought out of the jail to the market of al-Halaqa in San'a' and put to death there. The man was brought out and those assigned to accompany him brought him to that place, his head lowered, his lips moving, looking neither right nor left. No one among those assigned to him dared kill him, for they were from the simple people who had been swayed by the Jews' claim that disaster would befall his killer.

At that time a man from the Bani Hashem, from the lineage of the Prophet . . . happened to be there. He laid [al-Aqt'a] down with his face in the ground, drew his dagger, and slayed him. The whole time he covered his face with his cloak and no man could recognize him, and finally he turned away and departed from the place. For some time the unbeliever remained lying in the marketplace. Eventually [Ali] ordered the Jews to drag the man off, face down. They asked his permission to carry the man rather than drag him but they were refused. They offered him a lot of money but he persisted in his refusal. Therefore, they dragged him from the market of al-Halaqa to the gate of al-Sha'ub. [Ali] ordered him hung on one of the watchtowers alongside the gate, at the crossroads, so that all who entered or left the city could feast their eyes; therefore, he was hung in that place.

For several days the man remained in that posture, until the fat of his body spread out along the wall and down its sides, for the man had been fat. When a stench began to rise from him so that people suffered from the odor, [Ali] ordered the Jews to bring him down from there. The Jews were filled with great joy and gathered *en masse* to bring him down and bury him. Every Jew who managed to touch the man and take part in carrying him was filled with unparalleled happiness; the Jews buried him in their cemetery. Ahmad ibn Nasr al-Zaydi, *Chronicle* (from Y. Sadan, "The Chronicle of Ibn Nasr," *pe'amim* 42 [Spring, 1990], 124–126)

Some points of particular interest in this text include Ibn Nasr's description of the Jews' view of Suleiman as "almost a prophet." This raises the question of the nature of his "anointment" in the synagogue. Ibn Nasr, at least, does not see him as a messiah. A bit earlier he describes Shabtai Zvi as "the false messiah" (in Arabic, *al-masih al-dajal*), a term that connotes a specific apocalyptic role, like that of the Antichrist. It seems probable that he does not mean "false messiah" (*mashiah sheker*) in the Hebrew sense, and that the anointing with perfume in the synagogue is not understood by him in its likely Jewish circumstance. He, rather, sees the clothing and the perfume as ornaments that befit one who is to rule, and perhaps they were only that. The procession to the palace recalls the parades of Shabtai Zvi, while the mention of Suleiman as being accompanied "like a bride being led to her wedding" points oddly toward Zvi's distinctly ambiguous sexuality. Ultimately, it is hard to say whether Suleiman is a prophet of Zvi or a messiah in his own right, but the ibn Nasr text seems to show him acting as a messiah in close proximity to the time and style of the Shabbatean movement, perhaps progressing from prophet to messiah, as many of these figures have. If he and the community thought of him as the messiah of the lineage of Joseph, certain occurrences would be explained: The "something great" that has happened to him would be a *gilui eliyahu*—a "vision of Elijah," such as those sought by the Safed Kabbalists (see chapter 6)—giving him the task of preparing the way for the coming of Zvi; he announces to the Jews gathered in the synagogue, "Happy are you," meaning that they, not he, will witness the coming of the messiah of the lineage of David; he weeps while waiting alone in the synagogue to be taken to prison, joyful that events are following the prescribed order, and grieving over his own predestined role; he mutters to himself on the way to the block, intent on holding to his conviction that this is what he has been destined to do for the salvation of the world. All this is speculation.[8] A single aspect of the event supports the theory that Suleiman thinks he is the messiah of the lineage of Joseph and that the community remains convinced of it after his death: the great distress of the community at not being able to carry his corpse away in suitable honor, combined with their great joy at lowering his corpse from the wall, at touching it and giving it a proper burial. They would not have been so concerned if they thought he was simply another failed messiah.

SHUKR KUḤAYL I

Mori' (Master) Yehuda (in Arabic, Shukr/Shukri) ben Salim Kuḥayl is famous due, in part, to Yakov Sapir's accounts of him in the contemporary press in Jerusalem (in *ha-levanon*, among other publications); in Sapir's travel journal, *even sapir* (*The Sapphire*, vol. I [Lyck, 1866]; vol. II [Mainz, 1874]); and in his *igeret teman ha-shenit* (*The Second Letter to Yemen* [Vilna, 1873]). As often happens, the attacks of the antagonist Sapir, who was brought up in two schools of thought (Lithuanian orthodoxy and the Enlightenment), served to make the messiah Shukr Kuḥayl more famous and to set his career in posterity. Sapir in fact spread new tales of wonder about Kuḥayl by refuting them, laying the groundwork for further elaborations. His own writings and collections of the testimony of others received wide distribution throughout the Jewish world.

Shukr Kuḥayl's career (1861–1865) began during a period of political instability in Yemen. He made a gradual transition from messianic harbinger to messiah. In the first stage he kept himself in poverty, divorced his wife, and left his family so that he might wander, preaching repentance and prayer within the context of his apocalyptic visions. Ultimately, calling both his followers and the tribe of Dan to him from out of the wilderness, he delivered his claim, displaying, on his right hand, the inscription "The Messiah of the lineage of David," and, on his left, the name of a Moslem king. He rectified errors in the texts of the Bible and the Zohar, unscrambling Isa. 45:1, where the messiah's name appears as /koresh/, asserting its "proper" reading, /shukr/. He lived alone, except for the company of otherworldly beings, on the heights of Mount Tiyal. He became all-knowing in the religious texts and their secrets and in the name and nature of every human, and his magic surmounted that of the magicians of Egypt. As a threat to public order and a bad influence on the Moslems, he was murdered and his head was brought to San'a'. His followers, however, refused to believe in his death. As in the case of the conversion of Shabtai Zvi to Islam, we find the followers variously attesting that (1) he was not killed and will return; (2) the murder was only a show, and he would return; (3) he was killed and will rise again to live and work wonders; and (4) he had predicted his decapitation and explained that it was only a ruse intended to allay persecutions against the Jews. His followers continued to propound these defenses until the next messiah appeared and took advantage of them, claiming to be Shukr Kuḥayl come back. Sapir himself inexplicably confused the two Shukrs in his accounts.

In his initial summary of the background to the events, Sapir excuses the credulity of the Yemenites (which is repeated in his other writings on the matter): They are, he says, oppressed and suffer from poverty and other hardships. He praises their larger vision, their interest not only in their own rescue but in the world's as well, but he returns to his apology for their behavior when he writes that Shukr Kuḥayl "[communicated his message] to those who were impatient [regarding the coming of the redemption] and whose hands were weak [i.e., who were politically powerless] in the land of Yemen." This circumstance was sufficiently common; Sapir notes that "Ishmaelites [i.e., Moslems] as well as Jews speak of his signs and are not estranged from him."

Sapir is aware of one of the more common processes in messiah events—the ambivalent claim to the title "messiah." He writes that Shukr would say sometimes that he was the messiah and sometimes that he was Elijah's messenger. (Another source, Moshe Ḥanoch of Aden, an adherent of Shukr II, writes, "The people of Yemen believe that he is the messiah but he says he is not and merely obeys Elijah and seeks to awaken the people to Redemption.")9 In his earlier *Letter to Yemen*, Sapir praises the stratagem as cunning: "Kuḥayl was wise not to call himself messiah [p. 6], . . . but any[one] who possesses an eye that sees and a heart that understands will conclude from his words that he thinks he is a prophet sent from God and the redeemer, the messiah of the lineage of David (and that Elijah is his companion) [p. 10]." He repeats the tale that Shukr wrote "the Messiah of the lineage of David" on his right hand and the name of a Moslem king he would conquer, on his left, though it seems that Suleiman Amar's letter (cited later in this chapter) tells a slightly different story. In Sapir's version, the message written on the right hand has to be taken in the context of the inscription on the left hand; the two hands would have been employed together in a prophetic demonstration (perhaps with one hand laid over the other or erasing the other by rubbing it out, for example).

Letter from Mizrahi to Sapir

In his letter to Sapir, R. Yahya Mizrahi, a Yemenite who had emigrated to Egypt, summarizes the results of an inquiry he carried out at Sapir's request. The account tells the story of a single Shukr Kuḥayl, preparing for, and then incorporating the appearance of Shukr II as Shukr I and justifying the acceptance of the pretender as the original. We see here how the two Shukrs were joined together, not only by the assertions of Shukr II himself, but by sources acting within his design and enlarging on it independently. Perhaps the most important aspect of this account making can be found in the successful suppression of any information regarding Shukr Kuḥayl II's real origins—his separate history has been nullified. Mizrahi, as author of the letter, is ultimately responsible for the fully decorated and credible narrative and also for the unique elaborations concerning the legendary lost tribe of the Bnei Moshe and the messianic prophecy known as the prophecy of the child (*nevu'at ha-yeled*) from medieval Spain. Several other sources mention Shukr's response to the question the rabbis posed, "Why were the good tidings brought first to Yemen?," so we can assume the response was made public. Shukr I—having become "a different man," one to whom Elijah made revelations, one whose teaching was called "new Torah"—answers that there were particular shards (*klippot*) or sparks (*nitzotzim*) in Yemen that were the last to be raised in order for the repair of the cosmos to be complete. This reference to the Lurianic Kabbalah is amplified here by the mention of the *negi'a,* the contact between the shards and the sparks, or between the outer and inner aspects of the Sefirot—i.e., between evil and good. Amar's letter makes it clear that the interrogation by the rabbis took place in the synagogue after Shukr I had narrated his apocalyptic vision, and adduces additional material from the Lurianic Kabbalah—in particular, that Shukr I spoke of reincarnations or soul-wanderings (*gilgulim*), telling each man whose soul he had. This corresponds to what Mizraḥi's letter mentions: that Shukr I knew "each man's quality and name."

. . . I will write you [Sapir] the substance of the matter and if anything new happens with God's help I will write it all to you in order; it was the testimony of the people of his city San'a', some twenty men each testifying apart from the others, some who came from there and went back, some who have stayed on here in Alexandria and [elsewhere] in Egypt, that the man was one who feared Heaven utterly his whole life, who got along on very little, whose mouth never filled with jest, who never walked raised to his full height, a proper diligent student of merit. When he entered the *bet midrash* he would sit in the humblest corner, when he was honored to go up to the Torah he would refuse, when he was invited to dine—even to take part in a ceremonial meal—he would not go, he never profited from any creature but only his own labors. He is a poor man; his work was to stitch hides. He would sit in his shop a brief time; as soon as he had earned what would suffice him the day's expenses he would close and go to study. Now he is about forty years old. He takes no pride in his dress. One night there was revealed to him our lord Elijah the prophet of blessed memory who commanded him to divorce his wife, and then he set out to travel through all the towns of the wilderness of Yemen, to bring the people to repent and to betide the coming of Redemption to them that they should repent so that the period of the travails of the messiah might not be required, from mountain to mountain and from valley to valley in order to fulfill the verse, How beautiful upon the mountains are the feet of the harbinger, etc. [Isa. 52:7]. A man's messenger is like him. Elijah, may his memory be a blessing, himself traveled throughout the mountains and from city to city [as did he]. He tarried the greatest part of his time at last in the city of Tan'im. . . . He has a married sister and has given his wife a divorce and he has a grown son studying Torah at school. During his travels local people sought to give him bread to eat and clothing to wear and he would not take any favor or profit from any creature and this was according to the command of his lord the prophet Elijah, may his memory be a blessing, who commanded him not to take anything from any creature. At that time there appeared to him a column from the earth to the sky and he sat for some twenty-four hours.

And [recall] what I wrote concerning the towns of Yemen, those lands are not [even properly] called a habitation with respect to [the other] habitations known to all. . . . And when the rabbis of San'a' asked him why the betiding and the [call to] repentance were made to the towns of Yemen and not to other inhabitants of the inhabited [earth], he said to them that the sparks which require repair are in this wilderness, and [spoke of] the contact of the shards, etc. And when this matter shall be finished everything will be simple. And they asked him concerning the Ten Tribes and he said they were present but there was no need for them now, neither for them nor for the [lost] tribe of Moses, may his light shine, and that since the time Elijah the prophet may his memory be a blessing had appeared to him he had become a different man as concerns his learning in the Torah and double and doubled and redoubled what he had been and that no secret escaped him, [that he was an] overflowing fount of Torah and everything they heard from him was for them new Torah such as they had not heard nor seen in books and he knows everything in the world and knows all of the names of every human in the world and their essence and their quality. During the three years whenever they saw a Jew wearing a weapon the Gentiles were jealous of him and they made the Exile harder on the people of San'a'. And [the Jews] would say to them, Here he is before you, and [the Moslems] would try with all their might to kill him but they would not be able to do anything at all. If one were to write all that they did to him and that he did to them paper would not suffice for the story; in short he did many deeds among the people. He performed outside the laws of nature; even the great magicians of Egypt have limits and bounds on their ability but these his deeds were outside the bounds of nature's law and of magic. And the Gentiles that would come to [attack] him many thousands of them: after they had been cast back and fallen corpses he would summon [other] Gentiles to carry away their bodies. They would plead with him that he forgive them and he would raise them up for them and they would bow down to the earth before him and go on their ways.

At the beginning of his mission he ascended a high tower a distance of several hours walk distant from San'a' that no man was able to ascend, and set a great tent there and during the time when he had nothing else to do he would go up in the tower and sit. During the nights he would go into the old synagogue there alone (and he would not sit with any man, nor profit from any man) and when they would look upon him through the holes in the door at night they would see a great light inside as if there were many men studying there. And [if you] examine the Prophecy of the Child, the son of R. Pinchas may his memory be a blessing, you will see that the messiah must first be revealed in the wilderness and from the wilderness he will come to the inhabitation.

And at the end of the three years he was dwelling in the city of Tan'im in the Jewish lane. Thereafter he entered a special room in order that no man come in to him nor call him. He entered and sat within and closed the outer door behind him for some ten or twelve days, and when they would look behind the door from outside they would see a great light within and would hear [sounds within] as if there were many men studying, and thereafter he opened the door and came out alone and said to the people of the house, Know that I go to ascend a great mountain most difficult to ascend and that I must be invisible there for a year or more, and he went up the mountain. As soon as the king of San'a' learned that he had gone up the mountain alone he gave an order to his soldiers that anyone who killed this Jew Shukr Kuḥayl and brought him his head would take away a great gift and many people went and ascended the mountain of his dwelling. They stayed there some two days and came down saying, We found him and we cut off his head. Here it is in our hands. They brought it to the king of San'a' and received reward and the king hung it in the Jewish lane for three days. And a proclamation went forth among the peoples that they had cut off his head. And yet his sister and his son would not mourn for him for it was clear to them, for he had said to them previously, Do not believe that they have cut off my head. I only make it seem so to them so that they will not trouble Israel during the time of my disappearance, until I reveal myself with God's help.

When a year and a half had passed and he had not been revealed I wrote to the city of Aden to ask about him if he had been revealed and they answered me that many people had already despaired of him since a year and a half had passed and he had not come, so it must be that they had really cut off his head. And thereafter one of San'a' came to Egypt, a man called Moshe Hashash, and came to me to the city of Alexandria and sold me a Torah scroll and bought some books and stayed in my house for several days. He told me in secret that the rabbis in San'a' know that he is alive, that a paper from him [had been brought] to [a certain] rabbi by a messenger and that he had taken away an answer, but that they were afraid to let the secret that he was alive out among the Gentiles for they were in the Exile. Since then I would write occasionally to make inquiry and after two and a half years more or less had passed he was revealed in the sight of all and sat in his tower near San'a' for two hours in his tent. He had with him a Torah scroll and from below they saw that he was praying among ten men and they did not know who they were. No man was able to go up to the tower except if he'd been given permission. He would betide to Israel and say, Repent, repent for the time is near with God's help, and the deeds he did were very, very exaggerated and the Gentiles tried hard to kill him but could not overcome him and a great many believed in him and [still] say of him that he is a prophet. . . . (From Y. Sapir, *igeret teman ha-shenit* [Vilna, 1873], p. 6)

The details of Mizrahi's letter could be used to reinforce the idea of the non-death of the messiah; putting words in the mouth of the messiah—before he disappears—that are then shown to have been prophetic serves to establish a plausible narrative. No other account mentions Shukr Kuhayl's reason for making it seem that he had been killed—so that the Arabs would not bother the Jews during his absence. Mizrahi gives an example of Moslem anti-Jewish legislation (the decree that prevented Jews from bearing weapons), that had been activated by the appearance of Shukr I. Shukr II's tale of what Shukr I had told his wife is thereby validated: the Arabs did deal harshly with the Jews. It also accords with the reason given by the rabbis of San'a' for not "letting the secret [about the imminent redemption] out among the Gentiles," for "[we] were in the exile." This all made sense to the Yemenites who heard the stories; they knew what it was like to be in the exile under inimical power, to suffer and to conceal certain matters. Hearing these facts, they accepted the tale of Shukr I's intentional, apparent suicide. Even though there is a hint, in the background, of Maimonides' Yemenite messiah and his willingness to have his head cut off, it seems preferable to conclude that the prior event motivated the present tale rather than the teller.

SHUKR KUHAYL II (YEHUDA BAR SHALOM)

The case of Shukr Kuhayl II (Yehuda bar Shalom) is surely the most extreme and most convincing example of one messiah learning from another messiah's account. Although the accounts of Shukr II's proponents can generally be distinguished from those of his opponents according to whether they join Shukr II to Shukr I or keep the two separate, there were cases in which the two are apparently confused even by Shukr II's enlightened would-be detractors. The tales of Shukr Kuhayl I and of his non-death served Shukr Kuhayl II quite well from the beginning. The second Shukr Kuhayl took up the calling along with the name of the first, whom he claimed to be. Of course Shukr Kuhayl II's parentage was never clarified, certainly not by himself, since his patronymic as well as his personal name and epithet (if Kuhayl is that sort of appellative) had to be the same as Shukr I's. In one place (see his letter to Jerusalem), Shukr II refers to himself, in a rhyming couplet, as Yehuda ben Zerah—a messianic styling. Those who actually knew the first Shukr repudiated Shukr II. They criticized him for demanding tithes and then wasting the money on high living. Shukr II held feasts for those who came to visit him, many of his guests being Moslems who were adherents or objects of his charity. It was said that a very little food and wine multiplied to satisfy many. Because the presentation of this motif—the loaves and fishes, as it were—makes the feast a miracle, it excuses the profligacy he displayed in comparison with the ascetic conduct of his predecessor. Shukr Kuhayl II throws much light on the dark side of the messiah as he preys upon the gullible. He seems to have been a swindler and a conscious cheat. The descriptions we have of him, the letters he wrote, and letters from others that ask about something he said or did—these all show him to be insincere, out for power without a sense of responsibility. His claim to be the messiah does not rest on his having inherited the soul of his predecessor but on his being that person corporeally. If he had been less self-seeking and less cunning than he seems in all the sources (notice how briefly he exposes himself to the attention of Shukr I's wife and, one presumes, to the skeptical acquaintances of the first as well), one might argue that he really believed himself to be Shukr I. But Shukr II appears to be a confidence man; aware that he is not Shukr I, he does not make a convincing messiah for others or for himself, in the end. Nevertheless, he seeks to do good. Some of it merely fulfills what is commonly expected of a Yemenite messiah: preaching for repentance, prayers, righteous conduct, and penitence. Seeking to appease the Moslem powers is his innovation but is not only in his own interest; it serves his community as well. Klorman sees his tithing scheme as closely related to the scheme of religious purification through tax reduction that was put forward by Moslem religious reformers (and messiahs), whose traditions were shared by the Yemenite Jews. Followers of these Moslem figures had in fact proved willing joiners of Jewish messianic movements since the time of Maimonides.

We will never quite know what Shukr Kuhayl II thought of himself. He seems to have been taken in by the opportunities that were available to him—the inclinations of the Yemenite Jews, the death of an admired figure that could be appropriated, the accident of Sapir's adverse publicity—and not to have been beyond the reach of his own propaganda. His own public-relations activity was in fact quite wide-ranging, gaining adherents in India and Egypt and particularly among the wealthy Jews of Aden. His fortunes declined after he was savaged by Sapir; he was forced into poverty and died miserably in San'a' in 1877 or 1878. The two tales of his end are contradictory; neither of the tales makes him out to be a hero, exactly. One tale is quoted below; the other, more pathetic, more ambivalent, and more revealing of what he might have thought of himself, is from a traditional, oral account: "In February 1983, in Israel, I heard from Mr. Qarawani, a great-great-grandson of Shukr Kuhayl II through his son Salim, a family tradition about the last moments of Kuhayl. Mr. Qarawani told me that one night Kuhayl II sent his son Salim outside and asked him, to look up at the sky. When his son came back, he asked him: 'What did you see?' His son answered, 'I saw an eclipse of the moon.' At that moment, Shukr Kuhayl II clapped his hands and died."[10]

Letter from Suleiman Amar

Sapir's own condemnation of the Yemenite messiah(s) and community leaders is preceded, in his pamphlet (titled, bumptiously, after Maimonides' letter), by the following report, to which Sapir adds an introduction. This letter, a long eye-witness account of the careers of both Shukr I and Shukr II, was written by Suleiman Amar, one of the San'a' rabbis, and was delivered to Sapir while he was writing *even sapir*; Sapir then made use of it in that work. It contains an account of the apocalyptic vision that Shukr I described in the San'a' synagogue. The vision includes an Antichrist figure, as it were—an opponent who will be defeated in a final battle, though not immediately; he is a Moslem king. Shukr also mentions an earlier Moslem king in an attempt to fit his vision to the political disturbances of the period. Shukr also refers to local imagery—the "stone of the foolish" and the pilgrimages to Mecca. Amar seems to purposely fabricate a contradiction in Shukr II's use of the stone image; he offers two possibilities—that it represents the inimical persona, Armilus, from the Book of Zerubbabel who slays the messiah of the lineage of Joseph; or that it refers to the well-established tradition that regards the "great stone" as Rome—but he neglects to mention the Ka'aba, the black stone at Mecca that is the focus of Moslem pilgrimages and the obvious object of Shukr's reference.

Penitent practices associated with purification, and also with Karaism, appear in Amar's retelling of his informants' accounts. The communal fast in the graveyard (with the aim of substantiating Shukr II's claim), like the three-day period for it, can be associated with rites of purification. But the darkness of the New Moon recalls the Karaites' strictures on fire and their preference for a dark Sabbath. Graveyards as sites for communicating with Heaven, through the agency of holy ancestors, are emphasized in the Lurianic Kabbalah (as *yihudim*), and they are fit sites for the dolorous expressions of the Mourners of Zion. As we see in this letter, mourning practices inform the pose of Shukr I: His inattention to clothes, his preference for tasteless food, his unbarbered hair, and his untrimmed nails—all those belong to the traditional comportment of the bereaved. The community and its messiahs share these traditions.

[*Sapir's introduction*] (This letter is from a Yemenite man of the city of San'a', one of its great sages and teachers, a man of reputation in matters concealed as well as revealed, he is one of the two rabbis and teachers who on account of their making light of this false prophet and those who believe in him were forced to flee for their lives and leave their native land, and their houses and their possessions in San'a' were destroyed and ruined, and let this matter be for a sign and a wonder in the eyes of the fools there, that when he was passing through Egypt and Alexandria he saw that there were many there who believed in his vanities and spoke of him as holy, as mentioned above, and this master restrained the truth and lied concerning his belief for which ridicule they had plundered him in his city, but when he came to Jerusalem, and saw that may God be blessed our eyes were open to investigate and to make inquiry concerning all of his deeds and the tricks of this scoundrel, he revealed to us all that he had done and all of his plots, as he had seen with his own eyes, and wrote us this as a memoir and so that we might publish it in Israel, as he wrote it and in his own language.)

The opening of my speech and the first of my saying, to praise God, my might and my rock, who has brought me from a distant land, and led me through many nations, and shown me his wonders and his signs, and saved me from the Red Sea and brought me through, and brought me to the land of Egypt, and comforted me greatly, and set me down among great men, and there before all I found favor, and dwelt in quiet and security for a year studying some Torah, some Talmud and some Mishna, and surely I recalled and my soul spoke within me of my holy land and my ruined Temple, and I lifted my feet in my humility and in my poverty and came to Alexandria and went down to the great sea, and in the city of Jaffa there I came out, and to the holy city of Jerusalem may it be rebuilt and reestablished have I now come. And since the day of my coming forth from my city have I studied this my language . . . to tell what my eyes saw and what my ears heard may I stumble not in my lowliness. . . .

And here I, the hind [driven] from the city of San'a', tell the tale as it happened without addition or reduction that this aforementioned man, one who feared God more than others and nourished himself in hardship on the labor of his hands as is the way of the men of Yemen but lacked a bit in knowledge as is known to all of those who come to my city, yet found wisdom from nowhere for he would pursue the sages in their yeshivas to learn from them whatever he could. In any case about twelve years ago the spirit came unto him that he should divorce his wife and they went to the judges and they spoke with him in order to rebuke him for divorcing his wife on no account and bring him back to the straight way, for there was no quarrel between him and her, but he would not and he did not heed their speech but wrote her an unconditional bill of divorce according to the law of Moses and Israel. And after some two years according to what people said there appeared upon him a spirit, it was in the month of Sivan after the holiday of Shavuot, and the great sage as humble as Hillel, his name well known in the gates, the seed of the upright, teacher of Torah to the multitude, the sage Master Yahya Hayim Sharabi may his light shine found me and said to me, do you know or have you heard of the tales concerning Master Shukr Kuhayl, that he speaks wonders and secrets in matters of betidings and in matters of soul-wanderings, and speaks thus concerning this man that he is the reincarnation of this man, and concerning this man that he is the reincarnation of this man, and goes on saying so of some twenty men, and I on account of the honor of the rabbi mentioned set my ear as a catch-all to hear all that was said and it went in one ear and out the other . . . [Amar here discusses the tradition of the Lurianic kabbalah] . . . but our rabbi since he has no learning in the works of the Kabbalists almost believed his vanities and confabulations without further investigation. And this matter took place on the third day of the week, and it must be said that in that same year one of the progeny of the king had arisen and grown strong and taken the kingship for himself, becoming stronger and stronger according to the report, and that all of the Gentiles were frightened by what they had heard of him and all the more so the Jews scattered there and that they placed their confidence in the Creator of Light, but this matter is too long to tell.

Let us come back to our matter, and on the Sabbath at noon I went as was my custom to the yeshiva of our teacher Salem Yahya Ḥabshush may his light shine, and there was Master Shukr Kuḥayl sitting and with him our teacher and rabbi Yahya Ḥayim Sharabi may God protect him, and our teacher and rabbi the son of our teacher and rabbi Shukr al-Sarem may his light shine, and his peer our teacher and rabbi Suleiman the son of Salem Saleh, and his honor our teacher and rabbi Avraham the son of our teacher and rabbi Saleh may his light shine, and another three or four men, and he opened his mouth to speak matters of the future which came forth steadily as if they were words of prophecy, and these were the first of his bitter words: Know ye that this man who has become king now, soon the kingdom will not be his; he is an official and a judge but the main king for whom reign is destined by signs and wonders will come forth in this year, from the land where the Ishmaelites go on pilgrimage every year, and he will surely come with a mighty force and the sound of song and his coming forth will be from that stone of the foolish which is fixed there, and he will seek to destroy the faith and the established foundation, and the dwellers of the city of San'a' will find neither rest nor relief, until he drives them out to a great black mountain, until they cry out with embittered soul, three days without eating or light, and then the messiah of the lineage of Ephraim will be revealed. And I have come to make warning and to call all to repent and be redeemed, for the hour requires it so that he not press upon us the many decrees and destructions that this king will decree and know you that repentance and prayer will be helpless to cancel anything at all for the decree of expulsion mentioned will not falter, for this is how it must be. But the aim of all of this prayer is that he might allow us to take with us our household vessels. And if we do not do so he will drive us forth naked and barefooted possessing nothing. And those people mentioned sitting there asked him, When according to your words will this matter be, he said to them, Ninety days from today this thing will be nor will it tarry nor will this judgment pass away.

And I, when I heard his words fearsome and frightening and stupefying, was not able to restrain myself for I was not afraid and oh how I knew that it would be a bitter thing in the end, but those men who were with me neither saw nor understood how easy destruction comes at first, and oh how the fool leaps into the lead, I determined that I would speak unrestrainedly, and so I said: None of what you say is believable for books and scribes refute you in many claims: for one thing it is not for the simple people to suffer the travails of the messiah; and for another what has the messiah to do with making himself known in this land, the opposite of what R. Shimon bar Yoḥai has said in several places; and third what is this stone of the foolish of which you speak, is it Armilus who according to our sages is to kill the messiah of [the lineage of] Joseph, then it is out of order, and if this stone is none other than Rome then it is not in that place where the Ishmaelites make pilgrimage; and several other things which I do not have the time to say. All in all, your words are nothing but vanity which have no worth.

And when he heard what I had to say he became mighty wrath and rose up in his anger and went out and when he went out the rabbis and his comrades seated there reproved me: Why is it that you quarrel with him, are his words not aimed at repentance and prayer, if he helps not neither does he harm, and they silenced me as was neither the will of God nor my own, and they begged him to come back and to finish his speech and his nonsense, and when he came back he faced me and thus answered me: Know you that this king who comes forth in this year will come and winnow the important men of the congregation some ninety-three men and at the head of all of them he will speak to none other than you, for it will be his decree that they fall from their honor, tell me what will you say? I said to him I will answer you as R. Yehoshua answered when they asked him concerning the dead that the Holy One blessed is he will resurrect, will they need sprinkling or not? He said to them, When they arise then we will know as concerns them, so in this matter when he arises we will answer. But those who heard his words believed his vanities. And I kept my peace but I thought that since the time is close we will soon see what becomes of his dreams.

Ultimately everything he said collapsed, and even the remembrance of his words was not and after some month and a half he went outside the city and wandered through all of the cities and villages of Yemen and called them to repent and pray, and there were some places where he stayed a month, and some a month and a half, and some two weeks, and in all of those places where he set his foot he would set himself apart dwelling at a distance from all pleasures and clothed in rags, and if they gave him presents and clothes he would refuse them, he even grew his hair long, nor did he trim his mustache or nails. And after two years he went and established his dwelling in a certain place called Bani Jabr about a day and a half distant from San'a', and there dwell some ten Jews, and in that place dwell a fierce and hard people, and this place is a long wadi some twelve days in length and very hard people live there, some of them dwelling in houses, and some in tents, the place where he dwelled was at the beginning of the wadi, and even though they are men of war and heroes, nevertheless they are kindly disposed toward one who lives among them, and he lived there a year and a half. And during that time we heard wondrous things, there was one who would say that whoever sought money from him he would reveal to them hidden treasures and say that he did not at that time have permission to touch them until the proper time came, and there was one who would say that he saw written on the palm of his right hand the messiah of the lineage of David, and on the palm of his left hand the name and title of the king of the Ishmaelites, who according to their words was about to reveal himself. And among all of these, rumors that at every time and at every moment there were those who conspired against him to kill him but they could not. There were those who said that his face shone so like the sun that they were not able to see him, and more such wonders, that in that place where he sat was a very high mountain, and I know that mountain from when I went there before on my own business and I asked about that mountain, and they told me that it was the dwelling place of demons, and that no man could ascend that mountain, and that he who ascended it would not descend again—and this man mentioned would go up to the top of the mountain unafraid and there slaughter goat demons. And the goat demons would dance there. And if I were to go on with such stories the paper would not hold all of what foolishness men speak, but one thing I will tell, that in his great wisdom he would correct the holy Zohar, and say, This is not the correct version of the book, and besides this even the books of the prophets that we have, there is confusion and error in them. As in the verse, "thus spake the Lord to his messiah, to Koresh," (Isa. 45:1), there is an error in the word "to Koresh" and it needs to be erased and to read another name (he meant "to Shukr"), according to his wretched opinion, . . . and after he had been there some two years he ascended the mountain as was his practice, where some ten armed men lay in ambush, each man with his weapon in hand until he had come up some thirty steps and they threw stones at him, and he fell on his face to the ground and they came near him and took his head from upon him and they sent it to the city of San'a' to display their might to the princes and judges, and the Jews took his body and buried it, may his death be his atonement—and I investigated this matter well and it was true but those who believe in him say that the death was nothing other than a display and that no hand touched him, and there are some of them who say that truly he was killed but he will rise and do wonders.

And in the year 1867 the rumor went about that he was already alive and that he was dwelling in the city of Tan'im a day's walk to the east of San'a' and had sent for his son and his wife and dwelt with her several days without betrothal and marriage according to the law of Moses and Israel. And he responded that there had been a condition in the divorce, and since so many things had happened to him and that behold she was pregnant he had married her to save her honor. In any case I investigated and made inquiry about the matter among people who knew him previously and behold there was not in him any sign of Master Shukr the First who had been killed there at the mountain of the Bani Jabr (which is to the south of San'a'). And when they would say to him, We know you well from before yet now we see in you no sign, he would say to them wait a few days and you will see me as I was at first. Nevertheless neither sign nor wonder did he have nor any novelty nor any salvation but only what people who came to him every day to greet him from various places would tell him. Sometimes there would be fifteen people and sometimes twenty and he would send out to them from his house a feast that would suffice for only four or five people and they would eat and be satisfied and there would be leftovers. This is what I heard from several people who speak the truth.

And at the holiday of Passover of 1868 a rumor went forth among the Gentiles and the Jews, that on the eve of the New Moon of Iyyar he and all his army would come to besiege the city of San'a'. And he had with him a great and mighty force, some of the Gentiles dwelling near him, and some of the members of the tribe of Gad and of the tribe of Reuben as many as the sand that is on the shore, and on account of this rumor a king of one of the nearby cities sought to destroy and to kill and to wipe out all of the Jews God forbid, and wrote a judgment against them that they were to be punished by death, and many of the princes of the cities made treaty with him to bring this about, and it was a time of distress for Israel and we had no hope for our lives, except for God that he be with us as he had promised us in his Torah and so forth, and he established a spokesman to speak for our righteousness before him a prince of the capital city of San'a', who would not make treaty with them and the spokesman spoke well for us, and after Passover the prince of this city summoned the rabbis and judges and leaders of the city of the Jews, he said to them, you must pray to God concerning this thing—for you are answered when you call out—and if he is one sent from Heaven we too will receive him upon us, and if these are matters that have no substance his strength will grow weak and he will no longer confuse the world, and thus they did and they went out three days to the graveyard to prostrate themselves on the graves of the righteous, and they called out in great cries unto God may he be blessed and on the third day which was the eve of the New Moon of Iyyar the whole community men and women and children, fasted, and God heard their cries and of those fearsome rumors nothing remained, and no more was he heard of nor was his place known for some months, yet the Jews of San'a' had great expense on this account owing to the prince of the city—and then after this it was said that he dwelt in the city of al-Tawila and was despatching couriers to all sorts of places that they [should] make tithe to him.

And I traveled on thereafter to Aden and from there to the land of Egypt as mentioned, and while I was in Egypt letters came to me from my family saying that they were unable to determine the quality of the matter absolutely, whether it is witchcraft or some other thing. And he who does know would be blessed. Yet he who has received discernment from God ought not waste his time in these things, for such matters lead to a diminished belief in one who is a fool and without understanding, but the sage has his eyes in his head and knows that this is not the way and this is not the city mentioned in several places and particularly in what Maimonides, O.B.M., wrote in [Mishne Torah, "Laws concerning] Kings," and I do not come to warn but only to recall and know no more than do you, for I am a witling and know not, one who comes gathering after the reapers. So my word grovels in the dust at the feet of sages and their students.   Suleiman b. Suleiman Amar (From Sapir's The Second Letter to Yemen, letter 13, pp. 31–38)

In Amar's version of the writing on his hands, Shukr I seems to contend that his coming as the messiah of the lineage of David would coincide with the coming of a righteous king of the Moslems. Even though this interpretation conflicts with Sapir's account, Shukr I's use of his body as a proof text is established, and it reemerges in the accounts of Shukr II.

Amar's account makes a careful distinction between Shukr I and Shukr II. His narrative joins the two figures only in that he shows them to be different people. He mentions the testimonies of people who knew the first one and asserted that the second was not the same man. Early in the letter, while telling the tale of the first Shukr, he is careful to point out that the bill of divorce was unconditional; when he turns to tell the story of Shukr II, he introduces the latter's defense of his remarriage to the woman who was his wife when he was Shukr I—his claim that the bill of divorce was conditional—into the story. Though Amar mentions the miraculous provision of food and drink at Shukr's feasts, he does so in the context of Shukr's inability to produce signs and wonders to support his claim. From Shukr II's own letters (one appears below), we know this is a sore point; he responds to his followers' desires for miracles by saying that he is not yet permitted to do them—the time is not right. Nevertheless, miracle tales abound, most with the object of inculcating faith among his followers. A tale of another familiar sort relates the birth of his son—that is, the son of Shukr II and of the wife of Shukr I. The child is born after a single episode of intercourse. Eight days before the birth, Shukr instructs his wife to seclude herself and tells her that a mysterious woman will help her bear. She bears a male, and eight days later at the circumcision ceremony, Shukr presents his son, already circumcised by Elijah.[11] In this tale, the father doesn't disappear so that the son can be the messiah; we hear nothing more of the son, and it is the father who is the messiah.

Amar does not mention the tithe Shukr II demands (not even to connect it with the feasts he gives) until Shukr II is forced out of San'a' and is settled in al-Tawila, and he does not make an issue of it. Other opponents also did not look on the tithe as anything especially pernicious; it seemed a trivial matter, accustomed as they were to tax exactions from their governments. Shukr II does, however, make a number of explanations of the practice, indicating that it was at least an issue for him. In a letter to Yahya Mizrahi and the Alexandria community, Shukr II actually comes up with a fine justification appropriate to the dominant theology: The money is for an offering to Sama'el and his troop. The background to the metaphor is in the Lurianic Kabbalah and what it says about the sacrifice that is to be made to the demon Azazel in order to appease and busy evil so that, meanwhile, good may be done. Later, he makes it seem as though he does not actually seek a tenth but only some small symbolic amount, though from everyone.[12] Elsewhere (see his letter below), Shukr says that the tithe, like repentance, will purchase some release from the period of the "birth-pangs of the messiah." Amar sees Shukr II's public-relations network as a way to provide the messiah with information on distant events and people that he could use to demonstrate his uncanny knowledge.

Amar is critical of the rabbis and sages of San'a'—a tradition for the opponents of Yemenite messiahs since the time of Maimonides. They defend themselves, after Amar has driven an enraged Shukr out of the synagogue, saying: "[After all], are his words not aimed at repentance and prayer?; if he helps not, neither does he harm." Shukr's anger is unusual for him, but it is rare for messiahs not to express anger occasionally; they are avengers of their wronged people, after all, and their followers and opponents must feel the constant undertone of rage. The rabbis here are cowed by Shukr's rage and seek to appease him and silence Amar. Shukr does not hold out a promise of peace and ease to his followers. The best he can offer is that he will perhaps avoid some of the hardships of the period of the birth pangs of the messiah and the travails of the apocalypse.

The image of the messiah's face as so bright that no one can look into it oc-

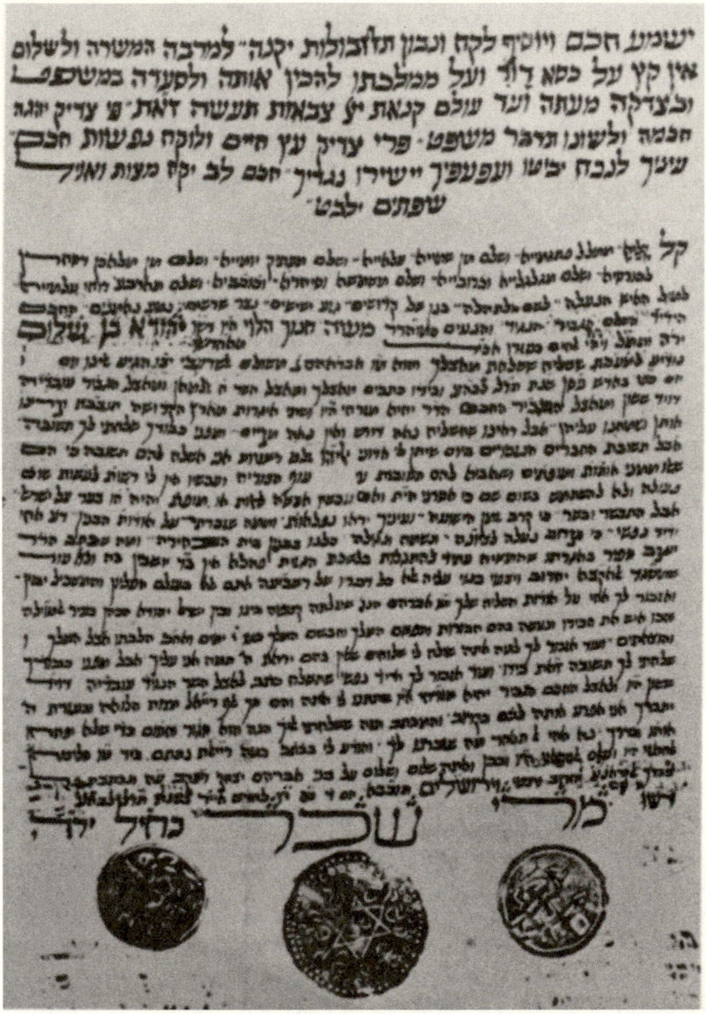
ישמע חכם ויוסף לקח ונבון תחבולות יקנה׳ למרבה המשרה ולשלום
אין קץ על כסא דוד ועל ממלכתו להכין אותה ולסעדה במשפט
ובצדקה מעתה ועד עולם קנאת יי צבאות תעשה זאת׳ פי צדיק יהגה
חכמה ולשונו תדבר משפט׳ פרי צדיק עץ חיים ולוקח נפשות חכם
עינך לנכח יביטו ועפעפיך יישירו נגדך׳ חכם לב יקח מצות ואויל
שפתים ילבט׳

Figure 10.1: The Sasson letter from *Jewish Quarterly Review* (1907) 19:163. This is another letter written by Shukr Kuhayl II to Moshe Hanoch. D. S. Sasson describes it as follows (pp. 164–165). "The letter was found among our family papers in Bombay a few months ago. It is preceded by five Biblical verses of a messianic character which the writer obviously applies to himself. These messianic pretensions also explain the words, "May his glory be high and his kingdom be exalted" [referring to himself in the body of the letter], and also the letters *qof shin* on his seal, which cannot mean anything but *qadish shmaya* 'the holy of the heaven.' According to Sapir, he called himself *mashiaḥ ben david*.

The letter itself begins with a few rhymed sentences in Aramaic, probably owing to cabbalistic influence. The letter is addressed to Moses Hanoch ha-Levi, in reply to a letter which the messianic pretender received from him. He states that he answers this letter only curs in this account as well. The onlookers are blinded because they cannot face the unpredictable fierceness of the messiah's wrathful attention. This image comes from Moses' shining countenance, yet one must ask why the image is associated with Moses (and, before him, with the gods of the ancient Near East). In addition to protecting them from the messiah's glance, the radiance also shields the thoughts of followers or antagonists, their own eyes, from him—a great benefit if they fear exposing doubt, for example, or threatening his supremacy with a look. There is no place to hide from Shukr, though: "He appears in many forms at every moment."[13]

Armed enemies of Shukr have no protection at all. Their swords turn into staffs, and other weapons, into firewood; they all wither into corpses, though he can resurrect them if he is assured they will become adherents. Indeed, death has no dominion over his justice: Decapitated, he can borrow a head and appear before the one who ordered his execution. His followers have good reason to fear him. One letter in Sapir's collection relates the tale of his punishment of the faithful Moshe Hanoch for a drunken utterance against him, "I don't believe the messiah will come from Yemen, I only believe that Haman did"; he punishes Hanoch by causing him to tumble from a ladder and fall into a five-day coma. Shukr provides both positive and negative incentives to reinforce his control over his following. There are many stories of Shukr's messengers: They are miraculously released from capture, protected from harm, even rewarded with riches for their loyalty. The letters that they carry for Shukr, bearing his words and signature, act as amulets to keep them safe.

Letter from Shukr Kuḥayl II

The text that follows is one of several letters that were written by the messiah himself. The first of these was sent to the rabbis and sages of Jerusalem after Shukr had become aware of their support for Sapir and had been informed of Sapir's arguments against him. His letters to other communities used the first one as a model. This letter was sent on to Sapir by R. Hayim Faraj Mizrahi, who copied the letter as it was contained in another letter, which had been sent by Moshe Hanoch, of Aden, to Rafael Suares in Alexandria in the early spring of 1870 (Figure 10.1).

It is a long letter that flows from subject to subject, in a single argument on Shukr's own behalf and as a justification of his deeds. Initially, Shukr promises the

---

out of consideration for the writer; but he will not pay any attention to the other people who, in reply to his petitions for money, wrote asking him to perform miracles, and also to send the replies by a bird, things which he could not do then, having no permission from his lord Elijah, and being altogether forbidden by God to perform miracles. It seems he had previously written a letter to Moses Hanoch ha-Levi asking him for money to build the Temple at Jerusalem. He asks for a loan of 1,000 Reals, and begs to be informed how much money had been collected previously by his representatives in India. At the end of the letter there are three seals: one on the right, with the initials for "holy one of Heaven"; the second one, on the left, is in Arabic but illegible; and the one in the centre has a Magen David surrounded by some mystical letters."

redemption, composing a mosaic of biblical verses that are traditionally associated with the messiah's coming. At times his versions of the texts reflect a common Jewish understanding of the verses; at others, he provides a reading that is less common—but still possible—and which corresponds to his own view as he argues his case. He praises the virtue of patience and connects it with his followers' demands for him to work wonders; then he lauds the rabbis and sages for their discernment and says that all true Jews rely upon them. He then moves on to his own role as spokesman for the Lord and emphasizes his sufferings to fulfill his obligations (actually the sufferings of Shukr I; Shukr II is himself the exemplar for his adherents to follow in artfully linking him with his predecessor). At this point he recites the narrative of his call vision, and then gives an updated history of himself as Shukr I, who is killed at the mountain of al-Tiyal and resurrected by Elijah. Elijah orders him to leave off his Torah study and preach. He recites his own adventures and concludes by saying that all his wonders and miraculous rescues were the work of God, through Elijah, and pleads with his audience to act properly and thereby speed the redemption. In a codicil addressed to Yahya Mizrahi, Shukr encourages him to remain faithful in the face of the opposition of his enemies, some of whom are community leaders, and of the spreading rumors accusing him of witchcraft.

The letter which that man sent to the sages and rabbis of the holy city of Jerusalem
How beautiful upon the hills are the feet of the harbinger sounding forth salvation, sounding forth peace, saying unto Zion, Your God has become king (Isa. 52:7), Behold they are the very first of Zion and you are the harbinger of Jerusalem (Isa. 41:27), Israel is saved an eternal salvation by the Lord, they shall not be ashamed nor embarrassed to the end of time (Isa. 45:17) . . . just as it is for me so is it for you. And this is my good advice for you, the Lord of Hosts will do it, for in only a brief time his anger will be ended (Isa. 10:25), therefore wait for me (Zeph. 3:8), the Lord of Hosts, sanctify him (Isa. 8:13), therefore the Lord will give you a sign (Isa. 7:14). Why should you be despondent, my people (Isa. 3:15), for I have not yet permission to make use of any doing, for the Lord has bound me not to make use of the Torah, for first Israel must gather together and thereafter the Lord will do wonders, this determination concerns the whole earth (Isa. 14:26). For the Lord of Hosts has determined and who shall annul it and it is his hand stretched out so who shall withdraw it (Isa. 14:27)?
. . . As concerns you all of you the children of wisdom and knowledge, go unto the light of the fixed menorah, enlightened ones, understanding that which is foretold and in this wisdom the salvation draws nigh, and you will gain merit and your degree will grow great and the lovingkindness of God will be extended unto you and the "secret" [truth] is inscribed in your hearts, may the Shekhina of God be upon your heads and the Lord will be your aid. Let it only be as in the days when God looked upon me, then he elevated me and he sanctified me and my eye looked upon all that is precious and he thrust me aside and he shattered me. And in every generation he draws me near; he aids me and he will rescue me and will lead me forward as a people. Unto you great men I call out, those who wage the war of Torah in the gates, the Lord is mine and I shall not fear. . . . He will show his wonders, for his words are pure words, he will subdue the cursed shards, and he will

free us from our heaps of bonds and he will conduct me and work to his own purpose and not for our purposes, amen, may it be his will.

Every man whose soul longs for the way of truth and Torah will pursue it through the sages, will participate with a low and humble soul neither longing for vengeance nor despising, then will he establish words of preference, words of Torah. Hear o sages my words and make them known, give ear to me, understand o people and elders, attend young men and youths, for my palate utters truth and my lips put forth straightforwardness. I left my household and abandoned my inheritance and gave up my homeland and family, my brothers rebuked me [and dealt with me harshly] but indeed I had hope in the Lord and he inclined toward me and he heard my call to be rescued and I saw that there was hope for me in the end, I suffered tortures and torments and they were trivial for I was sure of the Lord may he be blessed, and all this on behalf of Rachel and her children, for they are the ones who have put aside the works of Heaven and engage in nonsense, and there is none who asks and there is none who seeks and there is none who makes request. Hear this my brothers, hear this my companions, How long will you chatter uselessly, your words against me are already bountiful, and I have no strength to answer you until that one come who has sent me unto you and he will demand of you compensation for my shame. For they have sent me to make known to you that [the Lord] has not abandoned his lovingkindness for you in your Exile and has given to you a savior to redeem you and then your eyes shall see, and we shall rejoice and be happy, I and you, amen, may it be his will. . . .

Thus saith Yehuda ben Zeraḥ: My rose has flowered, and the light of the Lord has shone upon me, and my suffering has fled. Now have I come to say to the nobles all that has happened to me from the day that I have set out on the mission of the Holy One blessed is he when my lord [Elijah] may he rest in peace was revealed to me when he sent me forth to go unto Israel, he and Michael the prince of Israel, while I was yet dwelling in Uzal [i.e., Tan'im] impoverished and depressed, groaning and in sorrow.

Thus says the groaner: in the year 1861 upon a Sabbath, I was sleeping and awoke from my slumber and there was before me at my feet the figure of a man. And I looked and my soul took fright, and he said to me, Be not afraid, my beloved, for the Holy One blessed is he has sent me unto you that you go and give tidings unto Israel the holy people. And I said in response to him, What strength have I, what mightiness? for I am despised and the weakest of men. And he responded to me, Know my son that it is for this that you have been created. Know my son that on the day upon which you were born all of the sages of all of the peoples gave prophecy concerning you and said, today has been born the savior of Israel. And upon that day the crown of the king fell from his head, and he sent men to seek you out but I hid you away. While he yet spoke with me I heard another voice say, Before I made you in [your mother's] belly I knew you, and before you came forth from the womb I sanctified you, I made you the *redeemer of my people* (Jer. 1:5). And I looked at my body and it was altogether filled with points and names, and my blood was frozen within me. I went to the synagogue and I spoke to the sages of the people of my city and they came near to read the scripture that was written upon my flesh and not one of them was able to read it except for his excellency our teacher

Rabbi Yaḥya al-Sharabi, may his soul be bound up in the bundle of life, he read some few of [the points and names] and the people were greatly astonished. From that day forward my lord Elijah may his memory be blessed came and urged me, but I did not want to go, it was against my will, and he decreed upon me that I divorce my wife my beloved and do his will whether I wanted to or not. And he decreed upon me that I leave my house, my son, my land, and my inheritance and go willing or no to scramble afoot over mountain and hill, and I have challenged Israel that they repent and they have not wished to obey me and they have ridiculed me and they have handed me over to governments, yet they have not been able to work any evil against me, for the Lord was with me for he had promised me aforetimes that no man would be able to cause me harm. And so I went from city to city and from country to country as my lord commanded me and I was many times in great distress and I would eat and yet taste nothing at times and at times I would sleep in a settlement and at times on a mountain or a hill, and all this was on behalf of Rachel and her children and in order to set free the sparks of holiness as my lord has commanded me.

And one day I was dwelling in the city whose name is San'a' and my lord came to me and said to me arise, go to that place which I say to you, and I refused for I said to him, I have not the strength to suffer it, and he said to me, It is for this that you have been created, and he bound me in bonds of iron until I agreed to go. Thereafter he opened my bonds and I went to the place which he had said to me. I came to a town named Ḥarib and all of the Gentiles gathered to kill me but they were not able to do anything to me for the Lord was with me. They ordered me to profane the Sabbath, and I would not, for I spoke with them hard things and rebuked them and defamed them and ridiculed their faith. And after the Sabbath they caught me, put an iron collar around me and sought to put me in prison and my lord Elijah came and aided me and put the iron around the neck of their servant and they were greatly astonished. And they came and bowed down to me [asking me to] open the binding from upon him. And they feared me greatly for terror had fallen upon them and I dwelt there many days.

And a certain king from the town of Ma'rib, a great sorcerer like Balaam the evil one, came forth. His name was al-Raḥman, an evil Ishmaelite, and with magic he came to me and [would have done me harm] had it not been for God's aid unto me for they have a certain Name of Impurity but the hand of the Lord the God of Jacob was with me and I harmed him and the people were greatly astonished. The fear of God had fallen upon them, and they came and bowed down before me [seeking that I] cure him and so I cured him for this is what my lord commanded me. And thereafter I ascended the mountain whose name is al-Tiyal and the blessed one would have made unto me a great salvation had it not been for the sin that Israel brought about. And there came against me enemies and they killed me and they cut off my head and all this was on behalf of Israel. And my lord Elijah came and revived me and from that day forward has decreed upon me that I no longer engage with [matters of] the Torah. He said to me immediately Arise, go forth in the land as at first. And I dwelt in the land some five years and a half wandering through the country as my lord had commanded me and no man knew of me in all seven parts of the land and I left no town or city unvisited and came at last to the city of Alexandria where I fell ill. I dwelt there some months and no man knew me except for one woman whose name was Brakha and would bring me as I dwelt in the courtyard bread to eat and water to drink. And my lord Elijah gave me a cure and from that day forward I and he went walking until we came to the town "Mah'a," may it be destroyed and captured, and did that which we did [i.e., an act of magic]. And thereafter we went from there and he commanded me that I reveal myself in a certain city of Yemen whose name was Tan'im . . . in the year of 1861 in the month of Nisan and the Jews went and turned me over to the Gentiles. They sought to kill me and the Holy One blessed is he saved me from them and I dwelt there nearly a year and the Jews came to test me and a certain evil Jew, a great sorcerer whose name was Yehuda al-Shaqi came against me and sought to do me harm with his sorceries but was not able for the hand of the Lord was with me and he had [only] with him a Name of Impurity. Thereafter I left the town of Tan'im . . . in great honor and some few of the Gentiles came with me. But there were some of the Gentiles who set ambush for me along the way, whom the king of Uzal had hired to kill me, but they were unable to do anything to me, neither to me nor to those men who were with me, until finally we came to the city of al-Tawila. And I ascended and dwelt in a part of it against the will of the Gentiles, and I dwelt there in great honor. There was in it a certain great Gentile sorcerer, may he be cursed, whose name was Azazel, may his name and memory be obliterated. He came to me with his sorceries and sought to harm me but was not able. Thereafter my lord commanded me that I send emissaries to all of the cities of Israel to gather a tithe and I sent and there were those of the Jews who brought the tithe and there were those who ridiculed me, and it is fully known to the one who spoke and the world came into being [i.e., God] that I did not do so for my own honor but for the honor of Israel I did so, that they redeem themselves, and all of this was at the orders of the Holy One blessed is he. And the king of Uzal decreed against Israel that they should stand outside the cemetery and pray that the matter be annulled. I entered the city of Uzal on that day and the whole city was in an uproar against me and they sought to kill me but they were unable, for one would say, I saw him here, and another would say, I saw him there, and I laughed at them the whole day long, and they were astonished and frightened. Thereafter the Jews of the city of Uzal sent to me a certain sage whose name was Yeshua al-Ḥamdi who had with him [an instrument to] nullify sorceries, for they said that I, God forbid, was a sorcerer. And the Gentiles hired one to kill me but he was not able, neither he nor they, for my neck was made like a pillar of marble and their swords and spears were turned to wings. Whenever the Gentiles would ascend against me, sometimes when I was awake and sometimes when I was asleep, the Holy One blessed is he would save me from them, for my lord Elijah would come to me at every moment that I needed him. All my deeds that I did were according to the speech of the Holy One blessed is he; and the orders of my lord Elijah of blessed memory could neither reduce them nor release me from them. Now the time has come near, the moment for the redemption of Israel has come near. This is only a bit of what has happened to me, Yehuda ben Shalom. I bless the Lord who has directed me (Ps. 16:7) . . . and give thanks to God that he has not abandoned me and that he fulfills the promise that he promised me, when you cross through the water I am with you, the rivers shall not drown you, when you walk through the fire it will not burn you and its flames will not scorch you (Isa. 43:2). This is what Elijah my lord of blessed memory has permitted me [to tell you] and thus may you be at peace, amen, may it be his will.

Hear this, my brothers and my companions, engage yourselves in the prayers of King David may he rest in peace and in the composition of Rabbi Shimon ben Yohai may he rest in peace, gather together o proud ones and take strength, return, oh return from your evil ways, return with oppressed soul, call out your heart in a shout and summons, awaken the unsteady ones, arouse the sleepers, make entreaty of your spirits, return with your whole hearts unto the Lord your God and he will respond to your voice. I plead with you that you do this for the honor of the Holy Land. Remember this, be not afraid nor fearful for the Lord your God is in your midst and he will fulfill what he has promised you exactly as he has promised you, he will illumine your eyes as it is said, Behold I send to you Elijah the prophet before the great and terrible day of the coming of the Lord, and he will return the heart of fathers to their children and the heart of children to their fathers (Mal. 3:24). May it be in our life and days, amen, may it be his will.

(This is the letter that was sent to the sages of the Land of Israel; at the end of it [Shukr Kuhayl] turns to Master Yahya Mizrahi may the Lord watch over him as follows): And you Rabbi Yahya Mizrahi speak peace in my name to Hakham Yahya head of the yeshiva of the great man Yakov Baghdadi Nero, he and Hakham Mercado Nero, and say to them that their greetings have come to me and that order which they commanded upon Moshe Hashash when they said that I lay down [my] folly and that I am a fool to bring myself into such an affair as this, [that] our sages have said, he who brings himself into that which he is unable to do, his blood be upon his own head. And I know that they curse me but I do not take it to heart for thus spoke the prophet may he rest in peace, they will make a plan and it will come to naught, let them say a thing for it will not take place, for the Lord is with us (Isa. 8:10) . . . for our redeemer the Lord of Hosts is his name, the Holy One of Israel. And so may you have peace, amen, may it be his will.

[signature] His Excellency Master Shukr Kuhayl, may his kingdom endure forever

And concerning that which many of our people consider me to be, saying that all my deeds are those of witchcraft and demons, my witness is he in the heights that all my doings are at the order of the Holy One blessed is he. But of him who does sorcery and deeds of demons, the one who extracted retribution from the generation of the flood and the generation of the quarrel, and from Pharaoh the evil one and from Sihon and Og and from the 31 kings he will extract retribution from such a one, and all of the curses written in the Torah and in the Mishne Torah and the excommunications and expulsions mentioned in the words of our rabbi of blessed memory fall upon their heads and leave the people of the Lord in peace and may the Lord your God fulfill upon you and upon Israel your brothers the scripture that is written and I shall turn to you and I shall make you fruitful and I shall multiply you and I shall establish my covenant with you (Lev. 26:9) the Lord the God of your fathers, may he give you a thousand times more than you have (Deut. 1:11) and bless you as he spoke to you. Written here in the section of al-Qar'ani may it be destroyed and taken into captivity and may Jerusalem be rebuilt and established soon in our own time, amen, in the year [1870] in the month of Kislev on the thirteenth day of the month. (From Sapir, *The Second Letter to Yemen*, pp. 14–20)

The first part of the letter to the rabbis speaks of the "brief" delay in the promised redemption and of Shukr II's lack of "strength," his inability to work wonders. It is largely a weaving together of biblical verses, a technique that may have arisen from an inability to write fluent Hebrew on uncommon subjects or, equally, from traditional expectations for the epistolary genre. Shukr's own additions stand out vividly, as can be seen, but his biblical mosaic itself is not without art. One example of his technique should suffice; what he relates in such a letter is often only the cue for a verse or a passage that continues it but is itself not quoted. The summary of the points Shukr is defending (delay, inability to work miracles) is reached in the sentences that open the third paragraph. Initially, there is an interplay between the pronouns: "you" and "they" referring to the weak-handed rabbis and sages; then "our," as Shukr identifies himself with them in possessing the Lord; concluding with his demand to the sages and all the people that they give him their confidence. These are included in straightforward, carefully chosen biblical quotations. The statement "Just as it is for me, so is it for you [plural]," is not a biblical one. The closest matches to it are two passages from Kings; they differ from what Shukr says only in the number of the second-person pronoun (singular), but in both these biblical contexts, false prophecy and vain desires bring about a disastrous end. The phrase Shukr employs is easily understandable and does ring with a biblical tone, convincing to the unwary, useful to the artful. What immediately follows is the crucial message: God will see to the redemption; it will be soon, wait for it; miracles are the Lord's and Shukr is not yet permitted to do them. Shukr has played a trick with the pronouns, one that was set up at the beginning of this passage. He uses a phrase from Zephanaiah 3:8, "Wait for me," where "me" refers to God, but here Shukr, speaking in the first person, means to have the listeners wait for *him*. Moreover, the phrase summons up the most famous of biblical verses on the delayed coming of the messiah, Hab. 2:3: "If he tarries *wait for him* for he shall surely come and will not be late." The listener is surely confused into identifying Shukr with God. Shukr replaces the biblical ending of Jer. 1:5, "I have appointed you a prophet to the nations," with "I have made you the redeemer of my people."

In this letter we read again of the messiah's body itself as a text. Secret messages, barely decipherable to a skilled practitioner, can be discerned. Shukr II does not mention the traditional tale of the hand-written messages of Shukr I. In his account of his appearance as Shukr I, before the men of the synagogue, the writing covers all of his body and is only barely readable. Shar'abi was actually able to read one phrase: "the voice of my beloved herald."[14] A very late account says that Shukr Kuḥayl was a true prophet who predicted the emigration of the Yemenites from a land that had become a written text itself, testifying to Shukr's role: "Redemption will come [in Tan'im], located on the mountain's slope when three stone buildings are built in the shape of a *segol* [a Hebrew vowel marker in the shape of three dots in a triangle]. . . . [When the emigration took place it did so there], where the three buildings in the shape of a *segol* were built."[15] This is the zenith of the account tradition: the messiah makes an account of his own body and the land itself bursts forth in script. This last account is composed in retrospect, when looking back to find that there was a messiah, or at least a prophet, active in the redemption of the world, toward which the ingathering of the Yemenite Jews to Israel is a momentous stride. In R. Amram Qorah's account, quoted below, the image has already reached its sad nadir.

Account by Qorah

The next account is from the history of Yemenite Jews that was written by R. Amram Qorah, the last chief rabbi of Yemen before the community immigrated to Israel. Qorah was a leading figure in the Maimonidean enlightenment movement in Yemen and defends the rabbis of San'a' against the claim of weakness, or conspiracy with any of the messianic figures, laying the blame for the people's messianism on their poverty, the oppression of the governments, and their ignorance.

> When he would pass through the streets of the Jewish quarter in San'a' they would look mockingly upon him. His clothes were stained with a dark indigo, and his face and body were black from the indigo which spread from his garments, and he had a cord of wool tied around his neck at the adam's apple, to keep the spot from being discolored, and when he would go out in the marketplace he would remove the cord and the place where it had been tied remained white, so that he might show that this was the mark left when he was beheaded. Even the children of the town caught on to the ugly trick and would ridicule him, and he would struggle with anyone who looked at him askance.
> He rented a house whose walls were against the walls of the synagogue al-Ksar on the west side. In his attic room there was a lattice-work window open to the synagogue. . . . He would not enter to pray for fear he would be ridiculed, and there was doubt among the public whether he prayed at all. . . . And thus he lived some few days more and in 1877 or 1878 he died a final death in this house. When I was about sixteen I came out one evening from the school of R. Hayim Qorah and saw his bier passing and some ten men accompanying it. The students of the school danced behind his bier, saying: *maat al-masih! maat al-masih!* [the messiah is dead.].
> (*Tempest in Yemen*, ed. Sh. Garidi [in Hebrew; Jerusalem, 1988], p. 37)

YUSUF ABDALLAH / YOSEF EVED-EL

Yusuf Abdallah, the last of the Yemenite messiahs, appears in Habshush's account as a prisoner, though he is soon to be liberated through lobbying, as he was several times. Preaching repentance and atonement, Abdallah (who called himself Eved-El—the Hebrew translation of the Arabic name, meaning "slave of God"—more suitable to his role as a Jewish, as opposed to a Moslem, messiah) demanded gifts be brought to him. He was highly critical of the dress and jewelry fashions of the Jewish women because they were styled after those of the non-Jews, and he required that these objects be surrendered to him, warning that if they were not, the Shekhina would continue to be held in exile. The exile of the Shekhina, the female presence of God, was an important theme in Yemenite messianism, and this particular argument and demand is familiar from its biblical basis as well as from R. Hayim Vital's complaints against the clothing and fashions of the women of Damascus. Habshush says that neither Abdallah nor his followers drank alcohol, but that, gathering in the darkness after nightfall, Abdallah would bray to his believers like a donkey and that the believers would bray back. From the letter below (from an unknown antagonist) and from two of Abdallah's own letters in the same volume, we learn that neither his Hebrew nor his Arabic were of a learned quality; that he had Moslem followers; and that he worked a sort of swindle on some of his followers; having the latest creditor pay the next latest. The two letters from his followers show their Hebrew to be of the same quality as his; they come from the same background he does. While remaining faithful to him, they express their concerns about debts he owes and about problems within the community of believers.

Account by Habshush

Oh who will cure our wound? Will it really be that the new messiah who has now been brought to trial on the seventh day of Passover in 1893 and before whom was laid open the record of his misdeeds and follies on account of the sins of his vacuous lovers and believers is today set proudly at the head of those found guilty by the court? Even if the government should promise us that he would be led away once more into the wilderness, we would not yet believe it, for they might clear him by the merit of the silver of his disgusting [male] helpers and his abandoned [female] helpers just as he was saved from jail in the past month of Shevat. Woe for the messiah of the poor fools taken captive in his dissipations, who thought they would live among their brothers eternally in the shade of his folly, yearning for his deeds, alien to us and fit for them.

Once he lodged in the town of Ahla'l, one of the towns of the land of Aanas, and sent for the Jews of those towns to come have audience with him and have atonement made for them at the price of whatever they had, goat or sheep or silver or the like, and to rejoice with him at the celebration of the anointing of Master Yahya al-Akbal in whose house he stayed. And by dint of their labor at earning their keep with tanning hides and sewing them they made themselves ready at sunset, and walked in the dark from all the towns and villages, Zimran and Yokdan, so they might rejoice there; and when they were made merry by the faith of their false messiah, not by wine or liquor of any sort for they had none, but only by foolery and stupidity, [Abdallah's] servant stood alongside Master Yahya al-Akbal who owned the house and reproved them for their sins in the name of the messiah: You have sinned a great sin, that your wives and daughters imitate the women of the Gentiles among whom you live in their jewelry. On account of your transgression the Shekhina is in exile. Now take off the foreign gods from upon you. Every woman who has a bangle, bracelet, ring, earring, or nose-ring bring it to me and that will be your atonement. With a good heart and longing soul they fulfilled his harsh decree and accepted it, that he might exploit the jewels of their wives and daughters, so that the little silver and decorations of copper, iron, bdellium and lead which they had on them would make atonement for their sins. And after he had robbed them and put their goods in his sack he ordered the aforementioned Master to pray for them while they were gathered together, and in the mood of madness the messiah brayed like a donkey and said, Respond like donkeys: 'a'a'a, 'a'a'a, 'a'a'a, and at the command of the madman they responded to him, 'a'a'a, 'a'a'a, 'a'a'a, just like him. (*History of the Jews of Yemen*, ed. Kafaḥ, p. 278)

The sacrifice the women are called on to make is like that of the women who offer their jewels in the wilderness to build the Tabernacle and is a reminder that such ornaments endanger the unity of the community, especially when they are styled after the fashions of other communities. When the messiah and his followers bray at each other in the dark, it lowers all of them, but it brings them together in their devotion. The donkey bray is probably drawn from the tale of the "donkey of Ezra," and from the association Moslem literature makes between Ezra and the messiah.

Anonymous letter to Kafaḥ

The letter that follows is from an enlightened Jew, an opponent of superstition, who writes to another who is like himself. The explanation that is so common in many later studies of messianism appears in the letter: that messianism, or at least following a messiah, is in general the preoccupation of the ignorant and poor. Critiques like this one against superstition are often made by those who feel shame at being members of the same uneducated, unmodernized society that those they criticize belong to; when the criticisms contain an element of conservatism along with their enlightened skepticism, the impression one gets is of a writer caught unaware between the two tendencies and under some tension. In this letter of 1888, the (unknown) author makes the conservative complaint that Abdallah is creating new prayers and rituals. The rain ceremony takes place in a graveyard and includes the use of an ark draped in black, the sounding of great shofars, and courses of prayers and psalms. The author of the letter derides this use of symbols from the long-past holiday of Sukkot. Yet almost all the components of this ceremony can be found in other traditional rituals meant to break a drought. Such ceremonies have no prescribed form but are performed ad lib from suggestions and recollections. Admittedly they seem to be magic, intended to force a response from God or a divine agent, but they are quite an accepted practice in many forms of Judaism (the end of Sukkot entails a canonized rain ceremony; hence the dried lulavs and etrogs that are used in Abdallah's ritual). The modern reader of this letter will feel the force of the ceremony here as it brings the community together to share its pain and renew its social commitments. This community is indeed under stress, unable to keep up with the rising price of food, along with the reduced earnings. The radical renewal of the symbolic language of faith and community strength that is offered by a messianic event is traditional in the society. This event follows quickly on the heels of the double-messiah movement of Shukr Kuḥayl, and the phenomenon of the voice or sound heard in the streets played a part in that movement—perhaps as shofars, but more likely as an angelic voice—as well as here. So did the image of the messiah as someone of many forms, appearing in many places. The tales that elaborate these aspects of a messiah event involve the tellers in important roles and expand the reach and strength of the movement.

My dear, it is not unknown to you how oppressive this time is, lowered earnings and rising prices both, for from the end of Passover until now we have had neither rest nor quiet. Since the onset of the grain blight the price has doubled and the famine is strong. Once the price rose it never lowered again. Together with this we have had no rainfall from the end of the aforementioned holiday until now. And all these sorrows were but the opening and opportunity for the fool and worthless man, the false messiah, Yosef Abdallah, to swindle the fools and those who pose as pious and righteous with his lies. Vain and hasty people joined themselves with him and they too beheld the empty aspirations and lures; his words made an impression in the hearts of many of those who hate the Lord and rebel against the light. For such is the character of all superstitions, that they are founded on a lie and impress only those who are weak-minded and in love with the impossible and wondrous. As is known and published in the works of the Enlightenment. From that base the [infection] spread to the rest of the community, and the root took hold, bearing gall and wormwood. The man managed to hire some few known as diligent students of Torah with silver and copper he'd gotten from the letters he sent. He made up an order and regimen which he invented himself for the repair[ed arrangement] of the prayers, verses, and psalms. He and his followers inclined the heart of Master Suleiman [Q'ara] to take part with them in these matters. They decreed that our brethren the House of Israel should all come out to the cemetery. The messiah with all his lovers and acquaintances and arms bearers all came down to the Pit. Some of the bearers of this deceiver carried the ark covered in a black shawl above their heads as far as the cemetery. They sounded seven shofars of kudu horn as they walked and the sun and moon split at the sound. The groups of the false messiah's bearers brought their dry lulavs and etrogs with them and waved them about in the cemetery as if it were a festive day, calling out the *hoshannot* prayers as if it were Sukkot. It's a wonder they didn't bring bitter herbs, haroset, and matzot. They did this every Monday and Thursday and, when the New Moon of God's mercy [Av] brought early and late rains sufficient for the weary land, the sect of his lovers believed his lies, that if it hadn't been for him not a drop of rain would have fallen. And he went on conducting himself so, embittering our spirit. For last month he carried out a contemptible and vain deed, leading astray the hasty of heart to believe in his disgusting vanity: at midnight as people fell deep into their slumbers he, or one of his servants, came out and ran and skipped from alley to alley, from courtyard to courtyard, calling aloud, Return errant children! Redemption is near if you will awake from your sleep! Awake, awake from your slumber! and other such speeches. Thus it was that his cry was heard in several alleys, leaping from one to another with wondrous speed. Thus the sect of his lovers was astonished and astonished [others]: Did you hear the voice call out from Heaven thus and so? . . . and some of his servants said that they had looked out the window and seen him standing with his feet on the ground and his head reaching to the clouds. And some of them believed in their idiot minds that they saw fire springing up at the sound of the call. And some saw a man riding his horse and raced after him to see him and when they came to a wall he disappeared. And many other such nonsensical things. Thereafter he stood before all his lovers and attendants and spoke to them: Oh brothers! Oh companions! Have you heard the voice through the streets of the city? This is not the time to tarry. It will be awful if you do not awaken! Do this and live (Gen. 42:18): the entire congregation as one must go out to the cemetery seven times, Mondays and Thursdays, and sound the shofars of kudu horn and read the Song of the Sea [Exod. 15] while standing as well as many other charms and verses and psalms. . . . (From Y. Ratzaby, *Come South/to Yemen* [in Hebrew; Tel-Aviv 1967] pp. 204–213)

The quote from the Bible, "Do this and live," comes from Joseph's admonition to his brothers as he gives them instructions on how to avoid the drought and famine in their homeland, but the intricate and skillful use of quotations and their contexts that earlier Yemenite messiahs had made is not a feature of Abdallah's event. The call to repentance that Abdallah makes shows that he is not so set on swindling the community—if that is his aim—as to neglect the traditional language of redemption: You can escape the hardest trials of the birth pangs of the messiah if you will earnestly seek pardon and abandon your evil ways.

Account by Qorah

In the next document quoted, R. Amram Qorah (cited previously) writes a brief history of the time Abdallah spent in San'a'. The leading rabbis of San'a' were, as usual, not strongly opposed to Abdallah. The official chief rabbi, Suleiman al-Q'ara, in fact made it possible for him to act in the Yemenite capital. Abdallah had a substantial following in San'a' and in central Yemen. The passage below was written by Qorah after al-Q'ara died and the opposition (led by Qorah and Habshush, among others) finally managed to persuade the Ottomans to expel Abdallah:

In 1895 a man calling himself Yosef Abd-Allah sprouted up. He was some thirty years old, of ruddy appearance and sturdy physique. He kept the name of his village secret when he arrived in San'a' and spread it about that he was the emissary of the messiah, come to betide the End and the arrival of the messiah to release the captives soon, and that he had preceded him in order to carry out his own mission, to cure the sick and make the blind see, to make barren women fertile and so on. Every gullible fool was taken in by his vanities. He began to do his deeds and got a great deal of payment for his work in the form of whatever his followers possessed, money, vessels, clothes, and jewelry. He spent what he took in on meat and wine and all sorts of delicacies. Every glutton and drunkard attached himself to him and became one of his helpers.

R. Hayim Habshush, consumed with zeal against the deeds of this man and his deceptions, followed him about. Once when I [Qorah] was passing through the market on Saturday night I encountered Habshush. He said to me, It has become known to me that Yosef Abd-Allah is staying at the house of a certain man surrounded by women, eating and drinking and getting drunk and singing songs of praise, and I plan to go in there all of a sudden and catch them in their shame. [He gathered some others] and all of us went with him. we knocked on the door of the house, waited a bit but were not answered. Perhaps they had decided not to prevent us from entering but, rather, to flee and let us in thereafter. They opened the door and we came into the inner room where they had been seated but no one was there. Lights burned and showed painted sheets hung from the walls of the room and at its entrance, goblets of wine and all sorts of nuts, almonds and seeds laid out before the seats of the participants.

[The Ḥabshush party left and the owner of the rented room complained of the deeds of the Ḥabshush group. They were brought in and interrogated by the chief of police. Ḥabshush explained to him the danger of such men and their followings, giving the policeman a brief history of Shukr Kuḥayl I and II, stressing the harm they did the civil order, "by witchcraft, drawing wives away from their husbands and young girls into their embraces" and by preaching insurrection. The vigilantes were released and the policeman promised to investigate further.]

Ḥabshush continued to entreat with the police and the ministers of government until he succeeded and it was decreed by the wali [Ottoman governor] that Yosef Abdallah was to be expelled from San'a'. After he left he went to Shib'am and lived there, took a wife from there and sired a son, whom he named Yadid [Beloved], and never returned to San'a'. (*Tempest in Yemen*, ed. Garidi, pp. 53–55]

The Frankists, too, also were accused of an orgy shortly after they had gathered as a group (see chapter 8). There, too, the expectations and reports of the opponents failed to match what was actually demonstrable. In the case of Abdallah, Qoraḥ (quoting Ḥabshush) reveals that a central point of concern for them was the seduction of the women of the city by this hardy, ruddy invader. In the account, there is yet more about the women, in particular, as adherents of Abdallah. They don't seem to have quite abandoned themselves to his blandishments, but suffer his recriminations for their shameless conduct, having agreed (in the previous account) to give up their jewels to him.

Both the most positive and the most negative accounts of the deeds of the Yemenite messiahs contain important information, directly and indirectly obtained. The accounts of Sapir and Ḥabshush, along with all the other testimonies, mix the estimable data with the despicable and the strange in their descriptions of the conduct of these people. When he comes to summarize the situation in Yemen, Ḥabshush writes: "Our land conceives and bears messiahs at every moment; one falls, another rises. Likewise, those easily seduced give up their possessions to them and others arise in their place to satisfy the desires of the messiahs with their silver and what they own. And why is this? Because of the hardships of exile, because of the paucity of income, because of the lack of education, because of the lack of rabbinical supervision; and so folly reigns and enlightenment stands off afar and when one wolfish government falls, the Turks sprout up."[16] Others find Yemenite messianism a benign and vital element in the Yemenite Jewish tradition. Folkloric accounts of the messiahs—in particular, of Shukr Kuḥayl I and II (the last published in 1982)— along with folk songs, maintain them in esteem among many Yemenite Jews. It is noteworthy that another Ḥabshush, Yeḥiel, has, with the support of his family, published a novel, *The Messiah of the Lineage of Yosef* (in Hebrew; Jerusalem, 1988), which provides a detailed history of the family background, birth, youth, and deeds of one Yigal (Ḥabshush), who leads the Jews of Yemen aboard the flights they take to Israel in 1949. Though the work is fiction, it misses hardly a motif from all the messianic accounts as the author seeks to substantiate the making of the state of Israel and the ingathering of the exiled Jewries on grounds better than those of the social, political, and military movements that, owing little, if anything, to messianism, actually did create and maintain the nation. If we recall that messianic movements differ from other revitalization movements in two important ways—they have messiahs and their usefulness to society is in the tragic rituals they enact—the novel exposes its own fictive character. The real return of the Yemenite Jews to Israel was not a messianic movement: It had no messiah and it did not fail to reformulate the cultures of Jewries everywhere internally and in relation to other cultures.

The data of these accounts (as well as Klorman's analysis) are of special interest in supporting the hypothesis that messianic movements take place with the active participation of a larger society, as intense expressions of the greater society's reactions to stress as well as of the responses of the leader and followers of the movement. (See Chapter 1.) The Yemenite case, with its Moslem-Jewish interactions, involving stimuli that go from one group to the other, as well as a single common reaction to current social instability, clearly demonstrates the weakness of the mechanisms operating to keep the several societies within a single economic and political structure—particularly one under stress—and separate from each other.

11

CONCLUSION
The Characterization of Abandonment

Messianism has generally a particular outlook on the dimension of time: its temporal process leads to a change—or to a final concretion—on the heels of which the damaged present is annulled and a new world order that is wholly good replaces it, for if the present were good the necessity would be to ensure its continuation and not to endeavor to exchange it for a new world order. Since "this world" is evil, damaged, or ruined by negative elements, whether spiritual or real—such as suffering, death, illness, sin, and so on—a new world that would be entirely good is required.

Werblowsky, "Messiahs," *The Hebrew Encyclopedia*

The time scheme, the calendar, for a messianic movement has but a single date: now; a single agenda: complete change; and a single emotional character: desperation. Any departure from the agenda or any extension of the calendar marks the continuing victory of evil, so desperation to act correctly and finally and immediately conditions the activities of the movement. This new dispensation requires a new personal disposition, a new affect. The old bad self cannot last into the new good world, so the first step toward the new world, destruction of the old world, takes place initially in the follower's destruction of his old bad self. What can serve as a guide to the process of destruction and rebirth, since old behaviors are out of force? Only a single individual whose testimony can be taken concerning the process and its end, and whose behavior can construct the perceptions and deeds of his followers—only the messiah—can serve the following as a model. To do this he must be other than what they are, other than his own former self; this demands the destruction of his old self. His followers may then be able to do likewise. Both the messiah and his followers strive to destroy themselves and the world. Their awareness of what they are doing makes them desperate to drive their movement on to the rocks.

THE DYNAMICS OF SELF-DESTRUCTION

Despite the variety of details in the messiahs' lives and circumstances, one concludes, after reading all the accounts of them in succession, that they possess at least one feature in common: the messiah's failure to achieve his stated promises; from the beginning of every account, disaster is present and only awaiting its turn to appear. Hasidism spreads the risk around, multiplying messiahs and lowering the degree of disaster, less intent apparently on its own end. But a reckoning remains to be made with the part it played in the Holocaust. One tzaddik—the Satmar rebbe—ordered his following to remain steadfastly in Hungary, where they would be killed, and he then fled Europe. No messiah succeeds in leading his followers and the world to a harmonious existence—not on the political level, where independence and autonomy inside or outside Israel is not regained by the Jews; and certainly not on the cosmic plain, where disease, violence, and death endure as principal features of the human universe. No messiah is able to soften these perdurable actualities. The messiahs, during their lives, and the followers, after their leader's death, must push the successful fulfillment of their programs forward into the future in order to maintain themselves as microsocieties in the present, but their efforts merely inflect the unavoidable death of the messiah and the eventual collapse of his movement, leaving rationalizations on the ruins of the unattainable hopes they have raised. The texts themselves participate: they constitute the ultimate failure of these attempts; they may attack the messianic program as foolish or dangerous or recuse themselves from judging events in which they, too, wish to have a continuing role. Thus, the lack of success observable in the messiah's life is reborn in a linear description of his career, which proceeds along a definite course from one beginning to one end. The texts have been written to be read and to carry forth their authors' wishes to influence the future from an enduring vantage point. They are no more free than the messiah—they are bound by the aims and restrictions of the genre of historical narrative and counternarrative; and he, by the limits of life itself. The texts and the messiahs impose on each other's freedom in several ways.

The desire to avoid the inevitable end of their stories dominates both the reality of the text—its formal structure—and the reality of the messiah and the following. Indicating an awareness of what the end must be, the texts mask certainty in a guise of suspense, and the messiahs and their followings do the same—looking away from themselves in order to suspend their knowledge of the denouement. When we examine the texts and histories, their beginnings being determined by their ends, denial and the processes and yields of denial stand out as their common characteristic. The living messiahs and their followers are modeled by the texts as their activities add material to them; they do not misapprehend the nature of life or power, and before them they have the texts, which highlight what they know actually happens. The suspense serves to sustain the messiah and his following in the face of wary governments. Once the movement becomes fixed on a particular goal and gains enough power to be a threat, it can be dealt with easily. Jewish movements that took place in an Israel/Judaea, or a Persia, where Jews were enfranchised, though the subjects of foreign domination, were less flexible, more apparent, and, presenting more of a threat, subjected to quicker, surer, and harsher responses from the state authorities.

What the texts have known all along—the immanence and proximate emergence of doom—the authorities come to know at a particular moment, sooner or later. In the last act, at the point of recognition, they decide what they must do.

The messiahs and the followers continue along their course. The interplay of the three parties that occurs at this juncture advances the messianic ritual to its crisis. While pretense has underwritten all the relationships in the events until this point, now it is stripped away by the act of abandonment; "abandon," a verb in the middle voice, acts upon those who employ it, like the verb "marry." The verb "abandon" relates all the participants to themselves and to each other and contributes to a description of the ritual. It actually appears in some of the texts; it governs what happens even when it isn't used, since abandonment occurs whenever professed intentions are left unfulfilled. The recognition that the followers, along with those other Jews who stand outside the movements altogether (the potential followers), abandon the messiahs, and falsify them, comes as an important corrective to the widespread tendency to regard the messiahs as the betrayers who are seeking immediate gains under the guise of altruism. I argue that those who regard the messiah as the cause of failure are right; that those who regard the people as the cause are right; and that in the larger context, the whole society at every level contributes cooperatively to the abandonment, which itself defines the relationships. Ambivalence, ambiguity, reticence, equivocation, diffidence—in the end, betrayal: Messiahs had to go, along with their followings. A better path to Israel had to be found and was, one that discarded ambivalence and provided an opportunity for agreement among all the parties, permitting a role for weakness in assisting the designs of the powerful, and for compromise in the service of an ideal.

The themes of the abandonment of the self and of the other are present in many of the features that interrelate the messiah, the following, the context of a messianic event, and the texts that create the event. Along the way to the ultimate abandonment of the messiah by his followers, and of the followers by their messiah, virtually all vestiges of the old bad world have been stripped away, abandoned, themselves, in order to create the following:

A New Person

The messiah abandons the very physical being which is himself. His act persists in those texts which diminish his human nature in favor of his cosmic being and accomplishments. He is not the natural child of his parents, in the first place. He is an allogene; something other than his parents generates him. The texts usually efface his parentage in the period before the exile from Spain. In the later period, some special quality that makes the parents worthy of bringing the child into the world appears, a spiritual quality that replaces their physical defects. The most extreme examples of this are the virgin birth in the New Testament and the tale of Luria's birth. In fact, the messiah is not one self but two or more selves, and he cannot be born by physical means because he is not primarily a physical being, and thus known, but a being of capacities that must remain unknown in order to remain indeterminate, elusive. In the later period, he generally possesses a soul, his essential self, that is second-hand, either the eternal soul of the arch-messiah or that of an immediate-predecessor messiah; it is not new with him. The texts make his soul different from that of his followers; they believe that he outlives them, in a waiting zone of some sort, or that the eternal part of him, the soul that occupies him, holds itself in readiness for its next realization. In those cases where the messiah is more the type of the king-messiah, the military figure, where physicality plays such an important role, his parentage and birth are effaced; the texts may tell us nothing at all on the subject (e.g., texts on the anti-Roman messiahs; the oriental messiahs), or they may situate the birth and circumstances in a physical realm quite distant from the realm in which he is acting, in the land of the Lost Tribes beyond the Sambation river (e.g., Reubeni). As a principle, then, whatever the texts declare, or refrain from mentioning, concerning the messiah's antecedents and birth is integral to a presentation of the messiah as either decidedly more-than-human or so much like all of us that he has no particular lineage.

In the case of the mystical messiahs—those associated primarily with cosmos-wide times and end of the world deeds, those whose acts on earth have only twisted resemblances to their ultimate significance—the father's glory wanes as his son's waxes, to the point that the presence of the son's unlimited power ordains the absence of the father. The line of descent through the father is important to the son's pedigree; the father's deeds may likewise contribute to his son's holiness since it is due to those deeds that the father merits the honor of siring him. But the father, by the same token, cannot linger too long since the son's deeds must not depend on his father's; the son must not be hidden in his father's shade. In the birth-and-youth tale of Luria, his father merits him through his faith and deeds, then doubts whether he does actually merit him, thereby losing the quality that made him fit to father Luria. The father has thus cast doubt on his son's own merit when he is born (if the father is not worthy, then the son who is born must not be the one awaited); secondarily, through the part played by the father's faith and doubt, he has reinstalled the principle that others may determine the outcome of the son's deeds. Luria's success comes to depend on the righteousness and steadfast faith of others, and he and his efforts are doomed from the outset by his father's doubts. Isaac Luria cannot survive such a heritage; neither can his own son. But neither can Luria's father continue to live, a constant reminder that the son is but human. In the tale, the father is present at Luria's birth and circumcision and absent a few lines later, without doing anything in the meantime. Joseph performs a negative function in Jesus' story, as the father and not the sire. Abulafia says he actually comes to life (ḥay) when his father dies (met), and the end of that passage of the account relates his purpose as that of returning the hearts of fathers and sons to each other, a recognition of this tragic relationship. Molkho literally cuts himself off from his male lineage in his acts of name changing, self-circumcision (as opposed to being circumcised under his father's aegis), conversion, and emigration. Vital mentions the roots of his father's soul but nothing else; Luria assigns Vital a yihud to make with his father at his grave. After Shabtai Zvi's father, Mordechai, hands him over to his teachers as a child, the two have nothing to do with each other (Shabtai ceases studying with any teachers when he is young, and continues his studies in his father's house but is shut off from any contact with the rest of the household). Among the Hasidic messiahs, the Besht's father is away when he is born; Naḥman's father is a perfect Joseph, playing no part in his boy's education or upbringing; Israel of

Ruzhin's father dies when he is six; Safrin's father pleads for a son and is told, "If so, you will not live long, for there is no room in this world for both of you"; the true parent of the Rebbe, Menachem Schneerson, is his wife's father.

A New Name

As the messiahs assume their roles, another act—the assumption of a new name—separates them from their natural origins. Talmudic debates over the name of the messiah demonstrate the importance of the name in this context; they conclude that the messiah's name is a secret thing. Of course, some of the messiahs were lucky enough to be born with a name that serves their texts as evidence of their destiny, like Reubeni, of Davidic lineage; Yeshua (Jesus) the Savior; Hayim (Vital), both whose names mean "life"; Shabtai (Zvi), whose name refers to the Sabbath and the planet Saturn; Israel (the Besht); or Menachem (Schneerson), the comforter, the name of the messiah in the *Book of Zerubbabel*. Most seem to have changed their names, or their original names were effaced and changed in the texts and traditions of their followers and opponents and the surrounding society: e.g., the several Yehudas of the Roman period; Bar Kosiba (known as Kokhba); all the Persian messiahs (changed in several ways); Menahem/David Alroy; Abulafia (known to himself as Raziel); Molkho (who was Pires); Luria (the Ari); Zvi, Barukhia Russo, and Frank—the Holy Lords, Gods of Israel; Yakov Querido (the Beloved); Hayim ben Shlomo, (known as Malakh, the Angel); Yakov and Yosef combined by Frank; Yehuda bar Shalom (Shukr Kuhayl II). They leave their given names, and their family names, their families themselves in order to become new people, divorced and claiming the right to name themselves. In effect, these figures' names become the name of the messiah; he comes to be known by their (new) name, rather than they being known by his. Named Yakov, Frank constructs a whole salvation myth out of the family history of Jacob, his older brother Esau, and his son Joseph. (Though the messiahs change their names, their followers generally don't. Both Zionist leaders and followers changed their names to Hebrew ones when they came to settle in Israel, and this, too, is a manifestation of the nonmessianic nature of that movement.)

A New Family

The messiah's own family is rubbed out. Marriage is, if not unknown, at least uncommon, and with that there seems to be a smaller-than-expected number of children, particularly sons, mentioned in the accounts. Lusty Yakov Frank never remarried after his first wife died. The Ba'al Shem Tov did not remarry, either; the tzaddikim normally do, even must. An indication of the replacement, for the messiah figure, of a normal nuclear family unit with a different kind of group can be seen in the image of the table cited in the accounts: the mensa, the table of the Last Supper; the ones where Shukr Kuhayl ate as a lonely wanderer; the grand festive seatings where Reubeni sometimes ate, as did Frank and Zvi; and the rebbe's *tish*. At the Passover table, the messiah and his harbinger are always present, from Egypt to Crown Heights. The messiah belongs to his followers, it seems; they are his family. Frank calls the members of his inner circle his Brothers and Sisters and says to them that it is his wish that they be without blemish, all of them, so that when seated at a round table, none will distinguish him from them. Jesus offers himself to his disciples at the table, telling each one of them to take and eat a part of himself. At the rebbe's table, just as one raises the cup to him, hoping to catch his eye and his blessing over the drink, one longs for, and is blessed to receive, crumbs, bits, and pieces from his fingers, from his plate, which will enter one's own body and bring holiness with them. Foes, too, can be gathered in at table according to the practice of Shukr Kuḥayl II. As part of the messiah's family, the followers are promised a rebirth through the agency of his memory, his account of them.

A New Place

Just as the abandonment of their natural origins, names, and families frees the messiahs from normal appraisals, from traditional and local standards of judgment, so does the weight of their relationship with their home territory bring them to shake off its dust. All the messiahs of the Roman period are "Galileans," either according to them or to their Roman biographers, irrespective of their birthplaces; in the tales, Bar Kosiba loses his hometown (Kosiba) and becomes Bar Kokhba. Jesus remarks that no one is thought a prophet in his hometown (and this is doubly true of him, born in the Galilee, reborn in the texts in Bethlehem of David), and this serves well to direct attention again to the mutuality of denial and abandonment in this matter. The citizenry, who know too much about the messiah, are prone to repeat what they know and elaborate on it, in accordance with their support for, or antagonism toward, the messiah; the messiah, aware of this tendency, moves away, carrying his foreign background with him as a promise of the possibility of other, better, exotic lives; Reubeni does this (as does the land of the Lost Tribes motif in general).

Several messiahs are lifelong itinerants, but those messiahs who rise through addressing local concerns—after the requirement that prophets cannot be true prophets if they are not in the land of Israel has been abandoned, with a brief renewal of commitment in the sixteenth century—stay near their homes: among Marranos, emphasizing God's own marranoism; among Jews under Islam, emphasizing the virtues and motifs of Islamic traditions and their home locale as the way to Israel; among Polish Jews, proclaiming Poland, rather than the land of Israel, as the Place of the Ascent into the other world; in their shtetls, where their first followers live, to the point of carrying their shtetls with them when they move, in fact carrying the populations and their own local designations as the Bobover, Lubavitcher, Satmarer, or Belzer rebbe. Even these localist, populist messiahs usually end their lives away from home, buried abroad or disappearing into caves with no fixed address, or returning to the abode of their souls.

A New Escape

In the way messiahs model their prospective followers' hopes, they offer a whole menu of new responses to time-honored and inescapable oppressions. As long as Jews lack autonomy, these oppressions are always present, and range from physical persecutions to political and economic restrictions on their habitation, travel, occupation, dress; all such measures serve to formulate and maintain the submission of the self to an inimical other. After the loss of the land of Israel to the dominion of non-Jews, the return from the Diaspora had to be managed by miraculous travel; the land the Jews sought to reach was not the one in this world. The traveling is usually done over the waves but, in several cases, is to take place through the air, indicating that it is truly supernatural, unrestricted by biblical patterns of the Exodus and return; in some, the flight is not one of return from exile but simply of escape from a political situation that has come to be virtually identical with an imprisoning Nature. Alroy's sailing away from the pursuing king and ministers, in which he is borne above the waves on his handkerchief but not to the land of Israel, leads to a second trip through the air being scheduled for his followers (by a couple of swindlers who are obviously well acquainted with the expectations of their clientele). Frank swims across the floodwaters of the Totorozh on his horse, showing his observers the way to new freedom from nature itself—through self-confidence and a faith in him like his own. The extensive employment of miracles is, most of all, a demonstration of ways to escape oppression. Enemies of the messiah die, or he escapes from them or their prisons; the messiah penetrates the plans and plots of others; gates open of themselves. The most feared of oppressions is mortality, and all messiahs offer an escape from its rule. They are often willing to demonstrate their faith in their own power, offering up their heads and bodies or challenging overwhelming forces with a magic branch; sometimes they are not so willing and prefer to refute themselves, leaving the meaning of the refutation to be explained. Their ability to escape locales may be replaced by their ability to escape time in the way that prophesying correctly what will come to pass in the immediate future stands for knowing what will come to pass in a more distant, apocalyptic, time.

Knowing how to escape means recognizing, first, the need to escape from oppressive traditions; prodigious success in scholarship is a quality messiahs share with nonmessianic leaders, but only messiahs can come by their knowledge in an instant, with no preparation at all. Such miraculously gained new knowledge supports fundamental innovation—nothing less than a new revealed law. Magic deeds and miracles expected by followings, and performed by messiahs, challenge the confines of natural and traditional law. Maimonides decreed an end to miracle-working messiahs not only because he considered a more reasonable adjustment to reality more likely to improve the self and society, but also because he found the sorts of miracles commonly sought by such messiahs to be hazardous, and antagonistic to his scheme for rising to the prophet's role through scrupulous observance of Jewish law and devoted study of Jewish tradition, rational philosophy, and natural science. Unfortunately for Maimonides' preferences, biblical texts speak plainly of miraculous interventions in the natural order, and, out of the large number of predictions of wondrous events and, even, attempts at wondrous deeds throughout the two thousand years of Jewish messianism, some were bound to pan out. Bishop Dembowski, to take one example, after proclaiming Frank's victory in the disputation against the rabbis, ordered the burning of the Talmud and was immediately swept away by the angel of death, clearly a judgment made in Heaven. Moshe Ḥanoch writes a letter and tells how he became a believer in Shukr Kuḥayl II by falling from a ladder after insulting him, then learning it had happened at Shukr's command, for his own good. The pope dies seeking Abulafia's death.

A New Law

The notion that the days of the messiah, the messiah's apocalyptic reign, will be served by a new law is a Jewish one. Paul is quite Jewish in seeking to extend his new, more accessible, religion to Gentiles in the interest of time (Rom. 10:4) as did some of his contemporaries among the rabbis. In his essay, "The Crisis of Tradition in Jewish Messianism," G. Scholem reviews the most important rabbinic statements that look forward to a utopian messianic age governed by a new, relaxed law: Lev. Rabbah 9:7—"All sacrifices will be abolished except for the offer of thanksgiving"; Yalkut and Midrash Mishle on Prov. 9:2: "All festivals will be abolished except for Purim, which will never be abolished [and the Day of Atonement will be like Purim]"; Midrash Tehillim, in regard to Ps. 146:7: "The Lord allows the forbidden . . . and will one day allow the eating of all animals now forbidden to be eaten. . . . In the time to come, he will allow everything that he has forbidden"; Lev. Rabbah 13:3: "A new Torah shall go forth from me," and "the messiah himself will teach it (Yalkut in regard to Isa. 26:2)." Though these are all midrashic and speculative statements, they served Christianity well during the disputations against rabbinic Judaism and, along with Paul's writings, conveyed the idea of an abrogation of restrictions of all kinds to later messiahs. Those who made greatest use of the idea were the Shabbatean messiahs, from Zvi through Barukhia to Frank. Scholem notes that immediately following the proposal that all animals would be permitted as food in the period of the end of days, another rabbi takes the position that no animals at all will be eaten. Some messiahs also followed that line, and we can see that innovation in the law, including new strictures, also invested a new authority—the messiah—with the power to innovate independently. Abu Isa abolished sacrifices and altered other traditional requirements of the Torah, on the one hand, and forbade the eating of any animal and increased the number of prayers, on the other. Yudghan, Mushka, and Serenus (who decreased the number of prayers) followed Abu Isa in prohibiting distilled liquors. Many other messiahs (Reubeni, Molkho, Luria, Vital, the Yemenities) also promoted new abstinences; these extra restrictions, along with an enhanced emphasis on other acts of asceticism, repentance, and charity, continue the tradition of mourning for the destruction of the temple, as carried on in the circles of the Mourners of Zion. In regard to the new law, all these messiahs—not to exclude Shabtai Zvi, the performer of "strange acts"—increased restrictions, ensuring the continuation of the process of bringing on the end and establishing the rule of the messiah; at the same time, they abandoned restrictions, promoting antinomian behavior as if already living in the period of the end of days under the new rule. In either case, the messiahs are arrogating authority to themselves. But the new ethical and moral practices cannot be judged according to the traditions of this world. The messianic event has left this world for a new one. Just as old money has a new valuation put on it (see the discussion below), so do ethics, morals, and law gain new meaning in the "kingdom of Heaven."

A New Knowledge

The messiah may become a master of the new law by first learning the old and then building upon it, or mastery may come to him as a prophetic, revelatory experience; it may come upon him suddenly along with the tenets of the new law. Alongside the child prodigy—Jesus, Luria, Luzzato, and Safrin, among others—there are adult prodigies. Diogo Pires had no known Hebrew education; shortly after becoming Shlomo Molkho, he was studying mystic texts and expanding on them in his speeches and writings. The figure of one who has been illiterate, become literate, and expounded a new law is found in the messiahs Abu Isa, Yehoshua Heshel Tzoref, Yakov Frank, and perhaps some of the Yemenites and others. The story of Mohammed, who was illiterate, and whose masterful language in the Koran serves as proof of the book's divinity (the *'ijaz*), may have reinforced this pattern for messiahs rising in Islamic contexts, especially in the case of Abu Isa, who acknowledged the prophetic status of Mohammed. Both the child who is prodigious in his mastery of traditional texts, and the adult who suddenly acquires knowledge, expose the prophet's ability to dominate older scholars and tradition itself by providing evidence of a nonnormal destiny—a heavenly teacher or talent. Frank expressed the principle—one not unknown in Hasidism—that ignorance of the law and the tradition freed one for true knowledge of what the tradition, in its sophistry, had mistaken. (Beyond his signature, there's really no evidence, however, that Frank ever became literate.)

A New Status

Scholars have noted that rabbinic authorities rarely support messiahs, notwithstanding the cases of Bar Kosiba (supported by Rabbi Akiba) and Shabtai Zvi (by many) and the characteristic ambivalence of the rabbis of Yemen. The Jewish scholarly class is a leisured elite; messiahs don't belong to it and the challenge they present to it as prophets threatens its security. Since a messiah's followers—women and children, among them—also lack membership in this elite, the messiah's nonscholarliness, when combined with a background in unskilled labor, may persuade his followers to look upon him as one of their own and as a model of the new beings they will become in his reign. Some of the illiterate messiahs mentioned above earned their livings as laborers; to them, we may add other figures, from Etrog (Athronges) to the Ba'al Shem Tov. They offer their followers a type of leader who recalls a Golden Age.

A second group of messiahs, also lacking elite status, is neither illiterate (though they are unlearned by rabbinic standards) nor engaged in rough physical labor. They are not peasants, "cutters of wood and carriers of water," but artisans or craftsmen who do have some of the same opportunities that rabbis have but are not so far removed from the mass of the potential followers. (When Mahler alleges that class struggle motivates messianic movements, in *Karaites*, pp. 13–14, he confusingly lumps peasants together with artisans.) The artisan is not exhausted by his labor; he possesses leisure time; can read, write, and do arithmetic; has access to technology and knows the value of a new idea; must speculate in raw materials; amasses capital; and is in touch with fellow craftsmen, customers, and suppliers throughout the local, and even the more distant, communities. He presents a reachable goal for those in his community hoping to emerge from grinding poverty and labor. Meanwhile, he himself can look up and see an even easier life and so is more frustrated by social circumstances that deny him full opportunity and reward those who do not have his competencies. Where there are guilds, he may not enter them; he may do the same or better work than his non-Jewish equivalent but be paid less or not at all; he is, in any case, restricted from the most productive and most prestigious employment of the gains he makes. The burden of powerlessness weighs heavy upon him as a member of Jewish society when it is held captive by social and economic circumstances veiled as religious differences. Jesus was a member of a family that perhaps farmed but also worked with wood and possessed all the advantages of the craftsman. The Syrian Jew led launderers and weavers in a revolt against Christian institutions; the tailor, Abu Isa, was illiterate, at least in the sense in which the rabbinic society meant that term. Reubeni worked as something of a military man; Luria, as a merchant; Tzoref, as a jeweler. For the same reasons that an artisan may become a messiah, other artisans may choose to follow one. Crypto-Jewish artisans remained close to Judaism in Spain, and this class was particularly involved in the messianic ferment in 1500. While Ines of Herrera was not an artisan, many of her followers were; her father was a shoemaker, and another shoemaker spread her fame.

A New Economy

The economic scheme most people associate with messiahs and their followers is one of unbridled rapacity, with the clever former preying on the ignorant latter, but this is the exception rather than the rule. For the messiah and the followers, the dictates of time and place that govern worth function normally—by a given date, the new world will appear, with it, and a new coinage. It is economically sound, then, to prepare for the moment, purchasing and investing in what will be useful in order to arrive at and live in the new time and space (often, the land of Israel). The best investment during the season preceding the rule of the messiah would lie in whatever brings that rule to greater power. Demonstrations of faith in the earning potential of the movement in this period include charity and others of a more substantial character. Just as keeping money will be of no use, so, too, disposing of it becomes not waste but an investment in a new concern or a loan through which shares are acquired or insurance taken out against the period of travails. Guided by the festive spirit that led followers to take out loans, promising interest at high rates (which would not have to be paid back), or to sell local land at grossly reduced prices (since new land would soon be available) and use the proceeds for travel arrangements or for charity or for new clothes, parties and luxuries did not so much dispose of surplus capital as enlist the capitalists as new owners of a promising enterprise. The messiah was not milking his followers; with all his finery and pomp (and this posture had its companion, the impoverished ascetic, living on what the birds brought him, and drinking what water he could from creeks and springs), he was demonstrating how one should behave in the new scheme. How, after all, could the impoverishment of his followers benefit him, if wealth were his goal? He could be no better served by this, since his fortunes would fall with theirs, than he could by the loss of his followers in a war or by their imprisonment in a civil jail. The imputation of charlatanry to the messiahs, like the label "false," is not very helpful in understanding the economic activity of a group of people determined to bring on an immediate and drastic change in their common economic situation. The restruck Roman coins of Bar Kosiba's Free Israel lost their worth in one economy and were the only coinage of any use in the new one. (They remain precious today.) The hasty marriages contracted in the twilight of the old time, on the eve of the new, like the new clothes for the journey from the Diaspora to the old (new) land, were self-redeeming bonds and made good sense (unless, as Ines of Herrera promised, better mates were waiting on the other side).

A New Eternity

In the new time there would be plenty, and everyone would live a long, healthy life. Death, disease, poverty, and repression would all be conquered and forgotten forever. Of the many images of an endless future, none is so constant and, as an example, so important as the image of the messiah's own immortality. The messiahs are indeed immortal. The soul of the messiah is immortal. Even if the messiah seems to have been killed, the texts assure him of deathlessness. Someone else has been killed. He hasn't been killed, but has only gone and will return. He has gone into a cave to wait. He is waiting in the mountains. He is dead but will be resurrected. The soul, anyway, of the messiah is eternal, has been kept in readiness so as to be installed at the appropriate time and, if the time again turns out not to be right, will be reincarnated in some later messiah's body.

AMBIVALENCE AND ABANDONMENT

In a highly energetic dialectic, denying anything, even mortality, to the messiah denies him what he probably most desires. Like his following, but to an exaggerated degree, the messiah wants the power to define himself in a social context where that capability is severely limited. The unlimited scope of the messiah's desire directs attention to his feelings of denial and circumscription. Some of these feelings reflect conditions that are unquestionably present in Jewish Diaspora life, though perhaps exaggerated in the messiah's mind. The tendency toward exaggeration and feelings of denial may result from very early psychic damage. This is not the place for an extensive review of the literature on the psychology of the messiah, but approaches to his psychology as a damaged one, compensating for its injury through the manufacture of a "borderline" psychosis or neurosis, serve well to explain the messiah's actions when there is no other apparent cause. This also holds true for the psychology of the individuals who constitute his following and produces the peculiar relationship that the follower and messiah have with each other. The texts do not provide all the data necessary for describing the psychologies and their relationships outside the texts. However, a reading of the features extracted from the texts and mentioned so far in this chapter supports a messiah who demonstrates a highly labile affect—at times demanding and harsh; and at other times, appeasing and gentle—in his relations with his followers and his antagonists (they may be the same people) and establishes the source for this as a disorder in his self-concept associated with very early experiences. The messiah's denial of his parentage and his given name weighs heavily here. The richest resource for gaining insight into the messiah's psyche lies in his dreams as he retells them. They give hints of his fears but resist an easy explication. We are fortunate in having Molkho's and Vital's and Frank's here.

The texts often portray the messiah as a completely self-assured figure, yet a single text may portray him as both ambivalent and reticent, particularly in his initial assumption of the role. The one posture is as puzzling and revealing as the other, since in the first case, the texts know of the messiah's failure, and, though they may imagine him as immortal and returning, from one place or another, to complete his task, they cannot mention his success; and in the second case, the texts give no independent explanation for his reticence. When refusing the role, the messiah asserts his lack of some necessary physical, spiritual, or intellectual quality. Before going outside the text to propose a purpose or a motive for his making such a statement, it must first be said that the text itself is quite immodest in recounting the messiah's humility, ensuring that the reader will know of that quality, too, among his other virtues. Both themes—the messiah's reticence and his decided lack of doubt—betray the messiah as a result of their involvement with reality; the reality outside the text can be kept from limiting the text's possibilities, but the texts cannot break free altogether and at the end proclaim, "And so that was the redemption." Such a sentence would simply not be understandable. The texts then, do not believe in the messiah because they allow reality to check their freedom.

In reality, the messiah knows of the history of other messiahs and of the texts about and by them, oral or written. He has good reason to be ambivalent about taking on the task; he knows he can't do it and will probably die in the attempt. Again, the reality of the situation is observable and reputably recorded and predictable. A government, acting on behalf of the whole society, or any governing body acting for any constituent of the society, will not submit itself to a demand to restaff and reorganize without the application of superior force and will act instinctively to suppress messiahs and their followings. The degree of the government's fear is not rational, given the unequal distribution of power, but rises from its own knowledge that forces outside it—the consent of the governed, the will of other governments just like it, and even its own will—can determine its survival. It leaps at the chance to cooperate in drawing a limit. If the messiah has any success at all, he will be dealt with ruthlessly. Like the government, the messiah knows in some deep way that lack is inherent in his being and so is truly infinite and cannot be satisfied. He must desert his disabled self and is ambivalent since he knows what he will lose—the adaptations he has made—and does not know what advantages he will gain or what their price might be in terms of unknown disadvantages. It is simple to say that the messiah refuses his task in order not to threaten a potential following. If he allows the following to force him into the task, he is making no demands on his own and suggesting nothing about his divinity or the likelihood of his success. But something must have already happened before the messiah acknowledges his readiness to do that which others have forced on him; the idea that he wants the task and that he wants to be forced to do it has to be communicated, and only he—or others who know the pattern—can have transmitted it. His position says to his following that anything that happens is their responsibility since he didn't ask for the job, and his ambivalence, when it is stated, assures the followers that he will betray their expectations and that disaster will certainly result. It comes down not to his wanting to abandon them so much as his wanting them to abandon him. It is wrong to conclude that the following, unlike the messiah, are dupes and unaware of this dynamic. They, having all the messiah's knowledge of their own traditions and texts, know what they are doing. They have come into the relationship to betray the messiah, and their willingness to take this role rests on their certainty that he will betray them and that the forces that limit them—the government and their own damaged self-perceptions—will relieve them of their limitations and see to the execution of the sentence they have passed on themselves and their representative.

The following is often made up solely of people who are marginally attached to the society; such people always constitute at least the bulk of the following. They know, and so does the messiah, that they will revert to marginality, abandoning their new society under stress. They are of "profligate character," "wicked men," "gullible," "hasty," "unsteady" and can be counted on to betray. The movement makes use of this quality at first, forcing them to show their fidelity to a long-range goal—gathering in all the exiles, for example—by leading them to gather more people into the movement; and it rewards them by keeping them close to, ever more like, the messiah, betraying many others, an inner circle that can be threatened with becoming ordinary followers again, cast away from the fire that fuses the messiah and his closest adherents. The messiah makes use of the instability of the following, blaming them for every failure and particularly at the last, when they betray him to the government. The following in turn uses the messiah's betrayal as a stimulant to betray him since they know that he will run away or give up. The dictates of the tale in which they are all operating state at the outset that he will outlive them; his soul is not his; he is immortal in his essence. The recurrent theme of the land of the Lost Tribes, like the program that promises the return to an age of gold or the advance into an unlimited utopia where the only thing known is that everything will be different from what has been experienced, appears frequently in the tales, and in the assessments of the tales, to show that what is sought cannot be obtained by any human act.

The messiah ritual is largely a negative one by which identities and acts are restrained, contained and turned back at the borders the ritual establishes in retrospect. The productive aspects of Jewish messianic movements, as they have been reabsorbed into Judaism, are confined to the stimulation of self-appraisal, of self-knowledge that expresses itself in self-doubt, and of the desire to redress feelings of inadequacy, immediately, in the place where it is perceived, by helping others through charitable acts and self-restraint, and by resisting the desire to have what must be taken from others. One must say that Judaism possesses less complicated and less hazardous ways to promote this, though they may not be so colorful or even so instructive as these monstrous forms, born in such anguish. The ephemeral worth of such doomed creatures as our messiahs seems, finally, to be unequal to the real suffering endured to bear them.

NOTES

CHAPTER 1

1. Aeshcoly attempted to write histories of all the messiahs. The present work only takes up, at best, what Aeshcoly's death left undone in his *Jewish Messianic Movements* (1956, now republished [Jerusalem, 1992], with an important introduction by M. Idel).

2. My analysis follows that of Victor Turner, who considered the significance of ritual "both in respect to its meaning for those who carry it out and in terms of its contribution to the functioning of some social system" (*The Drums of Affliction* [New York, 1968], p. 26); his functional understanding of ritual as expressing and, in effect, resolving social conflict and change informs my own basic argument. Cf. Turner's idea of a "repetitive" social system, in which conflict and change are "contained within the society through periodic rituals. The conflicts did not generate structural change." See also, B. Morris, *Anthropological Studies of Religion* (Cambridge, 1987), p. 241.

3. An analysis of the co-occurrence of social disintegration and individual neuroticising effects as resulting in messianic movements can be found in F. Sierksma, *New Heaven, New Earth* (in Dutch; The Hague, 1961), as summarized in R. J. Z. Werblowsky, "A new Heaven and a new Earth: Considering primitive messianisms," *History of Religions* 5: 164–172.

4. An excellent review of the theoretical literature concerning the nature of the attraction of charismatic leaders and the relationship between leaders and followers, followed by three case studies (Adolph Hitler, Charles Manson, Jim Jones), is C. Lindholm, *Charisma* (Oxford and Cambridge, 1990).

5. This anthropological model was developed by A. F. C. Wallace, "Revitalization movements," *American Anthropologist* (1956) 58:264–281; see also, W. La Barre, "Materials for a history of studies of crisis cults: a bibliographic essay," *Current Anthropology* (1971) 12:3–44.

6. Religions as well as new messiahs may reconstitute a messianic event and incorporate it in their routine liturgical behavior. The messiahs use what they can from previous accounts and carry out their deeds in the public, political realm. The conventional religion may enshrine the event within the confines of the home or another sacred space. For Jews, the Passover meal (described in chapter 3) reconstitutes the Exodus as a prototype of the messianic redemption. Catholics in the United States reconstitute the passion of Jesus in their homes, churches, and, to a degree, outside those spaces. The Last Supper has of course been moved to occupy a constant centrality as the communion service, but some practices that recall the narrative of Jesus are associated with the season of Lent and the Holy Week, in particular. The stations of the cross are commonly walked on Wednesday evening, mapping the Via Dolorosa of Jerusalem and the churches of Rome onto the local church. The Eucharist remains in place as the Last Supper and the focus of the liturgy on Maundy Thursday. Ascetic practices—fasting, abstinence from meat (before Vatican II), and the pause in blessed marriages—recall Jesus' fast of forty days (like Moses' before Sinai). The communion is not held on Good Friday and many Catholics cease to engage in business at about 3:00 P.M. The period of the king-messiahship of Jesus on this Earth, which began on Palm Sunday, culminates on Holy Saturday at noon, when the abandonment of the Old Time is finalized with the relaxation of oaths of Lenten abstinence. Thereafter, catechumens are baptized, sinners are restored to their places in the church, white vestments are donned, as organ music sounds the Gloria and the New Time begins.

7. C. Geertz, *Islam Observed* (New Haven, 1968), p. 26, calls this situation "the time without order," "the time between times," as when the Indic civilization was dissolving and the Islamic forming in Java.

8. The institutionalization by the culture of the roles of the monarchy, the priesthood, and the prophet themselves as discussed below raises a problem. The king, for example, clearly arises in order to modify culture-threatening stresses—the Philistines, among others. The view taken here is that the way the institutions are received after the exile is qualitatively different from practices at the inceptions of the monarchy, the priesthood, and the prophetic role.

9. The discussion of biblical messianism here is brief since there are many works devoted to this topic (mentioned in other notes and in the bibliographic note). What is provided here is an outline that highlights the symbolic features of the accounts of the biblical messiahs that are germane to the study of the Jewish messiahs and the accounts of their lives, as they appear in the Bible, assembled in the mid-second century BCE.

10. The ancient Near Eastern background for the divinity of the king and its early developments in Judaism was described in S. Mowinckel, *He That Cometh: The Messiah Concept in the Old Testament and Later Judaism* (Nashville, 1955), pp. 21–95. The nonhuman character of the prophet and the priest—i.e., their function as agents of the divine and their consequent identification with the divine—is exhibited in their performances and becomes more and more evident as eschatological/apocalyptic literature develops. See John J. Collins, *The Scepter and the Star* (New York, 1995) pp. 112–122. Even initially, Moses, as the ideal type of prophet-leader in action, is associated with the divine by von Rad, for example, in his analysis of the Moses of the E document (G. von Rad, *Old Testament Theology* [New York, 1962–1965], vol. 1, pp. 292–293). J. J. M. Roberts, "The Old Testament's Contribution to Messianic Expectations," in J. Charlesworth, ed., *The Messiah* (Minneapolis, 1992), p. 48, puts the king-priest relationship succinctly: "If the Davidic ruler was Yahweh's regent for maintaining just political rule, the priests were Yahweh's chosen servants for maintaining the cultus that allowed Yahweh to remain in the midst of his city among his people." This sociopolitical relationship underlies the priestly role in the extensive developments after the exile. See Collins's summary of those developments, pp. 74–84.

The figure of the saoshayant of Zoroastrianism is often mentioned as a source for the Jewish messiah-figure, and, while this expected savior may have had some impact as early as the first or second century CE on Jewish messiahs and thereafter, practically on some of the accounts of Jesus, the dissimilarities outweigh the apparent resemblance. The Jewish messiah is a human being, anointed into his task, while the saoshayant is born of the seed of a god. Moreover, the Jewish figure is composed of three separate figures that combine aspects of kingship, priesthood and prophecy, each aspect and the combination of them having its own historical development within Jewish society from periods preceding contact with the Persians.

11. See the essay by Y. Zakovitz, "A poor man riding a donkey, Zech. 9:9–10" in *The Messianic Idea in Judaism* (in Hebrew; Jerusalem, 1982).

12. The idea of the return of the messiah, either in a second coming (the Parousia) or in a new form (the messiah of the lineage of Joseph, followed by the messiah of the lineage of David), came considerably later than the exile. Thus, Zerubbabel himself was not viewed, after his disappearance, as a messiah who would return. His image in fact changed following his disappearance, from messiah to prophet. This shift, like the idea of return, removed the necessity of acknowledging a failure and preserved Zerubbabel's messianic role along with the tradition of the messiah. He is seen as a prophet, telling of the future of Israel, in the frame story of the Book of Zerubbabel (in Y. Even-Shmuel, *midreshei ge'ula* [Jerusalem, 1953], pp. 56–88) and alongside the messiah in S. Kayyara's *sefer halakhot gedolot* (in the edition of E. Hildesheimer [Jerusalem, 1971], p. 223).

13. "[Along with the manna], one of the three things that Elijah will restore to Israel . . . is the jug of anointing oil." This is the text from the *Mekhilta of R. Ishmael*, Beshalah 5, (p. 51b in M. Friedmann's edition, 1968), perhaps the earliest of the Midrashim, instituting an enduring historiographic tradition. TB Horayot 11b and Keritot 5b "also state that until Josiah hid the sacred oil all the high priests and those kings who did not come to the throne by inheritance were anointed with the oil prepared by Moses. During the second commonwealth neither the kings nor the high priests were anointed with the 'oil of anointment,' though some of the kings were anointed with balsam." This is cited in L. Ginzberg, *The Legends of the Jews* (Philadelphia, 1968), vol. 6, p. 72. Ginzberg's conclusion, that "the emphatic manner in which many of the passages [from rabbinic literature, quoted above] state their view that neither Aaron nor the Messiah will be anointed in the time to come leads one to assume the probability that this opinion is directed against the Christian Messiah, literally 'the anointed one'" seems, on the one hand, unlikely and, on the other, an excellent example of intertextual reading (see below).

14. TB Pes. 6b.

15. La Barre laments the unavailability of the one particular, incomplete, study of the Jewish messiahs—Aeshcoly's (see above), which has yet to be translated for the wider body of scholars; Collins, p. 13, notes that "[in regard to the Jewish messiahs through 135 CE], it is unfortunate that we have no writings from the hands of messianic pretenders, or even from their followers, which would illuminate their ideology." This work attempts to supply what it can of those materials from the whole history of Jewish messianic movements. S. Sharot, *Messianism, Mysticism, and Magic* (Chapel Hill, 1982), for some reason does not mention Jesus or a large number of lesser figures, nor does he investigate and distinguish among his sources.

16. Yerushalmi, p. 24, n. 13.

17. Rosenzweig's commentary, *Ninety-two Hymns and Poems of Yehuda Halevi* (in German; Berlin, 1900), pp. 283–284. My thanks to my friend Thomas Kovach, for having brought this passage to my attention.

18. See Collins, pp. 11–12, 28–29. Metaphoric names, such as "shoot," (from Isa. 11) and "branch," (from Jer. 23), as opposed to functional titles, occur as well. They are chiefly

restricted to idealizations of the messiah in theoretical or poetic writing. When they occur in reference to an actual messiah, they are unmistakable indications of apocalypticism, as in Molkho's use of *yinon* for Reubeni (from Ps. 72:17), or in the several names Nathan of Gaza or other Shabbateans used for Shabtai Zvi. The use of such names is similar to the use of traditional nonmetaphoric or attributive personal names for the messiah, such as David, Menahem, and Shabtai, whether the names are chosen after the messiah's career begins or whether the career is lent support by the messiah having received such a name at birth. The name "David" possesses the character of a personal name and that of an apocalyptic-functional name, i.e., the name of, and the description of, the heavenly messiah (see chapter 2). For further remarks on this matter of nomenclature, see chapter 11.

19. D. Rhoads, *Israel in Revolution: 6–74* CE (Philadelphia, 1976), pp. 2–3, remarks on the polemic application of the terms. (He sees all those I mention as "revolutionaries.") Collins (p. 12) prefers to restrict the term "messiah" to eschatological figures.

CHAPTER 2

1. M. de Jonge ("Messiah," in *Anchor Bible Dictionary*, vol. 4, pp. 779, 787) provides a convenient summary of the distinctly different views of the messiah; Collins (pp. 20–41), a more detailed one.

2. No one exclusive body of scholars and lawyers dominated Jewish society in the land of Israel from the time of the return from exile through the second century CE, but the principle of government by a few who were scholars and priests was established by Ezra (with the support of the Persian government); and the reins of power over the culture and society, if not the polity, were held by one group or school which remained foremost among others, at least through the Bar Kosiba war against Rome. This group, eventually known as the Pharisees and, finally, as "the rabbis," composed the regnant doctrine of the messiah and defended its own authority to reject claimants.

3. Shaye J. D. Cohen, "The Festival of Hanukkah," in W. Hallo, D. Ruderman, and M. Stanislavsky, eds., *Heritage: Civilization and the Jews: Source Reader* (New York, 1984), pp. 55–56.

4. R. Yehuda (!) Ha-Nas'i, the patriarch and compiler of the Mishna, is referred to as the messiah (TB Sanh. 98b, TJ Shab. 16:1, 15; cf. Rosh Ha. 25). He was born after Bar Kosiba's rebellion and, like him, was known as *nasi'*. It is difficult to determine precisely the attitude of these references to him; they seem to be metaphoric ones. Sanh. 98b puts his messiahship in a conditional clause, for example.

5. *Antiquities of the Jews*, bk. 17, chap. 10, pars. 4–7, in W. Whiston's translation (New York, 1900).

6. He is referred to by Josephus in *Antiquities*, bk. 18, chap. 1, pars. 1–6, and again in his *Wars of the Jews* (New York, 1928), bk. 2, chap. 8, par. 1, as Yehuda, a Galilean.

7. The other three are those of the Sadducees, the Pharisees, and the Essenes. Rhoads, pp. 49–60, conducts an inquiry into whether the following of Judas constituted a sect, like the other three, and into Josephus' use of the term. He concludes that the evidence supports only the fact that "in a limited sense Judas the Galilean was one of the formulators of the later national call for freedom from the Romans." Even if the use of the term in Josephus is a retrojection, some of the qualities mentioned—especially those which go against characteristics of the "later national call for freedom from the Romans"—must have existed. I am using the traditional term from Josephus' studies with no further implications than that, but I tend toward M. Hengel's view (see Rhoads, p. 55, n. 17), particularly on the defining point of the movement's having had a unified leadership.

8. Whiston suggests that their names might actually have been the same, in a note to *Antiquities*, bk. 17, chap. 10. The confusion of these names, people, and dates occurs in Josephus' account itself; no one has yet sorted them out, though no one I have read accepts the identification of Theudas in Acts with any of the individuals known as Yehuda. Whiston's suggestion, like Josephus' confusion, can best be taken to indicate their feeling that the deeds of these men were similar, and their names similar, to such a degree that one is led to see them as in a stereopticon. The question of the one Theudas or two of them remains unresolved. See C. Jefford, "Theudas," in the *Anchor Bible Dictionary*, vol. 6, pp. 527–528.

9. The conclusion—that the messiah might have many names—guaranteed that he would never have any known name, that his name was a divine secret. See, among other texts, TB Sanh. 93b, 96b, 98b. Of course, some of the debates insisted that the name was that of some former scholar, the teacher of the proponent.

10. E. E. Urbach devotes the last chapter of his *The Sages* (Jerusalem, 1979) to the rabbinic theologies of redemption (pp. 649–692). Urbach explores all the important discourses and, in regard to messianism, reaches the conclusion that "the abolition of the figure of the personal Messiah is thus to be found in both conceptions of redemption—in that which regards it as the time of the End [of days], and also in that which integrates it with preliminary repentance" (p. 690).

11. The identification Rabban Yohanan ben Zakkai made of King Hezekiah as the messiah, like his deathbed assertion (repeated by others of the *tannaim*) of the near approach of this messiah (TB Ber. 28b), must be seen in the light of ben Zakkai's mysticism, on the one hand, and his practicality, on the other. It was, after all, he who said, "If you have a shoot in your hand and are told, 'Look, here comes the messiah!,' go on and plant the shoot first. *Then* come meet him" (*Avot de R. Natan*, Version B, ed. S. Schechter [in Hebrew; New York, 1967], p. 34). An *amora* (a rabbinic authority of the period following that of the *tannaim*) thinks of Hezekiah as the messiah who is already altogether gone: "There shall be no messiah for Israel, because they have already enjoyed [literally, "devoured"] him in the days of Hezekiah." (TB Sanh. 98b–99a).

12. The doctrine appears in *The Testaments of the Twelve Patriarchs*, where it was long thought to be so odd as to call for interpretations that would explain it away, until the doctrine actually surfaced as a belief in the Qumran material. See Collins, chap. 4, for a thorough review.

13. The rebellions in Judaea thereafter stem from this political, if not familial, lineage. The relocation of Jesus to Judaea in the birth narrative, and from there back to the Galilee, and then from there back to Jerusalem might reflect the ambivalent attitudes of his movement (as well as of the Davidic ideology) toward a policy of violence, associated with the Galilee, that was conducted in Judaea. For some other ideas, see Rhoads, pp. 48–49.

14. The origin and purpose of the messiah-of-the-lineage-of-Joseph/Ephraim figure is a matter of dispute. (The association with Ephraim, rather than Joseph, has to do with the lineage of Joshua, who followed Moses into the leadership of a community at war.) There is a clear connection to the idea of a "suffering messiah," and one is led to think of Jesus in the Gospels. The preliminary messiah frees the messiah of the Davidic lineage from suffering, torture, and death and may be a response to Christian doctrine. Perhaps the myth reflects some history. The myth which claims that the coming victorious Judaean messiah will have been preceded by a failed, northern one may develop from the association between the preliminary messiah and the northern kingdom, defeated in the eighth century, and the association of the second, southern messiah of the lineage of David with the successful southern kingdom. See Sh. Shavid, "Messiah, messianism," in the *Hebrew Encyclopedia*, vol. 24, p. 615 and the bibliography there. Lengthy consideration is given to the matter in Klausner, *The*

Messianic Idea in Israel. See, most recently, A. Elqayam, "The missing messiah," (*da'at* 38, 1997) (in Hebrew).

15. J. Neusner, *The Mother of the Messiah in Judaism* (Valley Forge, 1993), pp. 124–125.

16. This passage in Josephus may underlie the development in much later Jewish texts—outside the Gospels—of the term "false messiah." If the prophet were false and then became king-messiah, he would be a false messiah. Josephus does not himself use the term "false messiah" but this may be due to the natural confusion (mentioned above) of the prophet of a messiah with the messiah he prophesies. Compare Josephus' use of the term "prophet" for the "Egyptian" messiah.

17. R. G. Marks, *The Image of Bar Kokhba in Traditional Jewish Literature* (University Park, 1994), p. 22, n. 19, writes, "The exact nature of Bar Koziva's crime is unclear," and shows that as late as the thirteenth century, "Rabbi Menahem Ha-Meiri compares it with the crime of the *nevi ha-sheqer*, the false prophet punished in the Mishnah by death (Sanh. 11:5)."

18. In the foregoing summary of rabbinic views, I have mixed earlier opinions with later ones. What is said by earlier figures is often and, for a variety of reasons, put in their mouths by later ones. There are also many texts that continue to address reasonable expectations for national improvements in the situation of the Jews and for programs designed to influence individual and national conduct. Samuel says, "There is nothing that makes this world different from the days of the messiah other than our subordination to the foreign powers" (TB Ber. 34b). In several arguments that extend the role of propriety, restraint, and patient endurance from a daily to a cosmic ethics, authorities maintain that humans do have a part to play in bringing the messiah. They hold that repentance and charity hasten redemption and the coming of the messiah (TB Sanh. 97b–98a, Baba Bathra 10a, Yoma 86b). These positions reemerge in later events outside Israel. But the texts of rabbinic doctrines do tend massively toward the goal of making the messiah an apocalyptic figure, the creature of a fantastic time of great anguish, which is to be followed by a time of greater relief. He cannot be found and is not to be expected, only to be dreamed of. (They denied his coming [TB Sanh. 99a]; denied the Bible had messianic references to the exile, Sanh. 97b; held the matter hidden [Sanh. 99a, Yoma 9b, and cf. Acts 1:6]; required passivity of the Jews [Ket. 111a]; and set the messiah at the gates of Rome, suffering among leprous mendicants [Sanh. 98].) The basic rabbinic texts, as they are forming or already firmly in place, by the sixth century constitute the background from which the messiahs struggle to emerge.

19. See J. Klausner, *Jesus of Nazareth* (New York, 1925), pp. 17–43.

20. The first certain references to the idea of the *mashiah ben yosef* occur in the Talmud at the time of the Bar Kosiba rebellion; the proposition was already present in its parts but inchoate until then.

21. H. Shanks, ed., *Christianity and Rabbinic Judaism* (Washington, D.C., 1992). See also, his *Historical Image of Jesus* (New York, 1996). The synoptic gospels, for all that they differ from each other, make but one account as far as their impact on later accounts goes.

22. There are some problems with the story of Akiba's recognition of Bar Kosiba (and also with ben Torta's rejoinder). With the text from *Lamentations rabbah*, citing the story from TJ Ta'an. 4:68, compare TB Hag. 14a and Sanh. 110b, where Akiba seems to make statements about the messiah which would conflict with what he is reported to say about Bar Kosiba. See Urbach, pp. 674, 998, which prefers to dissociate the statements in Hag. and Sanh. from Akiba; and P. Schaeffer, "Rabbi Akiba and Bar-Kokhba," pp. 117–119 in W.S. Green, ed., *Approaches to Ancient Judaism*, vol. 2 (Providence, 1989), which dates the TJ Ta'an. and *Lamentations rabbah* later. See also the discussion by A. Oppenheimer, "Bar-

Kokhba's messianism" in Z. Baras, *Messianism* and *Eschatology* (in Hebrew; Jerusalem, 1983), pp. 153–165.

23. New York, 1971.

24. The brother of Jacob is known by three names biblically: Esau, Edom, and Seir; the nation Edom bears his name. As the native land of Herod, Esau/Edom comes to represent Christianity in Jewish texts.

CHAPTER 3

1. The connections between the new redeemer and the old one are drawn in later rabbinic literature (Ruth Rabbah, 2:14; Gen. Rabbah, 85; Exod. Rabbah, 1, 2:4; Num. Rabbah, 11; Deut. Rabbah 9:9; Ecclus. Rabbah 1:9; TB Sanh. 19b, 98b, among other texts). They include the statement that the first and the last redeemer will be the same and that the redemption will come in the month of the Exodus (Nisan). The text from Socrates Scholasticus above adds an emphasis on dating that recalls the Apocryphal work, *The Assumption of Moses*. In it, Moses prophesies to Joshua that after his death, the kingdom of God will come at the end of "250 'times.'"

2. Salo Baron presents this translation in his *Social and Religious History of the Jews* (New York, 1957), vol. 5, p. 184.

3. Cited in I. Twersky, ed., *A Maimonides Reader* (New York, 1972), pp. 460–461. This text directly influences Ibn Abbas's account of Alroy and, perhaps, the very event of the swindlers in Baghdad who themselves made use of Alroy's image (see chapter 4).

4. Twersky, pp. 458–459.

5. Ibid., p. 460.

6. Ibid., pp. 459–460.

7. From M. N. Adler, ed., *The Travels of Benjamin of Tudela* (in Hebrew; London, 1907), pp. 70–71. See chapter 4 for a description of this account.

CHAPTER 5

1. Cited in A. H. Silver, *A History of Messianic Speculation in Israel* (New York, 1927) p. 146.

2. Both this account and the one about Diaz are given in Aeshcoly, *Movements*, p. 435. Yet another figure, Goncalo Bandarra, a tailor from Trancoso, also became part of this confusion. See E. Lipiner, *The Cobbler of Setubal and The Tailor of Trancoso* (in Portuguese; Rio de Janeiro, 1994). See also D. Gitlitz, *Secrecy and Deceit* (Philadelphia, 1996) 58, 103–110. No study has yet appeared that places the crypto-Jewish messiahs alongside Christian popular prophets—male and female—of the same period. For example, Goncalo Bandarra, a close friend of the crypto-Jewish prophet/messiah Luis Dias, was held by his contemporary, the great humanist and Jesuit Antonio Vieira, to be a "true prophet." Vieira used Bandarra's prophecy as evidence that Vieira's own favorite millenarian king of Portugal, the deceased Joao IV, (as opposed to Sebastian who had died fighting the Turks in 1578, but was believed to be waiting on an island for the proper moment to return and liberate Portugal) was to be resurrected: "[Bandarra] prophesied that the king, Joao IV, would do many things which he has not yet done nor can do unless he is resurrected. Therefore the king, Joao IV, will be resurrected." (J. R. Maia Neto, "Epistemological remarks on Vieira's millenarianism," typescript of a lecture given January 24, 1998 at the W. A. Clark Memorial Library/ UCLA Center for 17th and 18th Century Studies sessions on Millenarianism and Messianism).

3. S. B. Liebman, ed., *Jews and the Inquisition of Mexico: The Great Auto-da-fé of 1649* (Lawrence, Kans., 1974), p. 105.

4. Ibid., p. 101.

5. Cited in Aeshcoly, *Movements*, p. 371.

6. Cited in ibid., p. 404–405.

7. Reubeni's immediate predecessor in this same role was Eldad Hadani ("of the tribe of Dan"), though this emissary from the Lost Tribes of Israel neither claimed to be of Davidic descent nor otherwise indicated messianic aspirations. This ninth-century traveler's tales of his own confederation of Israelite tribes—Dan, Naphtali, Gad, and Asher—and his description of the remainder of the Ten Tribes and of a distant kingdom of Jews appealed to Jews in Morocco, Egypt, and Spain. There may even have been a more immediate predecessor to Reubeni, dark, as he was, and also claiming to be a Reubenite, the son of a mother from the tribe of Dan. Such a figure appeared in Safed a few years before Reubeni, also relying on the Eldad legend. Like Reubeni, his origins were mysterious, and his adventures on his journey to *terra cognita*, marvelous.

8. Cited by H. Fraenkel-Goldschmidt, in her edition of R. Josel's *sefer hamikna* (in Hebrew; Jerusalem, 1970, p. 70), based on S. Stern, *Josel von Rosheim* (Stuttgart, 1959), pp. 112–113.

CHAPTER 8

1. Some of the works on these figures and their circles have appeared in English. The most important of it has not, unfortunately; the most significant is referred to in the bibliography attached to Y. Liebes fine piece, "Sabbatian Messianism" in *pe'amim*, 40 (1989). One must note as well the appearance of Moshe Idel's booklet, *Messianism and Mysticism* (in Hebrew; Israeli Ministry of Defense, 1992) which engages some of the topics of this book from the perspective of some of the messiahs and their engagements with theology or spirituality.

2. It is notable though, that unlike the Gnostic scheme of Marcion, with its good and bad gods, Frank never associates the material and the physical with evil. Some of the "doubling" (of gods, plants, images, for example) is similar to what little we know of Marcionite gnosticism as well as to many other dualistic schemes.

3. Sasportas, *Faded Flower of Zvi* (ed. Tishby, p. 95), reports a similar claim made by Shabtai Zvi.

CHAPTER 10

1. This number does not include Salim Shabazzi (b. 1619; fl. 1648), discussed in E. Brauer, *Ethnologie der Jemenitischen Juden* (Heidelberg, 1934), p. 375. Shabazzi was held to be the messiah on the basis of his birth date. Since he performed no miracles, and no wonders had appeared in the meantime, he was expected to become the messiah when he was eighty, but he never saw that day.

2. I am indebted to B-Z. E. Klorman's *Messianism and Messiahs: The Jews of Yemen in the 19th Century* (in Hebrew; Tel Aviv, 1995) for much of what follows (particularly in terms of bibliographic guidance). It is her study, among the many, that has made the most cogent case for the mutual influence of the Moslem and Jewish communities of Yemen on each other's messianic movements and apocalyptic literature and for the political and social background to such movements in Yemen.

3. See chap. 2, on "localism," for a fuller discussion of the Mourners of Zion, Karaism, and asceticism. Karaism as such never seems to have developed in Yemen.

4. A. Ya'ari, "Shukr Kuhayl," p. 124, cited in Y. Yeshayahu, A. Tzadoq, eds., *The Captivity of Yemen* (in Hebrew; Tel Aviv, 1975).

5. Cf. Klorman, pp. 25–27, 130–131, chap. 3.

6. From S. Halevi, *Chronicle of the Decree against Crowns* cited in Klorman, p. 37.

7. For the entire work with Arabic text, English translation, etc., and discussions of its bearing on the social and legal status of the Yemenite Jews, see P. S. van Köningsveld, J. Sadan, and Q. Al-Samarrai, *Yemenite Authorities and Jewish Messianism* (Leiden, 1990). I have preferred to follow Sadan's Hebrew translation of the text itself, checking it against the Arabic texts in *Yemenite Authorities*.

8. Cf. van Köningsveld et al., pp. 70–73.

9. Yakov Sapir, *The Second Letter to Yemen* (Vilna, 1873), p. 10.

10. Reported by Klorman, p. 157, n. 126.

11. Cf. Sapir, *Second Letter*, pp. 9–10.

12. Ibid., p. 26–27.

13. This reference and the following ones are to letters that appear in Sapir's pamphlet, pp. 9–13.

14. The informant was Sa'adia Hoze; see Klorman, p. 106.

15. Z. Baharav, *From Generation to Generation* (in Hebrew; Tel Aviv, 1968) 31–33 as quoted in B-Z. E.-Klorman, p. 107).

16. Habshush, "History," p. 249.

Index of Messiahs and Accounts

Index of Topics

Asterisks indicate entries related to motifs and symbols of messianic rituals.

Index of Places